Unprofitable Servants

Unprofitable Servants

*Crown Slaves in Berbice,
Guyana, 1803–1831*

Alvin O. Thompson

THE UNIVERSITY OF THE WEST INDIES PRESS
Barbados • Jamaica • Trinidad and Tobago

University of the West Indies Press
1A Aqueduct Flats   Mona
Kingston 7   Jamaica

©2002 by The University of the West Indies Press
All rights reserved. Published 2002

06 05 04 03 02   5 4 3 2 1

CATALOGUING IN PUBLICATION DATA

Thompson, Alvin O.
Unprofitable servants: Crown slaves in Berbice, Guyana,
1803–1931 / Alvin O. Thompson.

p. cm.
Includes bibliographical references.
ISBN: 976-640-120-9

1. Slaves – Guyana – Berbice. 2. Guyana – History –
1803–1966. I. Title.

F2384.T56 2002   988.102

Cover illustration: Detail from Whitney Miller, *Rejection* (n.d.).
Collection of the University of the West Indies.

Set in Adobe Garamond 11/14.5 x 24
Book and cover design by Robert Harris.
E-mail: roberth@cwjamaica.com

Printed on acid-free paper.
Printed in Canada.

To my immediate family:
Hilda, Sean, Brent, Abiola, Mandisa and Obadele,
and
my extended family whose names
are too numerous to recite.

Contents

List Illustrations / *viii*

List of Tables / *ix*

Preface / *x*

Abbreviations / *xiii*

Introduction / *1*

1 Berbice Slave Society / *12*

2 The Governors' Administration, 1803–1811 / *49*

3 Abolitionists Managing Slaves, 1811–1816 / *69*

4 Work and Industry, 1816–1825 / *103*

5 Material Culture, 1816–1825 / *140*

6 Social Culture, 1816–1825 / *172*

7 Oppression and Resistance, 1816–1825 / *209*

8 The Road to Freedom, 1825–1831 / *242*

Reflections / *262*

Notes / *269*

Bibliography / *308*

Index / *324*

Illustrations

Figures

1. Present view of a section of the *winkel* village / *xi*
2. Planter's tent boat / *20*
3. Plan of a coffee plantation / *31*
4. Coffee in the various stages of blossom / *32*
5. New Amsterdam in the early nineteenth century / *106*
6. Manicole palm / *150*
7. Plaited manicole fronds / *151*
8. Musical instruments of African slaves / *196*

Maps

1. The Caribbean and Circum Caribbean / *xiv*
2. Location of Berbice / *17*
3. Geophysical zones of Berbice / *19*
4. Distribution of estates in Berbice c.1804 / *23*
5. Selected locations in Berbice / *104*
6. Sketch of main area of New Amsterdam showing *winkel* village in 1826 / *143*

Tables

1.1 Berbice's Registered Slave Population for Selected Years, 1815–1834 / *27*
2.1 Summary of Revenue and Expenditure of Crown Estates, September 1804–December 1808 (guilders) / *59*
3.1 Comparison of Commodities Produced on Selected Estates in Berbice in 1813 / *99*
4.1 Disposal of *Winkel* People on 31 October 1823 / *110*
4.2 Employment of *Winkel* People on Selected Dates in 1822 / *112*
4.3 Commissioners' Estimate of *Winkel* Earnings (Value of Work) by Vocation, 1815–1824 (guilders) / *117*
5.1 Estimated Annual *Winkel* Expenditure on Food, 1816–1824 (guilders) / *159*
5.2 Estimated Annual *Winkel* Expenditure on Clothing, 1816–1824 (guilders) / *167*
6.1 *Winkel* Population at Selected Dates by Sex, 1819–1825 / *176*
6.2 *Winkel* Population and Berbice Slave Population by Age in 1819 and 1820, Respectively / *177*
6.3 *Winkel* Households in January 1825 / *189*
8.1 Deposits of Berbice Slaves in Savings Bank, 1 November 1826–16 March 1830 (guilders) / *252*

Preface

The main focus of this study is the way in which the administrators appointed by the British imperial government managed the enslaved Crown people located on four estates in the Guiana colonies and in New Amsterdam, the capital (the latter group were referred to as *winkel* or "shop" slaves). The main thesis of this study is that these people were badly mismanaged due to a variety of factors, including general lack of interest and inconsistent oversight, especially by the officers of the imperial government resident in London; lack of commitment by most of the officials resident in the colony to the ameliorative programme outlined by the imperial government; and greed on the part of some of these officials. By the 1820s the urban slaves possessed by the imperial government had become a financial burden and embarrassment to the imperial treasury and this had compromised the ameliorative effort, especially that aspect which sought to demonstrate that humanitarian principles and financial gain were not incompatible under slavery. In 1821 James Walker, the superintendent, declared, "The truth is the Winkel Negroes have not the character of having been profitable in any of the various hands through which they have passed." In 1824 the Department of Colonial Audit in London also declared that the *winkel* slaves were an unprofitable group of people.[1] While this study agrees with this conclusion, it argues that this lack of profitability was due to the mismanagement of the plant rather than to the inability of the enslaved people to earn more than their keep.

A number of interesting features of slave life among the government people and in Berbice at large emerge in the course of this study. However, in most cases we have chosen not to follow them up in great detail, because this would not only make the study too long, but would run the risk of distract-

Preface

Figure 1: Present view of a section of the winkel *village*

ing us from the central theme. Thus we have had to strip the study of a lot of the minutiae of day-to-day slave life in the colony, such as descriptions of buildings, varieties of planting methods and various types of clothing, except where these help to elucidate the main theme.

The trend in modern slavery and other studies is to deal with "gender issues", which often means specifically women's issues. The present study also adopts this focus where appropriate; in fact, the most detailed discussion of resistance (see chapter 7) concerns a group of women. However, in the main the study deals with male and female concerns holistically. Hopefully, this integrated approach gives a fuller and more coherent picture of what the slavery experience was like for those persons described here.

Even a cursory reading of this study will reveal the frequent use of such terms as "enslaved persons", "people" and "individuals" – all intended to emphasize the point that the focus is not on units of production but on sentient, thinking persons caught up in the trauma of slavery. We also employ the term "slave", which designated the unfortunate condition of their lives.

I am indebted to a number of persons and institutions who have played an important part in the production of this work. Professor Hilary McD. Beckles, pro vice chancellor of the University of the West Indies, and

Professor Barry W. Higman of the Australian National University made some valuable suggestions about how the work could be improved. Professor Winston McGowan of the University of Guyana and the late Ms Irene O'Jon helped me to locate valuable information in Guyana, while Dr Anthony Phillips of the University of the West Indies did the same in respect of the Public Record Office, London. Ms Claudette Foo of the University of Guyana kindly consented to draw the maps. The staff of the Public Record Office were particularly helpful in locating the documents in the T1 series that no one seemed to know existed until a search of the records was made. The ever-friendly staff of the Main Library, University of the West Indies, Cave Hill, Barbados, made my research there pleasant and rewarding. I express my gratitude to all of these persons.

The publication of this book has been made possible partly through a grant from the Research Fund of the University of the West Indies, Cave Hill, Barbados.

I cannot thank my wife enough for her patience during my toil, often well past midnight, in the effort to give birth to this work. Nevertheless, I want to record my thanks to her for understanding, or at least trying to do so.

To the Almighty I owe everything.

Abbreviations

CO	Colonial Office (British)
CPCJB	Court of Policy and Criminal Justice of Berbice
d.	dated
f	guilders
f.	folio
GNA	Guyana National Archives
LMS	London Missionary Society
MCPB	Minutes of the Court of Policy of Berbice
n.a.	not available
n.d.	not dated
PP	*Parliamentary Papers* (Accounts and Papers, House of Commons)
PRO	Public Record Office (London)
T	British Treasury

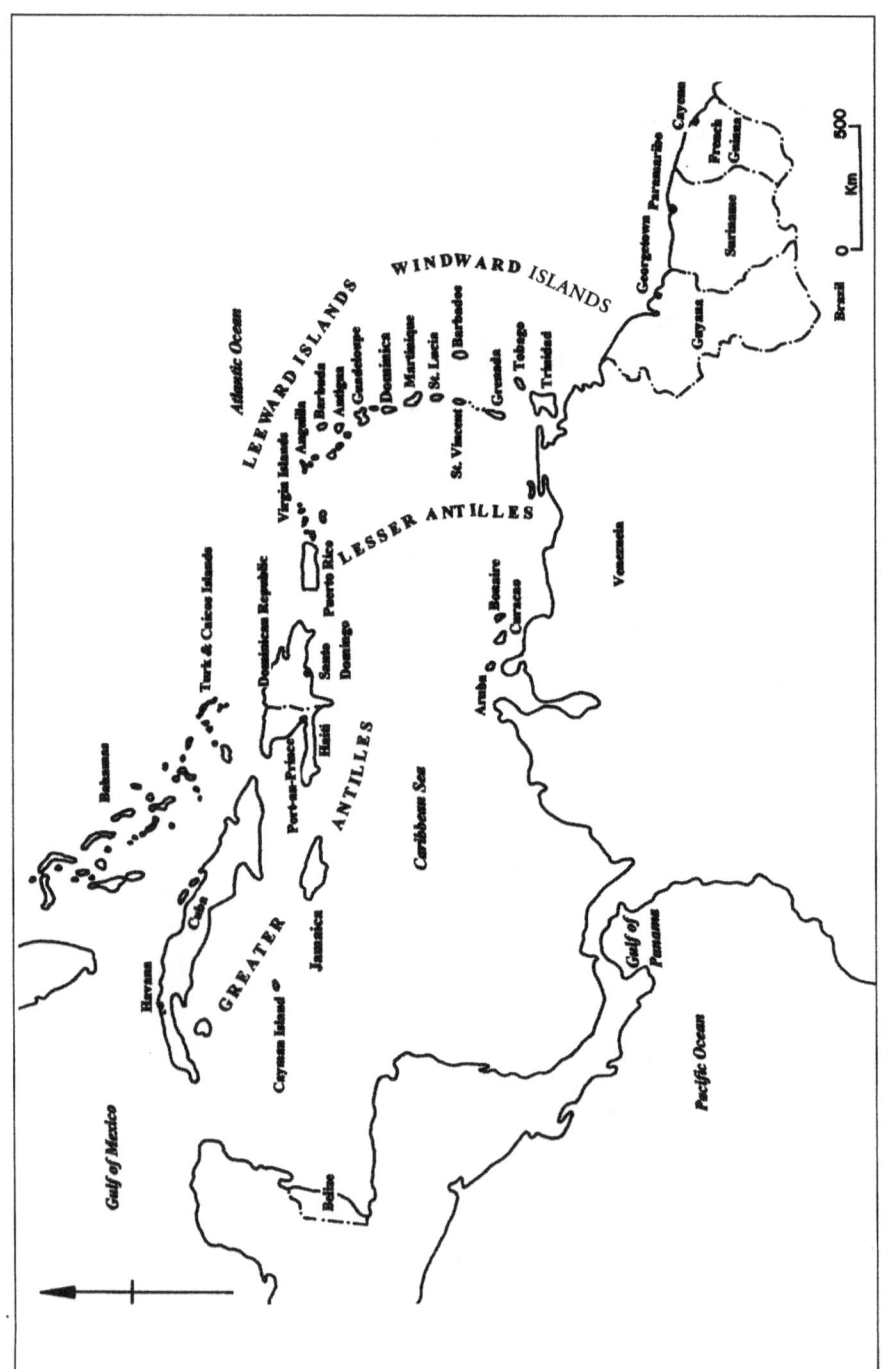

Map 1 The Caribbean and Circum Caribbean

Introduction

Slavery Studies on the Caribbean

In 1803, during the Napoleonic Wars, the British imperial government conquered the Dutch colony of Berbice and took over the management of a number of presumed government slaves. These comprised persons on four estates and others – mainly artisans – in New Amsterdam, the colony's capital, who were known as *winkel* (that is, "shop") slaves. At the end of the war the British government accepted the submission of the Netherlands government that the slaves really belonged to the Berbice Association, a private shareholding company, and returned the estates to that association. However, the negotiations did not encompass the *winkel* people because these were considered "public" slaves, that is, slaves of the colony's public works department (see chapter 3). They therefore remained the property of the British imperial government until their emancipation in 1831. This study will argue that the imperial government proved to be highly delinquent in overseeing the properties and often in appointing the right persons to administer them, and that it was only in the last few years before abolition that the government addressed the issue of the *winkel* people in any sustained manner.

The subject of slavery in the Caribbean has engendered a growing body of literature, especially since the late eighteenth century when the attack on the slave systems was commenced by philosophers, jurists, economists, humanitarians, evangelicals and others, and was, of course, repudiated by a large coterie of pro-slavers, especially the slave-owning fraternity. During the last two centuries this "peculiar institution" has come in for systematic critique. The early nineteenth-century writers were concerned mainly with specific and largely contemporary aspects of the slave systems. Within the British sphere, the debate spawned a number of works based on extensive research into the slave trade and slavery, two of the best known being those by Thomas Clarkson and James Stephen.[1] On the pro-slavery side, works by Edward Long, Bryan Edwards and James M'Queen were listed among the best polemics, at least by the pro-slavers themselves.[2] The debate also led to the publication of a large number of articles in popular and learned journals, and of British parliamentary papers by the House of Commons and House of Lords, based on evidence gathered from within and outside of the slave colonies. British works on the issue were complemented by a huge and diverse literature in other parts of Europe and the Americas, chiefly the United States. The strong biases in many of these works often limited their utility as scholarly analyses, though many of them were sources of highly useful information.

The 1920s through the 1940s saw the publication of important works in the historiography of slavery, such as those produced by William L. Mathieson, Frank Klingberg, Lowell Ragatz, Reginald Coupland and Eric Williams.[3] These works focused mainly on the late eighteenth century and especially the early nineteenth century – the period of the great debate on slavery. Mathieson, Coupland and Klingberg viewed the demise of the institution in the British colonies from a strongly humanitarian perspective, in which the British imperial government was considered to have made a tremendous economic sacrifice in order to introduce a new moral order into the colonies. While noting various contemporary economic arguments, such as those of Adam Smith,[4] that had been advanced to show that free labour was more efficient than slave labour,[5] this school of historians nevertheless concluded that humanitarianism rather than economics best explained the British imperial government's abolition of the slave trade and slavery.

Williams's thesis, published in *Capitalism and Slavery* and often referred to today as "the decline thesis", gave rise to a vast quantity of polemical literature on the abolition of British Caribbean slavery. His most notable antagonist in recent years has been Seymour Drescher who, in his work entitled *Econocide*, returned to the old theme of humanitarianism, using a wide variety of sources in an attempt to prove the assertion by earlier scholars that the imperial government had sacrificed its own economic interests, and especially those of the British colonists, in order to effect the abolition of the slave trade and slavery. As the title of his work suggests, he viewed it as "economic suicide" on Britain's part to pursue such an option. Within the last few decades more polemical literature, in the form of monographs and journal articles, has been written on this subject than perhaps any other aspect of slavery.[6]

More recently, scholars have also focused attention on demography, gender, material culture, creolization and urban slavery. Quite a body of literature has been produced recently on the first three of these, while a few important works have been written on the last two. Barry Higman's important study, *Slave Populations of the British Caribbean 1807–1834*, contains a large section on demography (including morbidity, mortality and fertility), and substantial information on all the other themes mentioned above.[7] The work contains a wide variety of useful data assembled from archival and other sources, and is enhanced by a large number of tables and figures. As stated, it embraces the entire British Caribbean and offers interesting comparisons with other slave systems in the Americas. It is unique in its assemblage of data and is compulsory reading for anyone doing research on that period of slavery. Higman's work reinforces earlier studies which have shown, although with less of a comparative dimension, that slaves suffered terribly in material and social terms, especially under plantation slavery, and that this suffering was reflected in numerous ways, not least in the demographic profiles of their communities. Other important works which address the subject of demography are those of Kenneth Kiple, which focuses largely on the medical and nutritional aspects of slave life, and Richard Sheridan, which probes more deeply into the impact of the labour and punishment regimes on the health of enslaved people.[8]

Gender (including family) concerns have become a fertile area of slave studies, with some impressive works being produced in recent years. These studies have been driven by the concerns of a number of scholars, especially women, that "herstory" has not been given the attention it deserves, and that women experienced and suffered from some forms of oppression peculiar to their sex. For instance, Barbara Bush begins her general study, *Slave Women in*

Caribbean Society, 1650–1838, with a section entitled "The 'Invisible' Black Woman in Caribbean History: An Introduction". Her study embraces such issues as women in plantation labour regimes, slave resistance, reproduction, family and motherhood.[9] She demonstrates, as does Hilary Beckles in a much more convincing way in *Natural Rebels*, that enslaved women played a major role in slave societies, even if their actual contributions have been marginalized in most historical studies. Beckles declares that, at least for Barbados, the multiple roles of women are much more clearly delineated in the contemporary historical records than those of men, but that they have simply been overlooked by gender-biased historians.[10] While much more work needs to be done on all aspects of the slavery experience of women, historians are no longer oblivious to women's central role in all aspects of slave life.[11]

Urban slavery is becoming an important theme in Caribbean historiography, but again few detailed studies have been written on this subject, compared with some excellent works on North America. The most detailed work is perhaps the unpublished doctoral thesis of Pedro Welch, but Barry Higman and Neville Hall are also among those making important contributions.[12]

As can be seen, slavery studies constitute a dynamic – arguably the most dynamic – area of historical studies on the Caribbean. A large number of studies on specific colonies and microstudies on plantations, towns and villages continue to enhance the historian's knowledge and understanding of the experience of slavery in the region. Comparative studies between the Caribbean and other regions also help to place the Caribbean slavery experience in the wider context of slavery in the Americas and the world at large. However, historians have paid almost no attention to state slaves (also variously referred to in the documents on Berbice and in this study as Crown slaves and government slaves). Therefore, an important aspect of colonial slavery still awaits detailed scholarly investigation, especially in those jurisdictions in which the colonial state was a substantial slave holder. It is important to know what differences, if any, existed between the colonial states' slave holdings and those of private owners, in terms of the management of slaves and the wider perception of slaves as human beings with certain basic rights.

Of course, state ownership of slaves was quite common throughout Asia, Africa, certain parts of Europe, and the Caribbean at different times. In Asia and Africa state slaves were often used as agricultural hands, traders, domestics, and generally as drudges. But they also formed important members of the ruler's domestic household, civil bureaucracy, bodyguards, army and the like. In the Oyo empire of Yorubaland (southwestern Nigeria), in the nineteenth century, the three most important court officials were eunuchs. They were placed in charge of the central government's administrative, judicial and religious affairs – including rituals to Shango, the chief Yoruba deity – and were themselves very wealthy persons. One of them, the *Osi Iwefa* ("eunuch of the left"), who was responsible for revenue matters, could substitute for the emperor in relations with subordinate kings. A host of other minor officials, known as *ilari,* fulfilled such roles as tax collectors, messengers and palace guards, under the *Osi Iwefa*'s authority.[13] The *lari,* their counterparts in Dahomey (modern Benin), performed similar state functions.

Important slave groups also existed in such African countries as Egypt, Sudan, Ethiopia and Bagirmi, and such Asian countries as India, Persia and China, at various times. Many of them became powerful military and court officials, often equalling and sometimes exceeding the power and influence attained by their counterparts in Oyo. Sometimes they were able to make and unmake rulers, especially in Muslim states. The *jannisaries* of the Ottoman empire and the *mamluks* (literally, "slaves") of the Egyptian sultanate were two such groups. In Egypt, where many of the Turkish and Circassian *mamluks* were incorporated into the army and administration, they become so involved in the high affairs of state that by the mid-thirteenth century – most of them now only nominally slaves – they were able to overthrow the Ayyubid rulers and establish themselves as supreme rulers until their power was broken by the Ottoman emperor in 1517. Moreover, even in the chaos of the Ottoman invasion their descendants were able to assert substantial control over the country and to remain a powerful force in Egyptian life until the early nineteenth century. Several centuries earlier, in the area of modern Iraq in the late ninth century, thousands of Zanj (East African) slaves – some of whom had been pressed into gang labour, while others had been incorporated into the army – revolted and set up their own government, which lasted for fourteen years. An increasing body of scholarly research is appearing on these state slaves, offering interesting comparative insights into the nature of slavery.[14]

In the Caribbean, since free labour did not exist on a large scale before emancipation, all governments utilized slaves for almost every conceivable task, especially those involving hard labour, such as building forts and roads, cutting canals and erecting dams. They obtained these slaves in various ways. In several instances the British government acquired them through conquest, as in the cases of Berbice, Demerara-Essequibo, Suriname, Martinique, Guadeloupe and Mauritius (Île-de-France) during the Napoleonic Wars.[15] The government retained those slaves in Berbice and Demerara-Essequibo that were considered to be part of the public works department of the colonies. They returned the other slaves (forfeited from absentee proprietors) at the end of the war. The notable exceptions are the three estates in Grenada that had been forfeited to the Crown as a result of treason on the part of the proprietors. The imperial Crown also acquired slaves through escheat, that is, as a result of their owners dying intestate, though before the 1820s the Crown usually delivered these slaves to the surviving relatives of the deceased upon application for them. Escheats existed in almost all British Caribbean jurisdictions, especially Barbados, Trinidad and Grenada. In a few instances, notably Trinidad, slaves were purchased by the colonial government for public works, since this was considered to be much cheaper than hiring slaves from private owners.[16]

The government also acquired labourers through judicial sentences against enslaved persons for committing various "crimes" against the state, such as desertion and participation in revolts. It might be argued that this last category of labour was not slave labour, in so far as the labourers were state prisoners. However, the differential treatment meted out to these persons when compared with white and free coloured prisoners and the tasks they performed indicates that the government perceived them as slaves whose labour had been forfeited to the colonial state on a temporary or permanent basis. Many of them worked on the roads in chain gangs with scarcely anything to cover their nudity: "only a coarse rag around their middle", according to Henry Bolingbroke.[17]

Apart from the slaves mentioned above, there were others who were acquired and utilized by the imperial government for various purposes. The best known among these were the enslaved persons who were bought by the government from their owners towards the end of the eighteenth century and incorporated into various divisions of the British West India Regiment.

Those in the Guiana colonies were often referred to as the Black Rangers.[18] There was also a group of apprenticed Africans that the imperial government had taken from vessels plying the illegal slave trade. Some of them were impressed into the West India Regiment, while others were deposited in a number of British colonial jurisdictions, including Sierra Leone, Mauritius, South Africa, Cape Coast, Antigua, Tortola, the Bahamas and Trinidad. Legally they were not slaves but the imperial government, through the collectors of customs of the various colonies, apprenticed them out to various free persons for periods of up to fourteen years. In the Caribbean, in particular, they were kept in conditions that replicated slavery, in some instances being integrated into the estate's work gangs.[19] Finally, there were numerous slaves who belonged to the "state" church. It is arguable whether these should properly be called state slaves since while on the one hand the material assets of the church theoretically belonged to the state, on the other the state made no attempt to dictate to the church how it should treat these slaves. They were also not included among the government slaves who were liberated in 1831, some three years before the general abolition of slavery in the colonies.

While the Crown acquired a number of slaves at different times and in a variety of ways, it was only in the case of Berbice that it assumed direct control over them. This was a peculiar situation that we have attempted to discuss in greater detail in chapters 2 and 3. However, we may say here that this peculiarity arose out of one imperial government official's interest in placing the slaves under the administrative control of a group of humanitarians resident in London, in what was clearly intended as an experiment in amelioration.

Government Slaves in Berbice

As mentioned above, the slaves who are the main focus of this study were acquired by the British imperial government through conquest of the Dutch colony of Berbice during the Napoleonic Wars. We know of only three short studies on them (although there is brief mention of them in a few other works, such as James Rodway's *History of British Guiana* and P.M. Netscher's *Geschiedenis*).[20] The first of these is Graham Cruickshank's article entitled "King William's People". The second is Donald Wood's unpublished paper on "Crown Slavery in Berbice".[21] Wood used several manuscript sources in the Public Record Office, London, but did not attempt a careful study of the management of these people and, moreover, did not access (perhaps was not aware of) the T1 series, from which most of the information for this study is drawn. The third work is an article by A.J. McR. Cameron, published in two parts recently in a Guyana newspaper, and drawn largely from Cruickshank's work mentioned above.[22]

The present work is a detailed microstudy of the Crown slaves in a small, largely underdeveloped slave colony, but it has wide implications for understanding the British imperial government's attitudes towards slavery in the era of "amelioration", and it raises serious questions about the government's commitment to the anti-slavery cause. Specifically, it seeks to make a contribution to Caribbean historiography in four main ways. First, it chronicles and discusses the management of Crown slaves in the era of amelioration. It deals with the government's perception of the slaves' readiness for freedom and indicates that in the case of at least one important government official (George Canning), the view was hardly different from that of the slave masters (see chapter 8). It demonstrates the government's reluctance to move forward with a programme of emancipation, even for its own slaves (of which there were around three hundred in the 1820s), long after the argument that they were economically important to the Crown or the local (colonial) government ceased to be valid. It also throws into relief the government's fear of plantocratic reaction to such a move. Second, it locates several leading humanitarians, including William Wilberforce, James Stephen and Zachary Macaulay, in the role of administrators of the Crown's slave properties between 1811 and 1816. This position gave these men a unique opportunity to demonstrate their skills as reformers. Their management of these properties was attacked by many pro-slavers inside and outside the British Parliament.

Third, the study attempts to give a much higher level of visibility and individuality to slaves than is common in studies on Caribbean slavery. The strong profiles and personalities of several of the enslaved people with which this study deals give them an identity that looms large. Michael Craton, in his work entitled *Searching for the Invisible Man*, attempts to give more specific personae to the slaves of Worthy Park estate in Jamaica, but what emerges is really a set of personality types, in so far as he constructs an imaginary (or imaginative) history of what slave life must have been for these persons.[23] In the present study, however, the actual details of several of the slaves' lives (or rather, aspects of their lives) are recorded, thus giving them much greater visibility than Craton was able to do. Unlike Craton's personality types, the cases dealt with here expose the reader not only to the actions of these persons but also to their thoughts on a wide variety of subjects, including food, clothing, accommodation, self-hire, the quality of management of the plant, and slavery as a whole. We have cited the views of more than fifty enslaved persons. We thus give a deeper insight than usual into their fears about and perceptions of the slave system, and their hopes for a brighter day. Studies on Caribbean slavery are, of course, not devoid of portraits of a number of individual slaves, the most significant of whom were those who emerged as leaders of revolts, especially during the rebellions in St Domingue. Thus, persons such as Mackandal, Boukman, Toussaint L'Ouverture and Dessalines have been the subjects of extensive research, and a good deal of information about them (sometimes combining fact and fiction) has been unearthed. Significant details have also been uncovered on the lives of other enslaved persons such as Nanny and Sam Sharpe (Jamaica), Old Doll and Bussa (Barbados), Kofi and Quamina (Guyana).

Finally, this study gives the opportunity to dozens of enslaved people to speak for themselves, through the testimonies of their experience, recorded by the Commission of Inquiry in 1825. Mary Prince, a Bermuda-born slave, was the first British ex-slave woman to record her experiences in print.[24] Almost complete biographies have been recorded of and by such North American former enslaved persons as Harriet Jacobs, William Wells Brown, Booker T. Washington and Frederick Douglass.[25] In fact, "slave narratives" (as they are often called by American writers) constituted an important part of the arsenal of American anti-slavery groups in the nineteenth century. However, nearly all these "narratives" were reminiscences of slave life, sometimes decades after the persons had achieved freedom. The present study utilizes testimony that the people gave while they were still enslaved. While there is a possibility of distortion in the documents, since the enslaved people were not the actual compilers, the greater likelihood is that the composite profile of their lives gives a fairly reliable record of their experience of slavery. It is particularly in this last respect that this study seeks to make an important contribution to the understanding of the slaves' experiences. The slave profiles included in this study relate to "ordinary" slaves, in the sense that they did not lead major revolts or become leaders of Maroon communities, nor have they been mentioned before in historical works. The profiles tell the story of how the average slave lived, worked and was treated (largely in the context of an urban environment).

It is useful to indicate the richness of the sources. The imperial government sent out a Commission of Inquiry in 1824 (arriving in the colony in January 1825), comprising Sir Charles Wyndham and John Kinchela, to look into the affairs of the *winkel* department and to report on the likelihood of the people making good use of their freedom, if given to them. That commission spent some twenty months in Berbice, investigating almost all aspects of the department, and recording the testimonies of every *winkel* adult, several of the children, all the members of the administration, and a number of other individuals previously or currently associated with the department. The commission also examined very minutely all the *winkel* records available and dispatched copies of a considerable number of them to Europe. These form the T1 series, cited so often in this study. I came across these records accidentally and concluded that they had not been opened since being closed in the nineteenth century. Certainly no previous scholar has used them. I had to pay special handling costs to have the voluminous sheets of paper unfolded, sorted, numbered and photocopied. The chronology does not always correspond with the pagination (higher pagination often being given for letters and so on written at earlier dates and vice versa), but the records have been properly preserved. They cover a large number of issues in considerable detail, but are deficient on such matters as slave families and slave culture. While I have managed to use fragmentary evidence from these and other sources to discuss briefly these aspects of the lives of the Crown slaves, I recognize that there is still an important lacuna in this study.

Disappointingly, in spite of extensive searches of several depositories and libraries in Europe, the records of the Berbice Commission for Management (the administration under William Wilberforce chosen to run the properties from 1811 to 1816) have not come to light. More puzzling is the fact that several biographies of Wilberforce, Zachary Macaulay and others fail to carry a single line about this commission, though their administration became a focus of debate in several English newspapers and the House of Commons published their report.

Introduction

Apart from quotations, the terms "Guiana" and "the Guianas" are used in this book to refer to the northern areas of South America between the Orinoco and Amazon Rivers, comprising part of present-day Venezuela, Guyana, Suriname, French Guiana and Brazil. The term "Guyana" is used to refer to the colonies of Berbice and Demerara-Essequibo that were merged into a single colony called British Guiana, in 1831, and to the modern independent state that bears that name.

1

Berbice Slave Society

The Caribbean Context

Berbice slave society was a fair microcosm of slave societies in the Americas, and especially in the Caribbean. These societies were based largely on the use of involuntary African migrant labour to service the tropical plantations. Large-scale importation of such labour in the Caribbean began around the mid-seventeenth century to facilitate the development of the sugar culture of Barbados and, later in that century, of St Kitts, Jamaica, Martinique and Guadeloupe. These constituted the main sugar colonies until about the mid-eighteenth century, when they were displaced by St Domingue. But that colony's plantation culture was itself destroyed at the end of the century by the effects of the French revolutionary wars (1790s) upon the region. More significant was the slave revolt which occurred in the colony in 1791, culminating in the overthrow of colonial slavery and colonialism itself, and the birth of the independent state of Haiti. The virtual destruction of plantation culture in Haiti and other factors led to the emergence of Cuba as the new sugar giant in the region. Within the British sphere, the capture and retention of Trinidad from the Spanish, and of Demerara and Berbice from the Dutch, led to the development of sugar on an increasing scale during the nineteenth century. These new sites of sugar production never rivalled Cuba, but they nevertheless resulted in a major shift in capital, personnel and slaves away from the older British sugar colonies.

The slave societies concentrated on sugar culture, but several of them also engaged in planting other tropical staples such as coffee, cocoa and cotton, as well as other export crops. However, the dominance of sugar has led historians and economists to speak of the region generally as an area of sugar monoculture. The cultivation of tropical staples was conducted within a plantation complex; by the eighteenth century the plantation was the institution that most clearly defined the political, economic and social relations of the vast majority of people living in the colonies. The plantation became an autarchic institution, in which nearly all decisions concerning the lives of the enslaved people were made by the management of the plant.[1]

Plantation society was characterized by a number of features, apart from the focus on tropical staples. These included a large African majority population comprising the labour hands and drudges of the plantation; a small white management corps, sometimes assisted by a few coloured persons; the command of the surplus production of the plantation for the exclusive benefit of the white group, while the blacks lived at marginal levels of subsistence; a severe punishment regime for the slightest violation of plantation regulations; and a general loss of rights. The enslaved people were by and large defined as chattel in the British and Dutch slave laws. While their personae were recognized under French and Spanish slave laws, in practice the slaves in these latter jurisdictions were treated with the same harshness and loss of rights as in the first two. There is now broad agreement among scholars that the treatment of the enslaved people in the various colonies had much more to do with the labour demands of the plantation regime than with the laws under which they were supposed to be governed. In other words, the more highly developed the plantation regime became, the greater was the degradation of the enslaved people.[2]

The plantation complex was the most common labour structure, but not the only one, in the slave colonies. Groups of urban slaves serviced the needs of the white community in the towns. The study of urban slavery is a relatively recent phenomenon, but it has opened up a new dynamic in the discussion of slavery in the Americas.[3] Already these studies have shown clearly that while there were broad similarities between rural and urban slave regimes, there were also significant differences in the treatment meted out to slaves under the two regimes. The overall view is that, in respect of both the material and the social bases of slavery, rural slaves were worse off, sometimes substantially so, than urban ones. The main area of uncertainty – a critical one – is whether the provision of food to urban slaves in general (apart from domestics) was at least equivalent to that of rural ones.

Most writers believe that urban domestic slaves benefited from the leftovers and sometimes from the general fare of their owner's larder, although they did not usually have access to kitchen gardens. On the other hand, writers suggest that for most other urban slaves the absence of kitchen gardens or of any significant livestock, and their total dependence on their owners for rations, made them potentially and often actually worse off than rural slaves. They also suggest that many slaves who were on self-hire might have earned just enough to pay their owners, leaving very little for food and other necessities.

Much depended upon the particular urban areas, the alternative sources of employment available, and the relative access urban slaves had to land on the peripheries of urban centres. In relatively developed urban communities such as those of Jamaica and Barbados, and in small nonplantation communities that were mainly commercial emporia, such as Tortola and St Eustatius, slaves had greater opportunities for a variety of jobs than in plantation regimes. On the whole, however, the range of jobs available was much greater in urban communities than in rural ones. Also, in some instances where similar jobs were available in both rural and urban areas, there was greater opportunity for urban slaves than for rural slaves to engage in these during their free time. The main jobs in this category were as domestics, artisans, stevedores, porters, tailors and seamstresses. Prostitution was also said to be more common in urban than rural regimes, although it does not formally enter the records of employment because it was illegal.

Skilled urban slaves on self-hire were usually the most secure materially because their skills were in great demand. This was particularly so of carpenters, masons, goldsmiths and silversmiths; in riverain cultures such as the Guianas boat builders were also in great demand. Generally, urban slaves had much greater mobility than rural ones to seek out the best jobs and to change jobs. Many owners did not worry about them too much, provided they paid their weekly hire. This was notably the case in Tortola and St Thomas, where such slaves were able to travel freely from one island to the other. This mobility, not only in respect of work but in all other aspects of urban slave life, caused great concern to slave owners and others who wanted to see strict controls placed on the movement of slaves (see chapter 4). This attitude, however, was one born of a general fear of slave unrest, rather than the experience of urban slave revolt. The reality was that such activities were virtually unknown in urban communities because (among other reasons) the towns had ready access to military reinforcements, and the urban militias were better equipped and drilled more often than the rural ones.

Urban slaves also had greater access to a variety of clothing than rural ones for several reasons: they (especially domestics) were given the "hand-me-downs" of their owners, those serving at table or as messengers were often given better attire as part of their employment, and they were able to purchase clothing sold in the urban shops. In fact, it was this access to urban shops that provided urban slaves with a greater variety of material goods than rural ones, including a wide range of jewellery and perfumery. However, this point should not be overstressed, for there were several instances in which urban slaves were seen going about in rags.

Individual slave owners in urban regimes had far fewer slaves than in rural ones. The average urban slave owner had fewer than six slaves, and some had only one or two. In general, they did not depend upon their slaves for their basic livelihood, in contrast to plantation owners. All white families, and some free coloured and free(d) black families, were likely to have a few slaves, at least for domestic purposes. In addition, "professional" persons such as doctors, lawyers, clergymen, company managers and high-ranking military officers were likely to have one or two slaves at their beck and call. The lives of these slaves were usually less rigorous and less hazardous than those of their counterparts on plantations. The main exception to this is those urban slaves belonging to owners who maintained "task gangs" that they hired out. These gangs usually comprised the most robust slaves, who undertook the most arduous tasks on the plantations, such as clearing forests and digging trenches; who had limited time for social interaction; and whose lifespan was generally considered the shortest of all slaves. In some colonies there was also a large number of government slaves engaged in both public works and domestic functions (for high government officers). The *winkel* people fall into this category.

There were many other ways in which urban regimes differed from rural ones. For urban slaves, these included greater access to medical care (since more doctors were resident in urban than rural areas), more opportunity for leisure and cultural activities, greater access to missionary religion and education, more opportunity to benefit from ameliorative legislation (especially from the 1820s on), and more opportunity for mixing and mating with other ethnic groups and social classes. This last factor was responsible for the substantial free coloured population in most colonies in the nineteenth century, who dwelt mainly in the urban communities and often vied with the poor white, slave and free black populations for space and jobs. Ultimately, however, plantation and urban slaves shared one fundamental feature: they were both unfree; this meant that the courses of their daily lives, and sometimes their fates, lay in the hands of their owners.

While Berbice society fell into the broad pattern of Caribbean slave societies, it had its own distinctive features, including the impact of its geography and environment on the specifics of its slave society, its slow transition to sugar culture in the nineteenth century, its relatively small enslaved population, its high slave-to-white ratio, and the almost total absence of social institutions among its white population. Visitors to Berbice (and Demerara-Essequibo) in the early nineteenth century commented on these and other differences in relation to the Caribbean plantation colonies.

Geography

Sometimes referred to today as "the sleepy county",[4] by the early nineteenth century Berbice's boundaries had been sketched out, from the Corentyne River in the east to the Abary River some sixty miles to the west (although lots were laid out for another twelve miles along the west bank of the Corentyne), between two other Dutch colonies, Suriname and Demerara-Essequibo. The Atlantic Ocean determined its northern boundary, while its southern boundary remained undelimited, save for the wide expanse of forest which restricted free access to certain places. The approach to the coastline is (and was) impeded by mudflats and sandbanks that make it very difficult for any but skilled pilots to navigate in large vessels. Moreover, sandbanks and drift mud often drift along the coast and interfere with the drainage of the rivers. The estuary of the Berbice River is accessed by a long channel, dominated by shoals that make it hazardous for even small vessels to navigate.

Berbice Slave Society

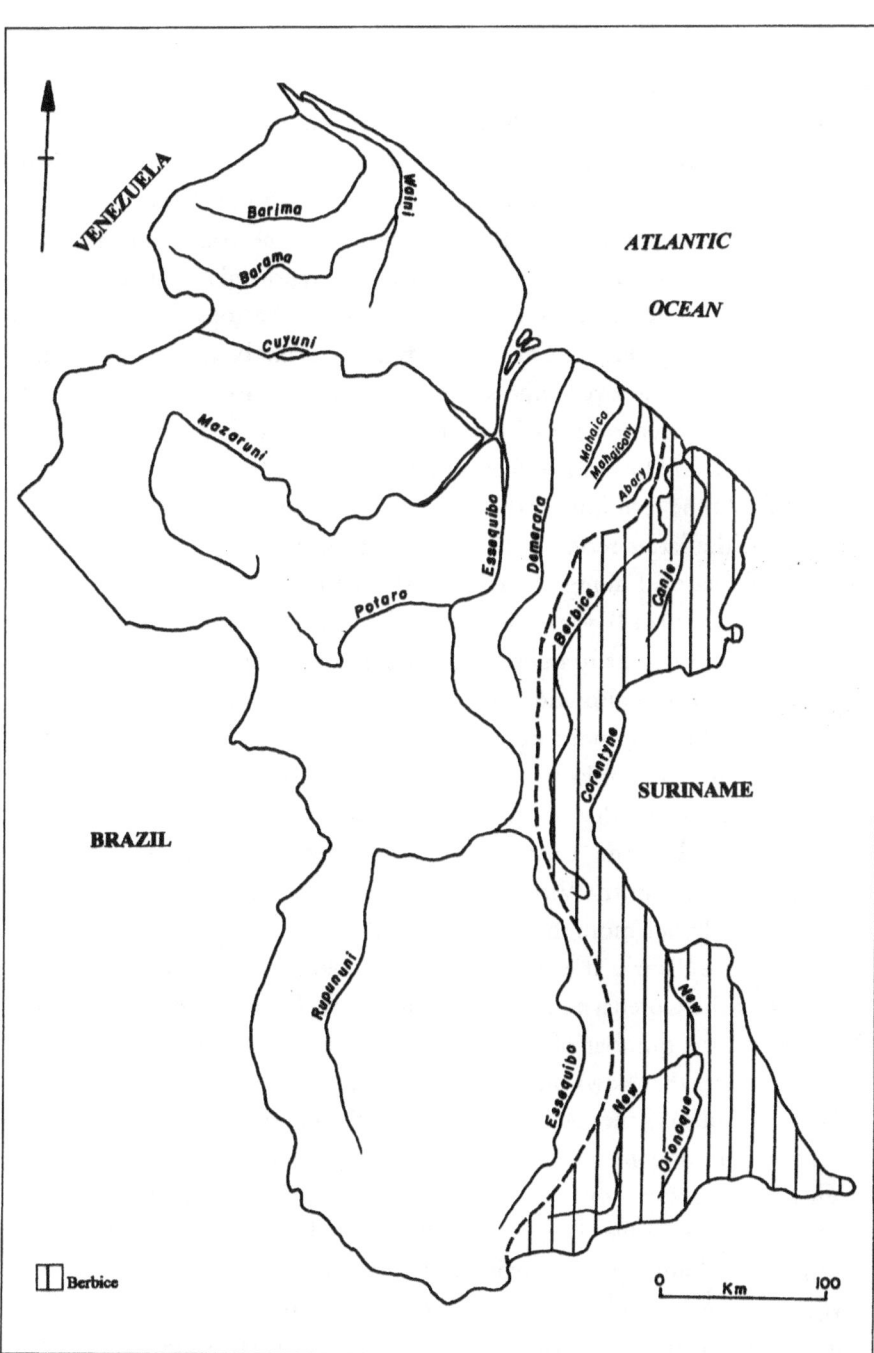

Map 2 *Location of Berbice*

The coastal area and the lower reaches of the river banks consist of alluvial clay whose soil is generally mixed and sometimes covered with foliage from the numerous trees which dominate the landscape. The alluvial area extends inland from 10 to 40 miles in different sections, and the soil is of differing consistency in various parts. It ranges from 50 to 200 hundred feet in depth, with the greatest depth being closest to the coast and the lower reaches of the rivers, decreasing regularly as it extends inland. The closer to the coast, the more saline is the composition of the topsoil. The land is almost level throughout the clay belt, with the gradient being very gentle and almost imperceptible over large stretches. A considerable part of this rich alluvial soil has been recovered over time by the natural deposition of soil from the tides, and by embankments or dams erected by the Dutch and later the British. At the terminus of the alluvial area the sand ridges and sand hills commence, the latter reaching heights of 120 feet.[5] It was widely believed that the alluvial soil along the coast and on the lower banks of the river (about 10 miles inland) was so rich in nutrients that the sugar cane could last twenty to thirty years, and in extreme cases up to fifty years, without requiring replanting. It was also said that with good attention it was possible to get as many as eighteen ratoons from the original plant. The rest of the alluvial land along the river banks was regarded as being very good for coffee production.[6] The remainder of the land is covered with very dense shrubs, known commonly as the "bush", and very tall trees that characterize the rainforest area of the country. Virtually parallel with the sand hills are a group of hillocks, usually not more than 200 feet high.

The Berbice River is the main river in the colony, which also shares jurisdiction over the Corentyne River with Suriname. Draining into the Berbice River are a large number of smaller rivers, the most important of which is the Canje River that flows into the Berbice on the east. Up to the end of the eighteenth century, the Dutch were still ignorant of the sources of these rivers.[7] The estuary of the Berbice River is divided by Crab Island into two channels, the eastern one being the more navigable. Even so, it is only between 17 and 20 feet deep at high-water level. The shallow draft of the river prevented any vessels drawing more than about 15 feet of water from navigating it for any substantial distance inland. While this factor offered the colony some protection from inland attack by frigates and other large vessels, the inability to accommodate large merchant ships was a negative

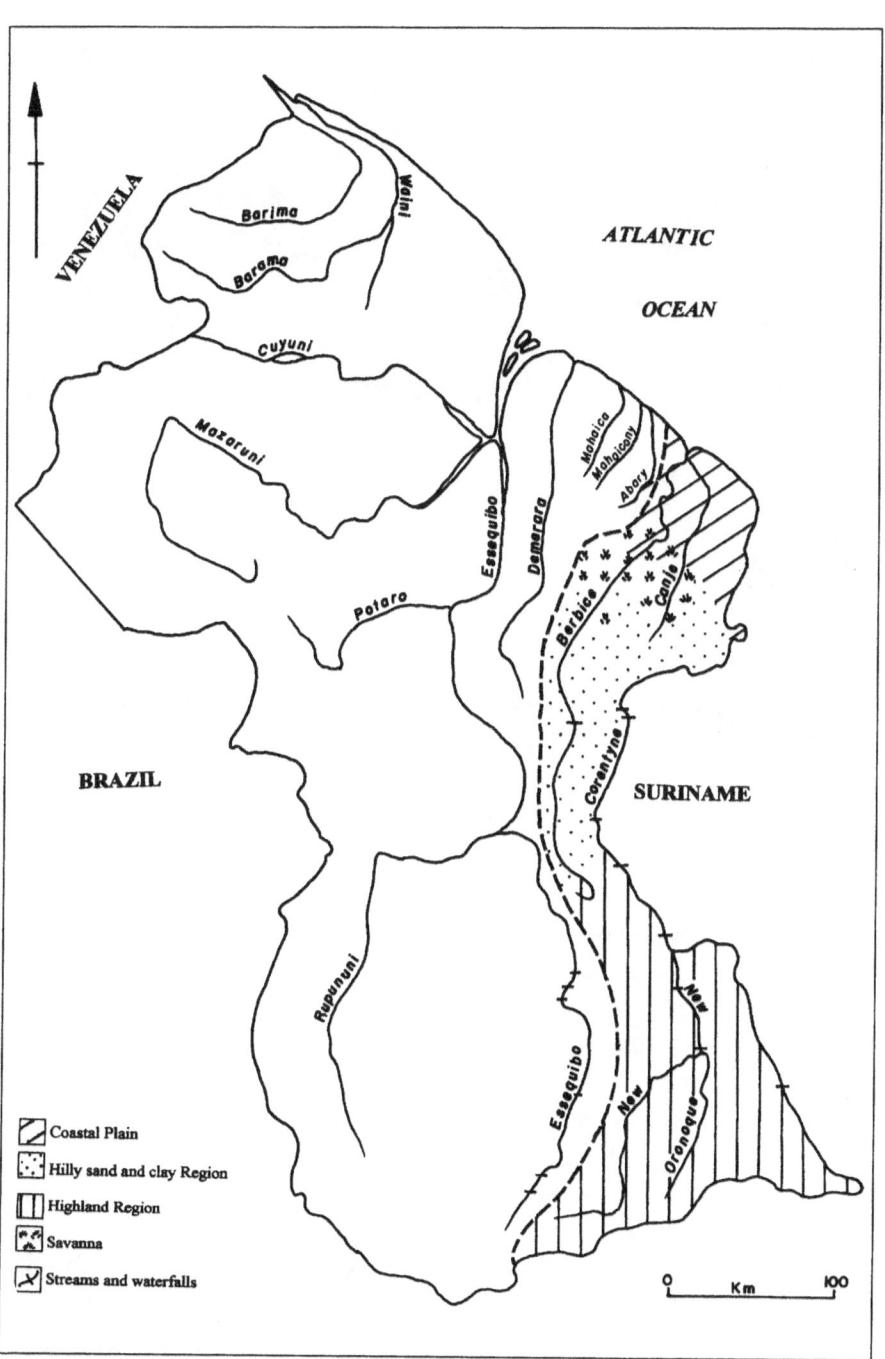

Map 3   Geophysical zones of Berbice

Figure 2 Planter's tent boat
Reprinted from Henry Bolingbroke, *A Voyage to Demerary, Containing a Statistical Account of the Settlements There and Those of the Essequibo, the Berbice, and other Contiguous Rivers of Guiana* (1808; Georgetown: Daily Chronicle, 1947).

consequence. As a result, planters preferred to transship their cargoes in small vessels to Demerara, which had a deeper and more commodious harbour. The result was that Berbice suffered considerably in terms of its mercantile and warehouse development, and ultimately in terms of its overall economic development.

Weather conditions vary considerably in the country, with an overall high level of annual rainfall. The country notionally has two wet and two dry seasons. The main rainy season is said to last from July to September, during which time, in the diseased environment of the early nineteenth century, the inhabitants were most affected by illnesses.[8] However, weather patterns are often erratic, with the wet seasons spilling over substantially into the dry ones and vice versa. Droughts in 1803, 1804 and 1823–26 wreaked extensive havoc on the plantation economy, while in 1809 an unusually long and heavy rainy season, which lasted well into the usual "dry season", carried away much of the produce.[9]

The fickle weather had its parallel in the equally fickle disease environment. The Guiana colonies were generally regarded as particularly adverse disease environments. Lieutenant Governors Van Batenburg and Beard listed the main diseases as "bilious fevers, fluxes, cholicks & liver complaints", and "Fevers, Dysentery and Bilious Colic", respectively.[10] Epidemics also visited the colony periodically. The early 1820s constituted a particularly difficult period in this respect. In 1822 and early 1823 the colony was affected by an epidemic of "pleurisy and dysentery". Around mid-1823 there was also an "epidemic of an inflammatory kind", somewhat like "European flu", while in 1825 measles struck, followed by whooping cough.[11]

Although the Dutch had occupied several areas of the colony since the early seventeenth century, it retained an essentially frontier appearance at the time of the British conquest. For most of the period Berbice was a society scattered among plantations, with no urban community whatsoever. Its main fort, Nassau (fifty-five miles up the Berbice River), was its headquarters until the last two decades of the eighteenth century when New Amsterdam, a small town that was designated as the capital, began to take shape. New Amsterdam was located roughly at the confluence of the Berbice and Canje Rivers, some five miles from the estuary of the main river. The frontier nature of New Amsterdam, the colony's heart, was symptomatic of its entire anatomy. Pinckard, while approaching the landscape from a few miles out at sea, commented that

> The view before us was that of a wild country, only just opening into cultivation. It comprized an extent of wood and water, with small patches of land breaking into incipient tillage, but it had nothing of the bold and romantic scenery of mountain regions. . . . No part of the territory of the island [sic] was visible, but from being flat and low, it appeared as a mere cluster of trees, growing out of the water, and causing a pleasant break in the wide embouchure of the river. . . .[12]

What Pinckard saw was partly mirage, but his description emphasizes the point that, from a distance, the hand of God so completely dwarfed the hand of man that human culture appeared nonexistent, and even from a closer vantage point the primeval forest appeared to overwhelm the plantations.

Actually, at the time of the British arrival in the colony the coastline was already laid out in a very basic way. A number of coffee estates had been carved out there, stretching almost as far as the Corentyne River. Older estates (several of them abandoned) dotted the geographical landscape up to about a hundred miles inland along the main river, while trade, woodcutting and other activities took some enterprising persons much further inland. In the early days the government granted each settler a plot of land, usually between 1,000 and 1,500 acres, with its frontage on the river. They could apply later for further depths, and some of them considerably extended their properties inland. Later on, grants were usually of between 250 and 500 acres.[13] Dams, irrigated channels or thick vegetation separated the estates from each other. The poldering of the coastal areas required a good deal of time, money and attention by both government and private interests, and it was therefore mainly the wealthier planters who occupied those areas. The process of coastal settlement received a fillip, especially after 1796, through British capital.[14]

The predicament in this small corner of the South American continent was how to tame nature and create not simply a settled existence, but a durable civilization. The Incas were able to do so in Peru, but in the Guianas the story was quite different. Everywhere the land refused to be tamed for long, displaying an almost defiant nature, and returning rapidly to its original state when abandoned or neglected for a short while. Even Suriname (where plantation culture became significant in the early eighteenth century) and Demerara (where it would become so from the early nineteenth) remained rude in their physical appearance and rudimentary in their political and social culture. This was certainly the case in Berbice where, on large stretches of the upper reaches of the rivers, nature returned to its accustomed habitat once the colonists had abandoned the estates for new lands on the coast. There, it took extensive poldering and constant reinforcements to keep the sea on the one front and the rushing inland waters (especially in the rainy season) on the other from wiping out what little gains human artifice had made. In spite of the more aggressive attempts at cultivation from 1796, following the British occupation of the colony during the French Revolutionary and Napoleonic Wars,[15] the colony did not lose its frontier appearance until well into the nineteenth century.

Early Colonial History

Given the situation detailed above, it is not surprising that Berbice never had an impressive colonial history. It was founded by the Van Pere family in 1627, transferred to the Berbice Association (Society of Berbice), a private shareholding company, in 1720, and wrested from the latter by the revolutionary government in the Netherlands, known as the Batavian Republic, in 1795. Sacked and ransacked several times during the eighteenth century, and victim of rumours about its adverse disease environment, it proved to be one

Berbice Slave Society

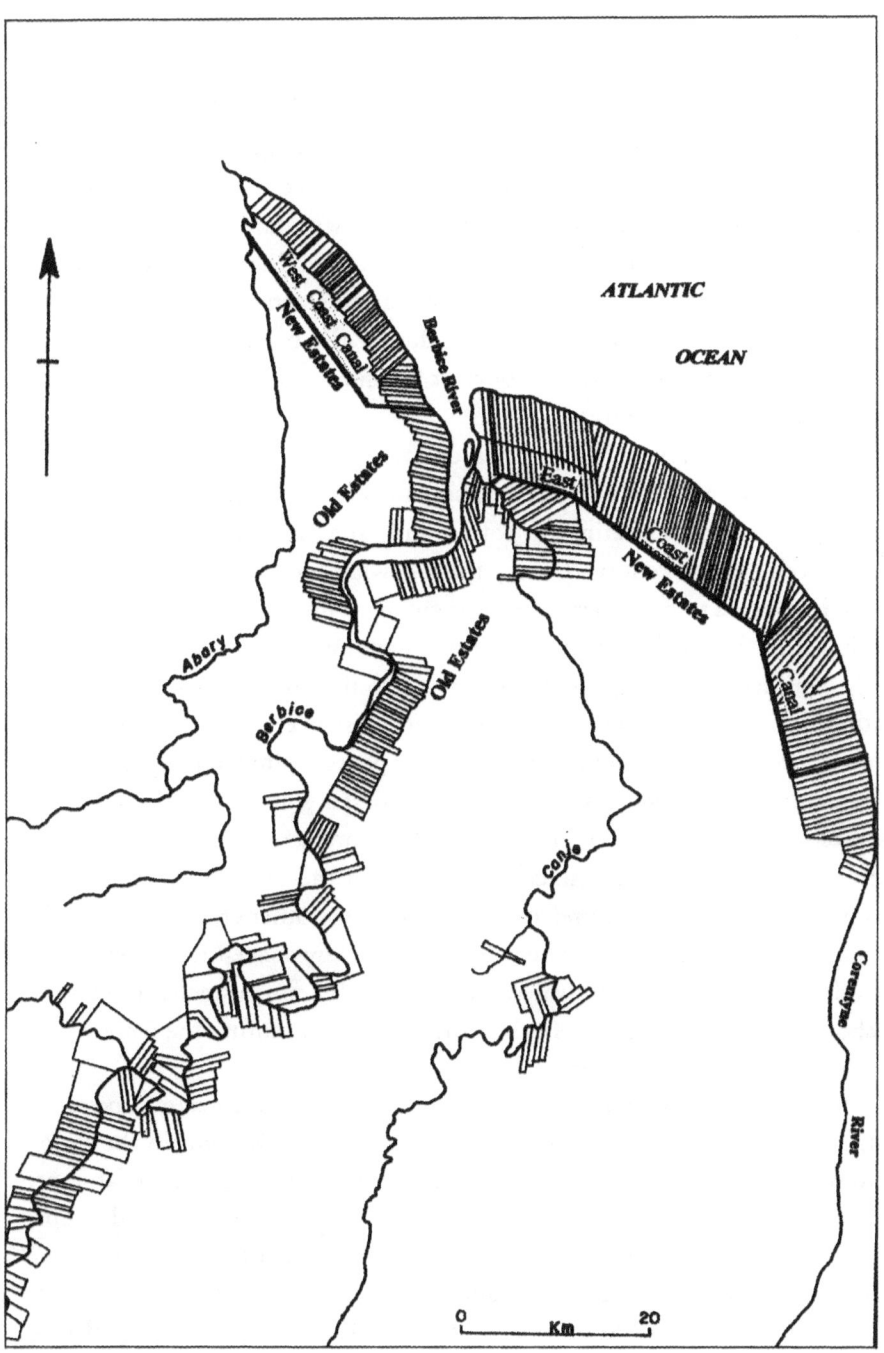

Map 4 *Distribution of estates in Berbice c.1804*

of the most unattractive colonies in the New World. The slave revolt of 1763, in which the insurgents held control of nearly the entire colony for almost a year, dragged Berbice briefly into the limelight. Other revolts chequered its existence before and after this date, notably in 1814, but these created only a few ripples. After each of them the colony lapsed back into anonymity, punctuated by small-scale marronage and brief British and French occupations during the American War of Independence and the French Revolution. After each of these wars the territory reverted to the Dutch. However, it fell to the British during the Napoleonic Wars which resumed in 1803 and, as noted above, it became a permanent British colony as a result of the peace treaty.

Berbice moved from being a tobacco colony at the time of its foundation to being a sugar colony in the late seventeenth and early eighteenth centuries, before concentrating on cotton and especially coffee production in the late eighteenth century. During the following century, under British control, it reverted to being largely a sugar colony. Thus, unlike most plantation colonies in the Caribbean, it did not maintain one dominant staple crop for any considerable time. This was due partly to the international market situation during the first phase of the colony's existence (sugar being preferred to tobacco), and soil conditions in the latter phase (cotton and especially coffee being deemed more suitable for the coastal soils where the colonists established most new estates in the late eighteenth century). Yet these factors do not fully explain the choice of crop, for in the nineteenth century the British showed a distinct preference for sugar over other crops, although the colony's fortunes might have been better assured by concentrating on coffee. Coffee estates could be cultivated profitably with a much smaller number of labourers than sugar estates. In the early nineteenth century the colony contained a significant number of small planters.[16]

In spite of the growth of Berbice's physical culture, Demerara superseded it, becoming one of the fastest growing plantation settlements in the region from the second half of the eighteenth century, and attracting far more British capital than Berbice was ever able to do. Because it possessed a superior harbour, it was also able to attract a larger quantity of shipping than Berbice, despite the fact that the number of ships trading with the latter grew from thirty-four in 1796 to ninety-four in 1798.[17] From the second decade of the nineteenth century a greater threat to the economic future of Berbice presented itself in the abandonment of a number of estates, because of speculation by Demerara planters in that colony for slaves. In April 1815 the Berbice Agricultural Society called a special meeting to determine "the most effectual means, of arresting the progress of the deterioration and ultimate destruction of this Colony, by the now frequent breaking up and abandonment of estates, and the consequent removal of the Negroes to the neighbouring Colonies".[18] In 1818 one government official complained that so great was the desire for slaves in Demerara that planters belonging to that colony were paying as much as £270 for prime Berbice slaves, and that sometimes they bought whole gangs, including the invalids, aged and children only one or two days old, at the fantastic price of £200 each.[19]

Population Profile

Berbice never had a large population, and thus almost any demographic decrease was significant. Indeed, demographically it displayed the same kind of inertia that characterized its economic development until the late eighteenth century. In 1785 the white population stood at around 280 and the slave population at 7,000. British occupation during the French Revolutionary and Napoleonic Wars increased the slave population significantly, from an estimated 8,232 in 1796 to 17,885 in 1802.[20] After 1806, with the abolition of the British slave trade to foreign and newly acquired colonies, Berbice's slave population atrophied, partly because of transfers to Demerara and partly because, as in other Caribbean plantation colonies with the notable exception of Barbados, the number of slave deaths was higher than slave births.

It is, nevertheless, extremely difficult to give an exact figure for the slave population of Berbice, even after the passage of the slave registry bill in 1817 and the first official returns under that bill in 1819. Again, the main problem is the number of transfers to Demerara, which officials guessed at rather than documented accurately, as indicated by the Registrar of Slaves in 1823.[21] For the earlier period a further complication arises, because the figures usually available are for the head tax, which excluded children under three years and listed those between three and ten years as half a person. Many slave owners also gave false returns of the slaves they possessed in order to escape the tax. There are likewise a few instances of official documents giving different figures for the taxable population in a specific year. These constraints limit the population data that we give below.

In 1815 the enslaved population was said to amount to 25,810 persons, comprising 23,723 on estates, 334 in the government's artisan shops, and 1,753 belonging to individuals.[22] In 1819 the figure stood at 23,255, while at the time of emancipation it stood at 19,359 (see Table 1.1). For some years in the 1820s slave births exceeded slave deaths, according to the registered returns of the population. This was the case in 1826, 1827 and 1828, when births exceeded deaths by 27, 124 and 55 respectively. Higman has calculated that registered natural increases per thousand of the population were -7.9 in 1819–22, -13.5 in 1822–25, +0.8 in 1825–28, and -4.8 in 1828–31.[23] This picture is not out of line with what was happening in several other slave plantation colonies, where births were rivalling and occasionally exceeding deaths among the now largely creolized slave populations. In the last years of slavery Berbice showed a much lower level of population decrease than Trinidad and Demerara-Essequibo, other newly acquired British plantation colonies.[24]

It is equally difficult to determine population figures for the whites and free coloureds. Official records show the whites in 1811 numbering only about 500, including 160 soldiers (not counting commissioned officers). The figures for 1822 and 1829 are 556 and 552 respectively. The free coloured population officially numbered 773 in 1822 and 1,151 in 1829.[25] A partial explanation of the great discrepancy in the number of free coloureds between these two dates is Lieutenant Governor Beard's observation in 1824 that free coloureds were in the habit of not registering, in order to avoid the head tax.[26]

Berbice reflected one extreme in plantation society, in which slaves vastly outnumbered whites, in contrast to Puerto Rico, which reflected the other extreme. In 1830, in Berbice, the slave-to-white ratio was 34.4 to 1, while in Puerto Rico the ratio was 0.2 to 1. Between these extremes were such colonies as Antigua (24.9 to 1), Demerara-Essequibo (21.9 to 1), Jamaica (16.9 to 1), Martinique (9.3 to 1), Trinidad (6.8 to 1), and Cuba (0.9 to 1).[27] The various Caribbean plantation colonies passed laws to ensure a minimum number of white adult males to slaves on any plantation. In 1732 the Berbice government set the ratio at 1 to 15, but by 1810 the reality had deviated from the law so greatly that the government introduced a staggered

Table 1.1   Berbice's Registered Slave Population for Selected Years, 1815–1834[28]

Year	Population
1815	25,810
1817	21,533
1819	23,255
1822	23,021
1825	21,464
1828	20,899
1831	20,645
1834	19,359

Sources: Berbice Gazette, 30 September 1815 and 12 April 1820; Council of Government of Berbice, Extract from *Sessional Papers*, 8 January 1818, PRO, CO 111/88 and enc.; "Slave Population in 1822", d. 23 December 1823, CO 111/97; Barry Higman, *Slave Populations of the British Caribbean, 1807–1834* (Baltimore, Md: Johns Hopkins University Press, 1984), 415.

ratio: at the lower end 1 to 79 and at the higher end 5 for any number above 451 slaves.[29] Planters frequently breached even these much more liberal ratios, because they were unable to attract any substantial number of whites to the colony. All these factors helped to prevent Berbice from realizing a real boom in its plantation development, unlike Demerara and Suriname, which could both point to some period of significant plantation growth.

Social Stratification and Socio-Sexual Relations

Berbice was a society that reflected many of the features of plantation societies in the Caribbean, where the whites could found colonies but could not establish a civilization. Their main (some would argue, their sole) preoccupation was gold in its literal and figurative forms. Their rough-edged philosophy caused them to wipe out much of the autochthonous culture and to suppress many of the African elements in slave culture. Everywhere they set themselves up as the new master class and built societies based on hierarchical political, economic and social structures that were themselves based on ascribed race and colour factors. They kept the subordinate groups in check, especially the enslaved people, by draconian laws and practices. The fact is that plantation slavery degraded almost all who came into regular contact with it, including administrators and missionaries who fought to humanize and even to abolish it but who nevertheless utilized the labour extracted from it. It also degraded the personhood of the enslaved people, sometimes in the most brutal forms, including the sexual exploitation of slave women, while demonstrating clearly that the racial divide in slave society rested upon conventional rather than providential factors. As Pedro Welch states, "All around them slaves could see evidence of the white man's infidelity to his own ideology of racism."[30]

Relatively few white women came to reside in Berbice, as in other plantation colonies. In 1829 the head count in Berbice showed only 126 white females, compared to 426 white males. The situation was far worse in some rural areas: 1 white female to 38 white males in the First River District, 2 to 23 in the First West Coast District, 0 to 18 in the Second West Coast District, and 0 to 23 in the East Bank and Canje River District. This adverse white female-to-male ratio contrasted sharply with that of the free coloured population, which in the same year showed a total of 688 females to 463 males. The proportion of females to males was significant in both instances, although tending in opposite directions. While the ratio of female slaves to male slaves was not as low, it showed a decided majority of males over females: 11,152 to 9,544.[31] What is important in this context is the large number of females among the free coloureds and slaves, in contrast to the situation that obtained among the whites. This encouraged liaisons between the white males and the females belonging to the free coloured and black groups.

Brutalities on Enslaved Persons

At the time of the British capture of the colony, the murder of an enslaved person was still not a capital offence.[32] Berbice would eventually rectify this situation and gradually pass a number of ameliorative laws, but planters did not easily relinquish their old ways. As late as 1827 (after the publication of the slave amelioration code in the previous year), planters still sometimes punished enslaved persons by placing their hands and feet in the stocks in such a way that their bodies were suspended from the ground and only held up by their limbs, for periods of at least one hour.[33]

In 1817 the government created the office of protector of slaves, an office in some respects similar to that of the *procureur-général* as embodied in the *Code Noir*, the French slave code of 1685. The protector, his deputy and assistants were to investigate slaves' complaints and, where appropriate, to prefer a suit against the transgressors in the regular courts of law. The protector was to submit detailed reports periodically to the lieutenant governor about his investigations. But during the first years of this office's existence the offices of protector and fiscal resided in the same person, the incumbent at the time being a plantation owner. Even when it became a separate office, the protector was still compromised for some time by his power to punish enslaved persons for making false or unproved complaints against their masters or managers.[34] The situation changed in 1829 when the secretary of state for the colonies instructed the lieutenant governor to rescind this aspect of the protector's authority. Thereafter, that official only had the authority to prosecute allegedly delinquent slaves in a regular court of law.[35]

The enslaved people suffered horrendous torture of mind and body, and had their senses sharpened by vulnerability and daily peril. One can hardly read the records of the protector of slaves without noticing the fears, anxieties and misery of most of the complainants. These records also indicate clearly a persistent spirit of slave defiance and struggle to define their own space and achieve some control over their lives. The vast majority of the complaints concerned inadequate food, clothing and rest; arbitrary, excessive and brutal punishments, including confinement in the stocks without permission to go to the proper place to relieve themselves; and punching, trampling and kicking by those in authority over them. Long and frequent punishment often maimed slaves for life, as happened to David, who had been cut up so badly that he ended up with permanent weals on his back.[36] What comes across strongly, even overwhelmingly, from a perusal of the records is a spirit of domination which accompanied the masters' dominion over the slaves, the masters demanding but not deserving respect, and the slaves striving to uplift themselves from a demeaning situation and to add some beauty to the texture of their daily lives.

The case of the enslaved woman America is one of striking brutality. In 1817 her manager, Jacobus Overeem of plantation Sandvoort, chastised her with 170 lashes because of a complaint by his wife that the slave had been insolent to her. The facts of the case underline Overeem's callous approach to discipline: America was about four months pregnant (had "young belly") at the time of the punishment; Overeem took her out of the hospital to punish her; he told her that he would only listen to her side of the story after punishing her; he lit a pipe and calmly smoked it until just over half the punishment had been meted out, following which he upbraided her and began smoking again until the end of the punishment; he employed two strong-armed drivers to cart-whip her simultaneously; and he subsequently placed her in the stocks for about a fortnight, forcing her to lie directly on her wounds. Some weeks later she suffered a miscarriage ("her belly turn"). In the trial that followed, he not only tried to lie his way out of the situation but encouraged two of his overseers to do the same. However, the court sentenced him to three months' imprisonment and also convicted one of his overseers of perjury.[37]

Overeem was not the only one on the "lunatic fringe" of society when it came to dealing with his servile charges. C.J. Grade, manager of plantation L'Espérance, displayed hardly human traits when he ordered his driver to flog the young lady Roosje (Rosa), who was eight months pregnant ("wanted one month of her time"), for not sorting enough coffee beans in the logie. The punishment was inflicted using a bush whip, doubled. Roosje had explained to Grade that she was too big to stoop and had to kneel down to do the job. So angry was he with her performance that he directed the driver to "Give it to her till the blood flies out." The next day he put her to work in the coffee field, where she began to feel a pain in her loins. The hospital doctor who examined her declared that he found nothing wrong with her and sent her back to the field. The following day she suffered a miscarriage. Her child had died in her and the black midwife had to force it out. Several witnesses who saw the dead child declared that "the arm was broken, one of the eyes out, and the head bruised". When Roosje informed the doctor of her miscarriage he replied, "I suppose you have been eating green pines." The fiscal took legal action against the manager, but unfortunately we do not know what sentence he received.[38]

It is necessary also to mention the notorious case involving Johannes Vander Brock, because of his influence in the society, the brazen way in which he flouted the law, and the judgement handed down by the court. He was a substantial planter, a former member of the colonial legislature, and had once acted briefly as governor. He was therefore well aware of both the

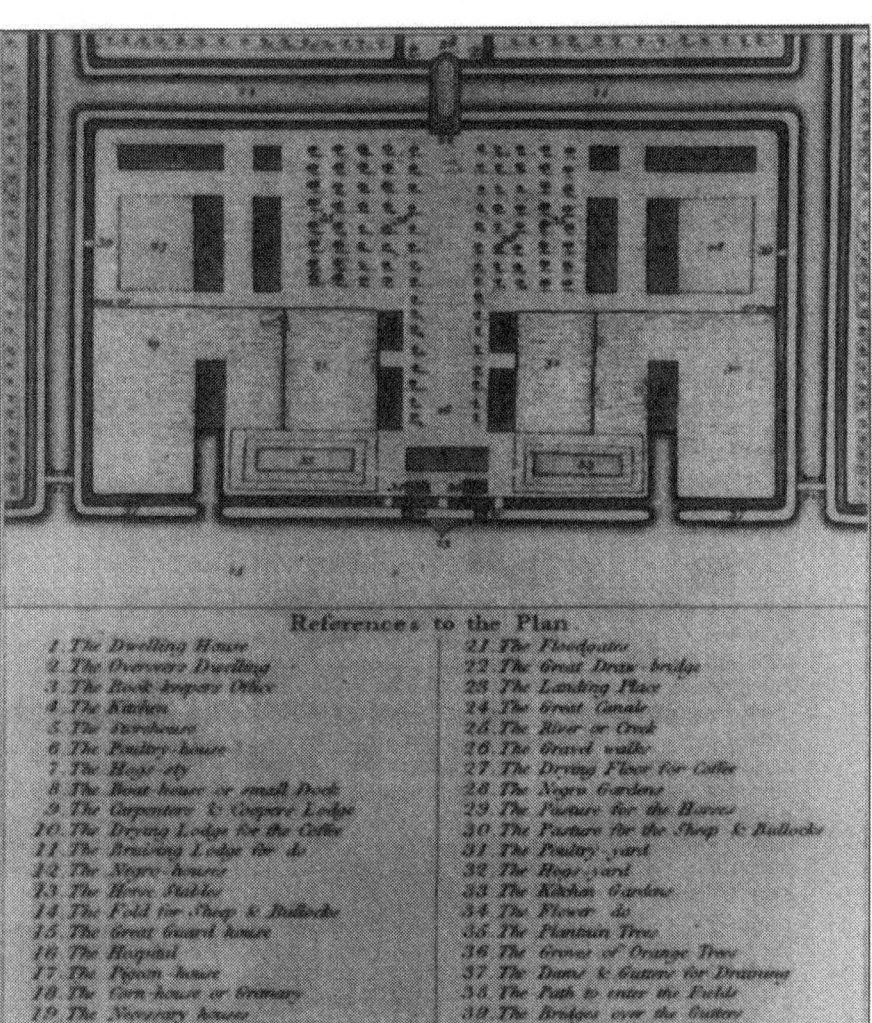

Figure 3 Plan of a coffee plantation

Reprinted from John G. Stedman, *Narrative of Five Years' Expedition against the Revolted Negroes of Surinam in Guiana on the Wild Coast of South America from the Years 1772 to 1777*, 2 vols. (London: J. Johnson and J. Edwards, 1796), 2: plate 78.

Figure 4   Coffee in the various stages of blossom
From a map of British Guiana by William Hilhouse, Demerara, 1827.

letter and the spirit of the colonial laws on the subject of slaves working on Sundays and holidays. Yet he deliberately violated these laws, alleging that he considered it more humane to punish his slaves by forcing them to complete work on these days which they should have completed earlier than to flog them. Worse still, he frankly admitted that he had punished Quassie, one of his slaves, by placing a chain weighing twenty-two pounds around his neck for a fortnight, while assigning him his normal duty of sorting beans, because Quassie had complained to the fiscal about being worked on holidays. The fiscal himself had to intervene to obtain the removal of the chain. Vander Brock admitted that the punishment was unheard of under the new ameliorative dispensation, but pleaded that it had not been unknown previously. His influence over the planter-dominated court was so strong that they found him not guilty on the charge of breaching the laws regarding Sunday- and holiday-work. On the charge of callous treatment of his slave, the court decided to remove the slave from under his jurisdiction, by selling him out of the colony and paying his owner the sale price.

Allegedly, the members of the court were disposed to sell the slave abroad because neither of the two persons involved wanted to have any dealings with the other, and they feared that the slave might fall under the influence of some relative or friend of Vander Brock, who might treat him roughly. However, the court paid no regard whatsoever to the mental and emotional pain that would result from removing the slave permanently from his friends and family.[39] The court's decision to banish him was the sentence sometimes passed on leaders of Maroon communities or revolts, habitual runaways, and persons considered hardened criminals. In effect, therefore, in this instance Vander Brock had committed the offence and Quassie had suffered the penalty. This is an outstanding example of the way in which the colonial judiciary sometimes functioned. Most disturbing of all was the sentiment of the court, in the preamble to the "sentence" passed, which indicated clearly that it was more concerned with the privileged elite than with handing down justice, although the offence was palpable. The preamble said, "In the weighing of offences and of punishment, the court would always wish to keep a steady hand; but if it at any time shake, they would hope that it may give a turn or impetus to the balance in favour of the defendant." The court was sure that in this case the defendant had acted "more on wrong judgment than wrong feeling".[40]

There was also sexual abuse. Louisa, the slave of L.F. Gallez, fell into double jeopardy, bearing a child for him and another for his son-in-law.[41] Children were also subjected to such abuses. Brutus and Aqueshaba told this story:

> The manager wants my daughter Peggy; I said no; he asked me three times; I said no; he kept the wife of Rule, and after having her a few nights, left her, therefore I refused. Manager asked me Friday night; I refused, and on Saturday morning he flogged me. . . .
>
> Peggy being sick, Acquasiba, her sister, attended; states, that manager sent aunt Grace to call Peggy, and to say if Peggy would not come, I must; we said, daddy said we must not, I was too young; Grace left us and went to daddy, shortly afterwards she returned, and tried to coax me to go, but I would not, as my daddy had forbid it. Grace went and told the manager. The manager sent to call Fanny. Fanny went up and found him in his room, and all of us (the creoles) got orders to be watchmen at his door; I was watchman, Peggy, Fanny, and many more.[42]

The protector of slaves declared that he found no hard evidence that the manager had punished Brutus for refusing to give his daughter to him, and therefore he simply admonished the manager on this score. That individual stayed on as manager,[43] probably using many of the other young girls as "watchmen" and taking "many more". This was the sordid side of human sexual relations. But the full story of sexual contact also embraces mutual amorous attraction between white males (and sometimes females) and the so-called inferior classes.

There were other kinds of brutalities. A one-legged slave who moved about on crutches complained that his master beat him with the crutch, threatened to shoot him with a pistol, locked him up for four months, and confined him in the stocks, after cutting his posterior with the whip. As the slave himself reasoned, "White people purchase negroes to work; but no white man is to kick and thump a poor negro with one leg." However, not surprisingly, his master convinced the protector that the slave was a sluggard and a liar.[44]

The people complained of a host of other annoyances and oppressions, including their superiors taking their property (chiefly livestock) without payment, and not giving them the legislated holidays or sufficient time to spend with their family and their nursing children – a common complaint among women. Here is Laura's complaint: "says, to have brought this child with great pain into life, it being of a weak constitution, requires of course maternal attendance; and as she is not allowed to provide fully for the same, she requests therefore assistance in obtaining this natural favour". The protector took no action other than recommending to the manager greater consideration to the complainant.[45] Oppression took other forms. On plantation Nieuw Stoop the owner kept "no women on the estate at all", according to one complainant, who was most likely suffering from sexual deprivation.[46]

The failure of the state to act more vigorously on behalf of the oppressed was due to a number of factors, including bureaucratic apathy and the fact that almost every colonial official, civil and judicial, owned slaves and had an institutional interest in preserving the system. M.S. Bennett, fiscal[47] and protector for a number of years, was part-owner of an estate, while Lieutenant Governors Imbyze Van Batenburg, William Gordon, John Murray, Henry Bentinck and Henry Beard were also estate owners. The governors also used the government slaves extensively, Bentinck having at one time sixty-seven of them under his control.[48] In addition, Fiscal Bennett dealt with cases from the viewpoint that Africans were natural liars and that they "are in the habit of exaggerating their complaints, and, indeed . . . very often they are unfounded; nine times in ten they proceed from the most indolent and worthless negroes".[49] It is plain, therefore, why the interests of the slaves were not impartially upheld and the efforts at amelioration were not advanced, with such a group in charge. Compromise and bias beset the judicial system, and most of the officers had only a fugitive interest in the welfare of the enslaved people.

Also, where laws existed protecting the enslaved from cruel, arbitrary and capricious acts by owners and managers, the vagueness of these laws on what constituted cruelty and the difficulty in eliciting evidence that the court would deem credible often defeated the good intention of the law. For instance, while the law prescribed a maximum number of lashes which masters or managers could impose on their own authority, it failed to define the severity with which these lashes could be administered, or the types of offences which merited the use of the whip. Thus slaves were frequently cut up by the whip, even when their masters stuck to the legal number of lashes. Moreover, the law placed no limit on the frequency with which masters and managers could administer such punishments, nor, until the last few years of slavery, did it prevent multiple punishments for the same offence – for instance, confinement in the stocks before or after a brutal whipping. The paramountcy of the proprietary rights of masters over the natural rights of enslaved persons remained a fundamental aspect of colonial and imperial law and practice until 1830.[50]

Amelioration?

John R. Ward argues that in the British Caribbean, and especially in the older colonies, planters initiated significant policies of amelioration, and that this was evident by the 1820s in such areas as food (quantity and quality), clothing, time available to slaves to tend their garden plots and engage in other personal activities, provisions and incentives for pregnant and lactating mothers, restrictions in the administration of the most brutal punishments such as severing of limbs and excessive whipping, and in a wide variety of other day-to-day practices on the plantations. He argues further that the ameliorative measures were perhaps both cause and effect of the improvement in the productivity of various colonies and of estates in particular colonies; that in the case of Jamaica, for instance, sugar and rum production per slave increased between 1750 and 1830 by an average of 40 per cent (elsewhere he says 35 per cent). This increased efficiency on the part of the enslaved people, Ward surmises, was partly due to the creolization of the labour force, which led to greater socialization of the slaves from early into the work regime, some reduction in the incidence of desertion and general unrest, and a stronger, healthier and more experienced labour force. He does point out that technical and limited scientific innovations in production partly accounted for this increase. However, he is clear that there was no "major advance in the design or quality of hand tools, so most of this difference must be attributed to greater physical strength and skill".[51] In attempting to explain generally increased indebtedness and poverty among planters in the old sugar colonies, Ward points out that they were divested of much of the fruits of their increased output by heavier imperial taxes, rising prices for overseas commodities, the vagaries of the wars of the late eighteenth and early nineteenth centuries, and absentee proprietorship that siphoned away a significant amount of the profits which should have been ploughed back into the economy to increase efficiency even further.

Ward concedes that the planters' policy of amelioration was driven in part by the pressure placed on them by the imperial government and the anti-slavery lobby in Britain, but he also sees it as a case of enlightened self-interest on the part of the planters generally. At the same time he notes that planters were inveterately opposed to the slightest interference by these metropolitan groups in what they considered as their private domain, especially since they believed themselves to be the most knowledgeable and experienced in how to deal with slaves. Finally, he argues that while "the growth of British West Indian productive efficiency accompanied a marked improvement in the slaves' material state", in social and religious terms, and ultimately in terms of the freedom of enslaved people to order their lives as they saw best, the planter programme was a clear failure.[52]

Ward's arguments are forceful and interesting. They constitute a combination of old and new ideas concerning British slave amelioration, and they are bolstered by a wide range of statistical details concerning production levels. However, Ward pays only peripheral attention to the newer slave colonies, especially Berbice, Demerara-Essequibo and Trinidad, a serious defect in a study that purports in its title to deal with the British West Indies as a whole. In addition, he does not treat seriously the possibility that, in fact, on a large number of estates (especially in Jamaica, from which he draws the best of his statistical information) the period after the abolition of the slave trade might have witnessed more draconian measures being applied to enslaved persons engaged in staple production. Finally, he relies too heavily on the testimony of planters and on the ameliorated slave laws for evidence concerning the significant improvement in rations and the increasingly healthy lifestyles of the enslaved people, although occasionally he does question these sources. Linked with this is the fact that the older colonies did not have protectors of slaves, as did Berbice, Demerara-Essequibo and Trinidad, who were required to listen to and investigate all complaints of slaves, and forward biannual reports to the Colonial Office on each case. As time progressed, the protectors were also required to include in their reports all returns to their office by managers and owners of punishments they had meted out to their slaves. This information for Berbice shows clearly that the number of punishments against enslaved persons increased significantly as emancipation approached, although the most extreme punishments occurred only infrequently because of penal and pecuniary sanctions against the perpetrators. We shall have to return to this issue in greater detail later on.

In Berbice, as elsewhere in the British West Indies, amelioration was the common topic among all classes of society, although discussed surreptitiously among the slaves. The Berbice planters, like their counterparts elsewhere, protested strongly against the issue of colonial slavery being dragged into the limelight in a way that put an unfavourable aspect on their government of their slaves. They resisted the proposals for a slave registry bill and for a more comprehensive slave code embodying ameliorative policies similar to those recently enacted for Trinidad and St Lucia. They asserted that they had already enacted several of the amelioration proposals before the imperial government had broached the issue of an amelioration code, and that these included abolishing the flogging of females, much more restricted use of the whip on males, giving slaves Sunday off as a day of rest, frequently giving them an extra day to cultivate their private gardens, and utilizing task work whenever practicable.[53] This was nothing but big talk, an instinctive rather than a reasoned response to the trenchant criticism made by the humanitarians of the planters' treatment of their charges. Their bitter opposition to the amelioration code indicated that they were not nearly as progressive as they tried to make out. According to Lieutenant Governor Beard, "Many disgraceful attempts have been made by the old Council to frustrate these measures and create dissension in the Colony."[54] Individual amelioration laws were enacted in a torturous and piecemeal manner, but the issue of a comprehensive slave code was weighed down for some time by discussion and inaction before its eventual promulgation in October 1826 (still, this was earlier than similar codes in Demerara-Essequibo, Barbados and Jamaica). The planters rightly saw amelioration – characterized by the humanitarians and the imperial government as a moral imperative – as simply an overture to the main act: the death of slavery.

From the early nineteenth century the Berbice colonial legislature, at the prompting of the imperial government, enacted a series of laws concerning food, clothes, rest and discipline. We shall deal with the first three of these in subsequent chapters. As regards discipline, the law of 1810 specified that no private person or his attorney should administer more than thirty-nine lashes for any offence. This limit was higher than that set by the Demerara-Essequibo regulation of 1784, which allowed private persons to administer no more than twenty-five lashes.⁵⁵ The Berbice law also spelled out the mode in which whipping should be administered. In order to prevent unintended damage to the slave, the individual was to be "laid flat on the ground his hands and feet tied sufficiently to prevent his vital parts being injured", under penalty of f500 (£38)⁵⁶ for any infraction of the law. The approved whip was the one in "ordinary use", and twenty-four hours' confinement of the slave in the stocks was to precede punishment. Management was to enter details of all punishments in the plantation or other appropriate book on the same day, along with the alleged offence and the person ordering the punishment. No punishment was to take place except in the presence of a medical practitioner, and punishment was forbidden if that individual indicated that it was likely to endanger the life of the slave. Finally, planters and attorneys were not to place slaves in chains, except with the consent of the fiscal.⁵⁷

As noted above, the problem was always how to give teeth to the ameliorative side of the law, which management flouted with impunity. The law concerning whipping did not indicate precisely to which instrument it referred. However, plantation slaves were apparently flogged most commonly with a *carracarra,* and less frequently with a "tar rope" and a cart whip. The *carracarra*, a sturdy bush rope, could have a damaging effect, especially when doubled or used to excess. The cart whip was a particularly brutal tool, and is described variously by James Walker (about whom much more will be said in subsequent chapters) as "the long cutting whip", a "beastly whip", and "that horrid instrument".⁵⁸ Pinckard recorded an instance in which a Demerara slave was being punished by two strong-armed drivers, who were cutting his bare skin with long, heavy whips, which conveyed the impression that they were tearing away pieces of his flesh with every blow.⁵⁹ The whipping of slaves with the same instrument used on horses and other animals is a striking indication of the legal perception of them as less than human beings. As the Lutheran minister Dr Conrad Schwiers pointed out in 1818, a slave was not regarded as a "persona" by the colonial laws.⁶⁰ According to Walker, the whip had become such a symbol of authority and a common instrument in the slave colonies that young white children commonly used it as a toy: "A stick or a stone is laid down as the supposed slave, and the pleasure of the young adept consists in lashing it with a whip."⁶¹ Thus "the young adept" was gradually initiated, or gradually initiated himself, into seeing slaves as objects to brutalize, and he would one day perfect that practice in the actual brutalization of his charges.

From the 1820s management used the whip less frequently in New Amsterdam,[62] but even after the promulgation of the slave code in 1826 a number of brutalities surfaced, sometimes leaving the protector powerless to punish delinquent masters and managers because technically their actions did not violate the law. At other times the colonial state itself erred on the side of cruelty rather than humanity. Thus the attempt to reduce the use of the whip as a tool of judicial punishment, as a result of imperial pressure on the colonial legislature, came with a sting in its tail. The treadmill became the chief instrument of correction in Berbice, as in Trinidad, Demerara-Essequibo and elsewhere, for slaves sentenced by the law courts. The Berbice treadmill had two motions, quick and slow: respectively 3.5 and 2.5 revolutions per minute. The quick motion was reserved for active youths. Those condemned to be "worked" on the treadmill could undergo up to four fifteen-minute spells in the morning and a similar number in the afternoon, at intervals of thirty minutes. They could also undergo four twelve-minute spells at noon, at reduced intervals of twenty-five minutes. Thus a slave could undergo as many as twelve spells per day, totalling two hours and forty-eight minutes. This was an exceptionally long period to be on the treadmill daily, but the records studied give no instance of any slave receiving anything close to the full measure of "work" on it. Still, a number of persons were worked for several hours weekly. In 1828 thirty-six persons (twenty-nine males and seven females) were worked on the treadmill.[63]

The treadmill was one of the most severe forms of punishment meted out to slaves, at least in Berbice. It was officially classified as "hard labour", whereas working on the public roads was classified as "employment not being hard labour". The treadmill was arguably as demeaning an instrument as the cart whip, although it never became the symbol of coercion, at least not in the same way as the whip. Higman links it with other instruments of "'official' brutality" used to keep enslaved persons in check. William Burn tells us that the spilling of blood commonly accompanied the use of this instrument.[64] The Berbice government officers considered it the most serious judicial punishment, short of execution, in the new dispensation (that is, more rigorous than judicial whippings and the use of the stocks, which remained in use for certain "offences"). They viewed the treadmill – which was sometimes combined with solitary confinement in the stocks – as such a terror that only the governor, the Court of Criminal Justice, the fiscal and the protector could sentence persons to be worked on it, under the direct supervision of the fiscal.[65]

A driver always had to be present to ensure that those being worked stayed on the treadmill. The regulations do not indicate how he was to do so, but later evidence on this point is telling. According to John Wray, in 1833 Sir James Carmichael Smyth, governor of the united colony, visited the jail and

> going to the treadmill, he examined the 'cats' with which females as well as males were flogged (some poor women of late dreadfully so), and quite shocked with those instruments of punishment, ordered them to be discontinued; these and other circumstances ending in the suspension of the fiscal and gaol surgeon.[66]

Such acts of institutional violence and brutality showed how easy it was for people who were responsible for upholding the law to be among the transgressors. The new dispensation of punishment employed the old personnel, and more brutal symbols of authority than had been used previously.

The issues of law and order, and crime and punishment, in the slave societies posed a dilemma for the imperial government, especially in the period of amelioration. In the late eighteenth century Bryan Edwards, the Jamaican planter-historian, made the point that "In countries where slavery is established, the leading principle on which government is supported, is *fear*, or a sense of that absolute coercive necessity, which, leaving no chance of action, supersedes all questions of *right.*"[67] This was a kind of Machiavellian approach to the problem, and while the imperial law officers did not go quite as far as Edwards, they admitted that as long as slavery remained in existence it had to be maintained by an extreme display of force. Stephen, reflecting on the "spirit of insubordination" that enslaved persons often displayed, rationalized that "if slavery is to be maintained at all, of course conduct of this nature must be repressed by severe punishment".[68]

This repression occurred throughout the entire system and may well have taken a turn for the worse in the last years of slavery. Stephen pointed out that during the six-month period from September 1827 to February 1828, nearly four thousand punishments had been inflicted on the servile population, which he estimated at twenty-two thousand persons. Exempting the very young, the very old and the sick, he concluded that about one-fourth of the entire servile workforce had been punished during that period. This, and other uncomfortable facts of slave life, caused him to declare that "a more deplorable condition of society can hardly be supposed", and that several harsh legal punishments for trivial offences highlighted "the extraordinary state of society, and the rude notions respecting the nature and punishment of crime existing in Berbice". He observed further that the most recent protector's report indicated "the absolute necessity of watching the administration of the law in Berbice with extreme jealousy", and that all the information available on the progress of amelioration in the colony showed that "whatever change is working in the condition of the slaves, proceeds with a pace sufficiently tardy to satisfy [sic] the most apprehensive caution".[69] This and several other circumstances convinced the cynics and critics of slavery that the more things changed, the more they remained the same.

This last observation was not entirely correct since, as we have seen, things did change, although the wheels of change turned slowly, sometimes imperceptibly, and at times seemed to be going backwards. This was the situation in relation to manumissions, an issue on which the planter class remained intransigent until the mid-1820s. The abolition of the slave trade exacerbated the situation, for now slaves became a resource of much greater value. In 1808 the estimated price of a healthy adult slave was f1,000 (£83). By the early 1820s that price could reach as high as f2,600 (£185).[70] Not only did owners increase considerably the prices they asked for slaves whom they agreed to manumit, but the government itself increased the legal fees for manumission. Between 1808 and 1820 only 151 manumissions took place, an average of just under 12 per year. It was only from 1826, with the provision of compulsory manumission in the slave code and a significant reduction of manumission fees at the prompting of the imperial government, that the number of manumissions increased appreciably, to 438 between 1825 and 1830.[71] The trend in Berbice was in keeping with what was happening in the last days of slavery in other Caribbean jurisdictions, such as Barbados, Jamaica, Demerara-Essequibo and the Bahamas. Still, impediments to manumission resulted from the very high appraisal of slaves whose prices, in cases of dispute, had to be settled by an appeals tribunal, representing mainly the plantocratic interests. The deputy protector pointed out one such instance in 1827, in which the panel appraised a six-month-old child at f500 (£34), although just seven months earlier it had appraised a child of similar age at only f200 (£14).[72]

On the whole, amelioration promised much but produced little. The main problem with amelioration was that it attempted to put a human face on an inhuman institution, but the mask kept falling off. The life of an average slave was not the comfortable one depicted by many pro-slavers.[73] A few slaves were better off materially and socially than the average, especially some drivers, domestics and specially favoured persons. In 1826 Frederick, former head carpenter of plantation Deutichem, now on pension of one joe (f22) per month, owned a slave whom he had bought for f500 from his owner. The urban slave Nancy Scott, owned by a free coloured woman, had a house with a "hall" and a "chamber", which she rented out to coloureds and others for fêtes.[74] But Frederick's and Scott's cases represented the aberration. The average slave found life to be nasty, brutish and short. Unlike peons or serfs, even creole slaves had no right to remain on the land on which they were born and had lived all their lives; nor until the last years of slavery did they have any rights to property that they had acquired. Owners could relocate, barter, sell or separate slaves from their families at whim. While the Council of Government alleged in the early 1820s that slave masters had stopped this last practice, instances of it occurred subsequently. The slave code of 1826 that sought to prohibit the practice was flawed in so far as it barred the separation of families in judicial sales but not in private ones. In 1827 Lieutenant Governor Beard cited two recent instances of the "long established usage" of breaking up families at sale, one by the receiver general and the other by the late deputy government secretary.[75]

The 1826 code also sought to protect the rights of slaves to property that they had acquired legitimately. But constant vigilance was necessary to maintain these rights, as the case of Friday illustrates. He had purchased a piece of land on which he had built a house, the whole costing about f1,000 (£71), from money obtained by self-hire. However, his owner divested him of this property and sold or transferred it to a member of his (the owner's) family. After the owner's death the matter came to the attention of the protector, who instituted proceedings to recover the property.[76] This shows how difficult it was to protect the rights of enslaved persons. A related problem was the expense entailed in enslaved persons' seeking to recover debts in the colony's law courts. Bird, the deputy protector, confessed in 1827 that "the efficacy of the Protector's attempts to recover their outstanding claims for the sale of pigs, poultry, etc. becomes each day more perplexing; few slaves if any are prepared to encounter the present heavy expense attending a suit before the Court of Civil Justice".[77] The Colonial Office suggested that the colonial legislature should set up a special petty debts court to deal with such matters, but the legislature refused for over two years to entertain such a suggestion. It was only in May 1830 that the lieutenant governor was able to report that such a court was in operation.[78] The attitude of the legislature on this score reveals the annoyance of the plantocracy at what it saw as continued imperial interference in local matters, and its lack of any real concern with the interests of the slaves when these did not coincide narrowly with those of the slave owners.

Religious and Educational Institutions

Berbice planters showed almost no regard for the development of social institutions at the nonmaterial level. It is true that few slave plantation societies in the New World demonstrated any major concern with social culture or displayed high levels of cultural attainment. The Spanish territories made some attempts to develop educational institutions from the early days, though in a rather perfunctory way. The French, British and Dutch paid much less attention to education, but the French appear to have paid more attention to religion – or at least the trappings thereof – than the other two. Up to the early nineteenth century no educational building of any sort existed in Berbice, while the only church buildings which existed were one or two small ones, or rooms in buildings (sometimes called "temples") on a few estates and in New Amsterdam. The few Reformed Dutchmen who bothered to attend church worshipped in a building the upper storey of which was used as the colonial surgeon's apartment, and the lower storey as a church.[79]

Here, as elsewhere, reforms came about slowly and haphazardly. In 1817 Wray stated that there were five places of worship in the capital, catering to Reformed, Anglican, Lutheran, Methodist and London Missionary Society (LMS) worshippers, and that an elegant Scottish church was being erected. In 1819 the LMS completed a chapel which catered to some three hundred souls, while in 1821 the colonial government erected an edifice for Reformed and Anglican worshippers to use by turns. In material terms, therefore, religion was gaining some attention among the white inhabitants of the town. However, the actual story is less impressive. The Lutherans had been without a pastor from 1779 to about 1816, the Reformed pulpit was filled only intermittently, and for many years there was only one incumbent Anglican priest in the entire colony. In 1823, in the aftermath of the slave revolt in Demerara, an anti-dissenting group burnt the LMS chapel to the ground, resulting in the scattering of many of the flock for a few years.[80] In later years Wray wrote about the drunken Lutheran and Anglican ministers, giving details which suggest that he was not simply casting moral aspersions on good men.[81]

As regards the enslaved persons, all denominations began to pay some attention to them from about the second decade of the nineteenth century, with the initiative being taken largely by the LMS. In fact, it was partly as a counterfoil to LMS activities that the Anglicans, Lutherans and Reformed people commenced missionary work. In such circumstances, it was not surprising that very few slaves entered the doors of the last three denominations, and even fewer stayed around long enough to become members and communicants. It is questionable whether these groups had any real interest in proselytizing among slaves, as this might have caused the slaves to believe that they were their keepers' brothers. The Reformed Church in Berbice owned slaves,[82] and while its doctrines are unknown to us in precise detail, it is plausible to conclude that they were similar to those of like faith in South Africa, who viewed blacks as the damned, fit to be only hewers of wood and drawers of water. From such a perspective, teaching Christianity to the slaves would be to cast pearls before swine.

The Lutheran Church, historically less sanguine in its condemnation of blacks to eternal damnation, for a very long time also found no place in its polity for its own slaves, whom it regarded as heathens and hedonistic. The church employed slave labour to cultivate its plantation Augsburg, and the management paid absolutely no attention to religious instruction. According to John Beatty, so opposed were the members of the Lutheran vestry to the pastor's initiative (around 1818) in offering religious instruction to the slaves that they removed him from the pastorate.[83] Reverend Johannes Vos, the Lutheran pastor in 1826, was quite frank about his total neglect of religious instruction to the slaves: "I have not till this day instructed any slaves in religion." However, he promised to do something about the situation immediately.[84] On the other hand, after the initial setback caused by the burning down of his chapel in 1823, Wray wrote frequently about the expansion of the LMS work, not only in town but also in the rural areas. He established new mission stations in several outlying areas.[85]

Educational institutions for both slave and free began to emerge in the 1820s, with the LMS work once again being the most significant, although largely confined to town and on a small scale. There were also about half a dozen small private schools by the late 1820s. However, the first government school was not opened until 1829. The school commenced with 31 boys and 38 girls, but showed hardly any signs of growth over the next few years. At the end of the first year enrolment stood at 89 (49 boys and 40 girls), but by 1831 it had dropped to 69 (44 boys and 25 girls).[86]

The Slave Properties of the Berbice Association

Berbician society was among the most backward of Caribbean societies in the nineteenth century. Only briefly and perfunctorily had it shown a disposition to awaken from its torpor. There was a strong sense of impermanence in the quick decay of buildings, the rapid return of abandoned estates to jungle, the high mortality rate of all segments of the population, and the absence of anything but the most rudimentary social institutions. There was no feeling of magnificence, no sense of high achievement, no cathedral effect, except perhaps in the lofty forests, mountains and waterfalls which marked the distant landscape. But this colony became the laboratory for the most intensive, though little known, "experiment" in slave amelioration conducted by the imperial government and a small group of prominent humanitarians. The subjects were a group of enslaved persons, belonging to the Berbice Association, who had fallen into the hands of the imperial government.

As noted previously, the Berbice Association had owned and managed a number of estates during the eighteenth century. In 1720 it possessed eight estates, which made it the largest slave-holding concern in the colony at that time. However, by 1796 the number of functioning estates had declined to four: Sandvoort, Dankbaarheid, St Jan and Dageraad. Sandvoort lay on the west bank of the Canje River, about five miles from New Amsterdam (or some ten miles from the mouth of the Berbice River). Dankbaarheid (later called Highbury) was about ten miles from New Amsterdam, on the east bank of the Berbice River. St Jan, before and after the period of our study, was joined together with Dankbaarheid as one estate. Dageraad (at its new site) was some thirty-five miles away, on the west bank of the same river.[87] While the association was still a major slave holder by the standards of Berbice, several private planters, such as Wolfert Katz, Paul Benfield and James Lambert, now owned more estates and a larger number of enslaved people.[88]

Attached to the association's property were a group of enslaved urban people, comprising artisans and field labourers (males and females), employed largely in New Amsterdam. The association employed these persons, known as *winkel* (that is, "shop") people, in various tasks. They belonged to one of several categories (originally called departments, each with a head over it), according to their specialities. The departments took in contracts for work, but did not usually hire out the artisans to private individuals or organizations. They also engaged in various kinds of manufacture, the products of which were sold to the public and to other government departments.[89] For instance, in 1791–93 they produced bricks for sale to the public. From January to October 1792 they produced 276,300 bricks which were used in building Fort St Andrew (Andries) and New Amsterdam. *Winkel* persons also worked on the forts and sometimes on the association's estates as bricklayers and in other capacities, some of which did not require specialized skills.[90]

From the early days of the colony's existence the *winkel* departments maintained the physical plant of the civil establishment. The departments were semi-autonomous units and received pay for all their services during the Dutch period (although the *winkels* themselves were not paid).[91] According to one source, under the Dutch the *winkel* departments held the monopoly on all artisan work done in the colony (but this probably means in New Amsterdam, the capital, and not in the rural areas), thus stifling the emergence of rival groups; the source comments, "their earnings were consequently considerable".[92] The departments were a major source of revenue to the colonial Treasury, and also contributed significantly to the governor's income through the commission that he received on their earnings.

As regards the association's estates, certain factors might have reduced their profitability. All of them were riverain, whereas coastal estates were deemed generally more profitable for cash-crop production and especially for coffee, the dominant crop by the end of the eighteenth century. The commissioners for management, who took over the administration of the properties in 1812, claimed that the estates were among the worst situated in the colony,[93] but this was not true of all of them. Dageraad was particularly unhealthy, but Sandvoort was no more unhealthy than the average Berbice estate.

Dageraad and Dankbaarheid cultivated sugar, while St Jan and Sandvoort grew coffee. Dageraad and Dankbaarheid were two out of only five sugar estates in the colony in 1807, and four in 1809.[94] Theoretically, the possession of two sugar and two coffee estates placed the association in a more favourable position financially than if it had concentrated on a single crop. It assured the association of a greater security in the event of the failure of one crop due to specific plant diseases or prevailing market conditions. However, this point should not be overstressed, since drought and other local and international circumstances often affected all planters and estates in the colony. A more obvious benefit from the possession of sugar estates was that as sugar, molasses and *kiltum* (a poor local rum produced in the colony) were often in short supply locally, they fetched relatively high prices. Questions would later be raised about the profitability of these concerns (see chapter 2), but at the time of the British takeover the estates constituted no burden to the colonial government, while it remains a moot point as to whether the *winkel* establishment was a burden.

2

The Governors' Administration, 1803–1811

The Situation around 1803

In 1803 a British naval detachment captured Berbice from the Dutch for the second time in the course of the French Revolutionary and Napoleonic Wars. At the time of the first capture, 3 May 1796, Berbice had been under the control of the Batavian Republic (the Dutch revolutionary government in alliance with France), which, shortly after it assumed power in 1795, took over the administration of the colony and placed it under the control of a body known as the Council for American Plantations.[1] This was the situation when the colony capitulated to the British in 1796. By the terms of the capitulation, the British agreed to retain the existing laws and to respect private property.

By the Treaty of Amiens (March 1802), which brought a temporary end to the war in Europe, Britain agreed to return Berbice to the Dutch, but several months elapsed before the latter actually resumed possession. Soon after, war broke out afresh and the colony surrendered once again to the British on 23 September 1803, under much the same terms as in 1796. During the first capitulation the British had been ambivalent as to whether the association's holdings should be classified as private properties. However, during the second capitulation they decided that the properties were state concerns, as a result of the association being "dispossessed [of them] by the Revolutionary Government of Holland".[2]

As under the Dutch regime, the British imperial government entrusted the oversight of the new Crown properties to the colonial governors from 1803 to 1811, but the latter developed no clear plan of how to manage them. In March 1804 the Colonial Department issued specific but not sufficiently comprehensive instructions concerning the administration of the properties to Van Batenburg, the Dutch governor retained by the British. He was to obtain an accurate account of their financial returns, including all credits and debits, from 1796 to the present, and to send any surplus funds immediately to the Lords Commissioners of the Treasury. He was also to send similar returns to the Treasury every six months, along with any surplus money, after the Court of Policy (that is, the colonial government) had checked and certified them. He was to consign all produce from the estates to Thomas Eden & Co. in London, from whom he was also to order all overseas articles required for the properties. He was given full powers to appoint and remove personnel connected with these properties. But the most interesting aspect of his instructions, in view of what transpired later, was the following stipulation:

> It is left to your discretion either to assign fixed salaries to the persons who may be employed under you or to allow a per centage upon the returns of the property under their agency, but the whole of the charges must on no account exceed the amount allowed under the former government, which, including the commission to the Governor, is stated to have been 10 per cent upon the profits.[3]

As regards the properties, the inventories in 1803 do not give sufficiently detailed profiles of their physical condition in such crucial matters as the slaves, fields and buildings, or of their financial prospects. While the inventories differentiate the slave population according to gender, fitness for duty and, to some extent, age (that is, adults, youths and children), they do not indicate the age distribution of the adult population or the various illnesses from which the slaves were suffering. In relation to the dwellings, in the cases of Dankbaarheid, St Jan and Dageraad the inventories only record the number of slave huts; in the case of Sandvoort the record only mentions "a sett [*sic*] of Negroe Houses", while for the *winkel* department the entry simply notes that there were "Houses serving for Negroe Houses". We cannot determine the type of accommodation on Dageraad. However, individual huts seem to have been the norm for Dankbaarheid and Sandvoort, with an average of 4.7 and 4.6 occupants respectively. On the other hand, St Jan seems to have used barracks, accommodating an average of 11.3 persons in each dwelling. The *winkel* village seems also to have contained individual huts, averaging 5.5 persons each in 1812. The records do not indicate whether these were laid out in an irregular fashion or according to some linear design.[4]

The inventories mention only one industrial building (on Sandvoort) as needing extensive repairs.[5] However, Colonel Robert Nicholson, temporary lieutenant governor of the colony, in commenting on the inventories, expressed the view that, although the estates possessed a "great number of valuable workmen", the buildings and houses were "in a very bad state". He stated further that the properties were "totally unproductive in their present states and something should be done with them".[6] However, Nicholson failed to explain that the drought of that year had played a large role in the estates' reduced productivity, and that estates in the colony as a whole had been similarly affected.[7]

Van Batenburg, writing a year later, added certain important details about the estates. In his opinion, Sandvoort was a fine coffee estate, endowed with an adequate number of slaves, and once the weather conditions were fine it would always be productive. St Jan had an "indifferent soil" and would never be productive. A new piece of ground had been put into cultivation there lately, and all the buildings had to be rebuilt as those existing were "only temporary ones". Dankbaarheid's soil was not as good as some other sugar estates in the colony, but the estate had a fairly good gang of labourers and tolerably good buildings. Dageraad stood on soil far superior to that of Dankbaarheid, but the buildings were in a shocking state of disrepair; it would require a year and great expense to rehabilitate them. On the whole, the estates would incur great expense and would hardly yield sufficient revenues, especially since they were heavily indebted.[8] He also commented that the *winkel* establishment comprised almost all old people, since for some time the department had not purchased fresh imports. On the question of the workshops and dwellings, B. Lohman, the person in charge of the establishment, had noted a few months earlier that they had been extensively rehabilitated.[9] Van Batenburg had perhaps given a more sober appraisal of the properties than his immediate predecessor, but his view still conflicted with official figures which showed the estates as having realized net surplus revenues for both the periods 1796–1802 and 1804–8. The *winkel* department had also shown a substantial profit during the first period, but rather dubious figures exist for the second (see below). This was the situation when the British took over the properties.

The Amelioration Question

The imperial government had now become the owner of over eleven hundred enslaved people, mostly engaged in plantation agriculture. Although the government did not recognize it fully at the time, and although the official records up to 1809 were silent on the point, the government had become involved in the task of making the estates profitable and ameliorating the conditions of the labourers. The government did not regard the undertaking as an experiment, and certainly did not issue any detailed instructions concerning the running of the estates and the treatment of the slave population, as the commissioners for management (also called the Berbice commissioners) were to do later. However, given the context in which the administration of the estates was taking place, it is obvious that several persons in both Europe and the Caribbean would pay careful attention to the manner in which the government, through its colonial officials, executed the task of running the estates.

The context in question relates to the general debate which was taking place in Britain and her colonies over two deeply emotive issues – the slave trade and slavery. Anti-slavery agitators were focusing attention at that time mainly on the abolition of the slave trade, but the system of slavery also came under attack. Among the main agitators were Thomas Clarkson, William Wilberforce, Zachary Macaulay and James Ramsay, who, along with many others, were calling for the amelioration of the economic, social and legal conditions of enslaved persons in the British colonies. The humanitarians (as this group was known) also argued that abolition of the slave trade would cause the planters, out of enlightened self-interest, to improve the conditions of their charges, thereby ensuring that the slave population increased by natural means rather than importation. The humanitarians were convinced that such improvement would lead to increased production of plantation staples, since the workers would perform better under improved conditions. Since the early eighteenth century, Barbados had been the only British plantation colony in which the slave population was increasing by natural means.[10] To the anti-slavery interests the high mortality rate among slaves was conclusive evidence that, when weighed in the balance, the plantocracy were found wanting, although the latter protested that they were being cheated at the scales.

As already noted, Berbice experienced the first blow of the abolition axe when the British abolished the slave trade to the newly acquired colonies in 1806 and, like other British colonies shortly after, it faced the challenge of introducing ameliorative policies to increase the population naturally. Up to this time the imperial government had not tried to enact any ameliorative legislation for the colonies; it had simply urged the colonial legislatures and planters to put in place more humane laws and practices. It also periodically disallowed specific laws that it considered prejudicial to the welfare of the enslaved persons.

The assignment of the lieutenant governors as the chief administrators on the ground was a sound decision but, left largely on their own without direct imperial oversight, they did a bad job. They, along with other colonial officials, showed more concern with profiting as much as possible from the properties than with effecting improvements. The physical plant depreciated further during this period. The *winkel* department fell heavily into debt with little hope of recovery, while the estates were barely making ends meet and were threatened with complete failure. Ill will, heated verbal exchanges, accusations, reprimands and open animosity became regular features of the administration of these properties. Slavery had become a sensitive political subject, and that sensitivity increased significantly when the enslaved persons belonged to the Crown. Van Batenburg, who, during his first period of administration, had ingratiated himself to the local plantocracy, now became the object of their disfavour by taking over the properties on behalf of the Crown, an act which they viewed as a violation of the terms of the capitulation.[11]

Winkel Work

Under the Dutch the *winkel* establishment comprised several specialties, referred to by the Dutch as different departments. Now, under the British, the entire plant was generally referred to as a single department, which is the way in which we shall refer to it henceforth. During the Dutch period the department received payment, usually in cash, for all work done either for other government departments or for private individuals. Under the British, the civil government assumed full responsibility for the upkeep of the department, but it did not pay the department in turn for maintaining the public establishment. According to Frederick Nicolay, the civil commissary,

> [W]hile the Winkel Department was under the charge of the Governor of the Colony ... the Government House, and all the public buildings, the public boats, stellings and wharfs, used to be kept in constant repair by the Winkel Dept, without any charge being made for such work. The mechanics were almost constantly employed in this manner, being even obliged to quit any other occupation in which they may have been engaged when Colony work was to be done.[12]

Payment for *winkel* work done for private individuals was made to the colonial Treasury. The department also worked for the Crown estates,[13] receiving estate produce in lieu of actual payment. The department therefore lost the semi-autonomous status that it had enjoyed under the Dutch.

The military governors removed several of the ordinary field people and artisans to work on improvements to the military installations. The number so removed amounted to sixty-three in 1804 and thirty in 1816.[14] Van Batenburg had alleged in 1804 that the removal of thirteen carpenters, in particular, had left the civil establishment with very few skilled hands to carry out much-needed repairs to Government House and the other public buildings in town. However, this was not the main reason for the general shortage of skilled labour which led to the very poor state of repair of some government buildings, at least up to 1810.[15] Over the years the *winkel* management had made little effort to train new artisans. In every one of the skilled trades the number of artisans in 1812 was smaller than in 1803. For instance, figures for the following categories in 1803 and 1812 respectively were boat builders 25 and 13, blacksmiths 10 and 7, whitesmiths 14 and 9, coopers 14 and 11, masons 9 and 5, sawyers 8 and 4, and carpenters 28 and 18.[16] The shortage of carpenters, in particular, about which the civil authorities complained so much, could easily have been reversed by training a number of youths in that skill, one of the simplest industrial skills to grasp. A more progressive policy would also have paid some attention to teaching young females skills as seamstresses, an activity only engaged in some years later.

Given the fact that the *winkel* people constituted the working arms and legs of the civil and military establishment, it is difficult to understand why the Court of Policy asserted in 1811 that "the Winkel department originally instituted for the convenience and comfort of the Colony, has long ago become oppressive and burthensome to it", and went on to suggest that the imperial government should get rid of the department by hiring the *winkel* people out, assigning them to the estates or selling them.[17] Actually, the Court of Policy did not wish to get rid of the whole gang but rather to retain a small corps who would service the regular maintenance needs of the colony, while hiring gangs for major capital and other projects.[18] On the other hand, the court had no interest in retaining or paying for those (thirty-five) persons who constituted part of the domestic staff of the lieutenant governor, and it would later campaign to rid the colonial legislature of the cost of maintaining them.[19]

Of the 251 persons comprising the adult population of the *winkel* department in 1812, 56 were "superannuated" officially.[20] Subtracting the aged, infirm and children from the workforce, this left at least 195 persons who were capable of remunerative work. It is therefore difficult to understand why the department was earning very little money, unless management was squandering their labour. The problem of determining the money earned from their labour is compounded by the fact that the officials kept records in a slipshod manner. Moreover, most of the records dating from after 1808 were not turned over to the agent of the commissioners for management in 1812, because of unavailability.[21]

The financial statement that Lieutenant Governor Gordon submitted to the Colonial Office in 1813 for the period 1804–9, though of doubtful accuracy, gives a vivid picture of financial loss by the department and heavy subsidies by the colonial legislature. The statement shows total receipts for the period of f87,759, as against total payments of f482,279, resulting in a deficit of f394,520.[22] These figures are in striking contrast to those for 1796–1802, which show f509,323 in receipts and f203,269 in payments, resulting in a net profit of f306,054.[23] From the first full year that the lieutenant governors took over the administration (1804), the receipts plummeted while the payments escalated. Overall, the differences between the two periods are so huge as to confirm the suspicion that something was radically wrong with both the system of accounting and the way the department was run. It is highly improbable that the expenses for just over 350 *winkel* people would have been almost as great as those for over 800 slaves on the estates (see Table 2.1, p. 59). The financial records themselves are sometimes ambiguous and occasionally contradictory. For instance, one official document gives the lieutenant governor's 10 per cent commission from the department's earnings in 1811 as f9,954.[24] However, a committee set up by the Court of Policy to examine the government accounts for that year declared that the total receipts of the department were "not quite f9,000", that is, less than the lieutenant governor's commission. Equally strange is the fact that the record shows the lieutenant governor's commission from the department in that year as being higher than that from all the estates combined for the same year.[25]

In reviewing the department's financial position, a number of other factors need to be considered. Contrary to the policy that the Colonial Department had established in 1804, that the total administrative charges on the properties should not exceed 10 per cent of the profits, Van Batenburg and his successors exacted a commission of 10 per cent of the gross revenue, in addition to the salaries and fees paid to other officers. This commission constituted a substantial part of the lieutenant governor's salary. Woodley's commission in 1809 (from all the properties) was f30,661 (£2,190), roughly 49 per cent of his salary.[26] Nicolay, in explaining why the department had been "so very unproductive", stated:

> In the first place, prior to the transfer of the properties to the Crown Commissioners [in 1812] there were a great number of Negroes attached to the fort – 30 – the hire of which was charged to the British Government – on the amount of which, as well as on the nominal hire of the 60 attached to the Governor himself, all Governors received a commission of 10 per cent. In fact the labor of the whole working gang was calculated, whether productive or not, and the Governor received the commission of 10 p cent [*sic*] on the whole, which amounted in general to f10,000 or f11,000 a year.[27]

Among the other causes Nicolay listed was the assignment of domestics to various public officers – the lieutenant governor, commissary, missionary, clerks and others – without paying any hire for them, while the department fed and clothed them. He estimated the total for whom the department received no remuneration whatsoever at between 115 and 120, leaving the "effective" labour force at the disposal of the department at about 50, when one discounts the aged, invalids and children.[28] No department could expect to pay its bills under such circumstances, and as the commissioners of inquiry observed (in 1826), the heavy debt burden with which the department was saddled "ceases to be a matter of astonishment".[29] Had the department received payment for all work done for public institutions and individuals, it would have realized a net surplus revenue. Based on the prevailing prices in 1812, the seventy men and twenty-five women employed year-round in the civil and military offices of the government would have earned an estimated f26,625 (£1,775).[30] The loss of this money constituted a substantial dent in the *winkel* revenue, even not taking into account the lieutenant governor's commission.

Graft and corruption were the frequent bedfellows of several officials involved with the department. A case in point is that of Webbe Hobson, the colony's receiver general, whom Lieutenant Governor Gordon discovered embezzling the department's funds, to the extent of at least f10,000 (£833). Gordon set up a committee of the Court of Policy to look further into the matter. The committee discovered that the situation was much worse than the governor had supposed. Hobson had omitted several payments to the department in the ledgers that he kept, thus showing a debit of f44,000 (£3,667) in that account, "totally different" from the documents that he had submitted to the court, which showed a surplus in the account.[31] Hobson sought to explain these discrepancies in various ways which did not prove satisfactory to the court. In the end the lieutenant governor, having already removed Hobson from office, decided to allow him to repay the outstanding balance within a specified time. The quantity of twenty slaves which he offered as security for repayment[32] was highly inadequate, since at that time a prime slave was valued at around f1,200 (£100).

Hobson was not the only culprit. In 1807 a committee set up by the court to examine the accounts of the department expressed surprise that there were no debts against Van Batenburg's estates from June 1796 to December 1802. When the deputy receiver general was requested to explain this circumstance, he declared that Van Batenburg had ordered him not to list these debts in the public books but rather in a separate one kept by the commissary. The committee could not determine what had happened to the book.[33]

Estate Administration and Finances

The situation in respect of the estates is more difficult to assess. Several discrepancies and contradictions exist in the statements of the various lieutenant governors (and sometimes in those of a single individual) concerning the viability of the concerns, a situation only partly explained by the instability of the international markets due to the war. Although the administration kept a large number of estate books, they were not in any systematic order and the accounts for several years were missing when De la Court, the new agent for the commissioners for management, received them in 1812. The financial statement dispatched to London in 1809 at the behest of Lord Castlereagh claimed that the estates collectively had realized a revenue surplus of £20,597 from 1804 to 1808. Sandvoort had experienced a loss only in 1805, but one that was sufficiently large to offset its gains in the following years.[34]

Lieutenant Governor Montgomerie boasted that during his regime (September 1807–March 1808) production rose appreciably on the estates,[35] and Dalrymple (January–December 1810) also conveyed the impression that the estates did quite well during his tenure: "I shipped one hundred thousand weight of coffee consigned to the House of Prinseps Saunders & Co. and left considerable quantity of produce on the estates when I delivered them over to Governor Gordon and have besides in my hands a small balance of money arising from sales of produce."[36] A few years later, Gordon declared that up to the end of his term of office the estates had managed to meet their expenses out of their own revenues; however, this view was in conflict with his earlier statements.[37] While the estates never became a burden on the Treasury, the extant records cast doubt on the accuracy of the accounts. The financial statement dispatched by Woodley contained a major accounting error which, when corrected, shows that the estates realized a significantly smaller surplus than he reported (£12,264 instead of £20,597).[38]

In 1810 Dalrymple estimated the lieutenant governor's annual commission from the estates at £1,200,[39] but Gordon in 1811, while also deriving a substantial commission from the estates, considered them unprofitable ventures which the Crown should sell or lease. According to him, the prices for colonial produce were low while the cost of repairing the buildings and other

Table 2.1 Summary of Revenue and Expenditure of Crown Estates, September 1804–December 1808 (guilders)

Year	Revenue	Expenditure
1804	53,239:8:8	44,322:0:0
1805	154,214:1:8	157,906:1:0
1806	181,114:5:4	110,655:8:0
1807	132,749:6:0	102,072:4:0
1808	125,382:17:0	84,571:15:0
Total	646,699:18:4	499,527:8:0

Source: "Account of produce", in Woodley to Castlereagh, 19 July 1809, PRO, CO 111/77.

works was high, and since no money was available in the estates' accounts to pay for these repairs, to effect them would result in substantial indebtedness for at least the next two years. He attributed this situation mainly to bad management.[40] Gordon painted too gloomy a picture of the estates, but he was quite correct in identifying poor maintenance and bad management as the main issues to be addressed. Nicholson, Montgomerie and Woodley had earlier pointed to the woeful state of the buildings, while Colonel Staple, with some exaggeration born of self-interest, had alleged that the estates were "gone to perfect ruin, the buildings . . . altogether destroyed and the whole . . . in a state of complete dilapidation". Gordon did not accuse his predecessors specifically, but Staple opined that a central reason for the deterioration was that most of the governors had no prior experience in managing Caribbean estates.[41] While Montgomerie had also noted bad management as a reason for the poor performance, he himself can be accused of the same.

Van Batenburg had made some effort to replace those buildings on Sandvoort that were beyond repair, but when Montgomerie took over the government in September 1807 he put a stop to this. He was only prepared to repair a few buildings which he stated were "very much neglected", and he claimed that a heavy expense was entailed by the repair. When Gordon took office twenty months later, he found the estate buildings "in a state of great delapidation".[42] The neglect of the estate buildings was symptomatic of the more general neglect of the government buildings.

Another alleged reason for the low profitability of the estates was the advanced age of their workers.[43] However, private efforts to lease the estates suggest that the invalidity (or lack of physical strength) of the labourers was grossly exaggerated (see below). The probity of the estate staff was perhaps a much more important reason for the modest financial performance of the estates. In 1805 Godlieb (alias George) Willem Unger, general overseer of the estates (under the supervision of the lieutenant governor), made serious allegations of fraud against Van Batenburg. According to him, Van Batenburg had instructed Van Hattem, the bookkeeper and clerk, to insert in the account books a governor's commission of 5 per cent dating back to 1796, although the British government did not place Van Batenburg in charge of the properties until 1804. It also showed Nicholson as receiving a commission, although Unger was certain that he did not receive one cent. The result of these interpolations was that the account now stood in a deficit instead of its former surplus position, to the tune of £2,460. Unger brought his allegations to the attention of the imperial officials in London, but it seems that they took no action on the matter up to Van Batenburg's death in November 1806.[44]

Gordon bemoaned inheriting a legacy of bad debts, which he estimated at about £3,200. He lamented being unable to meet pressing obligations for food and clothing for the people, short of a temporary loan from the imperial Treasury against a consignment of coffee recently dispatched to Europe by his predecessor.[45] He ordered an impartial appraisement of the estates, along with their servile occupants, but when he received the report he expressed surprise at the high value at which they had been appraised. He was not persuaded: "As I see not the least prospect of benefit to the Crown by holding these properties, I strongly recommend them to be leased or sold on almost any terms."[46] This was strong language from a man on the spot who presumably had the Crown's interests at heart. But he had erred in his appraisal of the properties, for eighteen months later he asserted that the estates had always met their expenses. The Court of Policy had also declared earlier that an amalgamation of the estates and the *winkel* department should ensure that they would meet all their expenses, so that the latter would no longer be a burden on the colonial Treasury.[47]

Gordon's most serious indictment against the managers and administrators was their neglect of the welfare of the enslaved people in respect of food, clothing and housing. He had this to say about the food situation on his arrival as lieutenant governor: "by some unaccountable bad management, the stock of ground provisions on the estates has been totally neglected, and the estates, being destitute, are obliged to purchase food for the slaves at a very heavy expense. I have made it my first care to remedy this evil, by planting provisions." He also charged that the *winkel* people had not received any allowance of clothing for the previous two years, a charge reminiscent of that made by Montgomerie in the previous year.[48]

In reviewing the performance of the estates and the quality of the management it is necessary to consider the general circumstances affecting the colony at the time, which impacted upon all the estates. From at least 1803 the colony experienced a series of natural and man-made disasters: cycles of drought and floods, fluctuating but generally low prices for colonial produce, and European warfare which spilled over into the Caribbean. Periodic cycles of drought and flood forced many a planter to "go under". In 1803 and 1804 drought wrought much havoc upon the estates, resulting in very low yields and a scarcity of provisions. The planters had to purchase imported flour for the labourers at very high prices. Many planters, unable to pay their debts, were sued in the local courts of justice. In November 1804 Van Batenburg indicated that the previous year's drought had taken its toll on the present year's crop of sugar on Dankbaarheid. In the following year he wrote that adverse weather had affected the colony's coffee crop so badly that "very little indeed was made last year, & the first crop was a mere nothing".[49] In 1809 Woodley commented that the colony had been "entirely under water" because of heavy rains which had fallen from November to March, and that as a result the cotton crop "is totally lost, and those of sugar and coffee are materially injured". This economic disaster had contributed significantly to the colonial Treasury being "without funds, and almost without credit".[50] The American merchants were demanding cash or colonial produce, which the colony could not supply. The local paper currency was worthless for such foreign transactions, and so the Americans had virtually deserted the colony. Not more than nineteen small vessels had visited the colony from January 1808 to February 1810, so that basic necessities were in short supply.[51]

In 1812 Gordon wrote that all the colonists were insolvent because of crop failures, low prices for colonial produce and high prices for supplies.[52]

By February 1813 the colonial Treasury was again in a virtually bankrupt situation: the receiver general needed f47,653 immediately to meet salary and other commitments but had "no funds of any description". Although outstanding debts to the Treasury were worth more than twice the sum required, there was little hope of realizing these in the short term. The government decided to relieve the problem through a new issue of f50,000 in paper money.[53] The situation was rather bleak, and might tempt us to conclude that, in the circumstances, the Crown estates had performed exceptionally well to remain solvent throughout the period. However, it is important to recall the statements of those who had first-hand knowledge of the condition and performance of the estates, and who alleged that under sound management they could have done much better.

Proposals for Rental of the Estates

It was with the prospect of making the estates viable that Colonel Staple approached the imperial Treasury in 1809 about leasing the estates for a stipulated number of years or until the end of the war should determine the fate of the colony and the estates. In return, he offered to pay a fee of £3,000 for the first year, and an additional £500 after every three years, to an upper limit of £5,000. He was also willing to guarantee that the properties would be maintained in no worse condition than they had been delivered to him. Shortly after this Wolfert Katz, the foremost planter in the colony and owner of about seven estates, put forward a counterbid to lease the properties for fourteen years at an initial fee of £3,000 per annum and increasing by £500 each year to a maximum of £6,000.[54] Meanwhile, Staple's offer had caused the Lords Commissioners of the Treasury to show great interest in the estates for the first time in about five years. They concluded that it was "evident from the amount of Mr Staples offer that they ought to have produced annually a very considerable sum". They therefore asked the Colonial Department to obtain from Woodley an immediate update on the financial position of the properties and to seek his opinion about leasing them to Staple.[55] The lieutenant governor's reply is quite interesting, in light of the prevailing view that the estates were not viable concerns and particularly in light of Gordon's views two years later.

Woodley replied that the estates had realized an average annual profit of £3,500 "clear of all expenses" during the period of British control, but that they had experienced some difficulties recently due to adverse weather conditions. He felt that, given the large contribution they were making to the civil establishment, Staple's offer was too low, but he also expressed the seemingly contradictory view that because they needed extensive repairs, a £500 increase in rental every three years was somewhat steep. He concluded by expressing a personal interest in renting the properties, as one who had resided many years in the Caribbean and owned property there. He hoped that if the imperial officers should decide to rent them they would consider him as being "entitled to a preference" on the same terms proposed by Staple. Dalrymple, successor to Woodley, also expressed an interest in leasing the properties.[56]

The Lords Commissioners decided to accept the tender of Wolfert Katz, who had put in the higher bid, but with the understanding that they could not guarantee him the lease beyond the period that the colony might remain under British control or "against the claims of any other Government upon account of this Transaction".[57] Katz found these terms unacceptable, and so the Lords Commissioners agreed to accept Staple's tender, subject to proper securities "for the payment of the rent & the performance of the Covenants".[58] At the same time Spencer Perceval, the prime minister and a fervent Protestant, decided to refer the proposed contract to James Stephen, who later became a well-known abolitionist, for a legal opinion on the matter.[59] Stephen advised the Treasury that the contract needed a clause "obliging the lessee to adopt the most probable means for keeping up the numbers of the slaves, by native increase, and to make periodical returns of the births and deaths; and enabling the Crown to determine the lease, whenever it should appear that the loss by mortality was so dangerously great as to demand that remedy".[60]

Acting on his advice, the Treasury proposed to Staple's attorney a contract containing a clause giving the former power to void it if at any time there should be a decrease in the slave population of more than 10 per cent on any single estate or 5 per cent on the estates combined. Staple's attorney responded that his client could give no guarantees respecting the depreciation of the slave population because their rate of decrease was exceptionally high.[61] This allegation startled the Lords Commissioners, who thought that such a situation called for urgent action. However, on seeking a clarification from Lieutenant Governor Gordon, they were informed that Staple's attorney had exaggerated the situation grossly. According to Gordon, there were 884 persons on the estates in 1803 and 791 in 1811, resulting in a net loss of 93, or 10.52 per cent over eight years – about 1.32 per cent per annum. The *winkel* department comprised 359 persons in 1803 and 348 in 1811, a net loss of 3.06 per cent in eight years or 0.38 per cent per annum.[62] Accurate figures are unavailable for the slave population in Berbice as a whole during this period, but Higman estimates a decrease of 9.66 per cent over the eight-year period 1807 to 1815 and 12.57 per cent from 1817 to 1825 (when the figures are less inaccurate).[63] The decline of the Crown slave population was therefore not out of line with that in the colony at large, although the death rates in both instances were high. These rates dramatically emphasize the point that while all humans are subject to mortality, the enslaved people were often tortured in life and swallowed up by death.

In the eyes of the Lords Commissioners, any situation not leading to the natural increase of the population was unacceptable. They also realized that it was clearly hypocritical for the imperial government to goad colonial assemblies to introduce amelioration while that government itself failed to do so when it had an opportunity.[64] Therefore they decided, even before the receipt of Gordon's reply, to abandon negotiations with Staple and to set up a Commission for Management, comprising humanitarians in London directly responsible to them.[65] The two main objectives of the Treasury were to effect the slaves' natural increase by improvement in their health and to effect their moral improvement through Christian religious instruction. The commissioners for management, themselves, added as a third objective the realization of a net profit from the properties.[66]

The members of the new commission, appointed on 23 April 1811, were William Wilberforce, Charles Long, Nicholas Vansittart, James Stephen, James Gordon and William Smith. They were all well-known humanitarians and abolitionists, several of them being members of the "Clapham Sect" that gave organizational structure to the campaign against the slave trade and in 1787 founded the Society for Effecting the Abolition of the Slave Trade. The most famous of them were William Wilberforce (1759–1833) and James Stephen (1758–1832).

Wilberforce was a member of Parliament for many years, and the main person carrying on the fight for abolition of the slave trade in that institution from 1791 to 1807. He was also a founder member of the African Institution, established in 1807 to ensure the effective implementation of the British abolition laws and the extirpation of the foreign slave trade. He was likewise a member of the Sierra Leone Company, which was instrumental in founding the Sierra Leone colony for repatriated blacks from Britain, Nova Scotia and elsewhere.[67] Stephen was the legal mind in the anti-slavery movement, until he was largely superseded by his arguably more illustrious son, Sir James Stephen. A member of Parliament at the time of his appointment to the commission, he had developed an acute hatred of slavery, having seen the brutalities meted out to the slaves in Barbados *en route* to St Kitts, where he practised law for some years. Like Wilberforce, he was a founder member of the African Institution. He wrote several letters and pamphlets on the subject of slavery and in defence of Africans against the charge of cannibalism. His two best known works on the subject of slavery are *Reasons for Establishing a Registry of Slaves in the British Colonies* and *The Slavery of the British West India Colonies Delineated*.[68]

Shortly after (date uncertain), the commission appointed Zachary Macaulay (1768–1838) as their secretary and accountant. He had vast experience as bookkeeper and manager of an estate in Jamaica, governor of the humanitarian settlement of Sierra Leone, and secretary and later committee member of the African Institution for a number of years. In 1823 he cooperated with Thomas Fowell Buxton in founding the Society for the Amelioration and Gradual Abolition of Slavery Throughout the British Dominions, popularly known as the Anti-Slavery Society. He was editor of the *Christian Observer*, the magazine of the Clapham Sect, and also of the *Anti-Slavery Monthly Reporter*, the official organ of the Anti-Slavery Society.[69]

An interesting point is that, contemporaneous with the attempts to ameliorate the conditions of the Crown slaves in Berbice, some of the members of the humanitarian group, especially Wilberforce, Macaulay and Thomas Clarkson, were involved in efforts, through the initiative of Henri Christophe, self-styled king of Haiti (1811–20), to improve the moral, educational and other aspects of Haitian life. The humanitarians were keen on developing this relationship, which they saw as an opportunity of proving that, outside of the context of slavery, blacks could advance in all areas of life just as other "civilized" peoples did. They could think of no more appropriate circumstance than a small nation recently liberated from slavery and colonialism. From 1816 they began to supply Haiti with a number of teachers, missionaries, agriculturists, technicians, doctors and other skilled personnel. They also recruited a few professors of classics, medicine and mathematics for a new Royal College. Wilberforce became the personal adviser of Christophe on matters of social reform and government, while Clarkson became his unofficial representative to the government of France. Religious institutions in Britain, including the British and Foreign School Society and the British and Foreign Bible Society, sent a lot of religious literature to Haiti. By 1820 an estimated 1,110 students were receiving a basic education through the medium of English in various parts of the country. While these numbers were small in terms of the educational needs of the nation, a significant start had been made in comparison with what had obtained before Christophe assumed office. However, the effort was short-lived; Christophe became terminally ill and eventually killed himself. Unfortunately, after his death the process of educational and wider social reform was aborted as Jean-Pierre Boyer (1820–43), Christophe's successor, repudiated British humanitarian influences and ideas, and got rid of the expatriate personnel that Christophe had recruited.[70]

Within the context of slavery itself, similar experiments at amelioration had been and were being carried out on a much more modest scale by various "humanitarian" groups and individuals. The best known of these in the British colonies was carried out on the Codrington estates in Barbados by the Society for the Propagation of the Gospel from 1710 onwards. The society failed dismally for most of the eighteenth century to carry out significant material or social (including religious) reforms among the Codrington slaves. It was only from 1783, when it granted a ten-year lease of the properties to John Brathwaite, one of the more enlightened planters, that any notable amelioration became evident and the estates became profitable once again, after being burdened by debt for some time.

Profiting from this example, the society determined to undertake major reform, which was partially underway when the Commission for Management was established. That reform included replacing the wooden houses with stone ones, improving the feeding regime of the people by assigning greater land space and labour to the cultivation of food, granting them slightly larger individual garden plots and greater free time, building new hospitals, regulating their workload more carefully, introducing new mechanical devices to replace manual labour wherever possible, and reintroducing religious and basic educational instruction. The society did not attempt all these innovations at once. Many of them actually began after the commission had taken office, while others were only in their embryonic stages at the time of emancipation. Nevertheless, the reforms, especially from the early nineteenth century, represented a response to the criticisms of the anti-slavers within and outside the Anglican Church, and more particularly those of Bishops William Warburton and Beilby Proteus, about the foot-dragging which had characterized the society's early efforts at reform.[71]

A less widely known experiment was that carried out in the late eighteenth century by Joshua Steele on his three plantations, Chester's, Hallett's and Kendal's – often jointly referred to as Kendal's – in Barbados. The evidence of this experiment lies largely in the letters and papers of Steele himself, some of which William Dickson later published in his *Mitigation of Slavery*.[72] Steele claimed that he was convinced that enslaved people, if motivated by self-interest and "adequate" rewards for their labours, did not need to be driven like dumb animals to their work, but would toil willingly and make the plantations more profitable. He therefore removed all the old coercive mechanisms on the estate, including the whip, and got rid of all his white staff. In their place he created a Council of Elders (a "slave magistracy") among the people, which dealt with routine matters relating to the plantations, and acted as an informal court to settle disputes, convening in his presence. He obviously acted as the court of final resort, except in those matters that required the intervention of the state.

Steele maintained most of the land in sugar cultivation, divided a substantial portion of the remainder into half-acre "copyholds" (that is, tenantries-at-will) and assigned them to each adult, for which they paid him an annual rent of £1 10s. He paid them wages for work in the sugar or main plantation sector, varying from 5d. to 7½d. daily, for 260 to 276 days yearly, according to their specialties and assignment to the two robust gangs. He also paid small sums of money to superannuated persons for doing light work around the plantations and gave the mothers of the children in the "grass-picking" gang 3d. per week for each child. The portion of the year in which the people were not required to work for him belonged to them to cultivate their plots. Steele set up shops on his plantations that bought the produce of the slaves' private plots at the current market rate and paid them in cash or goods, the latter at the lowest market prices. Out of their earnings they were required to provide for the full maintenance of their families (food, clothing, head taxes, and so on). They were also required to pay all fines that the Council of Elders imposed on them. Steele alleged that he was trying to recreate basically the kind of economic relationships which had existed under old English serfdom. The result, according to him, was that within a few years the plantations proved to be far more profitable than before, without the violence usually associated with plantation production.

Steele, an absentee planter for many years, began his experiment after he migrated to Barbados in 1780 at the mature age of eighty years. The experiment apparently ended around 1796, when he is believed to have died. His experiments produced considerable hostility among the Barbadian plantocracy, many of whom were no doubt happy at his decease. His successors seem not to have continued his experiment. The great flaw in his system, from the humanitarian viewpoint, was that he made no provision for the religious and educational instruction of his charges.[73] Moreover, the *raison d'être* of Steele's system, as of the typical New World slave plantation, was the profitability of the concern rather than the welfare of the labourers. In respect of the Crown properties, however, the Treasury now mandated the commissioners to focus on the welfare of the enslaved people. While the profitability of the concerns was now secondary, both the Treasury and the Commission for Management hoped fervently that they would at least break even financially.[74]

3

Abolitionists Managing Slaves, 1811–1816

Rationale for Acceptance of the Commission

The commissioners declared that sheer humanity and "strict moral necessity" explained their acceptance of the commission. While (perhaps contrary to their knowledge) the Treasury viewed their administration as an experiment in amelioration, they declared that such was not the case and that they did not want their credibility as spokesmen for the humanitarian cause to rest on the success or failure of that undertaking.[1] Berbice, they argued, was one of the worst choices for such an experiment since its unhealthy environment was a "most formidable obstacle" to such an enterprise. It was widely recognized as one of the most insalubrious colonies, where the mortality rate of both the enslaved and the free populations was exceptionally high; had they wanted to carry out an experiment, they argued, they would have chosen a more healthy environment. The miserable financial condition of the estates and the uncertainty of the British tenure over them constituted additional negative factors, since British rule might end before any positive results ensued.[2]

They declared further that they would not have undertaken the management had they thought that the estates would be returned to their former owners while Berbice remained under British rule. They recognized that the colony might be returned to the Dutch at the end of the war, but anchored their strategy on the hope that the British government would retain the estates. They hoped also that the imperial government would entrust them with the management of captured and other estates and slaves in other territories under British control, where in some instances a better field for experimentation existed. Perceval had intimated this to them, but he was assassinated shortly after the commission was established.[3] They sent a fairly long memorandum to the Treasury, elaborating their reasons for undertaking the commission and emphasizing that "they may not be understood as putting to a fair practical test any general opinions they may entertain, of the beneficial effects of humane improvements in the West Indies, by the issue of the present undertaking".[4]

They hoped by this memorandum to forestall attacks from the pro-slavery interests should their administration fail to reverse the misfortune that had beset the Crown properties, but had their administration achieved notable success, they would have used this as a springboard to launch further attacks on the plantocracy. However, many persons in Europe and Berbice regarded their administration as an experiment in amelioration, an opportunity to translate humanitarian rhetoric into humanitarianism. They themselves also really saw it as such, for in a letter to Alexander De la Court, the commission's agent in Berbice in 1813, Macaulay referred to the management of the properties as being "in some measure, a work of graduation and experiment". Further, he told the agent that "the comfort and preservation of the Slaves, and their advancement in intellectual and moral character, are so much the objects of the Commission, that if those ends should not in some measure be attained, the Commissioners would probably not persist in their undertaking".[5] The commissioners hoped to use the Crown slaves in Berbice to experiment with the "civilization" of blacks within a slave environment, just as the wider body of humanitarians attempted to do in a theoretically free environment in the cases of Haiti and Sierra Leone.[6]

Administrative Conflicts

The commissioners determined that this task required someone with a strong personality, but who was also courteous, diplomatic and charming. Experience in tropical agriculture and some acquaintance with Caribbean slave systems would obviously be additional assets. Above all, the person had to be committed to the ideas and ideals of the commissioners. However, as the commissioners explained later, they scouted the terrain in vain for such a person.[7] Eventually they appointed Lieutenant-Colonel Duncan Macalister, a former officer in the Scottish Brigade and erstwhile resident of the Netherlands. The commissioners felt that his long residence there and fluency in the Dutch language would be assets. At his suggestion they appointed as his assistant De la Court, a Dutchman "for whose talents and integrity he vouched in the strongest manner".[8] Macalister and De la Court had never visited the Caribbean, and lacked experience in plantation or slave management, nor were the commissioners personally acquainted with them. In Lieutenant Governor Gordon's opinion, appointing men who lacked tropical plantation experience constituted a major error of judgment by the commissioners.[9] It was like taking a voyage in the dark, and it certainly did not enhance the credibility of the commissioners in the eyes of their critics in Europe and Berbice.

Gordon, himself an experienced planter with estates in Demerara, did little or nothing to assist the work of the commission, despite the fact that the Colonial Department had instructed him to give the agent all necessary support. The commission and its agents engaged much of his negative attention. Even before the agents' arrival in the colony he sought to throw a spanner in the works. While promising the Earl of Liverpool to do all in his power to assist the commissioners in their task, he expressed "more fears than hopes" about their plans. In another dispatch about a month later he asserted that rumours about the formation of the commission had "occasioned sensations among the negroes that threaten to be productive of insubordination", and requested military reinforcements from the garrison stationed in Barbados until quiet should be restored to the colony.[10] So far he had no knowledge of the commissioners' reform plans, and so he was reacting to general planter perception in the Caribbean that the humanitarians were *agents provocateurs* of mayhem and insurrection.

Macalister's death shortly after his arrival in the colony provided Gordon with an opportunity to reinforce his prejudices. Since the late agent had assigned no executors to take charge of his belongings, Gordon took possession of them and so was able to peruse the commissioners' instructions. Without indicating what aspects of the instructions startled him, he asserted that he was now more firmly convinced that his earlier fears were well founded and that some members "aimed at other objects than simply the amelioration of the Blacks" in the colony. What Gordon wanted was an agent with a vested interest in maintaining the *status quo* and so he suggested appointing someone from the local legislature or judiciary, but the last thing that the commissioners wanted was to put new wine into old bottles. They therefore appointed De la Court in place of the late agent.[11]

Gordon also criticized the commissioners strongly for their instructions to the agent to send home all produce "which is adapted to the market of Europe" and to "make it an invariable rule to make no purchases on the spot of articles wanted for the slaves or estates . . . without the most urgent and unavoidable necessity". This rule was to apply to "food, clothing, lumber, medicines, or stores of any other kind". He was to pay always in cash when such necessity arose. The commissioners cited poor quality, high prices and usurious rates for goods purchased or credited locally as the reasons for their instructions.[12] In Gordon's view, however, their policy was one which "no other man, or set of them, follow in the West Indies, who have properties of the description of the Crown estates, the whole voice of the western world being against it!" The policy contained vestiges of the old mercantilism which Adam Smith and the new "school" of free traders were attacking. Gordon was no free trader but rather a pragmatist, for, as he rightly pointed out, the measure was extremely short-sighted since it robbed the agent of the opportunity, when circumstances permitted it, to dispose of some of the produce locally in return for goods needed on the estates. According to him, every estate in the colony, and indeed in the Caribbean, was run on that principle.[13]

Gordon also declared that the fluctuating prices of colonial staples on the European market since 1810 made it politic to dispose of produce in the colony when the price was right. He alleged that he once sold a quantity of coffee from the Crown estates to Wolfert Katz at six *stuivers* (about 6d.) per pound but that the buyer later received less than four *stuivers* in Europe.[14] However, the reverse was in fact more likely to take place, since prices for colonial produce were generally much higher in Europe than in the colonies. On the other hand, he might have been operating on the principle that a bird in the hand is worth two in the bush – which was not altogether unsound, given the vagaries of the war and the European market at that time. The commissioners, however, stuck to their trading policy, with the notable amendment, in December 1814, exempting rum from the arrangement when the agent deemed it more advantageous to dispose of it otherwise.[15]

Gordon had no doubt known about but had refused to touch upon an issue which later critics of the commission highlighted. Macaulay, the secretary and accountant of the commission, was partner in the shipping company Macaulay and Babington, trading with Africa, including Sierra Leone, and the Caribbean. The company became the shipping agent for all goods to and from the Crown properties. It was therefore in Macaulay's interest to have this produce sold in Europe rather than in the colony. While he was never found guilty of any wrongdoing, a conflict of interest was evident. One anonymous writer, in particular, virulently attacked the commissioners and Macaulay on this point, declaring that the company's coffers swelled as a result of the arrangement.[16] Joseph Marryat, member of the British Parliament and agent for certain planters in Grenada, criticized Macaulay for failing to lay before the House of Commons invoices giving the names of ships, prices of commodities and so on; instead he provided "bare lists of the articles without any particulars whatever".[17] However, Stephen defended Macaulay, especially in regard to his trade with Sierra Leone, declaring that he was involved in the very important enterprise of fostering the commodity rather than the slave trade.[18]

Gordon's dispatches on the commissioners' errors give the impression that his fears were grounded more in what he omitted than what he recorded. His studied evasion, however, could hardly blind them to the fact that as a planter his real source of worry concerned such matters as the abolition of the whip in the field, giving extra days to the workers, the introduction of task work on a wide scale, rewards to efficient slaves and incentives for early manumission. In the eyes of the lieutenant governor such innovations spelled doom for the institution of slavery and the colony, and had to be nipped in the bud. However, he dared not raise these concerns directly with the officials in Europe. Thus, by playing a careful if not a straight hand he kept his integrity intact. The commissioners regarded him as their most hostile antagonist; Stephen referred to him as "the bitter enemy of the Commission", while Smith viewed his opposition as "absurd".[19] The commissioners, believing that Gordon would seek to undermine their work, called for his suspension from duty and recall to Europe until their differences with him should be resolved, but the Colonial Office did not take such drastic action.[20]

Within Berbice itself matters were not going quite as the commissioners had hoped. De la Court became embroiled in a number of conflicts with public and private persons, including the managers of the estates, the fiscal, Reverend John Wray and three successive lieutenant governors. These conflicts could be explained partly by the anxiety of the white community over slave amelioration and the creeping fear of servile unrest. A slave revolt in the colony in 1814, though small-scale and not directly attributable to the commission's activities, made several whites view the commission's reform agenda as contributing to the general unease among the enslaved community.[21] There was thus covert hostility against the commission and its chief local representative. On the other hand, De la Court was irascible and at times too rigid when the situation called for compromise. He appointed three different persons consecutively as assistant agent or acting assistant agent during his brief tenure of office (January 1812–February 1815), and at the time of his dismissal he was apparently without any assistant. The reasons for the frequent changes are unknown but at least one assistant, Johan Frederic Obermuller, had conflicts with him.

The agent also clashed with Gordon and John Murray, though most of the blame for this lay with the lieutenant governors, both of whom displayed a less than friendly disposition towards the commission. Gordon handed over to Macalister and De la Court the estates, and the persons in the *winkel* department not employed by the military or civil establishments. However, he refused to deliver the books and other papers relating to the properties or to allow more than a temporary transfer of the buildings and equipment, on the contention that these belonged to the civil government. Murray, who became acting governor during Gordon's short holiday in Europe, maintained the same stance.[22] This was a very narrow interpretation of the instructions from the Treasury, for it was inconceivable that the latter would have turned over the people without the necessary buildings and equipment. Without a clear transfer, the agent might be unable or unwilling to carry out repairs, maintenance, replacements and so on without express permission from the governor.

The original dispute ended in December 1812 when Murray, on instructions from the Colonial Office, handed over the papers and buildings to the agent. However, fresh disputes broke out over his failure to transfer the land on which the buildings stood, and also over whether the houses occupied by the commissary of the *winkel* department and the colonial surgeon belonged to the *winkel* department or to the civil government. These issues remained unresolved up to the end of the commission's tenure. According to James Walker, the agent in 1816, the colonial government treated the *winkel* department as its tenant, and "appear to consider, for instance, that if a building is taken down, the land on which it stood reverts to them; nor are the Winkels supposed to possess a legal claim to a single inch of ground, even for the purposes of their business, beyond what the roofs of the respective buildings cover".[23]

When Henry Bentinck succeeded Gordon as lieutenant governor (1814–20), relations between the agent and the local government reached a new low. Bentinck, alleging that the agent dealt with a slack hand with those people in hospital by not preventing them from escaping during the evening and indulging in drinking in town, decided to set up his own hospital for the *winkel* people attached to his office.[24] Shortly afterwards De la Court applied to the lieutenant governor for a spot adjacent to the existing *winkel* hospital to build a new one. That individual, however, replied that the new hospital should be built some distance away from the main public road, and that the existing site was "miserable", "disgusting in the extreme" and "a nuisance to passengers, and persons living in the neighbourhood".[25] Tempers ran high, and in the sequel both parties let fly unkind and even biting words, but the agent showed a distinct lack of respect for the highest office of government. Bentinck himself opined that, "in a most marked and conspicuous way", De la Court represented the spirit of insubordination that had led to revolution in his country.[26]

A major part of the problem was that De la Court considered himself accountable to no one in the colony in exercising the office of agent. He stated as much when he refused to let Murray see his hospital regulations, "being not inclined to make myself responsible for any part of my administration to any body but my constituents".[27] More discourteously, he replied to the letter from Murray's secretary, inquiring when he would be available to receive the transfer of certain *winkel* property, that "from seven o'clock in the morning [I] expect your Excellency at my domicilium in town".[28] It is incredible that the agent should have expected the lieutenant governor to go to him rather than the reverse. Such a man, contemptuous of the highest colonial authority, was hardly suited for the task at hand.

Apart from direct conflict with the political administration, the agent came into conflict with several private individuals over legal issues that also led him into indirect conflict with the colony's legal officers. The legal problems were usually not his fault and sometimes were impediments deliberately put in his way to frustrate the commission's work. Many of these arose from difficulties in determining the outstanding credits and debts of the properties, a situation exacerbated at the outset by the lieutenant governors' failure to hand over the relevant records, which meant that De la Court had to consult them in the receiver general's office. Apart from the practical difficulties this raised, the agent alleged that the accounts were often defective, since several persons held genuine notes for outstanding debts owed by the properties, whereas there was no record of them in the relevant government books, a situation that did not change significantly after he received the books. The financial episodes were hardly worth all the litigation that ensued. Up to the end of De la Court's term of office, inherited debts amounted to f15,233 (£1,269), while inherited credits totalled f13,989 (£1,165), leaving a net debit position of f1,244 (£104).[29]

De la Court did not make a sufficiently strenuous effort to observe either the letter or the spirit of the admonition of the commissioners for management. Moreover, he had a misplaced sense of his own importance within the wider governmental structure of the colony, and regarded his administration as an *imperium in imperio*. Had his involvement in the conflicts occurred mainly because of his direct efforts to ameliorate the condition of the enslaved persons, his actions might have been more excusable. But most of the conflicts had little to do with actual amelioration, and the quantum of debits and credits inherited from the previous administration was not sufficient to justify the acrimony that attended their settlement. Actually, De la Court displayed little zeal when it came to implementing amelioration, in contrast to his high expenditure of energy on other matters. He proved to be a bad executor of a good cause, and this is the ultimate criterion for concluding that the commissioners had picked the wrong man for the job.

Instructions Concerning Reforms

The experimental nature of the reform programme appears in the instructions that the commissioners gave to Duncan Macalister, their first agent, which on the whole were quite revolutionary at that time. They included many of the ideas that the humanitarians were putting forward publicly on slave amelioration in the British colonies, and which the imperial government would later incorporate into the various amelioration acts of the 1820s. The instructions covered every major aspect of slave life.[30]

The agent was to consider the welfare of the enslaved persons as his overriding concern. He was expected to explore and exploit every opportunity that presented itself to ameliorate the condition of the people. At the same time, he was not to manage the properties with a view to any immediate emancipation of the people: "We would guard you . . . against all such behaviour and language as might be likely to give reasonable occasion for your being regarded or spoken of as one who has come out to effect a sudden and dangerous revolution in the general treatment of slaves, or to act with any view to their emancipation."[31] The commissioners might have had emancipation as their ultimate goal, but they never said so. In keeping with their stated goals, the commissioners laid down specific instructions about those matters that required reform.

Convinced that much of the mortality on the Caribbean plantations resulted from poor diets, they instructed Macalister to strain "every nerve . . . to provide on the estates a sufficient quantity of food". His first task was to put the provision grounds in a thriving condition, thus continuing what Gordon had set in motion. In order to enhance the quantity and quality of the food, they advised the agent to consider giving the labourers time off periodically, apart from Sundays, to cultivate their private plots.[32] He was also to supply the people with ample clothing, although the commissioners did not detail the types and quantities or the frequency of distribution. The custom in the colonies was annual distribution of new clothing.[33]

While the commissioners showed concern with proper housing for the people, they enjoined only the most necessary repairs to any buildings until they should obtain a sound picture of the building stock. They therefore instructed the agent to send home as much information as possible on the subject. Their attitude was due also to their uncertainty as to whether they would keep all the estates in production or make significant changes.[34]

The instructions dealt at some length with the matter of discipline, since the commissioners viewed this as one of the areas in which enslaved persons were badly abused and treated like animals. They absolutely forbade the agent and managers to whip their charges in the field, the commissioners expressing "an insuperable objection" to this method of increasing production. Instead, the agent might compel particularly indolent persons to complete their tasks by putting in extra hours, and might also withhold small customary indulgences, or confine them for limited periods. He was only to use the whip as a last resort, with "great moderation, and so as not to produce laceration of the flesh, or any ill effect to the patient beyond the present suffering". The guiding principle was to be persuasion rather than coercion.[35] In the commissioners' scheme, incentive was to be the principal means of achieving diligence and efficiency. One form of this was introducing task work for either individuals or groups, on completion of which the workers would be allowed the rest of the day off or would be paid for extra work. The agent was to ensure that tasks were manageable within a stipulated time and that the labourers were never overburdened with work. Task work was, of course, not new; it had been utilized in the Spanish colonies and elsewhere. It was regarded as a progressive form of labour utilization on slave plantations and was used on a wide scale in the post-emancipation period.[36]

Another proposed change was increased use of animals and machines, the rule of thumb being that people should not be given tasks which could be done by animals, nor animals tasks which could be done by machines.[37] Again, the commissioners were attempting to be innovative, for one of the main criticisms of the plantocracy for a large part of the nineteenth century was their general failure to introduce modern technology into agricultural production, thus reducing their dependence on and wastage of human labour, and enhancing their profitability.

The care of the sick was also to command the agent's attention. Hospitals were to be spacious, well ventilated, clean and supplied with drugs needed commonly. Persons with contagious diseases were to be isolated, and special diets provided for the sick, including wine and other cordials when prescribed. This last recommendation was nothing short of revolutionary, in a situation in which enslaved persons commonly suffered shortages of the most basic foods such as plantains, salted fish and salted beef. It emphasizes the point that they were now to be treated as *people*, and more particularly the king's people.[38]

The commissioners also addressed gender concerns. High infant mortality constituted a marked feature of Caribbean slave societies; the humanitarians considered it one of the fatal flaws in the slave systems. This situation was partly due to the planters' view up to the late eighteenth century that it was "cheaper to buy than to breed" a slave, but by the beginning of the nineteenth century pro-natalist policies began to take root, especially after the abolition of the slave trade in 1807. The commissioners were convinced that any serious policy of amelioration had to encompass this issue, and so they instructed their agent to ensure that adequate provisions were put in place for pregnant women. At the same time, they did not go into great detail on this subject, but advised their agent to keep "a watchful care of females during their pregnant state, and for a due time after their delivery, and also while they are nursing their infant children, including a great diminution of labour, and perhaps a total exemption from it during some part of these periods".[39] They also recommended that mothers who bore a certain number of children might be exempted from field labour and considered for manumission, thus allowing them to spend more time raising their children. They instructed the agent to advise them as soon as possible of the state of any lying-in rooms (if any) or hospitals on the estates, and also the factors that were responsible for the low birth rates on the estates, so that they could lay down more detailed pre- and post-natal regulations. As a rule, the commissioners wished to see a significant reduction in the work assigned to females.[40] It is, however, unclear whether they ever addressed these matters in greater detail. We surmise that their failure to include them in the list of documents that they published on their management of the plant indicates that they never got around to producing further regulations.

The commissioners also made known their views on religious instruction. No one in the colony had made any serious effort to convert the slaves to Christianity, although rooms called "temples" were set apart on the association's estates for this purpose.[41] The commissioners viewed Christianity not only as the sole means of saving people from eternal damnation in the life to come, but as the best means of civilizing them in this life. They would probably have refused to manage the properties had they not been given a free hand here. At the outset, however, they did not recruit a minister of religion but instructed the agent to emphasize the importance of the sabbath by refraining from assigning work on that day. He was not to forbid the people from cultivating their gardens, marketing their crops and doing other chores on that day, but the goal was to get them voluntarily to observe it as one of rest and worship. The commissioners realized that this would have to be accompanied by setting aside another day for the workers to conduct their private business.

The commissioners considered management the most critical variable in the success of the reform programme, and observed that personnel who did not share their vision could be the undoing of all their efforts at amelioration. They therefore authorized the agent to dismiss any persons who refused to obey his instructions, or whom he did not consider to be "fit instruments for cooperating in our plans of improvement". At the same time, because of the incumbents' presumed acquaintance with the dispositions of the Crown labourers and because a wrong move could have a baneful effect on the work, they advised the agent that "all hasty changes, in this respect, should . . . be avoided, except in cases of cruelty to the slaves; or other instances of gross misbehaviour".[42] They were also aware of possible difficulties in finding suitable replacements for those dismissed, although they were perhaps unaware of the extent of the difficulties that the Guiana colonies experienced in this respect. Whereas, for instance, in several Caribbean islands deficiency laws required the recruitment of one white adult male on the plantations to every ten slaves, in Berbice in 1810 the legal ratio was one to seventy-nine, and still managers often found it difficult to comply with the law.[43]

The commissioners advised their agent to keep the instructions a closely guarded secret, for they were aware that public disclosure of the details could lead to considerable opposition to their administration in both Europe and the Caribbean. They also made it clear that, although their experiments might serve as an example to others, they were only intended for the Crown people and were not to be used to assail the system of slavery. Still, the commissioners recognized that the agent would have to walk a fine line, for the slave-holding fraternity generally regarded any significant attempts at reform as revolutionary and even anarchic. While the commissioners did not specify those aspects of their reform programme that were likely to engender anxiety among the slave-holding fraternity, such matters as task work, the giving of an extra day a fortnight, the prohibition against carrying the whip into the field, the injunction to reduce corporal punishment generally and to find alternative sanctions, the suggestion that incentive to work should be based on rewards and not punishments, and the religious instruction of the slaves were the aspects of the ameliorative programme that would have been regarded as the most radical in the context of Berbice at that time.

During his early administration De la Court attempted to introduce some of the reforms mandated by the commissioners. Proper supervision of the estates was a demanding job, since travelling several miles up- and downriver could prove tiresome, apart from the necessary attention to the *winkel* establishment. Specific information is lacking on how well he stuck to his task initially. He did initiate partial reforms in regard to task work, the provision grounds, abolition of the whip in the field, and observation of Sunday as a day off for the people. However, by 1813 misgivings about his slowness in implementing certain instructions began to appear in the commissioners' letters to him. The agent increasingly retreated from his responsibilities and sided with the forces of entrenched tradition, especially after he married into a wealthy planter family and moved his residence from Sandvoort to New Amsterdam around October 1813. Contrary to the express instructions of the commissioners, he became involved in business transactions on behalf of private planters and merchants, acting as shipping agent for certain London firms, as executor of plantations and other property with slaves attached, and advertising the sale of "an assortment of dry goods, provisions, 2 field negroes, etc.".[44] He had really never shared the commissioners' vision, and once he had ingratiated himself into the company of influential persons in the society he quickly lost what little focus he had had on his original charge.

His administrative neglect, coupled with reports on his soured relations with various colonial officials, caused distress to the commissioners, who eventually had to remove him from office, his place being taken by James Walker of Edinburgh on 15 February 1815. The new agent, with a wife and five children (whom he would leave in London), was formerly a planter in Tobago and at the time of recruitment for the Berbice assignment was engaged in mercantile business in London. He was supposedly imbued with the commissioners' sentiments concerning slave amelioration and religious instruction,[45] although his statements and actions during his second period of administration (1819–25) cast grave doubts on his commitment to the humanitarian cause. He remained agent until the commission expired, with the return of the estates to the Berbice Association in July 1816. The commissioners attributed most of the main efforts at reform to him and his assistant, William Scott, commissary of the *winkel* department for several years.[46]

Food, Clothing and Accommodation

At the time that the first agents arrived in the colony only three estates were in cultivation, due to Gordon's abandonment of St Jan and the transfer of the people to Dankbaarheid, the neighbouring estate. However, the commissioners later re-established the provision grounds on St Jan.[47] De la Court addressed his early attention to increasing food production, in response to the commissioners' injunction that "every nerve should be strained to provide on the estates a sufficient quantity of food to supersede the necessity of purchasing imported provisions" and that this should be "one of the first and most important objects" of his management.[48] The commissioners also sent out rations such as salted pork, salted fish, barley and salt from Europe in 1812 and 1813. However, American privateers captured nearly the entire cargo of the former year, while a substantial part of the latter was damaged because the shipping vessel developed a leak. The evidence is ambiguous on the adequacy of the rations distributed in the first two years or so of the new administration, although the commission had inherited rehabilitated provision fields.[49] The available records do not give actual details about the quantities of food distributed, but they indicate that a major food problem developed as the agent and managers increasingly neglected the fields.

The agent did not immediately institute the commissioners' policy of granting the people an extra free day per fortnight to plant their private plots and do other chores as they saw fit, but the practice was partially in place by October 1813.[50] This put neighbouring planters under pressure from their slaves to grant a similar concession. In March 1814 the Court of Policy summoned Mr Henry White, the manager of Sandvoort, to explain the new policy of granting extra free time. He replied that he was granting the people a whole day every fortnight on Saturdays, instead of in the middle of the week, as De la Court had ordered him to do.[51] In effect, by modifying the agent's (and the commissioners') order, he was granting them only an extra half day per fortnight, since it was common practice to allow slaves in the colony

Saturday afternoons off from regular plantation work. No complaint surfaced against the two other estates, suggesting that they had not bothered to implement the commissioners' plans. However, Walker applied the instructions to the letter when he became agent in 1815.[52]

News gradually filtered through to the commissioners of De la Court's delinquency in providing basic foodstuffs for the people, which, in the case of those on Sandvoort, meant that occasionally they received only salt on rations day, forcing them to spend Sundays fishing and pursuing other ways of obtaining food. In April 1814 the commissioners strongly reprimanded the agent on this matter, but the situation, far from improving, deteriorated so badly that the provision grounds eventually failed to meet the minimum stipulations of the Court of Policy. In January 1815 Wray felt obliged to inform the fiscal about the neglect; when he had confirmed this report through visits to Sandvoort and Dankbaarheid, that officer fined the commission f1,000 (£83).[53] When Walker assumed office one month later he found the plantations "in a state of great destitution in respect of native provisions, and a heavy expense daily incurring for the purchase of the necessary food for the Slaves".[54] An inventory of Sandvoort, the main estate, taken on 18–20 February 1815 showed that there were two main plantain walks, besides plantain trees growing between coffee fields, and some areas planted in corn, but that none of the plantain fields was mature enough to yield fruit.[55] Wray claimed that several workers had run away because of lack of adequate rations, but that they returned shortly after the new agent assumed office.[56]

Walker's assumption of office led to the adoption of salutary measures, one of his first being to plant 150 acres in provisions, considerably more than the law required for the number of Crown people.[57] The primary emphasis was now on food production and only secondarily on cash-crop production. Besides the regular allowances, the agent allotted provision grounds to families, and allowed them adequate time to cultivate them, raise livestock and dispose of their surplus produce in the local markets. The agent also began to raise cattle and sheep, supposedly to increase the protein allowances to the people, although evidence from his second term of office tells a different story (see chapter 5).

It took several months to rehabilitate the provision grounds, and cost the administration £1,120 between February and November 1815. However, by the latter date the new energy and thrust saw the fields bursting with verdant life, although some of it must have been from the trees planted earlier by De la Court. Walker wrote in that month:

> I shall not in all probability have a guilder to pay for plantanes [sic], for we now have a great superabundance of them, both on Dankbaarheid and Sandvoort; although our young walks, which are thriving remarkably well, have not yet begun to bear . . . I feel pleasure in allowing them to enjoy plenty, even approaching to waste, and shall not therefore dispose of any plantanes except to the Winkels Department, till our young walks come into full bearing.[58]

This was not vainglory, for the independent testimonies of Scott and Wray confirmed that the people were supplied "abundantly with provisions" and had "plenty of every thing". In March 1816 Scott wrote to Macaulay:

> I feel much pleasure in having it in my power to inform you, that although a general scarcity of plantanes, and other provisions for the Negroes, prevails throughout the Colony, yet the Negroes on the Crown Estates enjoy abundance; notwithstanding the young walks, that have been planted since Mr. Walker and myself took over the Estates, have not yet come into full bearing. —As soon as they do, I expect to be able to sell several thousand bunches weekly.[59]

This capacity of the estates to produce a surplus of provisions despite the severe drought throughout the colony was the ultimate proof of the success of the new arrangement. In spite of the emphasis on food production, the cash-crop yield, particularly on Sandvoort, was higher in 1815 than usual (see below).[60]

Clothing was another problem to which the commissioners directed the agent's immediate attention and shortly after his arrival Macalister, the first agent, spent £1,500 on this item and on other necessities for the properties. Clothing, however, remained a major problem until at least 1814, because a cargo dispatched from Europe fell into enemy hands. The problems experienced with the shipment forced the local managers to purchase cloth in the colony. Unfortunately, no records of actual or alleged purchase or distribution have survived, so that there is no basis for comparison between the clothing received by the Crown people and that received by the wider population. However, the average quantity of cloth dispatched during the first three years combined indicates the commissioners' good intentions – roughly fifteen yards per individual.[61]

The situation is complicated by the fact that the colonial laws in Berbice, as in most other British Caribbean jurisdictions, failed to specify the exact quantities to be allotted.[62] In 1830 Charles Bird, deputy protector of slaves, observed that up to that date there was no explicit law on the subject, and that "the consequence is that scarcely two Estates, if they belong to different proprietors, receive the same". He went on to state that he encountered "much difficulty in arriving at any degree of accuracy on this subject". However, information that he solicited from various planters in 1828 and 1829 indicated that the most liberal planters gave their ordinary male field hands (not headmen) thirteen ells (about sixteen yards) of cloth and a jacket, while female field hands received eleven ells (about fourteen yards) and a jacket. Less liberal planters provided two laps (loincloths, length uncertain) and a jacket for males, and a wrapper and two petticoats (about thirteen yards) for females. Charles Kyte, a long-standing resident in the colony and manager of several estates, indicated around 1825 that slaves commonly received the scantier quantities of clothing.[63] Bennett estimates that during the whole of the eighteenth century, "in an average year" the enslaved people on the Codrington estates in Barbados received six and one quarter yards. In the early nineteenth century Mrs Carmichael claimed that on her estate in St Vincent the usual allowance was eleven yards.[64] As noted above, the average sent out by the commissioners for management was much higher than these figures but, on the other hand, the failure to send out cloth in 1815 could suggest that the commissioners intended the 1814 supplies to last for two years.

Apart from the absence of cloth in the 1815 shipment, the failure also to send out hats and tobacco pipes in that year caused the agent to comment that the "delivery extended only to a part of the articles these people needed".[65] Among the cost-saving measures introduced around this time was the training of the females on Sandvoort by Mrs Wray, the missionary's wife, to make much of the clothing required on the estates.[66] The *winkel* persons at the fort fared the worst, for the military officers kept them short of clothes, which, according to Walker, made them very ashamed to attend church with their peers.[67] While the available records do not specify the actual amount of clothing distributed, the independent testimony of Wray in January 1816 states that the people were clothed properly, which might simply mean that they were no worse off than the other slaves in the colony.[68]

At the outset the commissioners paid little attention to accommodation, for three main reasons: they wanted to use the little money at their immediate disposal on more pressing needs; they insisted on having full and detailed inventories of the various buildings and estimates of the cost of repairs or replacement before they would undertake any but the most urgent tasks; and the agent himself (De la Court) did not give such inventories and estimates. Marryat charged the commissioners with absolute neglect of the buildings: "As they found the buildings, so they appear to have left them."[69] He was, however, quite wrong, for Walker could point to a number of improvements and repairs, including a new row of houses erected on Dankbaarheid (to accommodate the people removed from Dageraad and St Jan, which had been abandoned at different times), and repairs to the buildings on Sandvoort.[70] The agents eventually repaired the houses, improvements which the commissioners attributed mainly to Walker and Scott, although the inventory taken of Sandvoort indicated that the houses there were in good order at De la Court's demission of office, and he had also repaired some of the other buildings. The people themselves played a major role in this regard, as Wray testified concerning those on Sandvoort in 1814.[71] On the whole, therefore, while the rehabilitation of the houses and other buildings did not receive the same immediate attention as food and clothing, it was not neglected.

Work and Discipline

Work and discipline were other areas to which the commissioners directed the agents' immediate attention. In keeping with their objective of substituting mechanical and animal work for manual work, in 1813 they sent out two ploughs, but the Americans captured part of the shipment that included these items. However, the inventory on Sandvoort in 1815 included three ploughs. Towards the end of their tenure they also erected a cattle mill on Sandvoort for "stamping" or peeling coffee, in place of manual labour.[72]

The commissioners had recommended the institution of a system of moderate task work and requested De la Court in August 1812 that his "attention may be sedulously turned towards it". The detailed instructions they gave on how the system should work indicate that they expected this to be the basic plan of operation. They also broached the matter of introducing payment in kind for extra work done after the completion of the task. De la Court claimed that he instituted it partially, but no evidence exists that he did so on any regular basis. In April 1813 the commissioners, noting that he had not yet applied it to the holing of land as they had recommended in their earliest instructions, tried to prod him into doing so, repeating the injunction that his "attention should be particularly directed to this subject". However, all the agents made little progress in this respect, or in regard to task work as a whole. They obviously considered it too revolutionary an experiment, given the "strong prejudices" of the plantocracy, as the commissioners noted, against this mode of work.[73]

Other recommended innovations met with a similar fate. The commissioners wanted to see night work abolished, but had to concede that "it was found impossible fully to obey our orders" because the Crown estates depended on the night tides to turn the mills for grinding the cane. In order to change this they determined to replace the windmills with steam engines, but they had to leave office before doing so. The problem also existed on the coffee estate, where the people laboured until 10 p.m. on some occasions, pulping and grinding the beans.[74] Sunday work declined appreciably, if it was not eliminated altogether, for official purposes,[75] but the commissioners were not entirely happy about its continuance for private purposes. This was a sore point with several members of the commission and also with their secretary-accountant, who held rigidly to the observance of the sabbath. Macaulay refused to take walks on Sundays.[76]

Another burdensome task for the field workers was the practice of "throwing grass" every evening after a long day's labour, as a result of which they often reached home very late and still had to prepare supper. In vain did the commissioners enjoin De la Court to assign this practice to other persons specially appointed for the task. Child labour also continued on the estates with very little change, except for the few who attended school a few hours daily.[77]

On the matter of discipline, the commissioners mandated the removal of the whip from the field, hoping that incentive born of self-interest would prevail over coercion. De la Court assured them that he had abolished this instrument as part of the driving system, but it remained the main disciplinary tool in other circumstances which they would not have tolerated. The main culprits were the managers, who were locked into the old system of control and who did not regard the slaves as sentient persons. De la Court removed one manager for excessive use of the whip, but Wray documented several other instances of such abuse by the managers. De la Court himself was not without fault in administering such whippings.[78]

Apart from the brutalities of managers and agents, the Crown people were subject to the caprice of law-enforcement officers. One such incident occurred when a magistrate ordered the instant administration of one hundred lashes with the cart whip because of the alleged impertinence of a Crown slave towards him. Walker took the matter to court, alleging that the victim had simply sought redress from the magistrate, when the latter visited Sandvoort, for an earlier theft carried out by one of the magistrate's slaves against the victim. In spite of the testimony of Wray and his wife, who had only witnessed the punishment, the court ruled in favour of the magistrate.[79] This incident emphasized how little protection even Crown people had before the law.

General Health and Maternity Care

Another important concern was the care and welfare of sick persons, pregnant and lactating women, and children, to whom the commissioners enjoined successive agents to pay special attention. The information available on these subjects is extremely sparse, and does not provide anything more than the bare outlines of how the ameliorative programme fared. The commissioners claimed that when their agents took control of the estates, the Crown people were suffering from deep morbidity: 204 persons were "wholly incapacitated from labour, either by old age, or inveterate leprosy, or by the effects of yaws, or lues venerea"; another 119 were suffering from consumption, chronic rheumatism and other conditions that only allowed them to do light work occasionally, so that the total number incapacitated was 323. Assuming that these included the *winkel* people, they constituted 31 per cent of the 1,041 persons directly under the control of the agents (excluding those assigned to the military and civil establishments). This "mass of disease", as the commissioners put it, excluded persons suffering from other chronic ailments, such as "inflammatory disorders, intermittent and remittent fevers and fluxes".[80]

Both De la Court and Walker felt that the situation would lead inexorably to a significant population decline in the next few years, but the former attributed this primarily to the climatic conditions which, according to him, made increases seldom on any but coastal estates, "where the air is more congenial to human nature than the rivers". He declared that the health of the Crown people had been managed badly and that the population included more aged persons, "corrupted in body and mind", than on the private estates. Walker, while also noting the influence of the climate and the neglect by previous administrators, felt that the problem was exacerbated considerably by the failure since the foundation years of the colony to limit the spread of diseases and provide proper care for the sick. This last statement had a familiar resonance in the Caribbean colonies during the slavery era. Whatever the explanation, both agents agreed that there was "more disease, and more effects of disease among us, than among our neighbours". According to Walker, the Crown hospitals were "distressingly full; for when a bad subject receives an accidental cut or bruise, or is attacked with a slight cold or feverish disorder, what would in other cases be a trifle becomes difficult to cure". Therefore, the commissioners could expect mortality and morbidity to be problems for several years.[81]

The commissioners, however, adopted a number of practical measures, such as the erection of a new hospital on Dankbaarheid, the rehabilitation of the existing one on Sandvoort, and an (unsuccessful) attempt to erect a new one or repair the old one in the *winkel* department. They also erected a yaws house on Sandvoort and sought to isolate persons with contagious diseases.[82] They recommended special diets for the sick, including port wine when prescribed, and shipped seventy-five dozen bottles of the same, along with various quantities of barley and medicines, in the cargoes dispatched between 1812 and 1815.[83] It is doubtful that De la Court regularly gave the first two items to the sick, and one can only speculate on the usage to which he put them. Other ameliorative measures after Walker assumed control in February 1815 included lying-in rooms for pregnant and lactating women, and "nurses" assigned to them. The commissioners never laid down detailed instructions as to how long pregnant women should remain in the field or when they should cease from work altogether. Neither did they suggest when they should resume regular toil after giving birth. These aspects were therefore left largely to the agent on the ground. However, the measures that

Walker instituted were considered to have an immediately positive effect: no stillbirths occurred on the estates during the remainder of the year. Children also commanded his attention, and he erected a new nursery on Sandvoort, as well as paying greater attention generally to maintaining their health. According to Wray in 1816, the children "that were almost sucked to death by chegoes & filth & the neglect of the Manager begin to be healthy".[84] But paediatric reform remained underdeveloped up to the end of the commission's term of office.

The commissioners attributed nearly all the ameliorative measures to Walker and Scott, while chastising De la Court for gross neglect which played a major role in the continuing high morbidity and mortality of the people.[85] They acknowledged that there was "a serious decrease in the number of Slaves" during their administration, and calculated the net mortality rate at just under 2.5 per cent per annum (that is, almost 10 per cent over the four-year period), less than half, according to them, of Staple's estimate in 1809. But Staple's figure was grossly exaggerated and the real figure was 1.04 per cent per annum. The rate of decrease during the commission's term of office was twice the absolute population decrease that the Treasury was prepared to tolerate in any private contract.[86] The commissioners asserted that had time permitted, they would have turned the tide of death into one of life. Although this cannot be proved, in March 1816 the acting agent indicated that the mortality rate had fallen appreciably over the past six months, while Walker stated that for the first seven months of 1816 (just before the Berbice Association repossessed the estates) the net decrease was one person on all the Crown properties.[87] An interesting observation on this score is the relatively large number of children among the *winkel* population, all of whom were locally born. In February 1815 they numbered 81 (or 33.6 per cent) of the 241 persons under the agent's direct control.[88] According to Walker, during the commission's tenure 107 children were born, of whom 23 died.[89] While the infant mortality rate was still much too high, the situation offered some hope of natural increase under a continued programme of amelioration. The Berbice commissioners had barely four and a half years to carry out their reforms, which they viewed as too short a period to expect significant improvements in a colony notorious for its adverse disease environment.

Schooling and Religious Instruction

The most crucial aspect of the reform programme was the conversion of the enslaved persons to Christianity and their preparation for heaven, which the commissioners referred to as "the supremely important object of their instruction". Associated with this was the establishment of schools for the young on the estates and in town.[90] Details of the curriculum and other aspects of schooling and religious instruction will be discussed in chapter 6. What is important to note here is that it was in these matters, above all, that the commissioners and their agents came into conflict with the vast majority of the planter class, to whom the idea of enlightening the slaves' minds and spirits was anathema.

Religious instruction, no matter how rudimentary, entailed teaching the people to think, to reason and to apprehend abstract ideas. It was not that the slaves were brainless beings before religious instruction began, although many planters chose to believe so or tried to argue that their minds operated incoherently and illogically. Some, of course, doubted that the slaves could ever grasp the other-worldly doctrines of Christianity, but felt that they might misunderstand or misapply to their physical circumstances certain concepts such as the fundamental equality of all persons, and freedom from spiritual bondage and oppression. Planters recognized that the institution of slavery could be undermined or reinforced, depending upon which portions of the holy writ were stressed. They would feel more comfortable if they could be assured that the evangelicals would preach obedience to masters, hard work, contentment with one's lot, honesty, sobriety and the like. On the other hand, they were dead set against those who denounced fornication, adultery, sexual exploitation of females and physical brutalities against enslaved persons. Most missionaries offered a mixed package containing both what the planters liked and what they resented, and this proved to be completely unacceptable to the majority of planters. Wray preached to his racially mixed congregation in New Amsterdam both on the duties of masters and servants and on adultery.[91]

Religious instruction to the Crown people was carried out with the express sanction of the imperial government and under the watchful eye of the commissioners. Wray, founder of the LMS work in Demerara at plantation Le Resouvenir in 1808 – an estate that gained notoriety as the womb of the slave revolt of 1823 – came to Berbice in June 1813 on the invitation of the commissioners and as a paid officer of the Crown.[92] This, in itself, was a revolutionary development, since only members of the established churches were so paid. His situation was therefore unique in the British Caribbean colonies, for he was in a real sense an "untouchable" with a captive community at hand. His specific mission was to instruct the Crown people, although in time his work spread beyond these boundaries and embraced small numbers of other enslaved persons, plus a few whites and free coloureds. Certain colonial laws (such as pass laws) impaired his freedom beyond the Crown properties, in addition to the apprehensions of the colonial governors and of the plantocracy generally.

The directors of the LMS, like those of other missionary societies, were aware of the feelings of the slave owners and routinely advised their missionaries not to act in any way which would upset the rhythm of plantation life. They were to preach spiritual ablution not physical abolition, redemption not revolution, and patiently await the time when God would choose to redeem the oppressed not only from spiritual but also from physical bondage. They gave such instructions specifically to Wray,[93] but this did not mean that they were attempting to reinforce the system of slavery. At least he did not interpret the charge that they gave him in this way. He was an anti-slaver at heart, but he realized that he was entering a sea of troubles, because his experience in Demerara and on three previous visits to Berbice had acquainted him with planter sentiments on religious instruction to slaves. The commissioners chose him not only because of the relative success of his work in Demerara, but also because of his indomitable personality, which was not easily daunted by private or official hostility.

Berbice at the time had more Dutchmen proportionately, and perhaps absolutely, than Demerara, and this might have produced greater resentment against Wray as a "Brit" – an alien – who wanted to reorder the world that they had created. Dutchmen in these colonies did not teach slaves religion. Therefore they were unlikely to welcome aliens with a new-style religion into their midst, and still less among their slaves. They also resented the presumption of superior sensibility or humanity by the British as implied by their concern with evangelizing the slaves, much as their co-religionists resented similar LMS activities among the Khoisan and Griquas in South Africa at this period. The colony, however, did witness occasional attempts by private planters to instruct their slaves. One such was a Quaker whom Wray met in May 1813 and who testified to the "good effects" that such instruction produced among them. Another planter wanted the missionary to instruct his slaves immediately, stating that he believed that in time this would allow him to dispense with drivers.[94] This planter was largely unconcerned with the other-worldly aspects of Christianity, but wanted a system which would internalize obedience among his slaves.

Wray's task was to establish a community of worshippers on each estate and among the *winkel* people. He resided at first in New Amsterdam, then shifted after about four months to Sandvoort, and then back to town after another nineteen months, all the while gradually establishing small groups of converts among the Crown people. In late 1813 and early 1814 he recruited two assistants, Meadowcroft and a literate young black man named Lambert, who resided at Dageraad and Dankbaarheid respectively, but the only available information about these persons is that he was pleased with their efforts.[95] As the work took root it began to attract persons from other estates and the urban community, while some planters expressed an interest in seeing similar work established among their slaves.[96] But the mission suffered many of the afflictions which beset the commission's wider amelioration programme.

Official enthusiasm for the work was lacking. Gordon wished to see numerous mission stations dotting the colonial landscape, but he wanted the enslaved people to be instructed only on Sundays during daylight, so that nothing would be done to alter their regular work routine or threaten the safety of the colony by their nocturnal movements. Wray responded that no meaningful instruction could take place only once per week and that it would be necessary to reinforce religious teachings by frequent repetition, at least three nights per week to those in town. According to Wray, Gordon did not approve of instructing the people "in misteries but [thought] it would be well if we could make them give over drinking rum". Wray, however, advised him that "the great things in which we instruct them are the depravity of human nature the great evil of sin & how offensive it is in the sight of God".[97] Murray's major reservation was about teaching the enslaved people how to read, a skill which he and most Caribbean planters feared would allow them to peruse subversive materials which might fall into their hands, especially at a time when so much anti-slavery literature was reaching the colonies. He reminded Wray of St Domingue, which in his view had experienced servile turbulence because of a few literate slaves. Wray replied that the St Domingue revolution had occurred because of the vast horde of illiterate persons who were led astray by a few designing persons, so that it demonstrated that there was danger, not safety, in ignorance.[98] Little room therefore existed for compromise on this matter, as both Murray and Wray were fully convinced of the right, if not the righteousness, of their cause.

Bentinck was likewise uneasy about teaching the slaves how to read. He had already run afoul of Wray in 1811, while lieutenant governor of Demerara, for introducing a law preventing slaves from assembling before sunrise or after sunset, which the missionary saw as a means of hindering the spread of the gospel. Far from submitting, Wray had returned to London and had received support from Wilberforce and Stephen that helped to ensure the repeal of the law. Bad blood still lingered from that occasion, and the lieutenant governor was not in a particularly forgiving mood when the two met again in Berbice, although he was more wary now and promised not to hinder the work of the commission. Some reconciliation eventually took place between the two parties in November 1815, when Bentinck agreed to act as patron of Wray's newly established Auxiliary Bible Society.[99]

The missionary, like his compatriots, felt that it was absolutely necessary to teach the enslaved people reading skills so that they could read the Bible and other Christian literature and be able to instruct others. In fact, the plan of religious propaganda involved raising up a local pastorate to spread the word of God, and a group of student-teachers to advance literacy. Swords were often drawn between missionaries and planters in the Caribbean on the subject of literary instruction for the slaves, which the planters viewed as too revolutionary a tool to place in their hands, for it would demonstrate their intellectual capacities, which the planters refused to acknowledge.[100]

At the outset the work on the estates went well, with the manager of Sandvoort expressing a willingness to have the people instructed and De la Court seeming to display keen interest in assisting the missionary in his endeavours.[101] However, once De la Court moved into town and Wray to Sandvoort the situation began to change visibly. It was at this time that De la Court married into a wealthy family and began to show greater neglect of the properties. On Sandvoort itself Wray soon found the young manager to be most unaccommodating. He described him as an ungodly, drunken and licentious man, seducing the girls on the estate, brutally whipping the people, neglecting to provide them with adequate food, and in general siding with the enemies of the commission. The missionary's efforts to intervene on behalf of the enslaved people caused the manager to accuse him of meddling in matters which did not concern him and undermining his authority, but Wray refused to back down.[102] For him matter and spirit were two sides of the same coin, and improvement in the one affected the other. The commissioners themselves had made it clear that the two were inextricably linked, that the task before them and their staff involved "the gradual amelioration of the temporal condition and the moral state of the people entrusted to their care", and that they "wish[ed] to see their domestic comforts increased, their minds improved, and their whole state ameliorated". The manager, who was not of a kindred spirit, began to make life a little hell for Wray, placing impediments in the way of religious instruction and sometimes refusing to pay the missionary.[103]

De la Court must have known what was happening, but he refused to raise a finger on the missionary's behalf. Wray made it clear that all was not well between the two of them, accusing the agent of having "a depraved conscience", disbelieving in "the authority of the Sabbath" and being generally hedonistic and heathenish in his lifestyle.[104] De la Court tolerated rather than supported the missionary's plan of operation, but the thin line of tolerance broke when the missionary preached a sermon concerning the sabbath, the details of which have not come to light but which the agent declared "was enough to make an insurrection in the colony".[105] Deliverance eventually came in the replacement of De la Court by Walker and of the manager by Scott.

Meanwhile, the community of believers had begun to take shape from the early days of mission work, although with some numerical fluctuations. In the beginning, because of its novelty, curiosity and the desire of some people to worship, the services in town attracted "a great many coloured and white people", while blacks also began to visit the mission, to the point where the little building became overcrowded. A day school set up in town soon boasted an attendance of eighty children, besides another thirty who attended evening classes. A few months later a number of adults enrolled in a reading class. Religious instruction through the use of catechisms was also showing some progress. In October 1813 Wray reported an urban congregation of one to two hundred people, with the estate schools also making good progress.[106] But gradually the numbers began to drop, and only a very few of the whites and free coloureds remained because of Wray's strictures against sin and against failure to observe the sabbath, and some unease concerning his insistence on teaching slaves to read and on holding nocturnal meetings. In February 1814 he bemoaned the fact that only a few persons had attended the recent service in town, and that among the absent were the *winkel* slaves whom he alleged were catching fish, trying to get plantains or pulling the chaise of the lieutenant governor to church (that is, using slaves instead of horses). The situation on Sandvoort was only slightly better, since the Crown people there were easier to assemble, but the few that used to attend from a neighbouring estate had suddenly stopped doing so. In June 1814 he again recorded a substantial drop in attendance at Sandvoort because the people, including the children, had to work sometimes until 10 p.m. to pulp and grind coffee.[107]

The aborted slave revolt of 1814 was an especially trying time for the mission. While no persons belonging to the Crown properties had been involved, rumours were rife that talk about amelioration had exacerbated the situation and that missionary activities had helped to inflame the insurgents' imagination. Thus the colonial administration and private planters kept a closer watch than usual on Wray and his flock, while the government issued regulations narrowly restricting the movement of enslaved persons, forbidding fêtes and the like.[108] As time passed, however, Wray became accepted into the community of whites, although many still had reservations about his style of preaching and his concern with literary instruction for the slaves. The commissioners' amelioration efforts had not produced the insurrection anticipated by the plantocracy, while Walker was proving to be a much more diplomatic representative than his predecessor. Wray also became slightly more accommodating of the prejudices of the planter class, although he continued to write home confidential letters about the vices of the whites and other groups.

The work experienced a new lease of life beginning in July 1815, with all shades, sizes and classes of people attending the crowded meetings in New Amsterdam, and with instruction in reading, the catechisms and needlework also progressing well. The missionary's first baptismal service, on 25 December 1814, involved nine adults and six children, while in 1815 he baptized sixteen blacks. He performed his first marriage ceremony of enslaved persons (not recognized by the colonial laws) in 1817, but the record does not indicate whether these were Crown people. Wray was quite satisfied with the progress of the work, given all the constraints under which it existed. The believers, in his view, were on the whole setting a good example to the rest of the inhabitants, white and black, by their greater diligence at work without the whip, observance of the sabbath, abstinence from revelry and solid attendance at worship during holidays.[109]

Economic and Financial Administration

The major financial problem facing the commissioners was how soon they could make the properties viable. They felt that if they could carry out their reforms and make the concerns profitable this would "furnish to West India planters an example of successful cultivation proceeding on humane and liberal principles" – in other words, it would show that amelioration pays. They therefore advised the agent to let economy rule in all matters of expenditure, keep accurate records and maintain a vigilant inventory of all stores.[110] The commissioners did not expect to realize profits in the short term, because of the debt burden on the properties and the need to rehabilitate the estates, including providing new equipment.

The recurrent expenses of the administration were also heavy. The commissioners themselves received no remuneration, but a large number of other personnel had to be paid. In Berbice these included the agent (£1,000 per annum), his assistant (£300), the estate managers (£300 each), the commissary of the *winkel* department (£300), the minister of religion (£300 plus other allowances), his assistant, Meadowcroft (approximately £90), and a number of other petty personnel. Besides all this, the secretary-accountant in Europe had to be paid (£300), and there were also the expenses of the office and clerks.[111] The number of salaried individuals was larger than during the previous administration and, as the commissioners themselves pointed out, also larger than was usually the case with Caribbean plantations. The records do not allow detailed comparisons between the two administrations, but the monies spent under the second must have been greater than under the first, even taking into consideration the high commission which the lieutenant governor had received. On the other hand, greater financial accountability reduced graft considerably, resulting in lower involuntary flight of revenue.

As already noted, the commissioners experienced initial financial problems due to the activities of American privateers who captured a cargo valued at £5,000, sent from Europe to the agent. Delays in sending out fresh supplies resulted in the agent incurring a debt of £5,800 for supplies purchased locally. The tale of woe did not end there. A vessel carrying produce from the estates in 1813 sprung a leak which prevented the produce from reaching the market when the prices for colonial staples were high, and also resulted in a loss of about £600 worth of goods through damage. While the commissioners eventually recovered from their insurance agents nearly the whole amount lost in the first mishap, they received no compensation for the second because the vessel was declared unseaworthy and the shipowners bankrupt. By the end of 1813 the debt stood at £10,000.[112] In spite of these setbacks and the vagaries of the European staples market, during the next two years the commissioners realized sufficient revenue from the sale of colonial produce to allow them to effect "more than making the income from the Estates meet the whole of the ordinary and extraordinary expenditure" during their tenure of office. By 1814 they had reduced their debt to £3,000 and while it stood at £2,000 at the time of their report to the Treasury in May 1816, they anticipated that this would be cleared off from the income of the produce soon to arrive in Europe. But during their term of office they never paid any money into the Treasury.[113]

Walker placed much emphasis on economy and the streamlining of management and production. Among the new measures introduced was the abandonment in 1815 of Dageraad, allegedly because of its particularly adverse disease environment, and the removal of the people to Sandvoort. This eliminated the need for one of the managers, while placing the assistant agent as manager of Sandvoort eliminated another separate office, thus resulting in a saving of £600 annually.[114] The influx of labour onto Sandvoort helps to explain the record production of coffee on that estate shortly after: 180,000 pounds, according to Walker. In reviewing the performance of the estates it is important to bear in mind that the colonial economy as a whole continued to experience a severe downturn, leading to the abandonment of several estates and the removal of the labour force, especially to the neighbouring colony of Demerara.

As regards the *winkel* department, the commissioners had hoped to realize a net profit from it, but it is difficult to determine its performance since

Table 3.1   Comparison of Commodities Produced on Selected Estates in Berbice in 1813

Estates	Slaves	Sugar (lb)	Coffee (lb)	Per slave (lb)
Sandvoort[a]	189	–	25,488	135
Zorg en Hoop	110	–	66,585	605
Standvastigheid	151	–	52,136	345
De Resolutie	143	–	88,732	621
Bestendigheid	171	–	80,831	473
Vryheid	339	–	182,427	538
Augsburg	143	–	33,037	231
Gebroeders	131	–	107,577	821
Dageraad[a]	133	196,918	–	1,481
Dankbaarheid[a]	296	225,578	–	762
Herstelling	164	165,220	–	1,007
Adelphi	38	34,838	–	917
Goldstone Hall	117	198,460	–	1,696
Mary's Hope	16	3,684	–	230

Sources: "Inventories of estates", October 1803, in Moncrieff to Hobart, 6 January 1804, PRO, CO 111/73; *Berbice Gazette*, 19 February 1814 and 1 October 1814; House of Commons, "Papers Relating to the Crown Estates in the Colony of Berbice", *PP*, 1816, VIII (509): 17.[115]
[a]Crown estates.

its accounts were amalgamated with those of the estates during this period. The commissioners were aware that some *winkel* persons remained attached to the military and civil establishments, and at the outset had instructed their agent not to remove them from these offices.[116] However, they soon discovered that these comprised the healthiest workers in the case of the military and a large number of robust ones assigned to Government House and the public works. Nearly all the sick, superannuated and young persons remained with the department. At the beginning of Walker's term 93 persons (62 men and 31 women) from the *winkel* department were assigned to the military and civil establishments. The effective workforce remaining in the department comprised 85 persons (63 men and 22 women), besides 22 apprentices, making a total of 107, or just 53.5 per cent of the total effective workforce. These, and mainly the men, who usually constituted the core of the department's labour force, carried the whole department, which included an additional 134 persons (53 superannuated adults and 81 children), besides its administrative personnel. According to Walker, there were really only 63 persons (adult males) who could be relied upon as steady income earners, or roughly 26 per cent of those persons under his direct administration.[117]

After the early frustrations of trying to make the department solvent, Walker recommended to the commissioners charging hire for the sixty-six at Government House and seeking the return of those attached to the fort. He was convinced that if the lieutenant governor continued to hold on to such a large number of labourers it was "in vain to hope that the Winkel Establishment is to be any thing else, during the whole existence of the present generation, than an unproductive and perhaps burdensome property". He also declared that he found the department to be the most unprofitable aspect of his administration. As usual, both sides felt some acrimony over the matter of payment for, or recovery of, the *winkel* people.[118] Finally, in June 1816, on the orders of the secretary of state, Bentinck reduced the number to thirty-two, declaring that "Those I have retained for domestic employ are fit for little else, having spent the prime of their life in such service to my predecessor in office."[119]

Review and Restoration

The humanitarian initiative attracted keen interest from several individuals inside and outside the British Parliament. Towards the end of the commission's term of office a group in Parliament called for a debate on the subject and requested that the final report and accompanying papers be laid before the House of Commons. The opponents of the commission condemned its performance, especially Marryat, who saw the humanitarians only as deluded persons with eccentric plans to reform slave society. However, Smith and Wilberforce, two members of the commission, stoutly defended their record.[120] The fact that Parliament decided to allot time to debating the matter underlines its importance in the wider debate on amelioration.

The commissioners had visions of a better life for the slaves, but visions in valleys are extremely difficult to realize, and slavery was a valley. The essential problem facing the commissioners was how to put a human face on an inhumane institution. The experience of Caribbean slavery proved that it was impossible to humanize the institution. The commissioners' decision to retain incumbent personnel in effecting the task of amelioration was politically correct but self-defeating. It was based more on exuberant expectation than reasoned thought. A fault line of separation needed to be drawn between the old and the new creation, but too much of the old life still clung to the new organism that was developing. Had time permitted, the commissioners would almost certainly have had to replace the old, dyed-in-the-wool personnel with a new breed of persons.

The reform programme spluttered and stalled periodically but did not fail completely. In the short space of four to five years important gains accrued in respect of task work, an extra day off for the labourers each fortnight, more rigid observance of Sunday as a day off, removal of the whip from the field and restrictions on its use generally, more liberal allowances of food and clothing, greater opportunities for individual accumulation of property, more adequate provisions for sick and pregnant persons, moral and religious instruction, attempts at literacy (although this entailed mainly reading), and training the adult females as seamstresses. All these innovations were in their embryonic stages when the commissioners demitted office, but they certainly improved the quality of life and self-worth of the enslaved people. It was the first time that management viewed and treated them as people rather than animals, and this was one of the most important features of the "experiment". It is impossible to say how far the slaves' material and social circumstances would have been enhanced had the commissioners had more time to conduct the experiment. The innovations placed considerable pressure on the owners and managers of neighbouring plantations, who expressed "considerable dissatisfaction" with what was taking place, for their slaves had begun to display "much jealousy" because they were not accorded similar treatment.[121] However, no actual unrest occurred from this circumstance.

At the end of the war the estates became the subject of discussion between the British and Netherlands governments. As noted in chapter 1, the status of the properties had been debated in the early years of British occupation.

The imperial government had ruled that at the time of seizure they had belonged to the Netherlands government (the Batavian Republic), which had recently taken over the colony, and as such they were fair prizes of war. While the war lasted the matter remained unresolved to the satisfaction of the shareholders of the Berbice Association. This was why the Netherlands government decided to raise the issue once again, arguing that the estates were private property. However, it did not enter a similar argument in respect of the *winkel* department because it had always constituted the public works department of the colony and for this reason was considered public property. The British government, clearly willing to rid itself of the estates, accepted the viewpoint of the Netherlands government. Thus, by the eleventh article of the convention of 12 August 1815 between the two governments, the estates were returned to the association. The convention said nothing about the *winkel* department.[122] Despite attempts by the commissioners to have the decision reversed, the colonial government formally handed over the estates to the representatives of the association in July 1816, with the exception of St Jan, which it restored a few months later.[123]

The restored estates were in a much better financial condition than at the time of their capture. Since 1732 the association had been forced to use the profits from them to subsidize the cost of the civil and military administration. After their return in 1816 unencumbered and rehabilitated, the association was able to dispose of them in 1818 to Donald Charles Cameron for £66,000 (f792,000).[124] This figure fell quite short of the independent estimate of f1,438,125 (£110,625) given to Gordon in 1811, but must be set against the fact that at that time the estates had some 791 slaves, as against 683 in 1818.[125] As indicated earlier, the Berbice estates in general were also depreciating in value, because planters were leaving for Demerara and elsewhere.

4

Work and Industry, 1816–1825

The Urban Context

The return of the plantations to the Berbice Association shifted the focus of attention firmly away from the rural to the urban context of life in the colony. We have already dealt with the differences in Caribbean society between the rural and urban complexes,[1] but it is important here to deal briefly with the situation in New Amsterdam. At the time of the British occupation of the colony this was a new urban centre with a very indistinct profile. While both the physical structures and the population grew appreciably over the next few decades, it never became an important urban centre comparable to Bridgetown (Barbados), Kingston (Jamaica) or even Georgetown (Demerara).

Up to 1818 the town was very much in its primary building phase and was still sometimes referred to as the "new town". In that year land was being surveyed for a number of new lots and the erection of a colonial church, while the court house had only recently been built.[2] In the mid-1820s New Amsterdam was a spot of land some one and a half miles long and just under a third of a mile wide, comprising roughly four hundred acres. It consisted of a main road built roughly through the centre of town, in a north-to-south direction, and two other trunk roads running in the same direction and commonly referred to as the "front dam" and "back dam", names suggestive of the hazards involved in traversing them during the rainy seasons. In 1826

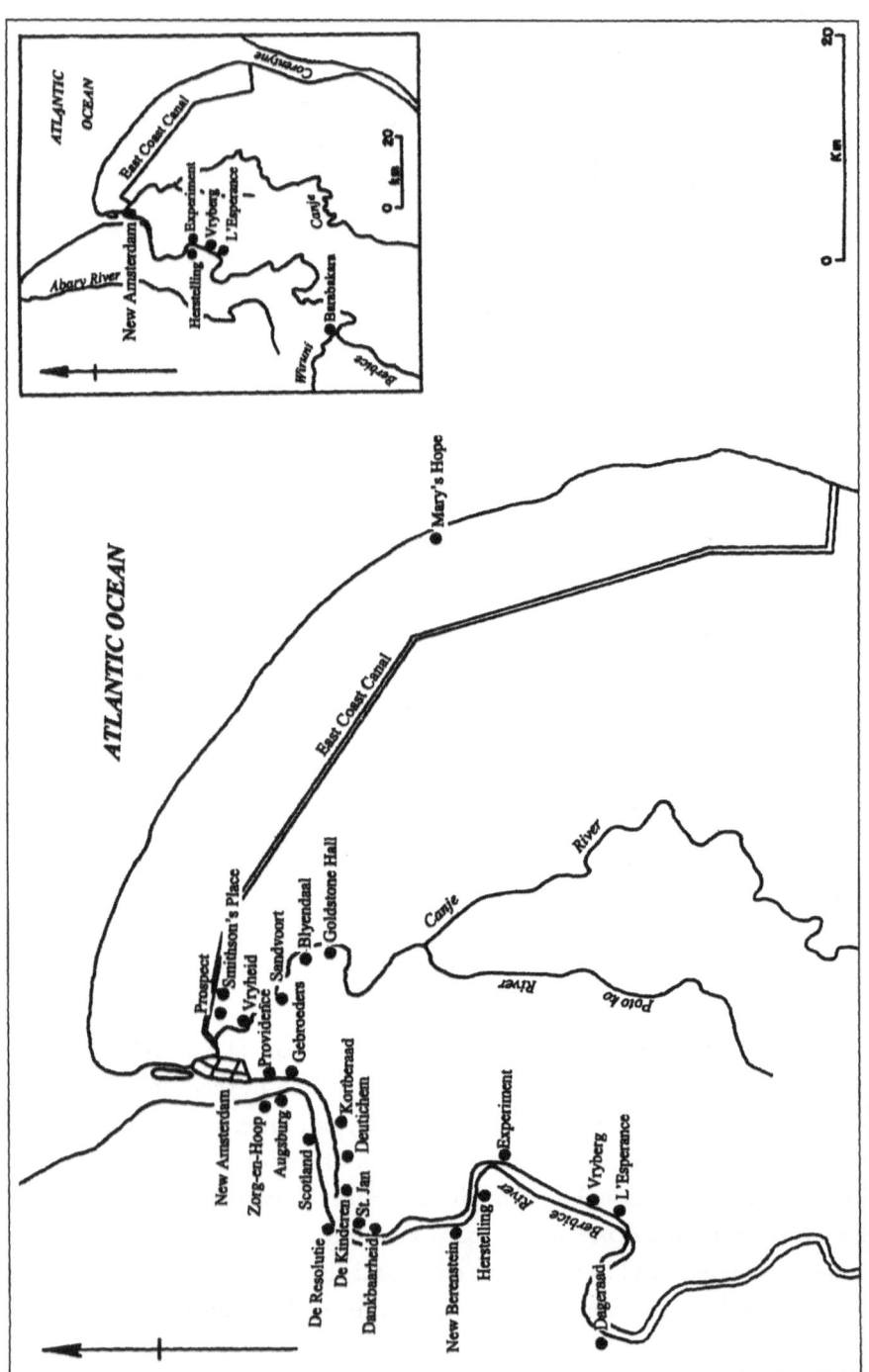

Map 5 Selected locations in Berbice

Commissioner Burdett described the town's drainage as being "in a most defective state".[3] No detailed description of the town during the slavery or early post-emancipation period has come to light. However, Henry Dalton, who lived in Guyana (pre-colonial British Guiana) in the late 1840s and early 1850s, described it at that time as being intersected by several canals. The houses were generally located on quarter-acre lots and were surrounded by trenches that provided drainage for the town. The stores and mercantile houses, located with their fronts towards the Berbice River, were provided with commodious wharves and warehouses.[4]

As noted in chapter 1, the town was located at the confluence of the Berbice and Canje Rivers, some five miles from the mouth of the Berbice River. In 1796 Dr George Pinckard described it as a town still in its embryonic stages of development: "The town is yet in embryo. . . . The land on which it is to be erected is in part cleared of its wood, and divided into lots ready for building; but, at present, only here and there a scattered house is to be seen"; and again, "the nakedness that prevails around the Government-house – the want of roads and paths – the swampy savanna – the heavy forests; in short all that meets the eye conveys the idea of a country just emerging from its original wildness, into civilisation".[5] At that time its perimeters were only mapped out on paper.

Most of the houses occupied by the settlers were constructed mainly from local woods, although local or imported bricks might also be used, while the roofs were made either of local boards or of shingles, usually imported from the United States. Most of the government buildings, including Government House, appear to have been constructed of a combination of bricks and wood with shingled roofs, although this did not prevent them from falling into rapid decay.[6] In 1796 Pinckard declared that Government House was "beyond all comparison, the handsomest and most spacious edifice" he had seen up to that time in South America.[7] However, by 1804, according to Lieutenant Governor A.J. Van Imbyze Van Batenburg, it was in "a shocking state of decay . . . scarcely habitable and threatened to go to ruins very soon", as were most of the government buildings in the capital. Extensive but not complete repairs were carried out on the buildings in that year, yet only five years later Lieutenant Governor William Woodley was making exactly the same complaint as his predecessor.[8] The government buildings generally suffered extreme neglect during this period, for similar complaints of dilap-

Figure 5 New Amsterdam in the early nineteenth century
Reprinted from Colonist, *Kort Historisch Verhaal Van den Eersten Aanleg, Lotgevallen en Voortgang der Particuliere Colonie Berbice* (Amsterdam: Sepp Jansz., 1807).

idation surfaced concerning the fortifications.[9] Decay and dilapidation were not unique to the government buildings. In 1814 De la Court wrote about many old buildings in town, including the *winkel* hospital, as in need of repair and painting.[10]

In 1818 Reverend Wray described the town as sweltering and not exposed to the sea breeze as was Georgetown on the Demerara coast. Accommodation for rental was also difficult to obtain. Eventually he was able to rent a dwelling that had once been a butcher's shop. According to his biographer, "it was a hot, leaky and filthy place . . . it had become infested with noxious vermin, rats, scorpions, [and] centipedes". Still, he had to pay a very high rental of £10 per month.[11] Over time, however, the town added landscaped beauty and human care to its natural surroundings. According to Dalton, around the mid-nineteenth century it presented a very picturesque appearance, especially when approaching it from the sea. The more exclusive dwellings were planted with fruit trees, palms and flowering shrubs.[12]

Since New Amsterdam was the only town in Berbice, all the administrative edifices and personnel, the professional offices, and the main retail shops were located there. As already noted (see chapter 1), up to the early nineteenth century there was no building dedicated entirely to Christian worship, the Dutch Reformed Church having to share a building with the colonial surgeon. In time a few church buildings were erected, but these lacked an imposing presence. The military headquarters, a military parade ground, Government House, the Court of Policy and Criminal Justice (later called the Council of Government), and a few government buildings occupied centre stage in the mid-1820s. Other structures included the *winkel* village and a small and poorly maintained jail, with a treadmill (from the late 1820s) used strictly on black inmates.

The town was administered by a council (called the "Board of Police", by a literal translation of the Dutch term)[13] appointed by the lieutenant governor and the Court of Policy. It had general responsibility for the good government of the town, including the raising of taxes, location and maintenance of physical structures (buildings, canals, trenches, debushing of areas and so on), and, along with other government staff, security matters. The board also had the power to impose sanctions on persons who breached its laws and regulations.[14] One of its main responsibilities therefore concerned movement in and out of the town, and particularly matters relating to urban slaves. In the early 1820s the management of the *winkel* department ran afoul of its regulations concerning the maintenance of the village and was fined for so doing (see below).

The population of New Amsterdam is difficult to determine. The deputy receiver general was only able to give the average for each year between 1812 and 1822, for taxation purposes, as 2,000 slaves, 460 free coloureds (no doubt including free blacks) and 245 whites. The commissioners of inquiry recorded figures for January 1824 (perhaps based on hearsay or conjecture) of 172 whites, 469 free coloureds and 202 free blacks. Official returns in December 1824 give figures, again for taxation purposes, of 3,913 slaves, 804 free coloureds and 240 whites.[15] Leaving a certain margin for the movement of people to various parts of the country and the elevation of children into the various tax brackets, there are still significant discrepancies among the various sets of figures. Lieutenant Governor Beard suggested that the low figures recorded in the official returns for the free coloureds between 1812 and 1822 could be explained partly by their habit of not registering in order to avoid paying the head tax.[16]

The figures for 1822, dubious as they are, indicate that the urban enslaved population constituted some 11 per cent of the colony's enslaved population; similarly, the urban free coloureds constituted 85 per cent of the total free coloured population, and the urban whites 44 per cent of the total white population in the colony. They also indicate that enslaved people constituted 74 per cent of the total urban population; while figures for 1824 indicate that they constituted 79 per cent. Higman did not look at the situation in New Amsterdam; however, he states that Georgetown (Demerara) and Port of Spain (Trinidad) were the two towns that deviated upwards significantly from the norm in regard to percentage of enslaved people in the total urban population. He estimates that in Georgetown they constituted 61 per cent in 1812 and 53 per cent in 1832, while in Port of Spain they constituted 50 per cent in 1808 and 25 per cent in 1832.[17]

These figures, while very high, are significantly lower than those for New Amsterdam around the mid-1820s. We do not have figures for 1832, but it is reasonable to assume that the percentages remained higher than those of the two towns just mentioned. New Amsterdam therefore showed a significant variation from the pattern of urban settlement that Higman indicates for the Caribbean as a whole. While it accords with his findings that roughly 9 to 10 per cent of the enslaved population lived in urban settlements, it varies significantly from his findings that whites usually outnumbered other categories, and free coloureds outnumbered slaves.[18] The implications of such differences, especially in terms of the slave owners' perception of the need for tight security in Berbice, are striking. The presence of the soldiers at the main fort, St Andrew (Andries), about two miles from the town, would have given only mild assurance to the whites that they would be able to cope with urban unrest, especially in the context of a general revolt. No such unrest occurred in town, but following the aborted revolt in 1814 and the revolt in Demerara in 1823 the government tightened its security measures for several months.[19]

Progressively, as time went by, amelioration became the subject of heated debate in the colonies and especially the urban communities where the majority of the whites lived. In New Amsterdam, and Berbice as a whole, the main focus of such amelioration continued to be the government slaves. Numbering more than three hundred in 1815, they constituted by far the largest single group of urban slaves in the town. The rest of this study will look at the management policies of the imperial government and its representatives in the colony towards these slaves, in the context of the abiding concern of the slave-owning fraternity in the colony with the problem of social control.

Profile of the Workforce

Central to the imperial view was the notion that the *winkel* department should meet its financial costs fully within a dynamic amelioration policy, but in this, as in other respects, management fell down badly. The department came to near financial ruin and became an increasing burden on the imperial Treasury, with the majority of the healthy adults being unemployed, or rather not gainfully employed, for long periods. This circumstance was due almost entirely to the poor way in which the officials on the ground, and especially Walker, the superintendent (as he was now called), ran the concern. Walker's attitude, actions and abilities during this period seem to be quite different from the individual revealed to us in the previous chapter, and at times it seems that we are dealing with an entirely different personality.

The imperial government itself was also at fault. It left the execution of its policy in the hands of the *winkel* administrators on the ground, and for the next few years paid very little attention to how they were managing the department. The Commission for Management ended its oversight of the property in 1818, and from then its former members took only a passing interest in the affairs of the *winkel* people. Walker, who had returned to England on learning that the estates were being restored to the Berbice Association, remained there until 1819; he continued to receive £1,000 per annum until February 1817, after which he went into (unspecified) mercantile business in London.[20] Meanwhile Scott, the assistant agent, continued to carry on the affairs of the department on a part-time basis, while also enjoying the office of postmaster, with a manager who was also deputy postmaster. The department was now left entirely in the hands of a slave owner,[21] something unthinkable during the commission's tenure. Scott himself, while maintaining a restrained regime of coercion, was never a great enthusiast for amelioration. He allowed the department to return slowly to its old ways, debt-ridden and simply drifting along.

The department experienced a number of controversies that had a devastating effect on its morale. Scott had expected an appointment as the department's agent, but in 1818 the imperial government appointed Walker as collector of customs in the colony and superintendent of the department. The appointment as superintendent took place with the distinct understanding that he would receive no pay for executing the functions of that

Table 4.1   Disposal of *Winkel* People on 31 October 1823

Disposal	Men	Women	Boys	Girls	Total
Artisans and seamstresses	32	18	3	22	75
Attached to Government House	14	14	0	0	28
Attached to Fort St Andrew	9	1	0	0	10
In service of *winkel* staff	4	10	1	2	17
Employed at provision plantations	9	9	1	2	21
Effectives sick in hospital	17	6	4	1	28
Aged, infirm, casually employed	27	23	0	0	50
Attending sick and children	2	1	0	0	3
Supporting self-considered manumitted	0	1	0	0	1
Apprenticed to trades or in-service training	0	0	10	0	10
Infants and children in school	0	0	41	14	55
Total	114	83	60	41	298

Source: Byng to Lords Commissioners of the Treasury, 4 August 1824, PRO, T1/3482/2.

office.[22] Walker returned to the colony in March 1819 and lived with Scott in the latter's house for the next eight months, intriguing meanwhile to eliminate his friend from the department and to secure Scott's emoluments. The battle was now joined, and for a short while there were virtually two administrations, with two sets of house and office rent being drawn on the department, and with Walker carrying out certain functions in a piecemeal way because of his failure to obtain some of the financial records.[23] Walker complained about his alleged failure to obtain Scott's cooperation and finally the axe fell on Scott's anxious head; in July 1820 the Lords Commissioners dismissed him from the department.²⁴ In manoeuvring Scott out of the post, Walker had played a risky game, and he would pay for it by the widespread social ostracism which attended his relations with public and private persons, to whom Scott was an old friend and long-time resident of the colony.

The *winkel* population stood at 335 in 1815 and at 297 in 1825.²⁵ We do not know how many of those in 1815 were considered "effective" labourers but the number in 1825 was 155.²⁶ Deducting those in the civilian and military establishments of the government would put the number of effectives at the disposal of the department at 124 out of 257. This constituted an effective list which represented about 48 per cent of the department's complement of persons, slightly short of what usually obtained on the colony's plantations. Charles Kyte, a long-resident planter and attorney, indicated that the number of effectives expected in a gang of three hundred was "something more than half" of that number. Henry White, another planter, stated that the number would be about one-half, while Andrew McWatt, the *winkel* manager, estimated it at one-half at the lowest.²⁷ The department often hired out the superannuated, invalids and children, sometimes for several months, to supplement its earnings. Therefore, its complement of potential income earners was somewhat larger than the figure given above. The year 1822 offers good examples of this, but we shall only use the first week of January as illustrative of most of the year. At that time the department listed 149 persons as employable out of 272 under its control, or almost 55 per cent.²⁸

The problem was that most of the effectives were either not employed at all as time went by or were in unremunerative employ, a situation that had little or nothing to do with seasonality, as is evident from Table 4.2 (next page). Kyte also stated that other owners did not experience similar problems with finding employment for their slaves.²⁹ Frederick Nicolay, former *winkel* bookkeeper-clerk (1805–14) and commissary (1814–17), testified to the commissioners of inquiry that as many as 115 to 120 persons were sometimes unremuneratively engaged while he worked with the department. They worked without any financial benefit to the department for various offices and individuals in the civil and military establishments, or in the *winkel* department itself. The result was that sometimes not more than fifty persons were available for remunerative employ, although, with the exception of those attached to the civil and military establishments (thirty-seven

Table 4.2 Employment of *Winkel* People on Selected Dates in 1822[30]

Dates	Hired Out					Department and Plantation				
	Men	Women	Boys	Girls	Total	Men	Women	Boys	Girls	Total
January 3	26	9	5	4	44	50	35	11	9	105
February 7	30	12	5	5	52	46	32	11	8	97
March 7	20	10	5	4	39	56	34	11	9	110
April 4	21	9	4	4	38	55	35	12	9	111
May 2	19	7	4	4	34	56	37	12	9	114
June 6	13	7	5	4	29	62	37	11	10	120
July 4	23	14	6	4	47	52	30	10	11	103
August 8	23	8	7	6	44	52	36	9	9	106
September 5	15	9	5	6	35	60	35	11	9	115
October 3	18	8	5	7	38	57	36	11	8	112
November 14	19	9	3	7	38	56	38	11	6	111
December 5	16	8	2	8	34	58	39	12	5	114

Source: Day Books 1–3, PRO, CO 318/90: 248–366.

in January 1825), all of them had to be fully maintained by the department.[31] On 20 January 1825, for instance, only twenty-six men and nineteen women were in remunerative employ, including officially superannuated persons.[32] This situation was not unusual.

Financial Mismanagement

The *winkel* accounts, more than any other feature, indicate in graphic outline the financial rut into which the department had fallen and which only worsened with time. Yet there is no guarantee that what Walker presented to the Department of Colonial Audit in London or what appeared on the books and other documents he presented to the commissioners of inquiry represented a reasonably accurate account of the department's financial transactions. Worrisome episodes of irregularity in the accounts, lack of appropriate vouchers and related documents, and the inability of the superintendent to give precise answers to specific questions caused the commissioners to doubt the integrity of the accounts. Rolfe testified that in 1820, when he and his senior officer examined the books, they found them in "the greatest possible confusion". The records of daily events had been kept irregularly, while the employment of the people had been "by no means distinctly stated; in fact they were so inaccurately kept, as to render it necessary for us to apply to the parties who hired them, to ascertain the periods, & the rates of hire – & in many instances, to examine the negroes themselves, as to the persons by whom they had been employed". The department never supplied them with records of the times or the rates of hire. They also encountered difficulties in determining what supplies the department had purchased, since several lacunae existed in the entry books and there was a deficiency in supporting bills.[33] At the same time, Rolfe exonerated Scott from any financial wrongdoing. He declared that Scott's accounts "appear to have been regularly kept up to the 30 June 1819", his period of unhindered administration, and that "all the confusion was between that period, & the 30th of September 1820". He attributed this to the conflict between Walker and Scott, "together with great neglect on the part of the bookkeeper".[34]

In spite of these findings and the superintendent's own promises, the situation did not change materially in the following years, although in 1824 the superintendent boasted that the accounts were "in a clear simple and condensed state". The commissioners discovered that he had not kept faith on this point. They complained of the "irregular mode of keeping the books & allowing the accounts to run on for a long period, which led to disputes and litigation".[35] In spite of the many and large indirect subventions which the department received, its health never improved. According to the reckoning of the commissioners of inquiry, its receipts for 1815–24 totalled about f229,594 (£16,400) and its payments about f459,374 (£32,812), a deficit of f229,780 (£16,412).[36]

Amazingly, the superintendent did not keep an office cash book. All the cash received, or rather what the superintendent remembered or cared to record, he entered in a small book in which he also kept records of the customs department and his private business, "blended and mixed together", and which he carried around with him. Periodically he dictated to the bookkeeper those items of income and expenditure which he expected that individual to place in a quire book, called a subsidiary journal, theoretically made up monthly. The commissioners for management had strictly enjoined their agents to keep "with precision and regularity, a set of books" which should contain all their financial transactions and comprise "full and distinct accounts of all . . . receipts and expenditure". The books were to be balanced annually, while the agents were to send to Europe monthly transcripts of their cash books.[37] The absence of vouchers on a number of occasions also made it impossible to verify the transactions. However, Walker excused his delinquency by declaring that it would have entailed considerable trouble and expense to keep the accounts in a more systematic way and that he relied "upon his character and integrity for the proper & correct application of every thing".[38]

The commissioners of colonial audit agreed with the findings of the commissioners of inquiry that the department's record keeping was very deficient in accounting terms and was not usually supported by vouchers. Dealing more directly with the superintendent's account, they expressed doubt that any efficient check had been kept on the receipts for articles sold and work performed by the department. They also observed that there was a large number of bad debts, and that these were not supported by certificates and the various other documents required by accountants. In spite of this, Walker was able to convince them that financial stringency had forced upon him the need to cut down on bookkeeping staff. Walker was also able to convince the commissioners of colonial audit that the charges made by the commissioners of inquiry, of misappropriation of stores and possibly of funds, were without foundation. The problem was that, while there was good reason for misgivings and suspicion about the superintendent's integrity in keeping the accounts and stores, there was no hard evidence on which to impugn him and the auditors were more disposed than the commissioners of inquiry to absolve him from wrongdoing. But, although they approved the financial statements, the auditors were not content to allow the existing system to continue, and they suggested to the Lords Commissioners that if they intended to retain the *winkel* establishment they should set up proper accounting practices immediately.[39]

The Labour Market

The woeful situation in respect of the *winkel* earnings had little if anything to do with the labour market, and much to do with the mismanagement of the plant. We need to consider several factors in dealing with this aspect, including the competitive nature of *winkel* labour, the people's work ethic, the department's training and marketing plans, and the general ambiance in which the people worked. Nicolay felt that a major factor in the low incidence of *winkel* employment was their high labour costs. He declared in 1825 that he could hire carpenters elsewhere for f300 to f350 (about £21 to £25) annually, while the department was requesting a fee of f3 (4s. 3d.) per day.[40] However, daily rates in the colony were usually substantially higher proportionately than monthly or annual ones.

Winkel rates of hire differed during the period under review. Samples of annual rates in January 1825 are as follows: Moses I, a carpenter, at f440 (£31 8s. 7d.); Jack, Primo and Pamba, grass cutters, and Pamba and Paul II, boat builders, at f360 (£25 14s. 3d.). Monthly rates were usually between f45 (£3 4s. 3d.) and f50 (£3 11s. 5d.) for males, and f27:10 (£1 19s. 3d.) for females. Daily rates varied between f2:10 (3s. 7d.) and f3 (4s. 3d.) for males; we do not have comparative rates for females.[41] In 1825 Wolfert Katz hired *winkel* artisans at the relatively low rate of 3s. 2d. (f2:4) per day and ordinary labourers at 2s. 4d. (f1:13). On the other hand, in 1826 William Campbell, attorney of plantation Vryheid, was willing to pay the department f450 (£32 2s. 10d.) annually for each of thirty *winkel* men alone or f350

(£25) for each of thirty men and twenty women, besides providing food and medicine.[42] This last instance demonstrates clearly that *winkel* labour could command a high market price.

Comparing the prices above with those for labour generally in the colony in 1825, the department's rates appear to be similar to and sometimes below the average market level. Nicolay stated that the usual monthly hire of artisan slaves was between f30 and f44 (£2 2s. 10d. to £3 2s. 10d.), and their annual hire between f300 and f500 (£21 8s. 7d. to £35 14s. 3d.). However, the labour of free artisans was much more expensive, since they worked for themselves and were therefore deemed to be more industrious. Nicolay estimated their monthly value at between f44 and f88 (£3 2s. 10d. to £6 5s. 8d.), and their annual value at between f600 and f1,200 (£42 17s. 2d. to £85 14s. 4d.).[43] Kyte estimated both male and female field and domestic labour at f350 to f400 (£25 to £28 11s. 5d.) annually, and artisan labour at f600 to f750 (£42 17s. 2d. to £53 11s. 5d.). The commissioners did not support the view of the high cost of *winkel* labour; in fact they alleged that sometimes the *winkel* people were hired out for low wages and that when the department wanted similar services it had to pay extravagant rates.[44] There is really no hard evidence to substantiate Nicolay's claim about the high rates being demanded for their labour. An interesting fact is that labour rates were appreciably higher in Berbice during this last period of slavery than in the early post-emancipation period, when the wage of ordinary labourers was thirty-two cents (1s. 4d.) and that of factory hands forty-eight cents (2s.) per day.[45]

Nicolay's second reason had slightly more merit. He alleged that there was depreciating demand for hired artisans since most estates now had their own artisans. He also alleged that with the increase in the numbers of free coloured men, most of whom were artisans, the demand for black artisans was declining continually. This argument found a faint echo in Walker's assertion two years earlier that the "respectable" plantation owners had their own artisans and that the number of solvent people in town was insufficient to employ all the *winkel* artisans. Kyte claimed that the number of artisans, and especially tailors, in the colony had increased recently, that there were too many *winkel* artisans in proportion to field hands, and that there was not as great a demand for the former as for the latter. He likewise asserted that "a permanent engagement never can be obtained for them" in town.[46] These

Table 4.3 Commissioners' Estimate of *Winkel* Earnings (Value of Work) by Vocation, 1815–1824 (guilders)[47]

Date	Carpenters	Smiths	Coopers	Masons	Boat Builders	Domestics and Labourers	Work Room	Gross Earnings	Actual Receipts
1815	6,195:0:0	11,442:4:0	6,174:0:0	4,568:0:0	9,370:10:0	3,626:5:0	—	41,375:19:0	11,223:5:0
1816	4,890:0:0	10,033:15:0	3,347:10:0	3,577:0:0	6,033:10:0	11,738:10:0	—	32,620:5:0	14,622:10:0
1817	4,207:0:0	10,180:5:0	4,501:10:0	4,971:10:0	5,606:15:0	5,167:10:0	—	34,634:10:0	27,947:13:0
1818	3,451:10:0	9,447:0:0	2,921:0:0	4,298:15:0	10,715:15:0	4,385:10:0	—	35,219:10:0	22,337:10:0
1819	7,549:0:0	5,070:10:0	3,150:10:0	3,601:12:8	7,105:10:0	6,149:0:0	—	32,626:2:8	38,547:18:12
1820	6,212:0:0	6,447:0:0	1,956:0:0	3,226:12:8	4,387:14:0	8,170:12:0	—	30,399:18:8	25,858:8:0
1821	1,480:0:0	2,085:0:0	1,190:5:0	1,649:0:0	880:0:0	9,856:18:0	255:0:0	17,396:3:0	12,130:11:9
					Artisans				
1822			10,576:11:0			8,519:6:0	683:15:0	19,779:12:0	35,664:5:0
1823			8,302:5:0			4,828:0:0	567:15:0	13,698:0:0	16,886:16:0
1824			10,252:10:0			4,648:8:0	427:0:0	15,327:18:0	14,825:4:0
Total								273,077:18:0	220,044:1:5

Source: "Winkel accounts", 28 February 1815–31 December 1824, PRO, CO 318/91: 301–14.

testimonies indicate that the *winkel* artisans were competing in an increasingly crowded market, but a careful analysis of the situation shows that it was not a closed or a rapidly closing one. As noted above, the price for artisan labour of free(d) persons was exceptionally high. Clearly, persons hiring labour would have welcomed the competition being offered by *winkel* labour, other things being equal. Several persons testified to the capacity of the *winkel* people to do excellent work. McWatt was sure that they were capable of doing as fine work as any other group in the colony. The commissioners boldly asserted that from inquiry and personal observation they were convinced that the men were good artisans and the women good seamstresses, and also that they were "decidedly the most intelligent body of Negroes in the Colony".[48]

George (born in 1797), a carpenter, was one such outstanding example. After five years of his life had been squandered as one of the superintendent's servants, he was finally hired out to Dr James Beresford. All who testified about him dubbed him an excellent craftsman. Walker regarded him as an excellent worker; the fiscal, for whom he had once worked, referred to him as "a capital workman" and a man of excellent character; Wray recommended him "in unqualified terms as honest, sober, & industrious, and of the strictest veracity". The commissioners noted that Wray had taught him and that "a good deal of pains seems [*sic*] to have been taken with his instruction".[49] Here was a man who had all the virtues of an excellent artisan and whose skill was in high demand in the colony. His reputation could have earned him a good price, but he was not alone, as we shall detail shortly.

In spite of his submissions above, Kyte refuted the allegation that the failure of the *winkel* artisans to find gainful employ resulted from the increased availability of artisan labour in the colony. According to him, every planter would be willing to pay for good and efficient, rather than sloppy and incomplete, work. He berated the free blacks and coloureds who in his view, with few exceptions, were given over to indolence, finery, dancing and general dissipation, and who often refused to work in order to demonstrate that being free, they could not be compelled to work.[50] His sentiments concerning the free blacks and free coloureds are clearly stereotypical, but this is not our focus of attention. However unkindly and obliquely, he makes the essential point that the labour market did not suffer from absolute constraints but was affected by a number of market forces, including the efficiency of labour and the social relations of production. Slave labour might be cheaper and more inefficient than free labour in general, but in a particular situation slave labour might prove to be more advantageous than free labour.[51]

It is appropriate to discuss here the issue of the efficiency of *winkel* labour. The majority of the evidence points to the fact that by 1825, and perhaps long before then, *winkel* labour hired out by the department (as distinct from "self-hire") had become inefficient and largely unproductive in economic terms. Already in 1822 Walker had observed that indolence was one of the primary reasons for the failure of the people to find employment. In 1825 Kyte attributed the unemployment problem principally to what he considered as the generally false impression among the inhabitants about the habits and dispositions of the *winkel* people. He himself testified that those whom he had hired had given him "great satisfaction – They were industrious, civil and attentive". Nicolay was even stronger in his praise of them, considering them in terms of sobriety and industry "the best Negroes in the whole colony in every respect". On the other hand, Dr James Beresford, one of the medical personnel attached to the department, viewed the majority of those whom he had hired as bad workers because of their idleness and absence from work. Finally, McWatt testified that the reason why the department was unable to hire out more people was that the employers complained that they did not perform the same quantity of work as other slaves. He felt that they were "very indifferent with respect to industry", that there was "a most material difference . . . in almost every respect" between them and plantation slaves, that they did no more than half the work of the latter, and that but for their idleness double the number would be hired out.[52]

McWatt made it clear that he was speaking only about the work ethic of the people, and that in other respects they conducted themselves "uncommonly well – I may even say better than they have ever done since I have taken over the Dept". He considered their bad work ethic as being because of over-indulgence by the superintendent, who spared the rod too much.[53] He had been in the department for a little over a year when he gave this testimony, and we are unsure how well acquainted he was with the problems that the department had experienced in previous years. These problems were much greater and deeper than any of those who gave negative testimonies cared or were in a position to articulate. If hired-out *winkel* labour was indeed inefficient, as the majority of persons testified, it had largely to do with the treatment of the people by the departmental staff and the lack of any coherent plan for their employment.

The commissioners had their fingers on the pulse of the department when they asserted that the root cause of the idleness and other problems which afflicted it had to do with the widespread discontent of the people, especially over food, clothing and housing, the neglect of the sick, aged and infirm, the brutalities meted out to them, the abridging of their holidays, and "pursuing a system of coercion & annoyance". They concluded that "no other result could well be expected than discontent, idleness and insubordination" in such circumstances. Even so, they believed that the extent of the negative response by the people was exaggerated. While they admitted the probability of some bad characters in the department, as in all population groups, they concluded (based on their residence in the colony for more than eighteen months) that the people as a whole were "willing, obedient & well disposed", and that all they needed to improve their industry was "encouragement & a proper direction to be given to their labour".[54]

Apart from the reasons given above, Walker claimed that insubordination at Berenstein and to a lesser extent in town in 1820–21 had a very adverse impact on the department, causing the business community to shy away from hiring *winkel* people. Up to 1825, according to him, the department was still recovering slowly from its effects – a circumstance for which he blamed Scott.[55] But his own poor accounting practices, which often led to litigation in court against debtors, real and imagined, also had a very negative effect on the disposition of business persons to employ the people. He himself believed that his duties as collector of customs also sometimes caused him to run afoul of would-be clients, and that this worked to the detriment of the department.[56]

Employment Policy

The department was guilty of a lack of any rational system of employment, which manifested itself in several ways. The administrators kept no coherent records of employment (or unemployment) and could give no indication of the quantum of labour utilized on a given task. They only kept a day book of hires, deaths, births and so on, and made a record of the employment situation at the end of each month in a rather irregular way.57 Failure to keep accurate records meant that at no time could the department review its employment profile and evaluate its performance thoroughly.

Instead of adopting vigorous measures to train the young people in various skills, Scott decided to take the easy course by leasing most of the smiths and carpenters to two private individuals, Thomas Keen and James Bone & Co., for modest fees. These individuals possessed little capital, and hoped to make their fortunes out of the sweat and blood of the *winkel* artisans. They never realized their objectives, but ran up huge debts with the department for nonpayment of the lease. Meanwhile, Scott had dismantled or sold the workshops and the site on which the smith's shops were located, so that the department could not readily reclaim the artisans without major problems of dislocation and unemployment.58

The *winkel* smiths were a versatile group of artisans, capable of working in iron, copper and brass, so that the department might have benefited substantially if their skills had been employed wisely. Walker finally obtained control of these artisans around November 1821, but for some inexplicable reason he did not commence erecting a new shop until 1823 and it was not opened until January or February 1824. His explanation for his tardiness was that when he finally achieved control of the smiths the situation was "too far gone . . . to make a speedy change in the want of funds & every other support".59 So he continued to job them (and the other artisans) out to private individuals while others moved in to fill the breach, and the department never regained any sizeable share of the market, with only five persons being employed in the smiths' shop on 20 January 1825.60 With the exception of the boat-builder's shop, the other shops suffered a similar fate, and while specific details on their demise are lacking, we know that up to 1826 the smith's and boat-builder's shops were the only ones functioning.61

The department concentrated on short-term hire instead of medium- and long-term contracts or doing the work in the department itself, as had been done previously. It had, in effect, become largely a jobbing firm rather than one which took in work contracts. The commissioners pointed to the "uncertain, desultory & irregular" nature of *winkel* employment: "sometimes in one place – sometimes in another – jobbed about the country and hired out to individuals, as domestics, or labourers, or to work at their trades – by the month – by the week – by the day – for half a day – for an hour – just as a job is offered, or their services might be required", a mode of employment which resulted in the people "leading a vagabond life".[62] This had a deleterious effect on the morale and self-esteem of a people once at the apex of the artisan group in the colony, making them, according to Commissioner Burdett, "the common drudges of the community".[63] While this was happening, and indeed largely as a result of it, other individuals seized the opportunity of creating niches for themselves in the artisan trades, sometimes utilizing *winkel* skills to do so. The situation with the boat builders offers the best example of the department being pushed out of a trade in which it once held a virtual monopoly. An individual named Da Costa, who had learned the trade and had developed his own firm in the womb of the *winkel* department by utilizing its boat builders, soon established a thriving concern, taking that business almost completely out of the hands of the department.[64] This happened in a colony where the demand for riverain craft was great and where the boat-building industry was thriving. What little of the trade remained within the department was dominated largely by the *winkel* artisan Louis.

The department had to compete for both private and government contracts, specifically those of the public works and military departments. The funds of the civil department came from local revenue, disbursed through the Council of Government (and additionally, in the case of New Amsterdam, the Board of Police or town council). As noted earlier, in strict terms the *winkel* department was not an arm of the colonial government but rather of the imperial Treasury. Still, mutual interest between the colonial and imperial authorities should have resulted in the Crown people being preferred in the colonial government's contracts, as had been the case up to 1811. Had this been done, a large number of the *winkel* people would have been employed year-round, which would have contributed substantially to the department's revenue. However, this did not happen, and so the department had to compete with other jobbing firms and individuals for government contracts.[65] The enmity between governor and superintendent, and perhaps other members of the Council of Government, did nothing to enhance the department's chances of being given such contracts.

The situation is more striking in the case of the military department, since that department was directly answerable to the War Office in London and was paid exclusively from imperial Treasury funds. Since the imperial

Treasury also subsidized the *winkel* department, it was even more logical to employ the people on the military works whenever possible and thus cut down on imperial subsidies to them. However, the king's men failed to see eye-to-eye on this matter, a circumstance best exemplified by the decision of the military department in 1825 to offer Katz a contract to build a new fort, although the department had made a bid for it. Katz, recognizing that he did not have sufficient skilled persons to do the entire job, subcontracted part of it, initially for a period of five and a half months, to the department. The entire job was expected to last for about three years, and had the department obtained the contract, it might well have been on the way to repairing much of the damage caused through unemployment in the last few years.[66] This signalled more than anything else the obloquy into which the department had fallen.

Training and Redeployment

The department did not think out carefully its training and redeployment policies. The boat-building trade again offers the prime example of "planless planning". According to the superintendent, in April 1825, because the boat-building business was slow, eleven of the twelve effective boat builders under his control (two others being attached to Government House, and two infirm but occasionally employed in the department) were temporarily or indefinitely relocated elsewhere: seven were employed "in the field or otherwise", two as painters, one sick in hospital and one convalescing. The activity of the last one (William I) was not mentioned. He was hospitalized in January 1825 and might still have been convalescing. In spite of the superintendent's allegations that he could find no regular work for these artisans, he was still training two apprentices as boat builders.[67] Other evidence given already (and which will also be given in the case of Louis) indicates that the boat-building trade was anything but moribund.

The loss of the former niche markets resulted in critical revenue shortfalls for the department. Walker indicated that one way out of this dilemma was to start a woodcutting establishment, which no doubt would have been a profitable venture, for the colony was accustomed to purchasing large quantities of lumber from abroad, while the huge local timber resources remained largely untapped. The demand for firewood in town was also evident.

However, the superintendent made little or no attempt to translate his vision into reality and his words into action.[68] The superintendent's lack of initiative also comes across in relation to grooms. Only a few *winkel* persons were employed in this activity, one of whom, Moses II (aged thirty-two), was allocated to Government House and considered by the commissioners as a good groom who "could never want for employment" because of his competence and the great demand for his skills in the colony.[69] Walker made no attempt to train grooms to meet this demand for them.

Walker might also have employed task work much more extensively for those persons who were field hands, since their tasks could be measured more easily than those of artisans and other nonfield persons.[70] The commissioners for management had recommended it strongly wherever it could be utilized, and the superintendent himself had declared that he was committed fully to this policy: "no plan seems equal to that of task-work". He had also opined that "when the negro has finished his task for the day, he must be regularly paid if he does any extra work".[71] The plantocracy's earlier concern about this arrangement, when the commissioners for management first introduced it on the Crown properties, had largely disappeared by the 1820s, and task work had become an important aspect of labour management in the colony, as in other parts of the Caribbean. According to Lieutenant Governor Beard, apart from harvesting, "the most considerable part" of plantation work was done by task, which was always moderate and could be completed by 2 p.m. by industrious slaves. The managers of Katz's seven estates likewise declared that task work was the system used on their estates, that the people usually finished work by 2 p.m., except during crop time, and had the rest of the day off.[72] Even if the plantocratic interests were exaggerating, these statements at least confirm that task work had become a common practice in the colony.

Walker affirmed that he used this system whenever possible, mainly in the field and the workroom, but the day books and other records suggest otherwise. True, problems occasionally occurred concerning the relative difficulties of tasks for artisans working as field hands, as against genuine field hands, but McWatt testified that the department got more out of the young people by this system: "The system of task work tends to promote industry among the people, as they work hard to finish their task and they have more time to attend to their affairs."[73] Task work therefore offered some incentive sorely lacking in the regular concourse of labour which required the people to toil all day no matter how hard or efficiently they worked. As regards payment for extra work, the department never implemented this suggestion.

Self-Hire

The people showed much greater industry when the department allowed them to engage in self-hire, that is, to work for themselves for a stipulated fee. Because of their reputation as highly skilled workers, they would have been able to challenge the free black and coloured population, whose rates of hire, it will be recalled, were usually higher than those of slaves. Done on an extensive scale, this practice would have gone a long way towards repairing the breaches in the department's finances and raising the people's standard of living. However, the superintendent was unable to see this, although he noted the ease with which the artisans were able to earn money when working for themselves during their free time. He testified, for instance, that the blacksmith Thomas – a frequent deserter – who otherwise was not very industrious, became highly so when working for himself. Thomas himself declared that he could earn f1 (1s. 5d.) during his lunch break (11 a.m.– 1 p.m.), and f3 (4s. 3d.) on Sundays.[74]

In order to appreciate the possibilities of self-hire it is important to give some estimates, however crude, of the cost of maintaining the department. The commissioners estimated the total expenditure of the department in 1824 at f42,000 (£3,000); this figure was very close to the assessment of the Department of Colonial Audit, which calculated the average annual expenditure from 1818 to 1823 at f43,594 (£3,113) in a situation in which, as we have noted, no strict accountability was the rule.[75] Estimates of the average annual cost of maintaining each *winkel* person ranged from f90 to f100 (£6 10s. to £7 3s. 4d.),[76] giving a total of between f23,400 and f26,000 for the entire group directly under the department's control. Administrative costs (salaries, medical costs, perquisites and taxes, based upon the figures for 1824) might be estimated at f12,000,[77] and to this might be added a rather arbitrary figure of f3,000 under "miscellaneous", putting the total cost of running the department at around f41,000 (£2,928). In fact, it is quite likely that the administrative costs could have been reduced substantially under proper management. On the income side, the commissioners calculated the average annual earnings over the period 1815–24 at roughly f26,290 (£1,877), and over the more restricted period 1818–23 at f23,393 (£1,670), as against f25,006 (£1,786) calculated by the Department of Colonial Audit for the latter period. But in 1824 the department grossed only f14,869 (£1,062), roughly 35 per cent of its expenditure. Nicolay estimated in 1825 that the department was capable of earning between f35,000 and f40,000 (£2,500 to £2,857) per annum under proper management.[78] This estimate was no exaggeration, and the income could have been higher under a system of self-hire.

Taking into consideration the potential labour force of the department, as discussed above, it was not unreasonable to expect an average annual employment of one hundred persons under self-hire, at a rate of f10 per (five-day) week, which would have realized an income of f50,000 (£3,571) per annum (a year actually comprising fifty work weeks). The system of self-hire was common at this time in urban Caribbean and American communities, including those of the Bahamas, Barbados, Cuba, the United States and Brazil. In Cuba it was estimated that one-third of the slaves in Havana worked under this system, and in the United States an estimated 20 per cent of the urban slaves were similarly employed. In Nassau, Bahamas, it had become the dominant labour market system by this time.[79] We have no record as to how common the practice had become in New Amsterdam, but there was no reason that it could not have worked efficiently there.

The situation of Louis illustrates some very positive aspects of self-hire, that of Frederick III the mixed blessings of self-hire, and that of Dominick the possible negative consequences of the refusal to grant self-hire. Louis (born in 1778), the father of eight children, was "headman over the people" and the department's chief boat builder. According to McWatt, in his younger days he used his free time to accumulate "a good deal of money". Now in his middle years (in 1825), the department often allowed him to be on self-hire, and he had "a good many jobs for building small boats & punts", frequently hiring the department's boat builders to assist him and always paying for their services on time. Louis himself testified that he had a comfortable house, some money saved and several debtors from whom he simply could not collect. He could earn f4:10 (6s. 9d.) per day when work was available. The commissioners declared him to be one of the best boat builders in the colony; he bore a "universally good character" and everyone spoke highly of him "for industry & general good conduct in every respect". McWatt summed up his character thus: "in short he is in every respect one of the best Negroes I ever knew, and his family are equally respectable".[80]

Frederick III (b. 1800) was an ambitious and enterprising young man who was able to seize the opportunity created by the demise of the smith's shop around 1819 to establish his own smithery. The department hired this shop from him in 1823 at a price of f88 (£6 5s. 8d.) in order to repair the militia muskets and do other work. He claimed in 1825 that he worked as a farrier under contract for f924 (£66) annually, but that other work was slow at the time. He was in favour of self-hire, but had a major grievance against the superintendent. His rate of self-hire was f52 per month (presumably translated into f624 per year), substantially more than if the department had hired him out to someone else, besides being totally responsible for maintaining himself. This left him with little money to save in order to purchase his freedom, assessed at £200. He claimed that since 1818 (clearly a wrong date, since Walker had not yet returned to Berbice at that time) the superintendent had promised to allow him to work towards the purchase of his freedom, if he behaved well. However, he saw little hope of remedying the situation since, according to him, Walker refused to put towards his freedom part of the monthly sum which he paid to the department. When asked by the commissioners to give an assessment of the young man Walker replied tersely that he was "very unmanageable – he expects to purchase his freedom".[81] Given the situation described above, it is hardly surprising that Frederick would be recalcitrant.

John Blassingame notes the driving power that the prospect of freedom had on enslaved persons: Josiah Henson asserted that "from my earliest recollection freedom had been the object of my ambition, a constant motive to exertion, an ever-present stimulus to gain and to save".[82] Perhaps Walker, never having been a slave nor deprived of his liberty, could not empathize with Frederick and felt that he was not yet ready for freedom. Frederick's case underlines the mental agonies of many enslaved persons who could not change their physical or social condition no matter how hard they worked. For Frederick, the cut of slavery was twice felt, first because of his sense of powerlessness and second because he was the only family member still in slavery.[83]

The two cases above dealt with *winkel* artisans who possessed the talent and desire to push themselves upwards against the odds. The first one was a stable and well-adjusted member of the department, while the other, in spite of the coldness between him and the superintendent, did not have any open strife with the department's staff or his colleagues. This, however, was not the case with Dominick (b. 1800), an equally talented artisan, whose life was virtually in ruins by 1825.

A mason and bricklayer by profession, Dominick was hired out by the department in 1822 at f4:10 (6s. 5d.) per day, the second highest rate of hire recorded in the department's ledgers. He testified that he was capable of making two bits (9d.) any day in his spare time, and Walker testified that he was an excellent bricklayer, suggesting that he was both highly skilled and efficient. In 1821 the department occasionally allowed him to hire himself for short periods, paying the department the very high sum of f3 (4s. 3d.) per day. On 3 November 1821 the day book records in its usual laconic way, "Dominick from being hired to himself to Dept." This might have meant that the job for which he had sought self-hire was completed or, more likely, that some disaffection had set in between him and the superintendent. In any event, within two months the day book recorded that he had been picked up on plantation Blyendaal (Bleyendall) as a deserter, taken to the barracks in town and charged with stealing plantains from the said plantation. He received fifty lashes on the fiscal's order, before being returned to the department. The superintendent dispatched Dominick, cast in the role of a rogue and a vagabond, to the dreaded plantation Berenstein as further punishment. From there the manager sent him on hire to plantation Vryberg, but he must have proved recalcitrant, for the same day he was back at Berenstein.[84]

In the next few months Dominick led a fitful existence – being hired out, finding himself sick in hospital and absconding from hospital. It is necessary to give here a brief glimpse of the purposelessness of his life at this point:

> 13 June 1822 – in hospital; 3 July 1822 – sent from hospital to Jansen at f4:10 per day; 10 August 1822 – returned from Jansen to department; 15 September 1822 – sent to Berenstein "under care, being afflicted with yaws"; 21 October 1822 – received twenty lashes for "repeatedly absenting himself when ordered to go to Berenstein"; 6 March 1823 – in hospital; 20 March 1823 – awaiting hire;

31 May 1823 – hired out at f3 per day; 9 June 1823 – in hospital; 28 June 1823 – hired out at f3 per day; 24 July 1823 – included in woodcutting gang in Canje; 12 July 1824 – hired out; November 1824–31 January 1825 – repairing workshop at wharf and clearing land.[85]

Dominick testified before the commissioners around mid-1825 that until recently he had been working at his trade on an estate but that he was lately hospitalized. Walker declared that he was unreliable, but this is hardly surprising given the kind of life that he lived, or was forced to live. The commissioners considered him to be "a shrewd intelligent man". Eventually, in 1828, he became more sedentary, marrying Antoinette – a *winkel* slave held for some years by the Maroons until she made good her escape – being baptized by Wray and becoming one of his faithful followers.[86]

Dominick was not the only deserter in his family, for both of his brothers, Thomas Harvey and Michael, also became deserters.[87] It is probable therefore that some conflict existed between his family and the superintendent, but whatever the situation, the result was the breaking rather than the making of a potentially very profitable artisan. This brings out forcefully the constraints usually associated with Caribbean slavery, which often destroyed the best initiatives and energies of its victims.

Several other *winkel* men testified of their good earning capacity. Hendrick I (aged twenty-two), a carpenter who doubled as a cabinet maker, stated that he could easily earn as much as four joes (£6) weekly by working for himself. This was a considerable sum for any artisan at the time, but he was probably not exaggerating. Carpenters were always in high demand in the colony because most of the colonial buildings were wooden and were in more frequent need of maintenance and repair than was the case with stone buildings. Both Walker and Graham, the late *winkel* bookkeeper, testified of Hendrick's excellent character and good workmanship. The commissioners noted that at his interview he wore a shirt of "good linen" which he had purchased himself, verified by the production of the receipt. Frederick II (aged thirty-six) claimed that he could earn f3 per day at his regular trade as a cooper and f4 for a molasses cask. He provided the commissioners with a written testimonial from Pryce Dyos, head cooper of plantation Providence, which declared him to be sober, steady, well-behaved and a good worker, an assessment confirmed by Walker. Balter, the head cooper, was another one anxious to work on his own. He complained about the lack of a cooper's shop which resulted in his being jobbed all around the country. He declared that if he had a lot of work he could pay the department f2 per day for self-hire, since he could earn f3. Others who testified of their ability to earn their keep under self-hire included Gorée (aged thirty-eight), Chanton (aged thirty-eight), William (aged twenty-nine) and Jacobus II (aged twenty-two).[88]

It was, of course, much easier for males than females to find self-employment because of the limited avenues available to the latter. The commissioners claimed that few outlets existed for the employment of females and that there was insufficient work for them as seamstresses, while clothing for the people could be bought far more cheaply than if manufactured in the department. Walker did allow some of the women to be on self-hire for short periods, but there is no information on how they employed themselves. Sophia I, Juliana, Rosalia and Tannetje, who were among those allowed this option for short periods, could have earned money as seamstresses in spite of the tight market situation, because they were highly skilled and efficient. Mrs Elizabeth Stanley, the workroom instructor, regarded Tannetje as the best seamstress in the department, and Tannetje, Juliana and a few others did a lot of (unpaid) work for the Walkers.[89] Other females could have hired themselves out as field hands, hucksters or domestics. Huckstering, in particular, was a widespread activity among females in urban communities, and would have offered at least some financial alleviation to the department. Lieutenant Governor Beard assigned a few of the *winkel* women attached to Government House to that activity.[90] The commissioners disapproved of female huckstering "with very few exceptions", and likewise of self-hiring or hiring them out as domestics, hinting that this might give them too much latitude and that some element of prostitution was involved in the last two arrangements. Wray had declared earlier that the colonists often accused the mission of existing on the wages of prostitution.[91]

Several *winkel* females testified that they could earn their keep, and some of them substantial sums, working under self-hire. Anna I (aged forty-two) declared that she could earn $10 (f30) monthly as a laundress, while she was also a good cook and needle-worker. Both Walker and a Mr Edwards, for whom she had worked, confirmed that she was able to earn a living on her own. Juliana (aged twenty-three), widely regarded as an excellent seamstress, stated that she could make a frilled skirt in two days for f2:10, which would have realized f25 in a twenty-day working month, all other things being equal. Sophia II (aged twenty-four) and Madelintje (aged twenty-one), other seamstresses, estimated their earning capacities at f6 per week.[92]

These cases and several others indicate clearly that the *winkel* people, especially the artisans and seamstresses, found the existing system of employment too restrictive and oppressive and wanted the opportunity to improve their material and social circumstances. Howard Johnson has shown how self-hire became an important means of ameliorating the condition of some of the Bahamian slaves. But both he and Higman have noted that self-hire was no guarantee that the slave's material circumstances would improve and that there were many instances when this was not the case – a matter which had partly to do with the high prices masters often charged for self-hire and partly with the fierce competition in the casual labour market.[93] As noted above, this problem also surfaced in the case of Frederick II, although largely in connection with his interest in accumulating sufficient money to purchase his freedom. Still, the *winkel* effectives generally were quite certain that they could improve their material situation under self-hire. The departmental staff could have assessed the earning capacities of those who wanted to work under this system and made a determination on that basis, but this was never done. Walker's failure to do so might well have been due to a desire to retain any surplus derived from individual *winkel* labour, although such a policy would only have militated against the wider financial interests of the department.

A major problem which arose in urban communities where self-hire became widespread was control of the slaves, which the colonial authorities viewed as an added dimension to the problem of the greater mobility of urban slaves when compared with their rural counterparts. As Johnson notes, "Slaves who worked on the self-hire system in the Bahamas enjoyed a considerable degree of independence"; and again, "The extensive autonomy which slaves on self-hire had achieved by the opening decade of the nineteenth century posed problems of control for slave-owners."[94] Higman regards it as "the most extreme form of independent economic behavior available to urban slaves" that "constituted a fundamental contradiction in the slave system. It admitted that economic efficiency required freedom in the market for labor and made the slave a free agent rather than a piece of property. It removed the slave from the direct authority and supervision of the master."95 Slaves mixing with free persons in a free market, in which they could negotiate the price of their labour, might no longer be satisfied with giving their masters a rebate and might seek to sever the ties that bound the two together, through either manumission or revolt, thus enlarging the possibilities of a social revolution. Some whites also complained that slaves on self-hire had more scope to steal, while others complained that easy subsistence under the system caused many slaves to work for only a few days and to spend the rest of their time in idleness and drunkenness.96

Masters who were concerned about the threat of a social revolution presented by self-hire, or who felt that slaves should be kept on the margin of material and social existence, were alarmed at the increase in self-hire, coming as it did at a time when anti-slavers were agitating for changes in the colonies. Some colonies, such as Barbados and British Honduras, passed laws imposing fines on masters who placed their slaves on self-hire, while others, such as Jamaica, Demerara and the Bahamas, sought to control the situation by requiring masters to register the slaves in question and receive a licence.97 We have seen no colonial regulations in Berbice on this matter, but it would be no surprise if such controls did exist. Walker might well have been pandering to the prejudices of the slave masters by restricting self-hire in the department, but the *winkel* finances suffered badly as a result.

The Workroom

The workroom was the main area in which the women were trained and employed as seamstresses, and from as early as January 1820 Walker expressed the desire to revive this aspect of the department's work which Mrs Wray used to conduct. On 9 October 1820, about one month after the conflict with Reverend Wray had broken out, the superintendent opened an establishment altogether separate from that of theWrays, employing Mrs Stanley as instructor. At first he expressed great optimism about it, declaring one year after its commencement that it was proving to be more successful than he had anticipated and that it might very well turn the females from burdensome to beneficial members of the department; a few months later he declared that it constituted "a radical part of the establishment".98 However, as in so many other instances, he was exaggerating. The unit never came near to attaining financial solvency, failing to pay its expenses and realizing only the miserly sum of f1,506 (£107) from work done up to 31 December 1823. Even taking into account the sewing done for other members of the department, largely garments for the females and shirts for the men (since little or no tailoring took place there), in the commissioners' view the department was unable to justify its existence as a financial undertaking. Needless to say, the superintendent could give no detailed information on the work done in the unit, the commissioners observing that its books were kept in a "loose and irregular manner".[99]

Walker produced a detailed statement only for 1822 and nothing more than total receipts for the other years, alleging that he had specified the particulars for 1823 and 1824 to the commissioners. However, the latter stated bluntly that he had produced no detailed statement. Walker also claimed that "the clothing for all the Negroes of the Department with the exception of woolen jackets and about a fourth part of the mens trowsers have been made in the workroom". However, Mrs Stanley contradicted this assertion, testifying that "the pupils are employed in all kinds of needle work, except tailor's work". But she immediately qualified her statement by explaining that the department also made jackets and waistcoats "for the servants in place, & trousers". This could hardly have meant more than a dozen persons employed in the superintendent's household or hired out as domestics. McWatt was unequivocal that all the men's clothing, except shirts, had been bought ready-made since he joined the department, a statement partly corroborated by the department's records, which show that it purchased ninety pairs of trousers in 1824.[100]

The workroom never attained a stable character, in relation to either the persons employed therein or the social relations under which production took place. McWatt testified that during his time the number of females in the unit varied from four to sixteen.[101] This was because management often removed them from the workroom and hired them to persons outside the department or to themselves, while at other times the superintendent relocated them to his domestic service or banished them to Berenstein as punishment. This had a negative effect on both the quantity and quality of their work, although, as noted above, some of them became excellent seamstresses.

Disharmonious Work Environment

The superintendent introduced a grave element of conflict into social relations within the work environment by setting the coloured persons to field work, especially the women, something considered as absolutely forbidden in the colony. Kyte testified that during his twenty years' residence in the colony he had never known mulattoes, male or female, being employed in such work, and went on to state that a proprietor who employed young coloured women in field work would expose himself to the general censure of the community.[102] There is much to be said for the superintendent if he was trying to break down colour barriers within the society, an almost impossible task because colour was delicately and intricately interwoven into the fabric of colonial society throughout the Caribbean. But Walker was not a reformer in this mould. In fact, his efforts at social reform veered in the opposite direction, for he adopted extreme measures at times to prevent the young ladies of the department from bridging the colour divide in their amorous relationships with white men (see chapter 6). He also regarded the colonial laws preventing coloureds from receiving commissions in the militia as "reasonable and sound".[103] Nor can we say that his major concern was with the efficiency of labour, for the degree of opposition that the coloureds put up negated his attempts at initiating field industry among them. He simply used such work as a form of punishment, by banishing the females especially to Berenstein, perhaps without considering fully the social consequences of his actions. The policy of reducing coloured females (and males) to the level of the blacks by assigning them to field work could have had an explosive effect on social relations between the two groups. However, this never happened, because the issues that united them against the superintendent were more pressing than those that had the potential to divide them.

The imperial government was itself unhappy about the employment of females in field labour. Already by an order-in-council of 16 March 1808 instituting the apprenticeship system for the apprenticed Africans, it had forbidden potential masters and mistresses to whom they might be attached to put females to field work, and had enjoined the collector of customs, their protector, "to take especial care that they be not employed in the latter on any account". This regulation obviously represented the government's attempt to shield the females from some of the worst abuses associated with plantation slavery. The government viewed light domestic work as more appropriate for the females, and suggested that they be employed as cooks, laundresses, seamstresses and so on.[104] Walker, as collector of customs in Berbice and guardian of a few of these Africans, should have known about this order and should logically have applied it also to the Crown people.

Walker also demonstrated his impolicy by his extensive use of artisans to do plantation work, a circumstance that Wray dubbed "a complete misapplication of labour as well as hardship to the people".[105] Walker also demonstrated his backward tendencies in his transformation of the extra day given to the people each fortnight from one which they were allowed to utilize as they saw fit into one in which they had to plant their provision grounds, although no clear evidence exists that they had personal plots, as distinct from the communal ones. He thus robbed this day of all its significance, making it another one of regular toil, although by this time a few planters, including Katz, were beginning to implement the practice of an extra free day.[106] While maintaining before the commissioners that he did not compel the people to cultivate their grounds on that day, Walker stated immediately after, in his accustomed equivocal way, that "a general inspection was maintained over them to see that they were on their grounds, whether they worked much or little". According to him, he placed an overseer over them on such occasions "to keep them to their work" and "not to exact any particular task from them", his principal object being "to keep idlers from wandering about to the annoyance of our neighbours".[107] This was a short step from admitting that he coerced them into working during their free day.

As for the workroom, the environment also became increasingly disharmonious and quite hostile at times. The incidents involving Matilda and Carolina II will be dealt with in chapter 7, but it is important to note here that these incidents helped to feed the spirit of resistance that remained unbroken for some time. As a result, their work habits and production dropped to the point where they were making on average only one shirt each per week.[108] The atmosphere was not conducive to high levels of production, and the superintendent seemed powerless to stop the drift downwards.

Several persons in the workroom and elsewhere indicated a preference to be employed otherwise. They were sentient and provident persons who wanted to enhance the quality of their lives and those of their families. They were locked in the jaws of slavery and frustrated by the restrictions of the slave system and an insouciant superintendent. Some of them also wanted to put physical and social distance between themselves and the departmental staff. Anna II (aged fourteen), on the verge of her adulthood and wanting to do something better with her life, bewailed the fact that the superintendent had assigned her to his household staff, doing nothing but mending "old things", while she might have been acquiring a skill in the workroom. Hector (aged thirty-seven), formerly a cooper but now working at the fort, expressed a preference to return to his old trade. Nancy (aged nineteen), another of the superintendent's domestics, preferred to be hired out. The superintendent had harassed her because of her amorous connection with a white man. Walker considered her an industrious and "civil young woman but spoiled for her station like the others" – a clear reference to those who had formed similar connections. Rosalia, mother of Adonis (aged ten), wanted her son to be transferred from his present apprenticeship as a boat builder to that of a carpenter, which would represent a break with family tradition, but she obviously viewed boat building as a dying trade in the department.[109]

Walker's Self-Interest

The heart of the problem in the department lay in the fact that the management, and especially the superintendent, were more concerned about their narrow interests than the wider interests of their charges. The full control of the department offered Walker a good opportunity to feather his own nest. The commissioners of inquiry reported:

> The Agent indeed appears to us, during the whole of his administration, to have been more actuated by motives of self interest, in providing for the domestic convenience of himself and family, & in converting the resources of the establishment to their use, than in paying that attention which was his duty, to the wants and comforts of the people placed under his care & superintendence.[110]

Although Walker did not receive a salary as superintendent, he appropriated the £200 per annum allocated by the Treasury for house and office rent. In order to save on costs, he integrated the offices of collector of customs and *winkel* superintendent as closely as possible. This, in itself, was sound management, except that he, rather than the Crown, benefited from it. For instance, although he was given £100 for annual rental of a customs house, he integrated the offices of the two departments in a single building which also served as the school premises, the seamstresses' workroom and his dwelling house. This resulted in a total rental in 1819 of £242, thus realizing savings of £58, which he pocketed.[111]

The commissioners of inquiry charged him with engaging in subterfuge by listing separate charges for the sections of the house he was renting, in such a way as to create the impression that he was renting multiple premises: agency dwelling house, *winkel* office, *winkel* store and *winkel* workroom. The commissioners also noted that the *winkel* office served as the customs house, while the *winkel* store was also a kind of customs warehouse. Similarly, *winkel* personnel sometimes served also as customs-house staff. Although there was a separate salaried *winkel* bookkeeper (at f2,000 per annum), the customs-house clerk was also designated *winkel* clerk, receiving f2,000 per annum for the latter office and only f400 for the former. A slave of the department, designated *winkel* office keeper, also acted as the superintendent's groom and as the customs-house keeper, the last post carrying a small but official allowance (of about £16 per annum) authorized by the Customs House Department in London, which the incumbent obviously did not receive.

The superintendent benefited in other ways from the assignment of several offices to a single individual. He employed a *winkel* man as both his butler and the porter of the *winkel* store, although he kept the key himself. Mrs Stanley, his housekeeper, also functioned as both the department's workroom instructor and the schoolmistress. She received f11 per month for the first office and f44 for the two others, besides an allowance of food (about equal to that of a headman), clothing, household supplies, free medical attendance and other small perquisites.[112] Walker also used *winkel* labour on an appreciable scale without paying any money, a practice which he justified on the basis that no previous administrator had paid for their services and that he was not receiving a salary as superintendent. This argument has some merit, but good sense ought to have prevailed in such circumstances. That this was not the case is evident from the fact that Walker usually had on his domestic staff between ten and thirteen *winkel* members.

The superintendent did not confine the use of *winkel* labour and materials to the cases mentioned above. He often employed the people to work around his premises. Sometimes an entire gang of not less than forty people could be found weeding the ground and trimming the fence at his residence, and carpenters could be found repairing and painting the house periodically. On one occasion he employed "the whole of the people" under the manager for three days in rehabilitating the premises. The boss also dispatched the people to cut firewood at an estimated annual cost, according to the manager, of 150 man days.[113] Mrs Stanley testified in July 1825 that the workroom had done no sewing for the superintendent's family in the previous year, but that in 1823 the seamstresses had made some clothes and sheets for them. Her testimony indicates that this was a regular workroom activity: "We make brown Holland sofa covers & mend them. Lady's dresses & clothing – shirts for the gentlemen – bed linen – bed curtains, and in fact all sort of needlework for a [sic] family." Tannetje, one of the seamstresses, also testified that Nancy, Harriet, Hannah, Juliana and herself sewed dresses, shirts, gowns and so on for the Walkers, who sent "plenty of work from the house into the workroom".[114]

After going over all the records and interviewing several persons, bond and free, the commissioners also accused Walker of a number of other improprieties, including keeping cows and sheep on the department's estate at Berenstein largely for his own use, appropriating for his domestic or other purposes cloth and food purchased for the people, furnishing his house (during his first assignment in 1815) partly at the expense of the department, purchasing Levantine jars (which he later carried away and only returned when asked about them) with *winkel* money, debiting the department's account of f330 which he alleged had been stolen while it was in his own possession, and contributing funds under his personal name to the relief of sufferers in Holland while charging the same to the *winkel* account.[115] "In short, everything was Winkel," was the commissioners' laconic remark.[116]

The fact is that the *winkel* superintendency was a lucrative post, netting its holder at least £700 per annum in salary, house rent and unpaid labour, not counting what an unscrupulous official might gain further by the use of materials or embezzlement of funds. It is no wonder that Walker accepted the post free of emoluments at the outset, and that he and Scott fought so bitterly over it. *Winkel* funds had been employed over the years, licitly and illicitly, to enhance the financial position of many government officials, but Walker was the greatest predator. He sought to justify his abuse of privilege by asserting boldly, "I am entitled to take and do take the services of the people for whatever purposes would require me otherwise either to purchase or hire slaves."[117] This was his ultimate and constant justification for whatever privileges he took with the department's assets. His personal interests frequently outweighed his sense of right and wrong. The commissioners felt that he availed himself too extensively of *winkel* labour, and in such a manner that it was "highly prejudicial to the interests of the property".[118]

Conclusion

Walker's skills as an administrator were not equal to the task at hand. The declining earning capacity of the department had more to do with his mismanagement than with the inability of the people to earn their keep. In spite of the fairly large number of invalids and superannuated persons, the department had a good number of effectives, highly skilled at their trades and anxious to work under proper self-hire arrangements. Had the superintendent pursued this option aggressively, the financial history of the department would have been quite different. But, far from doing so, he placed a number of impediments in the way of the people, creating unnecessary tension and conflict in the department.

The superintendent also fell short in a number of other areas. He failed to recognize the importance of re-establishing the shops dismantled by Scott – who himself had made a bad decision to do so in the first place – and allowed others to go to ruins. He also failed to retrain some of the artisans or develop a new corps among the young apprentices as grooms, timber cutters, tailors and so forth. He was more content to drift with the tide of misfortune than to swim against it. His poor attitude was infectious, and both staff and *winkel* people became afflicted by it. McWatt and others explained the apparent inertia of the people simply in terms of laziness which the rod of correction would rectify, and blamed Walker for using it too sparingly. On the other hand, Albert Memmi has noted that colonialism pollutes the best energies of people,[119] and colonial slavery was an even greater pollutant. The inertia of the enslaved people had much to do with their perception of the futility of their efforts to better their condition and most of all to attain freedom.

5

Material Culture, 1816–1825

Introduction

The material and social cultures of a people are the products of their innovative impulse. They are usually true indices of their world-view and their experiences in the bivouac of life: their hopes, fears, aspirations and achievements. Material and social cultures also normally enshrine the inherited values and traditions of a people's ancestors. They thus constitute the most significant expressions of their civilization and identity. Material culture is commonly manifested in such creations as buildings, food, clothing, icons, objects of art and a wide range of technologies. Social culture may also express itself in material terms, but at its highest level it is a spiritual or psychic phenomenon that finds expression in such forms as music, song, dance, religion and literature. But all this is only partly true of persons held under draconian regimes of bondage, which frustrate their ambitions, invade the cultural contexts of their lives and force them to develop subterranean cultures in order to survive with any measure of integrity. This is certainly the picture which emerges from a study of the *winkel* people, who chafed under the squalor and duress of slavery and who, while not suffering from the same level of deprivation as many plantation slaves, nevertheless found their physical and psychological space considerably restricted, and their hopes and ambitions thwarted.

The *winkel* plant constituted the place where the people were born, lived, worked, died and were buried. In traditional African societies the place of birth and residence was more than a material environment: it was equally a psychological and metaphysical environment in which the living communed with each other and with the ancestral dead. In African parlance, the people's navel strings and their bones were buried there, and thus the place acquired a deep social and religious significance not often appreciated by Europeans. However, in the context of the *winkel* department, it was also the place in which they were short-changed on food and clothing, whipped, brutalized and denied basic freedoms so that, as in the case of those slaves who lived on plantations, the village held poignant memories of pain which often outweighed the memories of pleasure. Life, of course, is a subtle blend of pleasure and pain, and both are necessities in the law of growth. But the slave system, with its emphasis on the grotesque rather than the beautiful, often reduced life to a succession of painful experiences for the slaves. The predicament of the *winkel* people underlines Orlando Patterson's observation that slavery is characterized by "powerlessness, social degradation or dishonor and natal alienation".[1]

The *winkel* people constituted the largest single community of urban slaves in Berbice, mainly creolized, larger in number than most plantation populations, but sharing a much smaller space. This, of course, allowed them greater scope for interaction with one another. Fictive kinship, developed by common experiences aboard the slave ship and in the colony, gradually gave place to biological kinship, forged through marriage and concubinage. At the same time, the urban dimension of their lives afforded them greater latitude to interact with other urban groups – slaves, free coloureds and whites – and thus to establish certain exogenous relationships. But this also exposed them in greater measure to white creole culture, values and aspirations in dress, religion, education and entertainment. There was also a greater degree of individualism in their daily lives than was the case with plantation slaves, who operated largely in gangs and who had less opportunity to acquire individual property. Thus the *winkel* people, like many other urban slaves, tended to show in much greater measure than plantation slaves the European elements of "creole" culture. Yet we must not overemphasize this point, for the extant records suggest that they retained a fair measure of African culture in language, music, song, dance, dress, names, medicine, religion (including rites of passage) and the strong gerontocracy of their society.

The Physical Environment and Buildings

The *winkel* establishment was located primarily in the northeastern section of the town, on a rectangular piece of land of roughly 2,556 Rhineland square rods (40,896 square yards), comprising some 8 acres.[2] However, it did not present a positive image of an urban or peri-urban environment. Between the village and the main town area lay many vacant lots overrun by brushwood, particularly black sage, and the same was true of land on which the village abutted. Walker described it in 1825 as a place "nearly surrounded by uncultivated lots of land".[3] Part of the site lay on savannah terrain which was prone to inundation during the rainy season, to relieve which the people used to burst the town dam, thus diverting much of the water into the town. In August 1821 the Board of Police (or town council) of New Amsterdam therefore ordered that those houses on the savannah be relocated.[4]

The *winkel* village or "negro yard" needed extensive drainage on all sides, including a system of dykes (*kokers*) in order to keep the water in check, but management erected them slowly and they were not complete until 1825. Maintenance proved to be a major problem, partly because of the looseness of the soil and the fallen vegetable matter which often clogged the trenches at the back of the village, and partly because the trenches were not cleaned regularly. In 1821 the Board of Police had undertaken to clean the town's northern trench regularly, a factor critical to keeping the village dry, but had done nothing about it.[5] The *winkel* people were also responsible for the state of some of the trenches, allowing hogs to run wild and to trample down the sides of some of the dams, and throwing debris into the trenches, so that the surroundings became unsightly.

The commissioners could hardly believe their eyes at their first sight of the village, shortly after their arrival in 1825, as this statement makes clear:

> The appearance of the Winkel village presented on the day of our inspection, in the ruinous & comfortless state of many of the houses – the accumulation of dirt and rubbish in the interior and vicinity thereof – the state of the trenches, some of which appear to have been a receptacle for broken pots, bottles, old rags &

Material Culture, 1816–1825

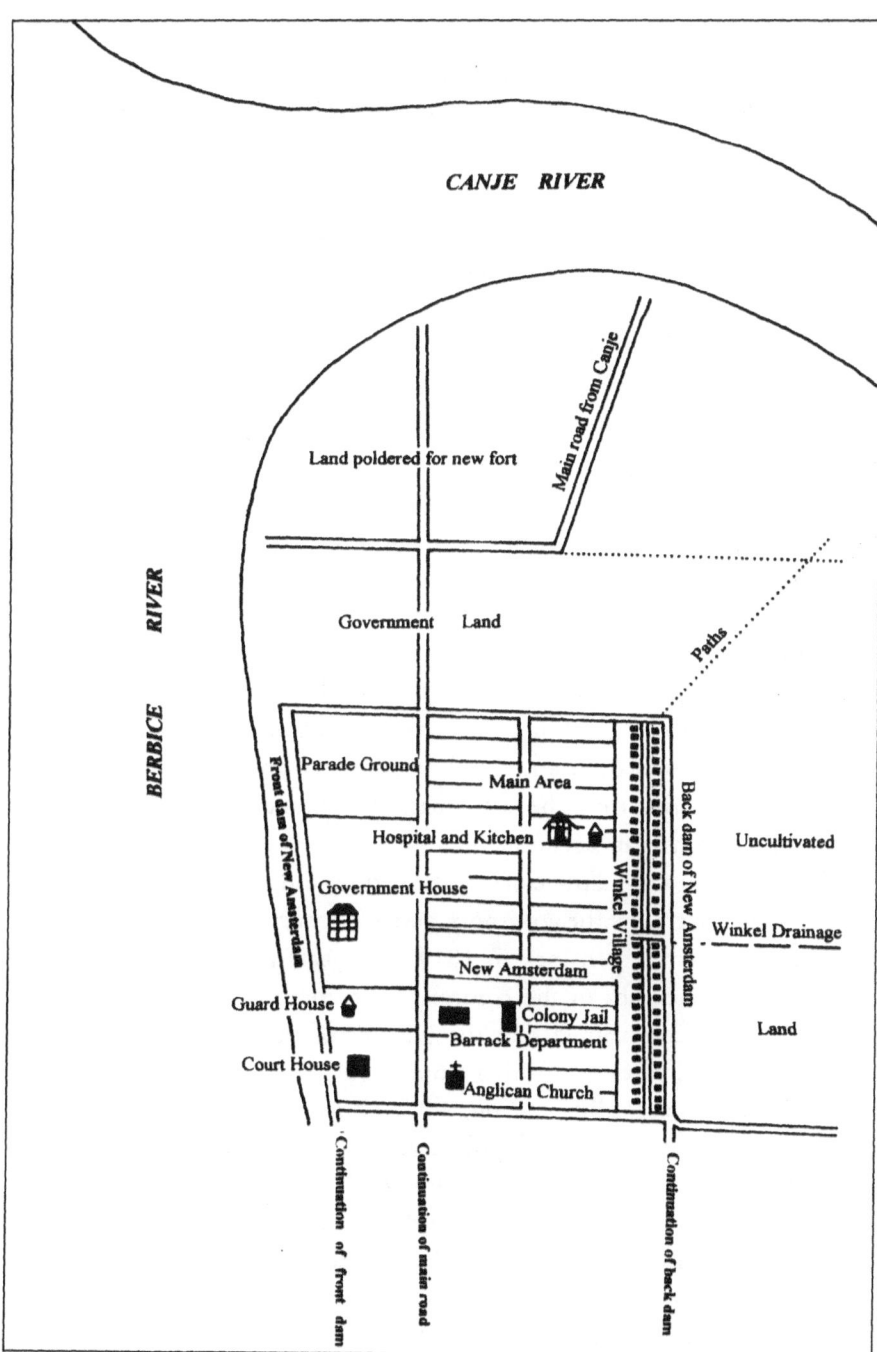

Map 6 Sketch of main area of New Amsterdam showing winkel village in 1826

rubbish of every description for years. – Others contained a quantity of green stagnant water, in which the pigs had been suffered to wallow – the drainage choked up – the ground near the dwellings covered with long rank weeds & brush wood – exhibited altogether the most striking proof of the inattention of the superintendent, & of the state of the establishment.[6]

They immediately gave instructions to have the filth removed and the trenches repaired, but it was not the first or last time that the *winkel* management received such instructions.

In October 1823 an inspection by the Board of Police revealed that the overgrowth in the *winkel* village violated the town regulations, for which the department incurred a fine of f200 and a threat from the board to remove the unsightly vegetation at the department's expense if it did not take measures to rectify the situation immediately. Six weeks later the board complained that the front (western) trench was filling up quickly and that its sides had been broken down by hogs; also that a portion of land around the houses needed weeding and that "only the sage bushes have been slovenly cut down – & besides that, the people are constantly throwing bottles & broken earthen ware, & all other rubbish into the trenches & about their houses", contrary to the town regulations. Walker responded that he had admonished the people on these matters and that he would take prompt action concerning the debris, noting that "the large quantity of broken bottles seem [*sic*] to be an evil of many years accumulation".[7]

The "evil" of poor maintenance of the surroundings went back at least to the period of control by the governors, and was reflected in the complaint of Lieutenant Governor Bentinck in 1814, two years after the Treasury had transferred the facilities to the control of the commissioners for management. Bentinck complained that the inmates of the hospital were accustomed to "air" all sorts of clothing ("many pitiable objects") in full public view. Worse still, according to him, with "all its easements flowing into a trench on the side open to the public view", the hospital was not only a social nuisance but also a serious health hazard.[8]

It was not only the surroundings but the buildings themselves which suffered serious neglect during most of the period under review. In 1825 the *winkel* establishment was located on four different pieces of land, all but one in very close proximity to one another. There was the village, occupying the northeastern section of the town and comprising four rows of buildings, dissected by small ditches and linked by bridges. It included all the slave houses, the nursery ("Creole House"), the smith's shop, and the commissary's (later manager's) living quarters, administrative office, storerooms, solitary cells and so on. Immediately west of the village on a double lot of land were the hospital and kitchen. The boat-building concern was located on the right bank of the Berbice River, with a good shed, two burnt-out sheds and a wharf. Finally, the provision grounds were located to the east (back) of the village, on a plot of land not exactly delimited, but some thirty to forty acres in size.[9]

The *winkel* housing stock and other buildings received little attention after they were erected and, like so many of the other buildings in the colony, went to ruin within a short while. In 1814 Lieutenant Governor Bentinck declared that the hospital, "a very low and miserably incommodious building", had become an eyesore and constituted a "nuisance", especially since the erection of the new public road in the centre of the town.[10] Although the hospital was apparently relocated in 1816, over the years its physical maintenance continued to be largely neglected. In 1826 it needed urgent repairs once again, while the fence that was supposed to enclose it was "full of wide gaps and one of the gates [was] lying down, broken and on the ground".[11] In 1819 the workshops had deteriorated so badly that their value was assessed at only f600 (£42), while their replacement cost was estimated at f3,000 (£210). In 1826 the Board of Police assessed the value of the houses for taxation purposes at f22,050 (£1,575), but Andrew McWatt, the manager, felt that the assessment should have been around f12,700 (£907) and that if the houses had been put up for auction they would only have fetched f5,000 (£375).[12]

In 1819 Scott began negotiations with the colonial government to relocate the houses, and expressed the view "that the present Negro Houses at the back of the town forming refuge not only for the necessitous but on their present extended scale offered shelter to runaways and vicious slaves should be constructed and built of materials less subject to conflagration".[13] However, they were never moved from their original location, as can be deduced from their dilapidated condition just one year later. Walker explained that the houses had been badly built in the first place and that they required constant effort to keep them in good repair. He never indicated the fault in the original structures,[14] but it might have been the materials of which they were made. The houses needed a planned programme of maintenance, but management carried out their rehabilitation on an *ad hoc* basis and mainly in response to the voices of discontent among the people.

The neglect of the houses started before Walker's return to the colony, and by 1820 the buildings had become so run down that one of the *winkel* people complained to the lieutenant governor about them. The superintendent himself recognized that the houses were in a miserable condition: "I should have been sorry to see any Negroes and was both sorry and ashamed to see the Crown Negroes so wretchedly lodged – especially in our formidable wet seasons."[15] He signalled his intention of erecting houses of more durable materials by employing Charles Brandes, a free coloured man, as overseer for several months in 1820–21, along with some of the department's people, to cut various materials in the forest for this purpose. They felled and dressed some of the finest woods, including cacaralli, crab (carap) and bullet wood, and also cut some manicoles (palms).[16] Unfortunately, most of the best quality lumber disappeared before it could reach the *winkel* village. Brandes testified that less than half the quantity cut would have been sufficient to repair the houses, and that he had heard rumours that some of it had been sold in town.[17] Although a substantial part of the lumber had been deposited in the superintendent's yard, about a mile away from the village, Walker was rather evasive about what had happened to it. He claimed that he was too busy to keep a proper inventory of what the woodcutter had delivered and so had assigned this task to John Scott, an illiterate slave for most of his life and a confused man, but whom Walker's predecessor had made departmental overseer. He also implied that the *winkel* people employed in the task and Brandes himself might have pilfered the wood, for which cause he had gotten rid of the latter and employed another person.[18]

The fact is that up to 1825, some four years later, most of the houses still stood in a deplorable condition, as the several complaints to the commissioners and the latter's own observations indicate. Old Adolphe asserted ruefully, "house fall down upon my wife". Dominick complained frequently but vainly to the superintendent about the bad state of his mother's house, in which he also lived. Primo II and Primo III testified about their houses being in a bad state. Sarah declared that she had begged repeatedly to have her house repaired. Most of the people found it impossible to tolerate the constantly leaking roofs during the rainy season. Marietje, Adrian, Jacobus II and Zacharias, among others, were mainly concerned with this problem, while Amelia sounded a plaintive note: "Bad house, Massa, all leak, when the rain fall, me obliged to wrap up all my blanket, and go and sit down. No place for sleep."[19] At least sixty-six adults complained specifically about the defective state of their houses during Walker's tenure of office – the largest number of complaints received by the commissioners.

The commissioners expressed surprise at finding the houses in such a "ruinous and comfortless state". McWatt testified that while the department had repaired a number of them, the greatest portion remained untouched and some were in very bad condition. In the face of this solid body of evidence Walker maintained that he kept the houses "in as good order as possible; repairing and renewing them as occasion required". He also asserted that the village was "considered of late years in the colony as distinguished by improvement and neatness, and the cleanliness of the hospital & nursery drew verbal confessions from the Commissioners themselves, tho' nothing is said on that subject in their letter".[20]

Some contradictions exist in the documents concerning the degree of rehabilitation of the buildings which followed upon the commissioners' instructions to have them repaired. Five months after Walker's dismissal in October 1825, Commissioner Burdett declared that very little had been done in this respect, while his colleague Kinchela concluded that the majority of the houses were in "good, or at least tolerable repair". Scott testified that when he took charge of the department once again in June 1826, he found that of the seventy-three houses, forty-eight required new thatching and many of them also needed new plates and rafters.[21]

Worse still, although in January 1825 Walker listed all the people as either living in *winkel* houses or (a few) residing in the main town area, Lizetta, forty-three-year-old cook for the manager, bemoaned the fact that she had no house of her own but slept in his kitchen. Zamore (aged fifty-two), an invalid, complained that because he did not have a house of his own he had to live in Moanda's house, and that the latter carried the key with him when he went out, thus locking Zamore out. Tellaway (aged thirty-eight), a former field hand, now a watchman of the provision grounds, testified that he had to live in "the watchman's box and hut" because he did not have a house.[22]

By the late eighteenth century, when the humanitarians were beginning to focus attention on the condition of Caribbean slaves, it was quite common for the pro-slavery interests to make comparisons between the lot of these slaves and the free working people in Europe. Charles Kyte was one of those persons who felt that the *winkel* people enjoyed superior domestic comforts to many persons in Europe: "I take the liberty of asserting, without fear of contradiction from any competent and experienced judge, that no Negroes in the colony, generally speaking, are by any means so well lodged as the Winkel people, . . . in fact they are infinitely better than very many of the cottages of the labouring poor in Great Britain, and (as I have read) in Ireland."[23] But Burdett had a ready answer for him: "[I]f the Colonial Negroes are not generally better lodged than those individuals of the Winkel Department, they are much to be pitied."[24]

Kyte's statement above is representative of the attitude of many Europeans who had lived for long periods in Caribbean slave societies. They came to accept that the Caribbean slave should live purely at a subsistence level, and that anything above that constituted "comfort". They generally failed to see the degradation to which they were subjecting human beings. In the specific case of the *winkel* village, the administrators had become so inured to its filth that they could live with it without realizing how demeaning it had become. On the other hand, the commissioners, fresh from Europe and with greater sensibility on the matter, recoiled at the squalor evident in the superior village that the *winkel* compound was supposed to represent. As Aimé Césaire observes, in the wider context of colonialism and oppression, "the coloniser . . . in order to ease his conscience gets into the habit of seeing the other man as *an animal,* accustoms himself to treating him as an animal, and tends objectively to transform *himself* into an animal".[25]

A question which logically arises is why the *winkel* people themselves did not seize the initiative to effect the necessary improvements to their surroundings. Moses I, like a few others, complained that he had no time to go into the bush to cut leaves for his house, since he only had Sundays off, and that "the parson no allow work on Sunday; – on Sunday sit down, do nothing but go to church, and hear God's word two times a day".[26] This insistence on Sunday as a rest day must have been enforced after Walker's dismissal, but the basic point remains that Moses alleged insufficient time to repair his house. However, he was one of the busier persons in the department; a number of others could not find gainful employment by the system that management had established, and so they should have had time to repair their houses.

A few persons did repair theirs, while others testified that they attempted to do so but received little or no assistance from the superintendent. Gorée (aged thirty-eight), a mason, built his own house. The case of Iantje (aged nineteen), a blacksmith, is striking. He testified that he had requested a house from Walker but that the superintendent only allowed him the assistance of three persons for four days to cut wood for that purpose. He was therefore obliged to employ two of his colleagues at f2:10 each on Sundays to assist him in building.[27] Perhaps the reason that more of the slaves did not repair their houses lay in the very nature of the slavery system and in the superintendent's attitude, which produced a deep malaise in them. The situation is thrown into greater relief when we recall Wray's statement recorded in chapter 3 about the attention that the people were paying to their dwellings during the first period of Walker's administration, when he was showing more interest in their welfare. The available information suggests strongly that while management was expected to erect and maintain the houses, in practice this was often left to families and individuals.

The better slave houses were generally constructed of various woods cut in the colony, including crab (carap) and cabacalli wood used for beams, bullet wood for posts, and cacaralli wood for rafters. The sides were usually enclosed with materials derived from the manicole, split in two, while the roofs were thatched with the fronds of the manicole, ita or troolie palms. This was how the *winkel* houses were constructed in the 1820s.[28] The village itself comprised two rectilinear rows of buildings, indicating that some planning went into their construction. We are not certain about the shapes and sizes of the houses. However, based upon the dimensions of the woods dressed in 1820–21 to repair them, they were probably fourteen feet square (length of new beams cut). From the ground to the beams they were probably seven feet high (new posts cut, nine feet long), and if they were built in gabled fashion they might have been several feet high from the beams to the top of the roof with very wide eaves (new rafters cut, twenty feet long). Higman informs us that the most efficient thatched roofs for causing rain to run off were those built very steeply, at angles of more than thirty degrees. This seems to have been the case with the *winkel* houses. The department also bought about thirty-six thousand shingles between 1823 and 1824. This

Figure 6 Manicole palm

Reprinted from John G. Stedman, *Narrative of Five Years' Expedition against the Revolted Negroes of Surinam in Guiana on the Wild Coast of South America from the Years 1772 to 1777*, 2 vols. (London: J. Johnson and J. Edwards, 1796), 1: plate 26.

Material Culture, 1816–1825

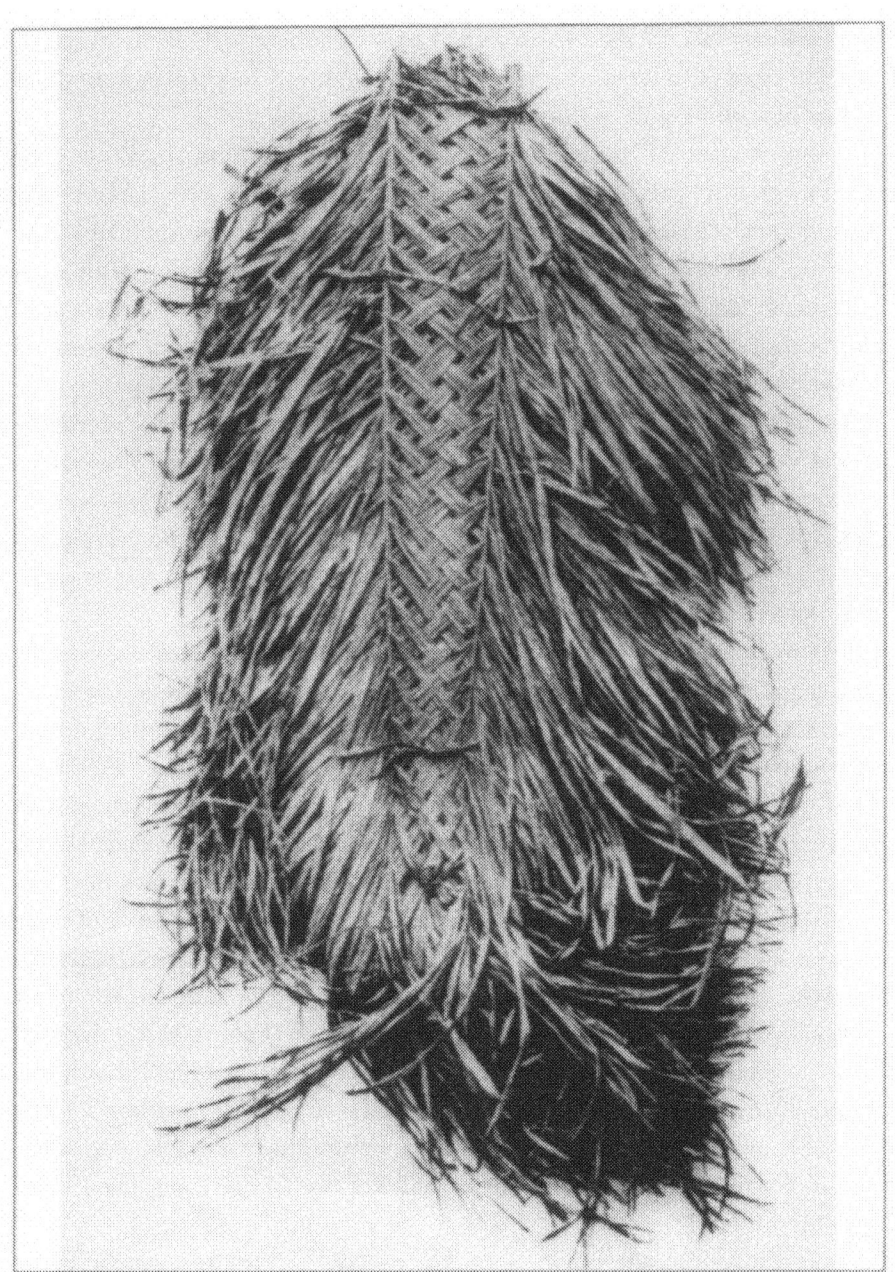

Figure 7 Plaited manicole fronds

Reprinted from Walter E. Roth, *An Introductory Study of the Arts, Crafts, and Customs of the Guiana Indians* (1924; reprint, New York: Johnson Reprint Corporation, 1970), facing p. 253.

material was usually used to roof the better buildings such as the hospitals and the manager's house, but the quantity purchased suggests that much of it was intended for the *winkel* houses.[29]

Slave houses of fourteen feet square were medium-sized ones by Caribbean and North American standards. The average occupancy in the seventy *winkel* houses occupied in January 1825 was 3.9 persons. However, Kyte claimed that they were jointly capable of accommodating easily one-and-a-half times the number of persons dwelling in them.[30] This suggests that several of them were significantly larger than the dimensions mentioned above. We know that several houses had a large number of occupants, with a few of them having nine to ten persons. This number of people certainly could not have been housed in such small units (see chapter 6). The houses of some of the higher-income-earners, such as Louis, the head boat builder, might have been significantly larger. It is said that he lived in a "very comfortable" house, a statement perhaps referring as much to its size as to its exterior and interior design.[31]

Almost certainly there was some variety of house styles and sizes within the broad pattern described above. No evidence is currently available on whether any of the houses were built mainly of stone, or about the number of windows, doors and so on. We can deduce from the evidence that decisions in relation to the houses in which they would live were left generally to the people. Walker's statement that several of them had made their houses "very neat" is perhaps reflective not only of the immediate environment in which the houses were located but of the exterior and interior décor of these houses. The instance mentioned above of Moanda having a key to his house, allowing Zamore to live with him, but refusing to give him the key to let himself in indicates clearly Moanda's control over the house. Walker declared that the people considered the houses as their own property and that it was "difficult to introduce the rules of a garrison into the Negro village".[32] The situation in respect of the *winkel* village reinforces the view that at emancipation Caribbean slaves generally considered the houses they lived in to belong to them.

Furnishings for the houses were left entirely to their occupants. Those persons who were less skilled, or who were old and had few relatives to take care of them, were generally in a worse position in this respect than others. Some of the houses had almost no furnishings, and their occupants had to sleep on the floor. Others, belonging to headmen and the "better sort of tradesmen", had "certain comforts, or even luxuries in furniture, which would not have been expected from their [i.e., the houses'] appearance". The people obtained these items either through purchase or through their skills as craftsmen.[33] No details about furnishings have come to light, but it is likely that they principally comprised furniture, household utensils, wall hangings, and sometimes objects of art.

Every slave society in the region had a few slaves who rose substantially above their colleagues in material terms, and whose owners allowed them to do so. One such instance was a slave on plantation Profit in Demerara whom Pinckard recorded as possessing a high bedstead, in the contemporary European fashion, with "deep mattresses", while the bedposts, drawers and chairs displayed "the high polish of well-rubbed mahogany".[34] Bernard Senior also referred to a coloured urban slave in Jamaica in the last years of slavery who earned a fine living as a saddler, shoemaker, barber, upholsterer, fiddler and horse trader. This was a highly skilled individual whose owner no doubt allowed him to work under self-hire. He is said to have possessed "a large house, well furnished, with a sideboard in his dining room, and a Grecian lamp hanging in his hall".[35]

Food

Walker's declared policy was to give the people the stipulated or customary food allowances in the colony.[36] Although these allowances were in the first place ungenerous, in Walker's case practice often varied from policy to the detriment of the people. As in the case of accommodation, complaints against management for small quantities and poor quality of food were quite common. Yet the records show that a substantial sum of money was spent on this item. Where much of the stock went remains a mystery, although the commissioners were sure that they had the answer.

Following the return of plantation St Jan to the Berbice Association, Scott purchased Berenstein in 1817 in the hope of making it the department's new food basket. However, the estate never yielded much under its new administrators for four main reasons: its distance from town, the questionable quality of its soil, conflict between the new superintendent and his assistant, and poor management. The estate was located about twenty miles from New

Amsterdam and, while plantation cultivation was estimated as extending about one hundred miles upriver, the *winkel* people and several objective persons still regarded the settlement as being too far upriver for persons who had spent all their lives in an urban environment. This fact alone was likely to make the estate a liability to the department for, as Walker pointed out in 1823, the people objected to living at Berenstein: "It has bred such discontent among the people as has sometimes been followed by a train of evils & losses of a very serious description." He found it exceedingly difficult to get forty people, males and females, to live there, since they regarded residence on the estate as "a remote & disagreeable banishment". The commissioners also noted that its location was one of the major setbacks to making the estate profitable, and thought that in this respect its purchase was "perhaps injudicious".[37]

There was some debate regarding the soil quality on the estate. There was not a correspondence of views about its suitability for growing plantains, but Scott was certain that he had made a wise investment. In May 1818 he had fifty acres under plantain cultivation and considered the estate as being considerably more valuable than its original purchase and rehabilitation costs.[38] He declared that before Walker took over the department the estate had yielded a surplus of plantains, allowing him to sell some of the produce, and also that when the superintendent visited the estate in 1819 he found twenty acres of cassava. Scott's statement is partly corroborated by the department's account books, which credited him with f13,450 (£1,034) for produce and stores sold.[39]

Walker admitted that the estate had produced a good quantity of provisions under a previous owner, but claimed that the land was now entirely worn out and that although he had employed "uniformly . . . planters of superior experience", he had not been able to improve its yield. He pointed out that the assistant agent had focused cultivation along the banks of the river, rather than further inland. He thought that the inland soil would be good for provisions, but felt that it might be prohibitively expensive to open up those lands and relocate the buildings, given the financial state of the department and the attitude of the people towards Berenstein.[40]

The conflict between the superintendent and his assistant was particularly detrimental at a time when cultivation was still in the early stages and some of the people had just begun to settle down to a regular agricultural regime. A large but unspecified part of the estate population comprised artisans who, even more than the regular field hands, resented estate work and, as events were later to demonstrate, would take any opportunity of abandoning agricultural work which artisans in all the colonies viewed as demotion. Thus, when the struggle started between Walker and Scott over control of the department, many of the people took the opportunity to do as little estate work as possible. Both men recognized the adverse effect that their wrangle was having on the morale of the people, but each blamed the other for it. Walker claimed that many of the people became rebellious and simply would not listen to him, being led astray by the assistant agent, while Scott declared that it was the superintendent's greed that was destroying the productivity of the estates.[41]

The last major reason for the poor yields was bad management. The plantation had six different managers between 1817 and 1825,[42] four of whom Walker appointed. Nothing is known about John McRae (or Mac Rae), the first manager, except that his tenure ended around mid-1818. He was succeeded by J. Finch (or Fink), whom Walker fired because he was "a foreign deserter, formerly a common sailor" who was constantly drunk.[43] Walker appointed Thomas Farley in his place. However, this individual left shortly after for a more lucrative field. The next three managers, William Gattarel, J. Deussen and William McConchie, were harsh, and the last of them was also morally reprobate. While Berenstein remained under this kind of management it proved to be a sea of troubles.

Finch's policy was to sell the good plantains and keep the bad ones for home use. Deussen (and other managers) kept a large number of cows, sheep, goats and hogs, although he declared that only the last of these (about fifty of them) belonged to him personally, the others being the property of the estate. The people hardly benefited from the raising of such stock, for only occasionally was a cow killed for them, and their rations never included mutton. The keeping of these animals was a major cause of discontent among the people. They had to devote much time and attention, which might otherwise have been employed in growing food, in building pens and maintaining the animals. In fact, several persons testified that Deussen grew food principally to feed the livestock and that he used most of the plantains to do so. Thus the *winkel* people found themselves competing with other slaves for the good plantains and with the hogs for the bad ones. Nor were they allowed to keep their own livestock (a common feature on estates), which Deussen viewed as competing for time, space and attention with his own stock, so that, according to the testimony of Susetta (alias Rosetta), he killed off the fowls and any other stock which they kept. The hogs also devoured a lot of the crops in the fields and trampled down the sides of the trenches recently dug. Michael testified that "as fast as he goes on, the hogs of the manager are spoiling his work". The managers' policies led to a critical shortage of plantains and other food for the people, a complaint made specifically by Betsey I, Leah I and Susetta.[44] This "hogwash" produced considerable grumbling and grunting on Berenstein.

The disciplinary problems on the estate will be dealt with in detail in chapter 7, but it is important to point out here that the situation was compounded by the superintendent's practice of sending recalcitrant persons to the estate, thus making it a sort of penal settlement for some years. The gradual transformation of the estate from a provision plantation to a place of punishment had a further deleterious effect on the work ethic of the people, and increased coercion followed in an attempt to raise production levels.

Natural events also played their part – though a small one – in the misfortunes visiting the estate. In 1817 the dry season lasted longer than usual, producing a great scarcity of plantains everywhere in the colony, as most of the crops dried up. In October 1819 a storm did considerable damage to some of Berenstein's buildings and provision fields, forcing the department to purchase plantains. In 1823 an unusually long wet season prevented new ground from being opened up and the long dry season that followed, lasting at least until 1826, added insult to injury. Thus, the estate succumbed to a combination of natural and human disasters from which it never recovered. Far from feeding the entire department, it proved unable to feed even those resident on it, forcing the superintendent to spend valuable money to purchase plantains for them and also to pay managers whose regimes were highly unproductive. Eventually, in December 1823, after seeking the advice of two respected planters, he abandoned the estate, leaving only a few persons to maintain the buildings. At the time of its abandonment its accumulated debt was f36,429 (£2,602).[45]

Walker then moved to re-establish the old provision grounds on the outskirts of the city which the department had abandoned some time before, but this was like reopening old sores, for the soil was poor. Still, Walker gave the impression that the department had become a hive of activity, preparing the plots to relieve the pressing food situation. The department spent April to August of 1824 digging trenches, clearing the land and preparing it for the planting of provisions, an activity that continued intermittently for several months. However, actual results were quite modest. Up to April 1825 only five or six out of the thirty to forty acres were ready for cultivation; this space would only have saved the department about f300 annually if planted in cassava. Worse still, only one acre was in actual cultivation at that time. McWatt explained the reason for this unexpected circumstance: when the land was almost ready for cultivation the superintendent took the gang up the Canje River to cut manicoles in order to repair the houses, during which time the land became overrun with weeds once again.[46]

The failure of the provision grounds to meet the ordinary needs of the department and the superintendent's poor management of the concern led to all sorts of unfortunate consequences for the people. Walker was forced to purchase plantains, sometimes at high prices based upon seasonal supply. The financial resources of the department being inadequate, by the end of 1823 he had run up a debt of f20,000 (£1,428) with Katz for two and a half years' supply of provisions. In the following year Katz was demanding payment, to effect which he proposed to draw a bill on the Treasury.[47]

Whether it was because of the difficulties that the department faced or from a miserly spirit, the superintendent skimped on the *winkel* food supply, breaching the stipulated minimum requirements established by colonial law and practice on this score. According to Fiscal Bennett in 1826, these stipulated that each adult, including invalids and superannuated persons, should receive two good bunches of plantains weekly or seven to nine pounds of rice, cornflour or wheat flour in place of plantains; younger persons were to receive half these amounts. Charles Bird, deputy protector of slaves, confirmed this statement in 1830 but added that children too young to be put to light work did not generally receive a specific allowance, since their food was prepared by nurses assigned for that purpose. The law did not specify the quantity of salted fish to be given, but the common practice was two pounds weekly to adults and half of that to children, although on some estates variations took place: one and a half pounds, in addition to salt and tobacco. Pork, beef, rum and tobacco were not specified in the law but were occasionally distributed to slaves at the pleasure of management.[48] An 1833 law increased the quantity of food for males and females over twelve years old, providing the following alternatives: three pounds of salted cod; four pounds of herring or shad; two pounds of salted beef or pork; four pounds of fresh beef or pork, with a half pint of salt. It also specified that the two bunches of plantains were to be at least thirty-five pounds each, otherwise the deficiency had to be made up to the tune of seventy pounds. Where plantains were not available "other farinaceous food" might be used, consisting of one of the following alternatives: twenty-five pounds of yams or potatoes; or twenty pounds of eddoes or tannias; or ten pints of wheat, Indian corn or rice.[49]

In practice in Berbice, as in other slave colonies, the rations distributed to the enslaved people differed considerably, depending upon the stinginess or otherwise of management. If the testimony of the managers of the seven estates of Wolfert Katz, the foremost planter in the colony, was truthful, he was perhaps the most progressive slave owner there. They testified in 1826 that he gave each adult weekly two bunches of plantains, one and three-quarters pounds of fish and one-tenth of a pound of tobacco; drivers and tradesmen received double allowances of fish and tobacco. Young people of about ten years received one and a half pounds of fish and one and a half bunches of plantains, while the mothers of infants received "some fish & plantains" for them, apart from whatever the children received in the nursery. Rum was distributed to the gang frequently, sometimes between one and three glasses daily, depending upon the weather conditions or the task in which they were employed. During crop time and holiday seasons they were given double allowances of fish and tobacco, and also pipes, two pounds of salted pork, some beef, and more liberal quantities of rum, besides their usual allowance of plantains. Every fourth Saturday they were given the day off to cultivate land allotted to them, on which they grew such crops as corn, yams, cassava and rice. In addition, they raised feathered stock (turkeys, fowls, Guinea birds and ducks), the proceeds of all of which, in cash and kind, they appropriated to their own use.[50]

Walker had spent sufficient time in the colony to make him aware of the slave laws and the customs on the provision of food. One would have expected him to conform at least to the minimum requirements of law and custom. Nevertheless, as he himself testified, he gave the people one and a half bunches of plantains if they worked in town and two bunches if they worked

Material Culture, 1816–1825

Table 5.1 Estimated Annual *Winkel* Expenditure on Food, 1816–1824 (guilders)

Year	Salt	Plantains	Rice	Salted Fish	Salted Pork	Salted Beef	Rum	Total
1816	n.a.	n.a.	1,187:11:0	2,124:3:0	n.a.	n.a.	655:0:0	3,966:14:0
1817	n.a.	4,820:0:0	5,268:13:0	2,233:11:0	264:0:0	n.a.	1,022:19:0	13,609:3:0
1818	n.a.	8,617:10:0	2,239:6:8	2,033:6:12	719:0:0	n.a.	816:7:8	14,425:10:12
1819	n.a.	1,320:0:0	137:4:12	3,355:17:0	429:0:0	n.a.	345:0:0	5,587:1:12
1820	10:0:0	2,024:0:0	753:16:8	3,527:19:0	578:0:0	40:0:0	336:15:0	7,270:10:8
1821	n.a.	7,520:0:0	2,693:2:8	3,581:16:0	586:0:0	n.a.	590:18:0	14,971:16:8
1822	n.a.	8,666:0:0	966:1:0	3,582:2:0	613:0:0	66:0:0	489:5:0	14,382:8:0
1823	23:0:0	8,372:0:0	90:0:0	3,252:18:0	234:0:0	n.a.	351:0:0	12,322:18:0
1824	11:0:0	7,784:0:0	43:10:0	3,409:15:0	258:15:0	25:0:0	174:0:0	11,706:0:0
Total	44:0:0	49,123:10:0	13,379:5:4	27,101:7:12	3,681:15:0	131:0:0	4,781:4:8	98,242:2:8

Source: "Disbursements for the Winkel Department", PRO, CO 318/91: 251–55.

at Berenstein, but he did not provide pipes and tobacco as some planters did in lieu of full allowances of food.[51] He justified his breach of the colonial laws by declaring that the townspeople had greater opportunities of earning personal income than those in the country, the former did lighter work than the latter, and he had adopted this practice from Lieutenant Governor Gordon, who had supposedly initiated it. He explained that Gordon had allegedly reduced the allowance because some of the people had once left a portion on the spot where it had been distributed. He also claimed that some time earlier he had increased the allowance of those in town to two bunches, but much of it had gone to waste and so he had returned to the old allowance. He offered no explanation as to why he gave the superannuated adults only one bunch per week, and the small children only half a bunch. He did provide the usual allowance of fish for effectives, and although he claimed that he gave the same quantity to other adults, *winkel* testimony refuted this assertion.[52]

Unlike fish, which was distributed by weight, plantains were distributed by bunches, the size of which depended very much on soil and weather conditions. When the bunches were very large, one and a half bunches could have proved adequately for the effectives, but this was not normally the case.[53] When the bunches were small, more enlightened planters supplemented the normal rations with rice, corn meal or cornflour, but this was the exception rather than the rule in the department before 1825. In March 1821, for instance, the situation was very bad for, according to Wray, the people received only one bunch of plantains and a little fish, while the old people received a little rice or cassava.[54] Walker's miserly approach to the distribution of food is exemplified by his own testimony that in the early period he gave the people seven pounds of rice as a substitute for plantains, which conformed to the absolute minimum specified under the law. Only later did he give them the slightly less meagre allowance of nine pounds of rice.[55]

In 1825, after the arrival of the commissioners of inquiry, Walker began giving the people some allowance of the supplementary foods, in addition to their usual quantities of plantains. In April 1825 effectives received their regular supply of plantains, plus two pounds of rice and corn meal, but other adults still did not receive allowances equal to those of the effectives.[56] Headmen in the department, as in the Caribbean generally, received greater allowances than the ordinary people. In December 1825, under the more liberal regime put in place that year, the seven headmen in the department received two bunches of plantains, four pounds of rice and four pounds of salted fish, plus one dram of rum every evening, except on Wednesdays and Saturdays when the quantity was doubled.[57] Walker tried to give the impression that it had been his usual practice to give the additional allowances of cereals, but Francis Dummett, his friend and a former manager of the department, refuted this, as did McWatt, the incumbent manager. There were at least twenty-four complaints to the commissioners about inadequate food supply. One of the most distressing complaints came from Roxanna, a woman well advanced in age who had given birth to thirteen children and who still tended the sick children and acted as a midwife when necessary. She complained of being given only half-rations.[58]

Apart from the commodities specified above, only rum was distributed by the department on a regular basis. The department distributed salted pork, salted beef or herring mainly on holidays, although occasionally beef from a cow or two killed from its small herd might be served as an alternative. It rarely distributed sugar, except a little to the sick children.[59] The enslaved people had to depend on their own resources to provide salt, vegetables, oils, herbal seasonings and so on for themselves, as well as the receptacles in which to cook and eat their meals. This was the typical scenario under colonial slavery, and the *winkel* people did not overcome it during Walker's so-called programme of amelioration. It was not until January 1833 that Lieutenant Governor D'Urban published a proclamation, without the approval of the colonial legislature, specifying that each adult slave should receive a saucepan for cooking, and each family a pot, yearly.[60] By that time the Crown people had been liberated.

The food regime in the department was a far cry from what the commissioners for management had intended when they urged that the people should receive liberal supplies of rations. Management supplied them with the same food – plantains and fish – almost every week, as if they were dumb animals. Wray, who was critical of the superintendent's failure to supply adequate quantities of food, nevertheless fell into line with the plantocracy in arguing that the rations stipulated by law were virtually all that the enslaved people needed to keep them in good health:

> [I]f the Negroes get two bunches of plantains & two lbs. or two & a half lbs. of salt-fish every Sunday morning they will think themselves well off . . . no food can be more excellent than plantains & Negroes cannot be badly off if they have plenty of them no more than the poor in England can if there be plenty of corn . . . plantains will make [that is, will be a good substitute for] pork, fowls, sheep, milk, butter, beef, bread, puddings, &c.[61]

Some of the people kept pigs and poultry within the precincts of the village. Some of them also apparently established their own small garden plots, for a good deal of uncultivated land lay behind the village, but this is only implied in the records, although they do mention the communal cultivation of the provision grounds close to the village.[62] The lack of specific evidence on this score in the extremely detailed records compiled by the commissioners of inquiry could only mean that few *winkel* people cultivated private plots. This is all the more surprising since the department could not find remunerative employment for a large number of them. Part of the reason for the lack of more kitchen gardens might have been that the artisans, who constituted the majority of the effective workforce, considered cultivating the land as below their status. But they could also have earned more money plying their trades during their spare time, as we have noticed in the previous chapter.

The people, like their counterparts in the colony generally, must also have fished extensively in the many rivers and streams that dissected the landscape, and they might also have engaged occasionally in hunting and gathering food from wild plants. However, the records are also silent on these matters. When food was in short supply some of the people must have credited provisions from the local stores, but there is only a hint of this in missionary Wray's laconic remark that "they are greatly indebted to some of the stores".[63]

The commissioners summed up the superintendent's food regime by declaring that he distributed plantains, "this absolute necessity of life" for the people, "with the most sparing and parsimonious hand".[64] The situation was worse for the females attached to the military department, who received only half-rations as a matter of policy. When the *winkel* woman Anna I (aged forty-two) complained about this, Captain George Gipps of the Royal Engineers Department promised "to use every exertion to obtain an increase

Material Culture, 1816–1825

[for her], in consideration of her not being married and not having any protector on whom she could depend for support".[65] This statement clearly implies that for married women or those with relatives to support them, army policy would remain rigid.

Clothing

People normally use clothing for a number of purposes, including health, comfort, decency, elegance and group or class identification. Arguably, in slave society its function was mainly for modesty and group identification, only secondarily for health and comfort, and very rarely for elegance. Higman points out that dress was often perceived as a form of art, and that "art and its underlying aesthetics serves to facilitate survival in a long-term evolutionary sense". He goes on to observe, "If this principle is accepted, there is no incompatibility between the harsh conditions of plantation labor and the existence of artistic creativity or aesthetic theory among the population."[66] Both plantation and urban slaves showed concern with the aesthetic aspects of clothing, especially on special occasions, as Steeve Buckridge has shown in his excellent study of the Jamaican slaves (including comparisons with slaves in other Caribbean colonies).[67] In regard to Berbice, Kyte noted that in the case of urban slaves "it is the ambition of a Negro at all times to appear dressed, and . . . the poorest field Man or Woman coming [to town] on their own affairs will endeavour to appear decently clad".[68]

Enslaved people looked forward to Christmas, in particular, which offered them the opportunity to display their best clothing, although other occasions such as Easter, Whitsuntide and (later on) going to church on Sundays allowed for similar display. Pinckard pointed out that at Christmas the distribution of new clothing was itself an occasion for merriment among the enslaved people, comparable to the joy that children displayed on receiving new toys. He went on, "Merry crowds are met in every quarter, dressed out in all the gaudy trappings they can collect, and with their hair cut, and fashioned into multitudes of whimsical shapes, representing figures of helmets, wigs, crowns and the like; decorated with a profusion of beads, bits of ribbon, and other tinsel ornaments."[69] Such occasions offered the enslaved people opportunities for individual social expression through dress and the reaffirmation of themselves as human beings rather than chattel or units of production. It was one of the few areas in which most owners and colonial legislatures did not seek to exercise close control over the slaves' lives, with the notable exception of St Domingue.

The fact that until the last years of slavery most slave laws did not specify the actual quantity and quality of clothing that owners had to provide led to a great variety of clothing being given, although most of what was distributed was scanty in quantity and coarse in quality. Several slave owners who regarded modesty as being of slight importance allowed their slaves to go about in rags. A few slave owners showed concern about elegance in slave attire, viewing it as dangerous to allow enslaved people to develop a "false sense" of their own importance. Domestics were the only category of such people usually given clothing of some elegance, often the discarded clothing of their owners. It bothered Walker, and others, that enslaved people, especially the females, should seek to obtain certain kinds of clothing principally for their aesthetic effect.

Berbice conformed to the common practice in the Caribbean of distributing clothing at Christmas, although an extra item might be given to a few slaves during the year. However, the *winkel* department often breached this practice, with partial distributions at Christmas and Easter, and randomly during the rest of the year. One reason for this was the lack of ready cash or good credit which prevented the department from acquiring all the necessary supplies at one time. But Walker also claimed that he responded to specific needs as they arose throughout the year in the case of adults, and that he preferred to distribute the schoolchildren's clothing allowance throughout the year in order to keep them clean.[70]

Due to the lack of funds to pay for bulk purchases directly from England, Walker usually purchased materials and clothing in the colony, a more costly measure, especially when he had to acquire the clothing on credit. For this reason the commissioners for management had strongly urged their agents to avoid purchasing clothing and other commodities in the colony, but it was only in 1825 that Walker managed to purchase clothing directly from England, using Dummett to do so on his visit to that country, at a commission of 25 per cent of the purchase price. According to the superintendent, this was well below the special mark-up of 33.3 per cent which that individual usually gave him for purchases made within the colony, still a price well below that of other merchants.[71] The workroom produced some clothing, although, as noted before, this section of the department became increasingly less productive as time went by.

According to the superintendent, each man received yearly a shirt, a jacket, a pair of trousers, two laps (loincloths used in African fashion) and a hat; in addition, well-employed tradesmen received another shirt. The women generally received a wrapper, an osnaburg petticoat, a check shift, a cheap gingham gown, a handkerchief, and sometimes a hat for field work. School girls received three dresses and one handkerchief, while school boys received three check-and-osnaburg "dresses" (or shirts and trousers). Younger children received smaller quantities of clothing. The adults received two blankets every three years.[72] Dummett and Mrs Stanley's testimonies, although differing in some details from each other and from that of Walker, substantially confirm Walker's statements; in fact, Mrs Stanley's statement indicates that the boys and girls received more clothing than Walker had detailed. Dummett added that the boys hired out as servants received "finer sort of trowsers of drill", while Mrs Stanley detailed the actual quantities of cloth given to the effective women: 5 yards check, 4.5 yards gingham, and 4.5 yards osnaburg; and to the old women: 2.5 yards sheeting and 3 yards check. All women received, in addition, a handkerchief.[73] The effective women therefore received the relatively "liberal" supply of some 14 yards of cloth.

As on the matter of provisions, the superintendent treated the invalids with scant concern, although his testimony once again betrayed his tendency to be vague when caught in a tight spot: "The invalid men receive a shirt, a pair of trousers, a hat & I think a lap."[74] It is difficult to imagine that he would have forgotten whether or not these people received a lap if he had been accustomed to giving them that item annually. Equally important is the fact that, once again, persons who had served the department during their best years were dealt with in a miserable way during their infirmity. While in theory Walker's allowance of clothing to the effectives was more liberal than that of the average planter, practice often went adrift from theory.

Walker's explanation to the commissioners suggested that he had some system of distribution, but the few instances in which relevant records exist suggest that the distribution was rather spasmodic and that very often he did not provide the alleged quantities. For instance, the extant records show that while the department made two distributions to the men, at Easter and Christmas 1824, it only made one to the women. Also, the men received no lap and the women no hat or handkerchief.⁷⁵ At times the distribution appears to have been completely random. Abrammaker received a shirt and a pair of trousers on 6 April 1822 and a hat on 28 May, less than two months later. Adam I received a pair of trousers and a shirt on 28 January 1822, shortly after the Christmas distribution period. In July 1822 a number of elderly persons received a jacket, a hat and a blanket.⁷⁶

The problem of determining what management actually distributed is complicated by the fact that no one in the department kept systematic records of distribution and that officials often made entries in the day books or other records long after the event had taken place, as Walker himself admitted: "records of the issues of clothing to the gang in general, were the part of our records kept with the least regularity"; and again, "When records were entered at all, it was generally in a memorandum at the beginning or end of one of the books in use – in a most irregular mode, I very readily admit."⁷⁷ Indeed, distributions on two or more occasions sometimes appeared in the records as a single distribution. Worse still was Walker's confession that often "one entry was made of the average annual supply" of clothing. When asked about the entries made in the ledger from 1821, he declared that they were simply extra supplies distributed to various persons, but he did not explain why he kept such a record and not one of regular supplies.⁷⁸ His distribution practice could hardly be called a "system". In the commissioners' view his supplies of clothing were "irregular and casual".⁷⁹

The superintendent excused his delinquency with the plea that he lacked the staff to do the job and that since the clothing was chiefly in his possession he was sure that it was in safe custody. While declaring his uneasiness at not keeping proper records now that the commissioners had begun their probe, he asserted confidently and even defiantly that the Crown had not lost "one farthing of benefit from the first moment of my acquaintance with the property . . . in respect of frugal outgoings".⁸⁰ The commissioners, however, concluded that he had skimped on the supply of clothing to the people. They based their conclusion on two main points: the testimony of *winkel* persons, and their own observation of the skimpy, worn and tattered garments of several of the people, some of whom were "almost in a state of perfect nudity".⁸¹ They concluded further that the superintendent had utilized a substantial part of the materials purchased for his own benefit and that of the other five members of his family. Their conclusion is not without

Table 5.2 Estimated Annual *Winkel* Expenditure on Clothing, 1816–1824 (guilders)

Year	Expenditure
1816	201:0
1817	715:5
1818	1,956:7
1819	842:11
1820	3,710:10
1821	4,955:2
1822	2,038:14
1823	2,440:6
1824	3,650:11
Total	20,510:6

Source: "Disbursements in the Dept.", 1815–24, PRO, CO 318/91: 255–60.

some merit, for among the items of clothing purchased for the department were a jacket costing f44 (in 1821), and a beaver hat and another hat costing respectively f7 and f9 (in 1819), all three considerably more expensive than the jackets and hats purchased regularly.

It is possible also that the department did not receive the quantities of clothing for which it had paid, the superintendent entering into collusion with the dealers to defraud the department. More likely, however, the department used part of the supplies to fulfil contracts to private individuals. The superintendent also allowed Mrs Stanley to enter into personal arrangements to supply clothing to outsiders, using the workroom and at least one *winkel* woman, hired to her at the nominal price of f16:10 per month.[82] This could have led to a train of abuses, including preferring her own work to that of the department and utilizing *winkel* materials without paying for them. The production of *winkel* clothing in the workroom was secondary to fulfilling outside contracts and other demands from the departmental staff. The situation was worsened by the small number of females in the workroom, the inability of the instructor to instil discipline among them, and the larger problem of unrest inside and outside that unit (see chapters 4 and 7).

Discontent over the clothing supplied manifested itself throughout the second period of Walker's administration (1819–25). His mean distribution policy helped to fuel the growing unrest in the department, especially from 1823. He became very uneasy when the Demerara slave uprising broke out in August of that year, and decided to distribute a fresh set of clothing in a hurry, although in a letter to the Treasury he couched his action so as to suggest that he was more liberal than other slave managers:

> I am taking this opportunity to distribute a fresh set of blankets and clothing – indeed within these last two years, although they cannot and do not complain, of any absolute wants, I should have been more liberal to them if it had not been necessary to be more economical – at present I feel the propriety of making them not only contented in their service but heartily attached to it.[83]

In spite of his assertion about the people's contentment, a general distribution at such an odd period in the year strengthens the view that deprivation of their full allowance continued to be a major problem in the department.

The commissioners received several *winkel* complaints of insufficient clothing, but we shall cite only a few of them here. Paul II (aged twenty-one) complained of not having clothes to go to church. At Christmas 1824 the superintendent had given him a pair of trousers, a shirt, a jacket, a hat and a blanket, but no lap. During the year his trousers "broke" and so he went to Walker and told him that if he received a lap "he would go in his skin" (that is, without a shirt), but the superintendent turned a deaf ear to his plea. Primo III (aged thirty-three) appeared before the commissioners "almost quite naked, having only a pair of old worn trowsers which he got from a mulatto man for working for him". February (aged eighty-seven) complained about lack of clothing (and food) and stated in the superintendent's presence that in 1823 he received no clothing whatsoever, that in the following year he was given a jacket and trousers, and in 1825 a shirt and a lap. Walker declined to respond to Paul's allegations at the time and never attempted to confute February's testimony.[84] As with the supply of rations, he issued more clothing after the commissioners' arrival than previously.[85]

Walker, while affirming that he had given the people their full allowance of clothing, explained the semi-nudity of some of them by asserting that Dutch custom held sway in the colony, by which slaves tended to view clothing more as ornament than covering and "decent clothing is not considered as necessary among the slaves". They were thus accustomed to going about almost naked, and management could hardly persuade the elderly men to wear anything more than a lap or strip of cloth around the middle or the women anything more than a petticoat. It is true that the Dutch paid scant attention to clothing their slaves properly, forcing some of them to go about the streets almost naked and sometimes making the young ladies serve at table in absolute nudity.[86] But this can hardly be taken to mean that the enslaved people went about naked as a matter of preference.

Quite apart from the quantity of clothing distributed to the people, there was the question of quality. On this score Kyte, an estate attorney of over twenty years' experience in the colony and temporary successor to Walker as superintendent, commented that the clothing on his predecessor's list "differs widely from that description of clothing given to other Negroes throughout the colony".[87] Walker must be commended for providing at least some of the people with superior clothing to that which was generally distributed in the colony, but again the wide variety and high quality of some of the material raise suspicion that they were not all for legitimate departmental use. The department purchased blue and white salempore, calico, penistone, flannel, check, osnaburg, britannia, bengal, gingham, dimity, derries, sheeting, drill, union stripe, white jaconet, linsey woolsey, linen platilla and canvas. The superintendent bought large amounts of gingham which the women supposedly used to make Sunday dresses and for other special occasions. The men also sometimes received lined jackets: seventy-four such items were distributed in 1820, seventy-five in 1823, and a large (unspecified) number at Christmas 1824. Persons in domestic employ received waistcoats and better quality jackets, trousers and white shirts.[88] While distributing better clothing, Walker made it clear that he did so to provide comfort for the people rather than to indulge them in finery, which he wished to discourage among them.[89]

The department also provided footwear periodically to a few persons. In 1815 it purchased a pair of laced boots for Emmanuel at a cost of f30. The extant records also show that between 1815 and 1823 the department purchased at least thirty-six pairs of shoes, each costing between f6 and f12. McWatt testified that during his time as manager, from mid-1824, the department distributed shoes to one or two persons because of their diseased feet, a humane gesture on the superintendent's part. It is likely that some domestics or favoured persons also received a pair occasionally.[90]

The most interesting aspect of the superintendent's distribution was the periodic handing out of red shirts. The records show that the department distributed at least five such shirts in 1819, four in 1820, twelve in 1823, two in 1824 and six in 1825. The shirts cost between f2:1:11 (in 1823) and f5:10 (1819 and 1824) each, as cheap as an ordinary shirt at the lower end and comparable to better shirts and medium-priced jackets at the upper end.[91] Red-dyed clothing was rare but not entirely unknown to the slave communities in the region. Slaves received red garments occasionally as special awards. In 1814 Alexander, who had betrayed his colleagues by informing the colonial government of a plot to revolt, received a red jacket, blue pantaloons, a silk handkerchief and a white shirt, among other rewards. In the case of Barbados, as early as 1698 Christopher Codrington's father had specified in his will that among the items each slave should receive was a red coat or jacket, while in the eighteenth century these slaves received a large number of red caps. North American slaves, both males and females, were fond of wearing red clothing to church, and the same might well have been true of Caribbean slaves.[92]

Apart from those mentioned above, the department distributed few other domestic and personal items to the people. The records mention only razors for four of the years between 1815 and 1824, forty-eight of them (the highest number) being purchased in 1818 and only one in 1821. Other items such as knives, scissors, beads, mirrors, needles and thread – all of which Katz boasted that he gave to his slaves – are absent from the department's distribution list and financial statements. However, the workroom received various quantities of thread, needles, thimbles, buttons and tape.[93]

Some *winkel* persons were able to provide better clothing for themselves and their children either because of the money they made through extra work during their spare time or because of their connections with their free relatives or free lovers. Hendrick I (aged twenty-two), a carpenter and cabinet maker, appeared before the commissioners of inquiry in a shirt of "good linen", while Walker mentioned that Sim (aged twenty-two), a boat builder, usually dressed in "a superior style" to most others in the department. Several children also appeared before the commissioners in fine clothing, quite above the ordinary fare distributed in the department.[94] One of the major problems that Walker encountered with a number of the young ladies was what he considered as their love of finery, which in his view gave them exalted notions of their station in life (see chapter 6). He noted that several of them were "well dressed" in clothing far superior to what was usually worn by domestics or handed out by the department. He attributed this to the fact that their white lovers supplied them with such clothing.[95]

6

Social Culture, 1816–1825

Introduction

At the beginning of the previous chapter we discussed briefly the social and material context of the lives of the *winkel* slaves and more generally of the Caribbean slaves. Now it is important to pay more attention to the social aspects of their lives. Some social historians and anthropologists view social culture as ultimately more important than material culture because it embraces the folk memory, myths and community psyche that are the very essence of being or belonging. At its most quotidian level, social culture embraces issues of health, household and family organization, but, as already noted, it also takes more aesthetic forms such as music, song, dance, religion and education. Information on the social culture of the *winkel* people is generally far less complete than that on the material culture. With the exception of religious proselytizing and schooling, the writers of the extant documents showed little direct concern with the *winkel* people's social life, while no archaeological work has been done on the site of the village, unlike the excellent work done by Jerome Handler and Frederick Lange in Barbados and more recently by Barry Higman on Montpelier in Jamaica.[1] Nevertheless, we shall attempt to discuss briefly several aspects of the social culture.

Social Policy

Any study that attempts to deal with the social culture of the *winkel* people would be incomplete without taking into account the department's social policy and the heavy hand of management on the people. The imperial government considered the intervention of management as necessary to wean the people from their perceived primitive barbarism and qualify them for freedom at some future date. However, very little of Walker's social policy had anything to do, at least directly, with amelioration, as this programme was called, and still less with preparing the people for freedom. In view of the burden of his mandate to prepare them for that important event, it is necessary to discuss briefly his views on social change.

Walker wanted to preserve the security of the colony at all costs, and this meant doing nothing that would create, or threaten to create, a social revolution among the slaves or even a ripple among the plantocracy. He was against abolition, viewing it as a danger which had to be avoided: "Emancipation I must confess has always appeared to me a fearful question to be much agitated"; "It had always humbly appeared to me that there was much of danger and mistake in agitating the revolutionary subject of emancipation".[2] Looking at his *Letters on the West Indies,* it becomes evident that he had always taken a dark view of emancipation. In that work he made it clear that while he agreed that slavery was "an evil", he had no objection to that institution in itself: "It is not, however, to bondage in itself that I object: this I am desirous of stating in explicit terms." He opined that since the majority of the colonial populations were in "abject slavery", it would be "impossible to give them sudden freedom with any safety even to themselves", and those prejudiced in favour of freedom might be "apt to act somewhat blindly". For him, freedom could not be rationally conceived for slaves in the foreseeable future: "*the less emancipation shall be spoken of the better.* All parties should suppose it to be a thing *in nubibus* – very much out of mortal sight at the present moment."[3]

Starting, therefore, "on the supposition that it is never to be any thing else than enslaved [*sic*]" for the mass of the people, he considered the great *desideratum* to be the provision of comforts for the slave that would make him view freedom as "the deprivation of a father's roof to a child", so that "knowing the blessings he has possessed in his former state, and fearful of the risks of a new condition, he would, in many cases, lay hold of independence with a timid hand".[4] Placing strong emphasis in his *Letters* on the relationship between master and slave, he enjoined that the health, comfort and happiness of the latter should be the main concern of the former, and material returns only of secondary importance.[5] In practice, however, he did almost nothing to ameliorate the condition of the *winkel* people during his second term in office.

He viewed religious instruction for the enslaved people in rather narrow terms: as a "prudent measure which has become so necessary for our safety". He wanted a religious society in the colony, administered by Anglican, Dutch Reformed and Lutheran ministers, and "subjected to the direction of the landed interest of the Colony". Recalling the discussion in chapter 1 about these denominations, it is reasonable to conclude that Walker saw religious instruction as principally an opiate for the people, a means of colonizing their minds to ensure their continued subjection to the plantocracy.[6]

As time passed, Walker's policies became increasingly divergent from those of the imperial government, as detailed in the earlier instructions of the commissioners for management. Although conscious that he was falling short of the standard of righteousness expected of him by his humanitarian colleagues in Europe, who increasingly saw him as lacking in courage, he was not moved to greater action. His own words speak eloquently to his limited vision of his task:

> My principles were never revolutionary – my utmost wishes for the Negroes of the West Indies were to see them christian slaves – and with respect to their outward condition to witness their enjoyment of the ameliorations which have of late been undoubtedly in progress. My friends in England have sometimes been disappointed that my sentiments did not go further.[7]

Such fossilized thinking was hardly congruent with the humanitarians' call for radical reform, and it indicates that Walker's spirit of innovation had died. At best, his policies were a simulacrum of humanitarianism. It is therefore surprising that Macaulay, who should have had access to Walker's *Letters*, published in 1818, recommended him in the same year for the superintendency.[8] It again raises the issue of the extent to which the humanitarians at this point in time were committed to a policy of slave emancipation.

Walker also showed a morbid concern with keeping the people as far as possible out of the main areas of the town, which he felt exercised a cor-

Social Culture, 1816–1825

rupting influence on them. This concern surfaces on several occasions in the extant documents. After the abandonment of Berenstein plantation (twenty miles upriver) he wanted to purchase a plantation closer to town but still some distance from it, feeling that this would allow the people to obtain hire in the town but restrict their access otherwise to urban life.[9] He also sought to exercise tight control over the social life of young females in particular, forbidding them to entertain amorous relations outside the village and often banishing them to Berenstein as punishment for disobeying his orders, as this and the following chapter will detail.

Demography and Health

As noted in chapter 3, fundamental to the programme of amelioration and the wider social policy of the imperial government was the improved health of the enslaved people. The ultimate yardstick used by the humanitarians, and arguably by most scholars of slavery studies, to determine the demographic success of the new social policy is the net increase of births over deaths, or a constant increase in the enslaved population. The *winkel* population declined consistently until 1825, following basically the same pattern as the slave population in the rest of the colony and the Caribbean – with the notable exception, among the plantation colonies, of Barbados (see chapter 1). However, from that year births and deaths were just about equal. The population stood at 335 in 1815, 297 in 1825, and 298 in 1831, at the time that the people were emancipated. The department manumitted or handed over to free persons for manumission another forty-six persons between 1820 and 1831, before the general emancipation, while three were handed over to the Berbice Association (following a judicial ruling in favour of that organization on the ownership of those persons), and one was imprisoned for life. If these fifty other persons had remained in the department, there would have been an overall increase of thirteen at the time of emancipation.[10]

The continuing disparity in the sex ratio of the *winkel* population, where males outnumbered females by a significant margin (see Table 6.1, next page), was arguably one of the principal reasons for the small natural increase. While the increase occurred after Walker was dismissed from office, it would be speculative to attribute the increase solely to a more enlightened

Table 6.1   *Winkel* Population at Selected Dates by Sex, 1819–1825[11]

Date	Males	Females	Total	Female % of population
27 Feb. 1819	186	132	318	41.5
1 Jan. 1820	185	128	313	40.9
1 Jan. 1821	183	129	312	41.3
1 Jan. 1822	181	129	310	41.6
1 Jan. 1823	179	126	305	41.3
1 Jan. 1824	175	124	299	41.5
1 Jan. 1825	169	128	297	43.1
10 Oct. 1825	171	129	300	43.0

Sources: "Report of the Commission of Inquiry", T1/3483/1: 12–13, 93–95; "Return of slaves", 27 February 1819, T71/438: 723–32.

regime in place after his dismissal. Clearly, under him the tide of demographic misfortune had begun to turn, although he could have done much more to facilitate this development. Factors which might have been responsible for the growth of the *winkel* population include increasing creolization, an increased birth rate, and possibly a lower death rate among the young people. Significant in the population profile of 1825 was the increase in the number of youths in relation to the total population: 75.43 per cent in that year as against 52.05 per cent in 1819.

By 1819–20 the *winkel* population was already older than the average for the colony as a whole. This is not surprising, for the imperial government had not replenished the *winkel* population by fresh imports since it took over the colony in 1796, while the period 1796–1806 was one of unprecedented imports for the colony in general and for its sister colony Demerara. The population of Berbice more than doubled during that period.[12] Thus, about 73 per cent of the *winkel* population in 1819 was local-born ("creole"), in contrast to 43 per cent for the colony at large in 1820.[13] The difference in the ages of the two groups of slaves might also be demonstrated by reference to age categories which show that the largest group of *winkel* slaves (34.59 per cent) were in the 41+ category, while the largest group of

Table 6.2 *Winkel* Population and Berbice Slave Population by Age in 1819 and 1820, Respectively

Years	Winkel Population	%	Berbice Population	%
< 3	20	6.29	1,556	6.69
3–10	43	13.52	3,308	14.23
11–20	57	17.93	3,175	13.65
21–40	88	27.67	11,113	47.79
41+	110[a]	34.59	4,103	17.64
Total	318	100.00	23,255	100.00

Sources: "Return of slaves", 27 February 1819, PRO, T71/438: 723–32; *Berbice Gazette*, 12 April 1820.

[a]For completeness we have assigned one person, whose age is missing, to this age category because the document seems to indicate that this was so.

the colony's total slave population (47.79 per cent) were in the 21–40 category (see Table 6.2). Unfortunately, the information is insufficient to allow for meaningful comparisons about the general health of the two groups of slaves, but Dr John Beresford, who was the medical attendant of the *winkel* people for a number of years, declared in 1825 that their health was "pretty much the same as in other parts of the colony".[14]

There was a high incidence of morbidity among the *winkel* people. This was not simply a function of aging, but had much to do with the general conditions under which they lived. A few of them became octogenarians and nonagenarians and there was also one centenarian, as the following brief details from the returns for 1819 indicate: Fruitje (aged 101, died at age 104), Lucia (91, died at 94), Lysje I (91, died at 98), Berbice (86, died at 90), Aaron (86, died at 88), Johanna (81, died at 90), Cadet (81, died at 83) and February (81), who was still alive in 1832, one year after the Crown had liberated the *winkel* people.[15] Curiously enough, the majority of the very elderly (over seventy years) were not listed in the 1819 returns as suffering from any serious maladies. Only four persons had major afflictions: Flora, very near-sighted and bent over; Fruitje, bedridden and nearly blind; Johanna, toes atrophied from gout; and Cadet, incurable ulcer. The children were almost completely free of permanent physical disabilities. In fact, only Hendrick II (aged thirteen), lame from birth, suffered from any disability or physical defect, an observation which the commissioners corroborated in 1825. They noted that the children were healthy and "remarkably fine". They also declared that the young people as a whole – perhaps the teenagers – were "serviceable and well looking".[16]

On the other hand, a large number of the adult population in 1819, especially those between the ages of twenty and sixty, seemed to have passed through the valley of the shadow of death. Here are a few of the more striking "defects" or identifying physical traits of these people, some of whom had multiple ones: Baatje (aged 29), lame in right arm from a dislocation; Abraham (aged 46), had lost part of his penis; Welcome (aged 57), marks of old ulcer on legs and feet and bedridden; Pontje (aged 46), had lost nose bridge; Primo (aged 44), poor eyesight, mark on back from a burn and leprous in his face; another Primo (aged 51), large scar on back; Simon (aged 56), large scar from burn on chest; Taylor (aged 36), scar from cuts on left side of chest and armpit; Bastiaan (aged 23), marks of old ulcers on both legs and feet; Betsey I (aged 22), Frientje (aged 18), Louisa (aged 18) and Sophia II (aged 18), all "pitted" with smallpox; Jacobus (aged 22), pitted with smallpox and marks of sores on both legs; another Jacobus (aged 16), marks of old ulcers on both legs and feet.[17]

The following is a classification of the identifying physical traits of the *winkel* adult population listed in the registration return for 1819: smallpox (4 persons), wens (3), loss of one eye (2), part or full loss of one or several toes (9), part or full loss of one or several fingers (2), lameness in arm (1), lameness in one or both legs (2), loss of leg (2), atrophied limbs (2), partially or fully blind (10), parrot toes (2), bow-legged (3), white spots on body or limbs (5), asymmetrical limbs (3), deaf and dumb (1), crooked back (2), leprous (2), incurable ulcers (2), scars on limbs (2), scars on other parts of body (13), old ulcer marks (8), loss of part of penis (1), swollen testicles (1), other traits (6).[18] Some of these marks were relatively trivial, but others indicate that the persons affected underwent deep trauma. The age range of those affected also indicates that the vast majority of identifying traits were not simply due to old age. Indeed, in a number of instances, especially in relation to scars from cuts and burns, it is probable that some of these were due to punishment inflicted on the victims.

The adverse disease environment accounted for some of the maladies, such as leprosy and smallpox, but we need to ask questions about the quality of the preventive and curative measures which the department took to promote the health of the *winkel* population, a matter which we shall consider in greater detail shortly. Whatever the reasons, the returns for 1819 listed some 93 persons, or 41 per cent of the adult population of 226, and 29 per cent of the total departmental population of 318, as having some special or "irregular" physical traits (exclusive of birth marks and scarification), a quite alarming percentage which indicates a high level of morbidity. The environment was a factor in the morbidity and mortality of the slave population in the Guiana colonies as a whole and, as noted in chapter 3, was often a major point of discussion. Periodic epidemics continued to play their part in attenuating the health of the Berbice population, as we can gather from the years 1822–23 and 1825.

In 1822 and early 1823 an epidemic of "pleurisy and dysentery" struck the colony, resulting in a high incidence of illness among the *winkel* people, more than one hundred at one time being affected, mainly among the young people. Around mid-1823 an "epidemic of an inflammatory kind", somewhat like "European flu", occurred, wracking the health of the *winkel* population, causing some eighty persons to be hospitalized at one point, and resulting in higher mortality than usual among the elderly folk. Two years later the invasion came in the form of measles, followed by whooping cough, which sent the colony's population to bed, including a large number from the department.[19]

The maladies from which *winkel* people died, as listed in the population returns for 1825, include apoplexy, convulsions, dysentery, contusion, asthma, consumption, leprosy, insanity, elephantiasis, dropsy, atrophia, bowel disorders, hydrocephalus, *paracentesis abdominis* (drainage of the abdominal cavity), hemoptysis, locked jaw, pleurisy, debility, scorbutic disease, fever, cancer, inflammation of the intestines and inanition. According to Dr John Beresford, the main diseases that afflicted the children were "worms and catarrhs".[20] Diseases frequently had devastating effects in the region because epidemiological knowledge was still very limited and treatment was often highly experimental. But for a long time medics also placed far more emphasis on curative than on preventive medicine, a situation which obtained in the British Caribbean up to the 1930s, as noted in the Moyne Commission Report of 1939.[21]

The discussion above emphasizes the point that life is a perishable commodity and that every action should be taken to preserve it. Walker did introduce some commendable measures in the area of health. He assigned a "nurse" to attend those sick in their homes, and hospital cooks for those invalids unable to fend for themselves. He also granted permission for convalescent persons to go upriver on the Canje where the climate was less insalubrious, while he initiated a system of allowing a relative or close friend to attend sick and pregnant women in hospital on a one-to-one basis – all highly commendable practices, although the commissioners criticized the last of these measures as being too costly to the department.[22] Taken by themselves, these measures seem to indicate that the superintendent took great care to ensure the health of the people. However, other circumstances, plus loud complaints from the people to the commissioners and the latter's own observations, indicate that his health policies and practices required much improvement.

The inadequate attention that management paid to health matters cannot be attributed simply to ignorance of the medical needs of the people, for the department paid much higher health-care costs for its staff. Between 1817 and 1820 the routine care of each *winkel* person cost f4 per annum, without medicine, as against f50 for each free person. Extra sums had to be paid for special treatment, such as amputations and autopsies. Departmental expenditure on medical care between 1 January 1817 and 17 October 1820 totalled f7,857 (£561), comprising f5,865 (£419) on the first category of persons and f1,992 (£142) on the second. Based on an estimated average of 277 slaves and 12 white persons (including the missionary and his family), per capita expenditure on the two categories was roughly f21 and f166 respectively. Thus the expenditure on medical care for each white person was almost eight times that for a black person, clearly indicating differential access to medical care on the basis of race and class, and forcefully reminding us of the observation of Juan Francisco Manzano, a Cuban ex-slave, concerning the planters' attitude to the slaves: "life is cheap".[23]

The department recruited European medical personnel to look after the health of the people. In the early days the colony retained the services of a doctor, referred to as the "colonial surgeon", who was responsible chiefly for looking after the health of all the government slaves on the plantations and in town. His perquisites included an office close to the *winkel* village. However, with the restoration of the plantations to the Berbice Association, his full-time service was no longer considered necessary, and so he was contracted on an annual basis to deliver health care for the *winkel* people and the departmental staff and dependents on a per capita basis. Dr John Beresford (later in association with his brother Dr James Beresford) performed these services for a substantial part of the period. Other medics employed for shorter periods or for specific ailments included Dr A. Johnstone, Dr Joseph Jeffrey, Dr G. Waring, Dr J.H. Eenhuys and Dr L. Theurer. The doctors on the permanent payroll were expected to pay two routine visits per week to the department and other visits as the need arose. As noted above, they and other doctors were paid additional money for specialized services.[24]

A common practice in the slave colonies and also in the *winkel* department was the assignment of African medical attendants to look after the sick; some slave managers simply left the people to take care of these matters as best they could, save in exceptional circumstances. The chief African medical practitioner in the department in 1823 was a man named Lambert II (aged thirty), a highly intelligent individual, according to the commissioners and Lieutenant Governor Beard (see chapter 7). He was referred to sometimes as the "negro doctor", a title indicative of a role much more complex than simply dispensing medicine and dressing wounds. Other hospital attendants were appointed periodically from among the aged and invalid. In June 1824 one female and two male invalids were listed in this capacity. Midwifery duties were also carried out commonly by African midwives, such as Roxanna (aged seventy-seven).[25]

Important individuals who did not enter the formal structure of slave management as medical practitioners were the African religious leaders, who often combined in their persons skills as exorcists and herbalists. These persons usually held the most important places among the African leadership, being feared and respected for both their knowledge and their powers to relieve or impose sickness on individuals. They were especially important in cases of supposed mental illness. A growing body of scholars believes that they performed cures of both a physical and a psychosomatic nature. The most celebrated of these individuals in Berbice during the nineteenth century was the exorcist Willem, who was executed in 1822 by the colonial judiciary for causing the death of a female in the previous year through exorcism.[26] The *winkel* establishment also had its own practitioner in the person of Hans (aged fifty-six), a Congolese, whose mystical powers were well known beyond the confines of the department. The activities of this individual will be dealt with more extensively under the section relating to religion, but it is important to recognize here the operation of African medicine at its highest, metaphysical level within the department for several years before Hans was finally apprehended in 1819.

By the 1820s, of course, the creole population had veered much more strongly than their predecessors towards "western" medicine, and this was perhaps also true of those African-born persons who had lived long in the colony and who had benefited from such medicine. They therefore looked mainly to this source for daily attention to their ailments and complained, sometimes bitterly, about management paying insufficient attention to their medical needs. These were second only to their complaints relating to housing. There were forty-one complaints by adults about improper diet and general lack of care during illness, including allegations that the superintendent did not comply with the doctor's prescriptions on this matter.[27]

Frederick IV (aged twenty-three), for instance, complained that while ill in hospital he received nothing special but a spoonful of sugar, and that his mother and sister had to provide him with soup at their own expense. Peter (aged thirty-five) alleged that during his illness he asked the superintendent for a little rice and sugar, which the latter refused, stating that he did not deserve them. He alleged further that the doctor had ordered him to stay off salt but that the only food given him was salt-fish soup and okra. He asked for fresh food but the superintendent replied that he could not afford it and further that the individual "might be thankful that he had so good a master". Diena II (aged twenty-two) asserted that the doctor had ordered sago and barley water for her but that she received neither; however, McWatt gave her soup, three tablespoons of sugar and a little rice. Betsey I (aged twenty-eight) testified that the doctor had ordered her to have a good diet or she would die, but that she received very little of anything that was "comfortable" – only cold, tasteless soup like water, which she could not consume, and on four occasions a small cup of chocolate and a slice of bread. She also testified that when she was ill with dysentery she received no sugar, barley, rice or wine which the doctor had ordered.[28]

Making allowance for complete fabrication and exaggeration, the number of complaints and the specific nature of some of them still indicate that the superintendent was delinquent in providing proper nutrition for the sick. Dr Theurer testified that he ordered arrowroot, barley, chicken soup and wine regularly for those hospitalized. He had witnessed arrowroot and port wine being sent to the hospital, but had heard some of the people complain about not receiving any. As a result he had spoken to Dummett, then manager, who had replied, "I will speak to Mr Walker, but what can I do?" Theurer had also heard complaints about the soup being cold by the time it arrived at the hospital from the superintendent's house. More complaints came from those sick in their houses than from those hospitalized.[29]

On the other hand, Dummett, whose testimonies usually weighed in favour of Walker, declared that those hospitalized were supplied with soup and wine whenever the doctor ordered these, and also brandy, gin, sugar, barley, candles and oil. He even specified the quantities of some of the items served – about ten gallons of brandy and three to four cases of gin during his tenure as manager (March 1821–April 1824). He could not remember any rum or porter being distributed, but recalled that a loaf of bread was distributed occasionally. He declared that the items were handed to the hospital attendant, a *winkel* slave, thus implying that he could not vouch for the way in which they were distributed and that any charges of misappropriation should be directed towards the attendant.[30]

McWatt, Dummett's successor, had a different story to tell. He stated that he had heard a few complaints from the sick that they had not been given the wine ordered by the doctor. While he could not vouch for the truth of such allegations, he declared that not even a bottle of wine ever passed through his hands prior to the arrival of the commissioners. Before that time he knew of only two bottles of wine being given out to each of four persons. A little sugar was also served to selected persons, and to a few others when they requested it, but the quantity of this item could not amount to more than four hundred pounds per year. He never saw black pepper, vinegar or turpentine, items purchased by the department, used in the hospital. Likewise, he never knew of even a glass full of gin, brandy or rum being officially given to the sick, although he had privately given them rum and gin on occasion. However, he was aware that Madeira wine had been served to them in September and October 1825 (after the arrival of the commissioners), Adolphe, an old man, receiving eight to nine bottles of the same, and various quantities being given to three other persons.[31]

The care of the invalids and superannuated persons was the area in which the superintendent displayed the greatest degree of callousness. He dubbed Abrammaker (aged fifty-two), formerly a boat builder, now tending the manager's cows, "a lazy old man", while the commissioners, more sympathetic, noted that the complainant suffered from "defective sight" and was "nearly useless". Bernard (aged thirty-one), a carpenter disabled by leprosy, received less than his allowance of clothing, the superintendent likewise considering him "lazy". The commissioners' appraisal of him was that he would need future care and support since he would be unable to provide for himself in a state of freedom. Also among the "lazy" ones were Mentor (aged fifty-two) and Nassau (aged sixty-two). While the latter was officially superannuated due to old age, the former was suffering from a seemingly permanent back injury and hernia.[32]

Adolphe II (aged sixty-two), a former smith, was another of the lazy ones, according to the superintendent, although he confessed that he knew very little about this man. The charge of laziness is particularly surprising given this man's age, the prevailing disease environment in the colony, and the often harsh conditions under which slaves worked during their active years. In this man's case, however, to old age were added rheumatism and a leg that had been broken when a house collapsed on him at Berenstein, an injury the effects of which still plagued him. Adolphe bewailed the fact that, having worked hard for the department during his healthy years, he received little clothing, had to put up with a leaky house, and was not properly tended when sick. Let us listen to him:

> [W]hen me ask any thing he wont give me – he tell me, he say, you go away, you go work – you don't bother me. Since Massa come he, he give me one round jacket, & one trowsers without hat – after that when me been sick, me tell to he, me not able to work, so long me sick – now Massa Walker give me half allowance, & say you don't work – so long me sick, me ask blanket, he no give & after that, this time get blanket – this trowsers – this shirt.[33]

These examples throw into relief once again the jaundiced approach of some slave owners and managers to the suffering of their charges. However, the commissioners, fresh from Europe and not imbued with the prejudices of slave society, were often able to view their suffering in more objective and humane terms.

All the cases cited immediately above, involving invalids and superannuated persons, had to do with individuals whom the superintendent considered as choosing slovenliness over industry. Difficult as it is to excuse his reaction to them, it becomes even more difficult to explain his treatment of other superannuated persons whom he did not regard as lazy and whose age would have made them the objects of special care in free societies. Simon I (aged sixty-seven) was one such person. He was formerly a cooper whom the superintendent described as once "an industrious man". Now Simon was complaining of the way Walker treated him. Whenever he asked the superintendent for anything he would be told to go and find work. Simon had to give one of his colleagues a fowl to replace his broken artificial leg, which the superintendent refused to replace.[34] Lysje I (aged ninety-eight), the oldest person in the department at that time, was a greater object of pity because of the abject situation in which she lived. She testified that she received no clothing whatever in 1825, and that what she had received in the previous year was inadequate and had to be supplemented by gifts from friends. Though she was ill and infirm the superintendent gave her no special diet – "neither sugar, soup, wine nor any thing else". Walker, when asked to give a statement about her, said that he knew little about her! Lena (aged seventy-seven) was a different case, in so far as Walker could speak about her with some assurance. She complained that her house was in a very bad condition and that she had received only a petticoat, and no "comforts" whatsoever from the superintendent. The latter's assessment of her was, "Troublesome old woman. Ill tempered."[35]

The above testimonies, in all their sad eloquence, constituted a solemn and sustained chorus of wrongs. But Walker was not uniformly heartless towards the superannuated. Jonetta (aged seventy-two) spoke positively about his treatment of her, saying that he had been good and kind to her when she was sick, giving her wine, sugar, soup, rice and other items.[36] We do not know what made the difference in her case, but clearly he had his favourites.

African society, in which the young respected and sometimes revered the aged as treasuries of knowledge and wisdom, would have revolted at this treatment of elderly folk. But in the *winkel* department (as in Caribbean slave society at large), although several of its members were African-born and others ("creoles") had imbibed the African traditions, the stark reality was that old age was often met with neglect, disregard and contempt by slave masters. True, African family ties remained strong in slave societies and helped to ease the suffering of the aged and sick, such as Lysje. But enslaved persons were generally desperately needy, and could often give no more than the widow's mite. The superintendent was in a position to do better, but was indifferent to the pleas of his charges.

The situation improved appreciably after the commissioners' arrival, the superintendent wishing to mute the complaints of the people on this as on other matters. The people began to receive wine and porter on a more regular basis. François II (aged twenty-nine) testified before the commissioners that during his recent hospital stay he had received soup every day, plus sugar and barley. Bastiaan (aged twenty-nine) testified that "[w]hen in hospital lately got soup & 8 bottles of porter. Was formerly in hospital for the same complaint and got no porter."[37]

Taking all factors and testimonies into account, it is difficult to disagree with the commissioners that the superintendent had skimped on the diet given to the sick. They suggested that he appropriated to his own use much of the department's supply of meats, wine, porter, brandy, gin, sugar, barley, salad oil and other commodities. They concluded that, with few exceptions, the nourishment served to the sick consisted of "a little miserable cold soup sent to them from his own table after dinner, at a distance of a mile from his residence".[38] His treatment of the people on this score, as on other matters, veered far from the instructions laid down by the commissioners for management:

> The health of the Negroes must ever be a particular object of your attention. . . . The recovery of the Negroes when sick, and their future health, will depend so much on the manner in which the hospital is conducted, that it will well deserve your utmost care to enforce, on the managers of all the Estates, an uniform and undeviating attention to this point. – The hospital itself . . . should contain every convenience for the sick. The medicine chest should be well supplied with the drugs wanted for common use. Above all, great care and liberality should be used in supplying nutritious and well prepared food for the convalescent patients, and wine and other cordials when recommended by the medical attendants.[39]

Other complaints surfaced against Walker concerning his insensitivity to the people in times of family sickness and grief. Sophia I (aged thirty-two) declared that the superintendent dispatched her to Berenstein and would not allow her to remain in town to look after her eighteen-year-old daughter, Catherine, who had suffered a miscarriage. Mrs Wray had to look after the young lady and send her sugar, barley, bread and candles. Elizabeth claimed that when her grandfather died she had to pay f1 to hire herself in order to attend his funeral. Juliana also asserted that she had to hire herself for four weeks to attend to her dying mother. The extant records likewise indicate the callous way in which the superintendent treated the young lady Susannah II (aged twenty-two). Her infant daughter died on 10 February 1822, while Susannah herself was still in hospital, but on the following day he hired her out.[40] These incidents were at once petty and tragic in terms of human relations.

In each of these cases the superintendent had developed strained relations with the females, and this coloured his sense of decency and propriety. Sophia had run afoul of him on the matter of her relations with a white man, while he considered Elizabeth idle and "spoilt" for her station in life because she was mistress to a white man. Juliana was actually living outside the village with a white man, and the superintendent alleged that this had "spoilt her industry" and induced in her a love of finery. Susannah had earlier been banished to Berenstein. While there she, along with eight other persons, had complained against Deussen, the manager of the estate, for which the fiscal subsequently placed her in the stocks. She absconded some months later and suffered confinement once again.[41]

The overall picture on demography and health is that of a population slowly bridging the gap between deaths and births, with a younger and healthier group gradually emerging. However, there were worrying indications that sustained health was not the norm as the youths moved into their twenties, a factor which had a lot to do with the vagaries of the natural environment, physical brutalities meted out to them, conflicts among themselves and with other slaves, and poor housing, food and medical care.

Social Relations

The social relations among the *winkel* people will be discussed mainly in relation to household and family organization, and social contacts with the wider community. Structurally, the household was the most important unit in the village. It bore close resemblance to the family, but with the important difference that several members of the family might reside in separate houses inside or outside the village, resulting in nonresidential family units. Some households might also include close friends rather than blood relations, as was the case with Moanda and Zamore, mentioned in the previous chapter. While average occupancy in the seventy houses which were occupied in January 1825 was 3.9 persons, household sizes varied considerably.[42] There were thirteen single-person households and another thirteen double-person ones; on the other hand, there were two cases of nine persons making up the household and three cases of ten (see Table 6.3).

Few couples were married according to Christian rites; in fact this did not happen before the early 1820s because the colonial laws did not allow it until that time. Thus, when Wray took it upon himself during his early ministry to marry a few couples, he was aware of the fact that he was doing so outside the pale of the law.[43] Dr Conrad Schwiers, a Lutheran minister resident in the colony for seventeen years, was amazed that Wray could be so bold as to marry slaves and expressed the view that "surely nobody would be so wicked or daring" as to convince the lieutenant governor that such a union was legal.[44] According to the departmental records, in January 1825 there were three legally married couples and twenty-two reputed couples living together in the village. However, there were as many as thirty-five (female) single-parent households. Interestingly, in married or cohabiting households in which there were stepchildren, only the children of the female partners are mentioned specifically, thus underlining the fact that the emphasis was on matrilineage and perhaps matrifocality.[45]

Many recent scholars have rejected the old view that slave children were generally neglected by their fathers who remained largely invisible and marginalized. These scholars have emphasized that slave families, especially in the amelioration period, were fairly stable, that there were coresidential and non-coresidential, nuclear and extended, units, and that children often had positive relations with their fathers.[46] Very little work has been done on the situation in Berbice, but the *winkel* records of the mid-1820s bear out these conclusions. Louis (aged forty-seven), the head boat builder, was perhaps the finest example of fatherhood in the department. He fathered eight children (by at least two women) and drew loud praise from the management for his

Table 6.3   *Winkel* Households in January 1825

No. of Persons	No. of Houses
0	3
1	13
2	13
3	10
4	9
5	10
6	3
7	4
8	3
9	2
10	3

Source: "Return of the number of houses", 20 January 1825, PRO, T1/3483/1: 893–95.

diligence, sobriety, recent marriage to Cornelia II (aged thirty-one) according to Christian rites, faithfulness to his religious obligations (as a communicant in Wray's church), and care for his children: "He is in every respect one of the best Negroes I ever knew, and his family are equally respectable", was manager McWatt's comment on him.[47]

Evidence from the *winkel* department in Berbice shows that some females had a large number of children, for example, Susannah, ten; Clarissa, twelve; and Maria I, thirteen.[48] Several other mothers had four and more children. Even allowing for the deaths of several of these children, some households must have had a large complement of living ones. While these examples do not offer a definitive profile of the *winkel* population, they reflect high levels of fertility and some retention of African traditions of large family sizes.

Most *winkel* people married or cohabited within the village. However, a significant number had relations outside the village, with children being born largely through unions between *winkel* women and free black, free coloured and white men.[49] Twelve children (of whom five were living in 1825) were born from the union of Clarissa (aged fifty-two), a black woman and domestic at Government House, and the free black man Tom Rose. In 1825 Clarissa was living outside the village with her reputed husband.

Arsenia (aged thirty-five), also a black woman working at Government House, produced five children with her free black reputed husband Ben Young. In 1825 she was living in the village.[50] The commissioners pointed out that many of the people were closely related to "some of the most respectable free colored inhabitants" of Berbice.[51] This statement should have included white persons, for over time there was deep penetration of the black complexion of the original *winkel* population by lighter hues: mulatto (middle), mustee (upper) and cobb (lower) shades of complexion, numbering twenty-six, two and thirty-four respectively around mid-1825, or some 21 per cent of the department's population.[52]

Prostitution, a common feature of urban life in the Caribbean during slavery, was also common in the small town of New Amsterdam, and *winkel* women became involved in this more unseemly aspect of town life. The commissioners declared that most of the adult females were "living in a state of prostitution",[53] but the context in which this statement was made suggests that they were referring mainly to reputed marriages as against legally recognized ones. Nevertheless, both Walker and Wray confirmed that prostitution did exist among the females. Wray wrote to his superiors in Europe:

> The Negroes houses in town belonging to the Crown we have reason to believe are a complete brothel & a scene of wickedness & vice . . . a receptacle of soldiers & sailors & the lower classes of Whites & others & furnish objects of carnal gratification for many . . . fornication &c is I fear going on among the Crown Negroes in town.[54]

During the time that Wray was on the department's payroll he asserted that he was sometimes accused of living on the wages of prostitution.[55] This implies that Walker encouraged the females in these indiscretions, but this was far from the case, as the evidence above clearly illustrates.

Walker acknowledged that the practice had existed at one time and asserted that Wray had been partly responsible for the situation by not exercising firm control over the females on his domestic staff. He also declared that he personally had been of clean hands and a pure heart in the matter; that when he returned to the colony in 1819 he found some *winkel* women cohabiting with white and free coloured men who paid hire for them; and that as the lesser of the two evils he agreed to allow the men to purchase them and their children, on the understanding that these men would manumit them.[56] At the same time the continued hiring out of females as domestics during his second administration, sometimes for long periods to white males, created a context that was conducive to prostitution (and also promiscuity and seduction). The department hired out even females in their early teens, such as Madelintje, Cornelia, Grietje, Elizabeth and Carolina II – all between twelve and fifteen years of age.[57] Conscious of this, the commissioners expressed great reservations about allowing females to be hired out as domestics.

Apart from the emotional aspects of some of the connections, tangible material rewards and some social prestige often resulted from the relationships. A few of the women actually lived with their reputed husbands (for example, Juliana, Clarissa and Susannah) in urban dwellings outside the village. We have already dealt with the material benefits that the women and the children often enjoyed from such relationships. They also received some social benefits, including greater opportunities for manumission, and for education and social advancement. The commissioners noted that Charles II, the mustee son of Juliana, was undergoing instruction at a private school at his father's expense, being thus able to read, say his prayers and recite the catechism well. Esdaile, son of Lucia II, was another lad sent to a private school by his father.[58] With very few exceptions, *winkel* men could not provide their spouses and children with these benefits. Walker expressed the view that more *winkel* men than women were willing to tie the knot within the department, and that the females were reluctant to do so because the men "were not able to purchase ornaments for them".[59]

Walker saw it as his duty to undo such relationships, even to the point of intruding into the very private lives of his female charges. The offensive manner in which he set about terminating these forbidden affairs threw into vivid relief his style of management, and elicited the revulsion and increasing opposition of the females. He, in turn, saw the persistence of the prohibited liaisons as a dangerous alchemy that had to cease. He locked up the young lady Tannetje for a total of about nine months in the "sick house", in "a little room" in the customs house, and in the gallery and the lobby of his house because of her relationship with her white lover. He also confined Juliana, Madelintje and Eliza along with her at various times. Cornelia III, Nancy, Elizabeth I, Betsey II, Janetje, Sanetje, Suzette, Catherina, Julia, Sophia I and Juliana were among those sent to Berenstein because of their connections with white or free coloured men.[60] For the same reason he placed Cornelia III in the stocks in town every night for four weeks, although she was six months pregnant. The same thing happened to Nancy every night for one month, during which period her mother had to smuggle supper to her. Elizabeth's story was that the superintendent promised that he would allow her to return to town if she agreed to marry a black man, but that nobody had proposed to her. While at Berenstein, Deussen had ill-treated and flogged her. The tapestry of female life in the department is woven with similar testimonies.

The superintendent's intrusive interest in the love lives of the females and his attempts to prevent them from stepping out of the perimeters that he had laid down for them underline the far-reaching and tormenting nature of the slave system. Persons were harried for relationships which in free societies would have been quite permissible. As one who upheld the social order of slave society, Walker might have been persuaded, as Roger Bastide points out, that miscegenation made "the lines separating the social classes dangerously unstable".[61] But the reality is that genuinely amorous relations often existed between black women and white men even within the constraints of slave society. What John Stedman said of Suriname in the late eighteenth century also applied to Berbice in the nineteenth. According to him, the European males "in their amours most usually prefer the Indian, negro and mulatto girls, particularly on account of their cleanliness, health and vivacity".[62] This is a dimension often overlooked in discussing the intimate relations between whites and other groups within slave society, although it emerges also in Thomas Thistlewood's relations with his female slave Phibbah.[63] Also generally overlooked is the fact that some white women did not possess the personal charm and appeal of a number of coloured and black women, but Stedman makes this quite clear.[64]

One might have expected the female members of Walker's household to be more sensitive to his invading the privacy of the *winkel* females and to the impropriety of his manner of dealing with the issue. However, a small window into their minds on this matter is opened by Betsey II's assertion that she was placed in the stocks at Mrs Walker's suggestion. Juliana also implied that the superintendent's wife was party to the treatment meted out to her.[65]

Any society that turns a blind eye to sexual promiscuity and moral laxity does so at the risk of engendering major social problems, but at the same time it has to proceed with caution and wisdom in addressing these issues.

In Caribbean slave society, where such behaviour was the norm among both the oppressors and the oppressed, the situation presented more difficulties than usual. In the context of the *winkel* department, Reverend Wray was the person best trained to deal with this situation, but Walker had virtually excluded him from the department's programme of counselling and rehabilitation without finding any adequate substitute, and Walker was clearly not the man for the job. The commissioners had this to say about his means of controlling the young women: "[W]hen he attempted to reform giddy girls, by locking them up at nights, & putting them in the stocks for weeks together, we think he evinced a very incompetent knowledge of the female character – thereby giving a stimulus to those propensities he was desirous of restraining, which were only increased by opposition." They added that Mrs Stanley had told them that in her opinion the young females often reacted as they did "out of spite" for the superintendent.[66] In a society convoluted by "caste", racism and sexism, the superintendent might have viewed the actions of the females as a challenge to him as master, white and male. It is certainly arguable that class, race and gender ideologies played a central role in his treatment of the females for what he considered their social transgressions. This conclusion, at least as far as gender is concerned, is corroborated by the fact that he never punished the men for similar activities, although about thirteen of them were in exogenous relations in 1825, at least three of these with free coloured women.[67]

Leisure and Pleasure

The social life of the *winkel* people also involved becoming immersed in other aspects of town life. As already noted, Walker was particularly concerned about the "corrupting" influences of the town on the people. The departmental records do not have much to say specifically about the nature of their involvement, but we know that the social life of the town embraced drumming, dancing, rum drinking and cock fighting, among other activities. Fêting was common in town on weekends and especially during the holiday seasons. Certain days during such seasons were officially declared by the colonial government as "dancing days",[68] with the Christmas season being the high point of such festivities. These were occasions when enslaved people could temporarily forget their pain and engage in some pleasure for a short while. They became so exhausted on such occasions that it was common in Berbice, Barbados and perhaps in some other colonies for individual owners to give them an extra day at the end of the holidays to recover. In Berbice these days were strictly "rest days", the slaves not being allowed to engage in any fêting.[69]

We have already noted in the previous chapter that such festival occasions included new clothing and extra allowances of food by the owners, but they also involved the enslaved people using some of the little money they had earned or the livestock they had reared to purchase items that they could not afford during the year. By the early nineteenth century the infectious spirit of Christmas had permeated all ranks and classes of society, bond and free, who became caught up in the giddy atmosphere. Pinckard describes the experience of the slaves in Berbice on such occasions:

> Parties of them go from the different plantations to spend the mirthful hours with their more particular friends or acquaintances of the neighbouring estates, and it is a happy meeting of relatives, lovers, and fellow-passengers who have voyaged together from their native Africa. The whole country exhibits one moving scene of dancing gaiety.[70]

Slave dances commonly involved those derived from Africa, with adaptations made as time went by. In the typical dismissive fashion of Europeans at the time, Pinckard referred them as "rude African dance[s]", while Schomburgk, writing in the early post-emancipation period, described them in more pejorative terms: "the dancers are soon transported with wild bacchanalian lust, when what with a series of disgusting jerks, 'winds' and contortions they resemble Furies rather than human beings . . . the dance waxes more fast and furious, even more demoniacal". But both writers were also aware that some blacks could just as easily convert to European dances. Pinckard was quite surprised to find that the slaves present at the governor's fête were able to perform "even minuets . . . in precise and stately step, and with a degree of ease and gracefulness of movement which is seldom witnessed among the common people in England". Schomburgk, too, noted their capacity to engage in "country-dances, quadrilles, etc.".[71]

Winkel people were fully immersed in the activities described above, with the village being a scene of "riot", "drunkenness" and "noise", according to Wray.[72] At Christmas and other holidays it was customary for the lieutenant governor to hold a fête at his official residence for his own slaves and others, including the Crown slaves, where both European and African dances were the order of the day. Wray's congregation, comprising mainly the Crown people, disappeared on Whitsunday in 1820 because of the lieutenant governor's fête: "They began at 8 on Saturday evening & continued it till 12 on Sunday evening. The Town was a scene of dissipation & noise and drunkenness. On Sunday Evening His Excellency the Governor had them before Government House till nearly nine oclock drumming & dancing & treated them with Punch."[73] It was not the last time that he would bemoan the effect of such fêting on his Sunday congregation.

Drumming accompanied virtually every fête, traditional or European. Scholars writing about musical instruments in Africa and among the African diaspora have singled out the drum as the most characteristic instrument of African musical tradition, and its rhythms as the lifeblood of movement for the people. In the case of Berbice, Pinckard, Schomburgk and Wray testified to this indirectly in their writings, the first of these noting the presence of the drum, the violin and fife, as the main instruments played at the lieutenant governor's ball in the great hall of his official residence. Schomburgk noted the passion of the drummer and his ability to set the tone and pace of the dancing.[74] Tambourines, banjos and others might be added to the list of musical instruments. Drumming often took place outside of fêtes. While there was no law prohibiting the use of this instrument in Berbice, there was some proscription of its untimely use. The *winkel* slave Cochrane once received twelve lashes for drumming and dancing, on the complaint of some members of the colonial administration, but Wray makes it clear that the playing of this instrument could be heard loudly and frequently in the village.[75]

Winkel people, like other slaves, gained notoriety among the whites generally for a number of other activities. Wray complained about their excessive drinking, card playing and cock fighting.[76] *Winkel* people mentioned specially in the departmental records as being alcoholics include William, who was punished twice for bad behaviour due to excessive drinking; Grieta, who Walker alleged was drunk at the time that she offered an impertinence to the manager, for which she was cart-whipped; Lambert, who was said to have attempted suicide while in the stocks as punishment for intoxication; and Lauw, who actually committed suicide while in solitary confinement for

196 | UNPROFITABLE SERVANTS

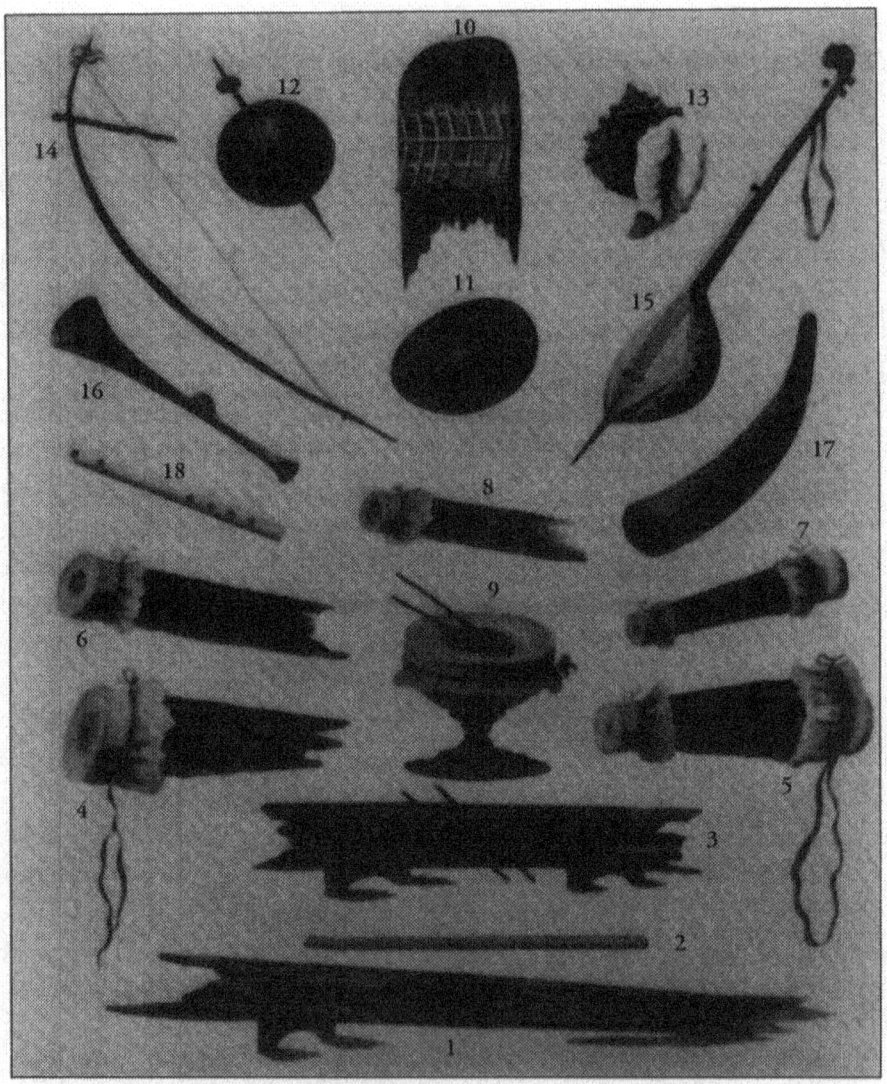

Figure 8 Musical instruments of African slaves:
1. Qua-qua; 2. Kiemba toetoe; 3. Ansokko bania; 4. Great Creole drum; 5. Great Loango drum; 6. Papa drum; 7. Small Loango drum; 8. Small Creole drum; 9. Coeroema; 10. Loango bania; 11. Large empty gourd; 12. Saka-saka; 13. Conch; 14. Benta; 15. Creole bania; 16. Too-too; 17. Horn; 18. Loango too-too

Reprinted from John G. Stedman, *Narrative of Five Years' Expedition against the Revolted Negroes of Surinam in Guiana on the Wild Coast of South America from the Years 1772 to 1777*, 2 vols. (London: J. Johnson and J. Edwards, 1796), 2: plate 69.

Social Culture, 1816–1825

brandishing a cutlass in a state of intoxication.[77] The colonial laws forbade the selling of liquor by or to enslaved persons, but these laws were usually not rigidly enforced in times of relative calm. While there is little doubt that several *winkel* people overindulged in liquor, the drinking of this substance in large quantities is often associated with pain rather than pleasure, as the cases of Lambert and Lauw suggest (see chapter 7).

Religion

Religion was one of the most important elements of African social culture that survived the middle passage and the plantation experience in the Americas. Because of official prohibition of African-derived religious practices in Berbice[78] and elsewhere, such practices became part of the subterranean culture of the slaves, usually away from the gaze of Europeans. However, some Europeans were allowed to witness certain practices or were informed about them in some detail. Reverend Wray was one such person. He witnessed a number of funerary rites where some of the most significant aspects of the people's religious culture were manifested. He attended one such ceremony among the government slaves in which the mourners engaged in a series of rituals, including the placing of pipes containing tobacco, eggs and other items in the coffin; drinking rum and pouring some over the coffin; and asking the deceased to carry messages to their ancestors. A few weeks later they held a dance and a feast in remembrance of the deceased.[79] Wray described these ceremonies as involving considerable financial expenditure on hogs, fowls and other food, "yelling dancing & drinking & sometimes carrying provisions to the grave some time after [the funeral]". McWatt added that several of the deceased were buried with a number of ornaments. One government slave informed him that it had cost that individual three joes (f66) to prepare a feast for his wife who had died a few months earlier.[80]

Government slaves shared with other enslaved people the view that disease and death were not natural phenomena, but rather the work of malevolent spirits and persons. In order to ward off such evil they often wore amulets.[81] Their intimate embrace of the religious culture of their ancestors was best exemplified by the presence of Hans in their midst, to whom reference has already been made. This fifty-six-year-old Congolese man, blind in one eye, must have been a member of the department before 1796, for after that year the imperial government ceased purchasing fresh slaves. Yet it was not until 1819 that his activities were brought to the attention of the colonial authorities. Although a field hand, he must have gained considerable influence first among the *winkel* people, where he honed his craft. Over time his skills as an exorcist became noised abroad among the other urban and plantation slaves. As a *confu* man he was much feared, some slaves refusing to touch him when ordered by their manager to apprehend him. The investigations carried out by the Court of Criminal Justice after his apprehension revealed that he was "in the habit of carrying on a regular obiah trade", and that he had "exercised his art on different occasions on several estates . . . assuming unto himself the possession of supernatural power derived from God".[82]

The influence of Hans among the *winkel* people might be inferred from his wider influence over slaves elsewhere. He visited plantation Deutichem on the night of 12 June 1819 at the invitation of January, one of the drivers, in order to discover the source of poisoning or some other evil practices which were believed to have led to the sudden death of a number of slaves there. His presence and performance had quite a mystical effect on the people who, from evidence collected by the estate's attorney, threw themselves on the ground, "biting the grass, tearing the earth with their hands, and conducting themselves like maniacs". A few days later, on Hans's return to the estate, renewed excitement followed. According to this same witness, "the minds of the people were in . . . a state of ecstasy, and [they] conducted themselves as possessed to that degree as to attract the attention of three gentlemen passing, who came and inquired the cause of this uncommon agitation".[83]

The actual details of what took place on the first night when Hans cast his spell, as detailed by several of the slaves who were present, are also interesting. Taking a tub of water, a bundle of wild canes and some grass, he dipped the last of these in the water and sprinkled the faces (or washed the heads, according to another testimony) of those present, at the same time directing everyone to dance what was obviously the *water mama* or *minje mama* (mermaid or water spirit) dance, himself also participating. What followed is taken from the testimony of Frederick, who clearly was not an accomplice to anything underhanded which Hans might have been doing:

[T]he negroes became as if crazy; some threw themselves in the mud – others jumped; they that were the most turbulent were flogged with the wild canes by Lindsay Harry, by order of Hans, and recovered; others more furious and not recovering from the stripes of Lindsay Harry, Hans struck with a bamboo, and they immediately recovered. He asked me if I was afraid; I said no, but I did not like this sport. . . . Venus was quite as a crazy person and could not recover the effects, for which she had been struck with the cane and bamboo, but not so as to cure her effectually. She danced in the circle, and coming up to me said, I was the bad man on the estate.[84]

Venus proceeded to Frederick's house where she, along with others, ransacked his kitchen, looking for the poison but finding none. Venus testified that she had fallen under a deep spell, as the partial paraphrase in the fiscal's records indicates:

My head began to turn, as if I were mad; don't know how occasioned this: the first dance she ever saw, whose heads turned in such a manner that they fell to the ground. Were flogged with the wild cane first; if not recovered he flogged them with a carracarra, and put guinea pepper in their eyes which he chewed. All this was done to me, but I could not recover. Had not, nor ever does drink rum. I could see and hear every thing, but was exactly as if I were crazy: I recovered a little after this last. Is not aware that she accused Frederick as the bad man. . . . I was in hysterics; constantly laughing, although nothing was said to make me laugh. . . . He [Hans] chewed some wild cane and put it in my mouth, and I recovered.[85]

The ritual was more complicated than the summary above indicates. Whether what Hans did was by sleight of hand or skill in the mystical arts, he did cast quite a spell on the people. However, the exercise had to be aborted because of the approach of the overseer.

Frederick, irate over being accused without proof, divulged the entire matter to the overseer, who apprehended Hans when the latter appeared on the estate a few days later. When apprehended he had f50 on him. He did not do the job for free; he was paid a handsome but undisclosed sum of money by the people, many of whom were forced to pay by January.[86]

He was arraigned before the Court of Criminal Justice on a charge of practising "obeah", a practice which the court declared as threatening to lead to "the total subversion of all subordination and ultimate destruction of the inhabitants of this colony". The court therefore imposed several punishments on him. He was sentenced to be placed in the colony's chain gang for life. In addition, while wearing his "obeah" paraphernalia around his neck he was to be severely flogged with rods under the public gallows and then branded. Finally, he was to be exposed to public view with his "obeah" paraphernalia sixteen times, for one hour on each occasion, during the sittings of the court over the next year. January and Venus were convicted along with him.[87]

It was the kind of influence that Hans and his fellow practitioners wielded over the enslaved people that slave owners, missionaries and the imperial government sought to counteract, although often in different ways and for different reasons. Theoretically, the hub of the imperial government's social policy was the moral and religious education of the people, which the humanitarians considered essential to get rid of their "superstitious" beliefs and prepare them for the boon of freedom, although the humanitarians did not generally accept that this was a *sine qua non* of freedom. The policy which the commissioners for management had laid down for De la Court and which successive agents were expected to follow unswervingly was the "moral, and religious improvement of the Slaves" by "all wise and prudent measures" and "with all possible vigour".[88] However, in this area also Walker failed badly in the task of amelioration. He never worked out any clear strategy of operation and was rather perfunctory in what little he did. Some of it was largely negative, especially in respect of the coloured females.

Wray himself, now located in town and finding his constituency among the former Crown slaves considerably atrophied, concentrated on developing a congregation among the urban and peri-urban slaves, and courting the favour of the coloured and white urban population. However, he soon came into conflict with Walker for two main reasons: first, the superintendent's reduction of the subvention to the mission; and second, the general management of the department. The cost of the mission constituted a substantial outlay in cash and kind for the relatively small establishment which the Crown property had become. It involved £500 per annum for house rent and salary, besides rations, medical expenses for Wray's family, and "expenses for instruction" which totalled around f152 in 1818 for Madeira wine, corks, salted fish and candles. The mission also enjoyed the services of several *winkel* persons.[89]

Soon after Walker's return to Berbice he reduced Wray's salary from £300 to £150 per annum,[90] in an arbitrary way which peeved the missionary and which was exacerbated by the irregularity of supplies for the school and chapel. Wray acknowledged that he could not expect to get the same emoluments as he had when the Crown property included the estates. However, he felt that the superintendent should at least have made some regular provision for the school and chapel, which he considered critical to the realization of the imperial government's plans for the intellectual and moral improvement of the people.[91] The directors of the LMS could give no assurance of any long-term subvention to the missionary, given the multitude of their other overseas commitments. While in 1819 they voted the sum of £100 to assist him (and gave him a total of £400 over the next two years), they emphasized that they did not propose to continue the subvention; they hoped that the *winkel* department's support and personal subscriptions would meet the full cost of the mission.[92] This policy was likely to, and indeed did, place the mission much more in the debt of the plantocratic interests than before and stifled much of its independence of thought and action.

The second main reason for soured relations between the two parties was the manner in which the superintendent ran the department generally. Wray felt that the financial malaise within the department was due largely to Walker's inefficient management, including unnecessary lawsuits, the purchase instead of the production of food, and the assignment of artisans to field work instead of making efforts to find suitable employment for them. He also criticized the superintendent for appointing severe managers at Berenstein, one of whom (Deussen) was constantly profaning the sabbath by sending down the punts (flat-bottomed riverain vessels) on that day. Wray had spoken to Walker about the matter, but the superintendent had simply replied that the manager was at fault, while the missionary felt that the superintendent should do something to stop the practice.[93]

The dispute between the two men led to the superintendent setting up his own school and needlework class (workroom), and also seeking to influence the *winkel* people to attend the Anglican Church rather than the missionary chapel. In fact, Walker tried in vain more than once to get the Lords Commissioners to recruit missionaries either from the Church Missionary Society (the evangelical arm of the Anglican Church) or the Moravian

Missionary Society to replace Wray, whose work, he alleged, had failed to instil moral values and godly living among the people.[94]

The majority of the slave-owning fraternity continued to look upon religious instruction to slaves, and especially teaching them to read, as dangerous. Moreover, although Wray did not generally teach slaves to write, there was no guarantee that some of them would not learn this art. Frantze (aged nineteen) testified before the commissioners that Wray taught him to read but that he taught himself to write.[95] Certain aspects of missionary teaching also reflected badly on the practices of the plantocracy and the white community at large. Wray's teaching that the sabbath was the Lord's day on which no one should work upset a number of slave owners who continually breached the laws on this matter. He often found it expedient to omit this part of the Ten Commandments when instructing the enslaved people, since this created much conflict with the slave owners, although he asserted that he always advised the people to do all "necessary work" on that day.[96]

A more sticky issue was his preaching against fornication and adultery. The prevalence of such practices among planters, managers, overseers and clerks stood in stark contradiction to his sermons on this issue. He cited Galley (alias Gallez) as one such example. Although that planter had invited the missionary to preach to his slaves, he himself was "living in open and notorious fornication"; he had "three wives professedly", two of whom were sisters and both pregnant at the same time. On Sandvoort the new manager had three or four wives and had fathered children by at least four women.[97] More directly affecting the morality of the department was the fact that Scott, while assistant agent, actually cohabited with the *winkel* woman Betje with whom he had at least one child. This practice was completely at variance with the instructions of the commissioners for management, who had stated a decided preference for married men as managers, enjoined that the departmental staff should set a high standard of morality, and directed the agents "to discountenance, and, if necessary, to punish" all sexual liaisons between the management staff and the slaves.[98]

Speaking more generally, the plantocracy attacked Wray on such basic aspects of Christian doctrine and practice as calling (baptized) slaves "beloved brethren", singing hymns of spiritual freedom, which would put notions of another kind of freedom into the slaves' minds, singing certain hymns which were "warlike", and giving slaves Christian literature – all of which tended to suggest to the plantocracy that missionary pedagogy taught the slaves insubordination.[99] Planters showed particular concern when the missionary distributed Bibles to the slaves. Several New Testament passages spoke to the issue of freedom, and indeed Patterson argues that, more than any other religion, freedom forms the core of Christianity's *soteria*.[100] While the focus in Christianity was on spiritual freedom, the missionary could give no assurance that the enslaved people would not interpret the various verses in terms of physical freedom. Such passages, for instance, as "Christ hath redeemed us from the curse of the law" and "stand fast therefore in the liberty wherewith Christ hath made us free, and be not entangled again with the yoke of bondage" might exercise a more powerful influence on the enslaved people's minds than "servants, be obedient to them that are your masters according to the flesh, with fear and trembling".[101]

More terrifying, from the planters' perspective, was that enslaved persons were likely to come across the story of the Israelite deliverance from Egyptian slavery under the mighty hand of Yahweh and his servant Moses. That deliverance had been accompanied by the "angel of death" destroying thousands of Egyptian slave masters and their families, and the Israelites seizing their goods. "Let my people go!" might become the battle cry of Africans under colonial slavery, with frightening consequences for their masters. In 1822 the enslaved "prophet" Denmark Vesey of Charleston, South Carolina, tried to prove that slavery was against biblical teaching, read to his followers the passage about the Israelites' deliverance from the Egyptians and plotted an apocalyptic revolt.[102] Slaves in Berbice might not have known about Vesey but they certainly knew about Moses, and several had named their children after him.[103]

In spite of covert and overt hostility, the missionary managed gradually to insinuate himself into the favour of a few members of the plantocracy and white officials, including Lieutenant Governor Beard, Acting Fiscal William Scott, five members of the Council of Government and Court of Criminal Justice, and Wolfert Katz, the biggest planter. These formed the backbone of his financial support.[104] By 1819 he had built a chapel in town capable of holding about three hundred people, but an infuriated white mob burnt it down in broad daylight after the slave uprising in Demerara in 1823, in which the colonial government implicated Reverend John Smith, Wray's coreligionist, and sentenced him to death.[105] It took a few years before Wray could rebuild a new chapel, a factor which had a deleterious effect upon the size and morale of his congregation.

Still, a number of the older *winkel* people continued to attend his services, many of them being attached to him and his family on a very personal basis. However, the vast majority of them retired altogether from church, while the youths and infants hardly attended chapel. Wray claimed that after the destruction of the chapel in 1823 Walker stopped them from attending church. While we have no evidence of any such prohibition, the people realized that Walker's attitude towards the mission was cold and distant, and this might have caused many of them to stay away.

Several of them, of course, could hardly speak English, or only a broken version of it. The lingua franca in the former Dutch colonies at this time was "creole Dutch", which did not encourage the population to attend services in English. But there had also been some coercion to attend services in the early days of the mission which, once removed, led to the significant drop in *winkel* attendance. The examination of the people by the commissioners of inquiry revealed numerous instances of persons who no longer attended chapel, or did so in the most irregular way, and who had practically forgotten what little they had learned of the catechism or the New Testament. Most of them could still remember the missionary teachings against the evils of stealing, lying, swearing, drinking and disobedience to their masters, but very few of them were committed to any of the ideals espoused by the missionary.[106]

A few of them attended the Anglican Church, which itself still had only a minor, sometimes barely visible, presence in the colony. True, the Anglican ministers, Reverend Austin (1817–22) and Reverend Whitfield (1822–27), baptized a large number of persons, mainly small children. Austin, in particular, showed great interest in instructing the slaves, but with his departure what little hope existed of finding an alternative pastor for the *winkel* people all but disappeared.[107] Reverend Whitfield did examine the children periodically in the church catechism on Sunday afternoons, an effort supplemented by those of the superintendent's daughters.[108] Nevertheless, the *winkel* people generally drifted away from Christian teachings and only began to return to the chapel after the commissioners' arrival and their apparent encouragement of the people to do so. In fact, a small revival took place among the people, several of them holding prayer meetings in their houses twice to thrice weekly.[109]

Schooling

Issues relating to schooling were among the matters marked by much disagreement between the missionary and the superintendent. It will be recalled that as a result of their conflicts Walker opened his own school in October 1820, gradually removing all the children from the mission school. By October 1823 Walker's school had enrolled twenty-six males and twenty-eight females.[110] The superintendent entrusted the task of instructing the children primarily to Mrs Stanley, a coloured woman who was once a slave and who, in the commissioners' opinion, from "her very limited education" was not at all qualified for such a post.[111] She doubled as the chief instructor in the workroom, and tripled as Walker's housekeeper. Walker declared that she was a full-time member of the *winkel* staff and only worked as his housekeeper during her free time. Her official work hours in the *winkel* department were ten hours daily (6–11 a.m. and 1–6 p.m.) on weekdays.[112] It is difficult to see how she could have fulfilled this obligation, performed her duties as the superintendent's chief housekeeper and found time for her own family. Clearly, she short-changed the department and relied heavily on the superintendent's two daughters, who at first taught in the school two and a half hours daily and later three times a week, and on Hendrick II the tailor.[113]

Walker periodically removed the children from the school and workroom to hire them out,[114] a policy contrary to the best principles of amelioration which the Treasury expected him to implement. Child labour was still prevalent in Britain at this time,[115] and more widespread in the slave colonies. Therefore, the superintendent might have felt justified in employing the children in this way. However, he must have known of the humanitarian opposition to child labour in the slave colonies, which in the view of the humanitarians was an important reason for the high infant mortality that prevailed. The rationale for hiring out child labour in the department is difficult to explain, since large numbers of effective adults were unemployed at the time (see chapter 4). Here again Walker was simply conforming to plantocratic practice, not willing to institute any major social reforms in this area.

While for a long time to come black colonial education would be criticized for its mediocrity and rote learning, especially at the primary level, the situation in the *winkel* school was, if anything, worse. A maximum of two hours' education daily in most instances could hardly have given the children any firm grasp of the basic principles of literacy. Mrs Stanley testified that "the children have the capacity to learn, but they cannot learn much because they are in school only from 11 to 1", while Walker confessed that the boys' education, in particular, suffered badly because of the lack of a schoolmaster. Mrs Stanley herself was often away in the workroom or in the superintendent's house, which were all in the same building. One pupil, Moses III (aged eleven), averred that Mrs Stanley could be found periodically in the superintendent's house making cakes for his family during school hours. This lad expressed a clear preference for the mission school.[116] The parents were also quite aware that the superintendent was short-changing their children in their education and that it would be more beneficial for them to return to the educational fold of the missionary, where they had been better instructed. Tom, one parent, opined that "the children were learning so well with Parson Wray, and Mr Walker came and took them away". Daniel, another parent, explained that in the *winkel* school the children were only taught to repeat things by heart, while in the mission school they were taught "by the book".[117] This suggests strongly that reading found little place the *winkel* school's curriculum, as distinct from the mission school where it constituted the principal method of instruction. On the whole, the commissioners were firmly convinced that the missionary school was superior to the departmental one.[118]

There were a few instances of "properly" educated children. Louisa II (aged eleven) was one such example. The commissioners summarized her attainment in this way: "Reads in the testament very well – taught by Mr Wray. Repeats the Lords prayer & Church Catechism very well – learned them at Mr Walkers – very perfect in her instruction." They gave an only slightly less commendable citation of the skills of Christina II (aged eleven). A few children benefited from instruction under private tutors, usually paid for by their free fathers or, as in the case of Harriet (aged almost five years), by some other benefactor. She attended a private school held by Mrs McIntosh, her godmother, and was showing good progress at the time of her examination by the commissioners.[119] The commissioners were firmly convinced that while a few of the children were afflicted by hebetude the vast majority of them were intelligent, and some even gifted, individuals, as a few of their observations will indicate:

Moses III (aged 11), "a very smart intelligent boy".
Mary Gordon (aged 13), "dumb looking girl".
Lavinia (aged 13), "a very intelligent decent girl".
Frederica (aged 10), "a smart intelligent girl – well instructed".
Nathaniel (aged 9), "a remarkably smart, intelligent boy".
Derrick (aged 7), "appears rather dull".
John Scott (aged almost 6), "a very smart intelligent boy".
Thomas Ferrell (aged 9 years 6 months), "not much instructed. Very backward for his age".
Jemima (aged 9), "a smart clever girl".
Lucretia II (aged 8), "a smart intelligent girl".[120]

The positive examples can be multiplied easily. Unfortunately, these young minds were likely to be soon polluted by the effects of slavery, the more so since Walker was increasingly disposed to pander to the prejudices of the planter class. This was clear from his view of writing: "Writing is a branch of instruction I do not think necessary in this school." Wray was slightly bolder, only teaching slaves to write with the consent of their masters.[121]

The commissioners concluded that, on the whole, the educational and religious efforts had yielded little positive result. The commissioners of colonial audit had said much the same thing earlier: "We do not think . . . the general tenour of his [Walker's] letters bespeak much religious or intellectual improvement in the Negroes." Walker agreed: "I must state with regret, that owing to the most peculiar adversities which perhaps ever surrounded any undertaking, my summary must be a catalogue of evils, rather than a report of success."[122]

Conclusion

The interviews of the *winkel* people by the commissioners showed a population comprising intelligent, sentient persons, with hopes, fears and aspirations common to humanity. They volunteered information and made suggestions on a number of issues relating to the department. Some of their views ran counter to those of the administration on matters such as the work regime, schooling and discipline. They showed a concern not only with elemental matters of daily existence such as food, clothing and accommodation, but with creating better economic and social opportunities for themselves and their children. They found the slave system galling and Walker's administration deficient in many ways. The interviews bring out more forcefully than any other event or circumstance the fact that the *winkel* slaves were people and not simply things to be treated whimsically and discarded when no longer wanted. Slaves could and often did exercise their minds rationally; in fact, although in many instances their bodies were mangled, their minds remained quite alert. The commissioners recorded a few instances in which some of the slaves appeared quite dull, and many more instances in which others showed sound intelligence.[123]

At times Walker tried to wrap his actions in the protection of the colonial law, but the naked truth was revealed by the probing of the commissioners. He was not an innovator and did nothing to challenge the *status quo*. He largely destroyed the small gains which had been made during the regime of the commissioners for management. During his second tenure of office he sought increasingly to insinuate himself into the favour of the slave-owning fraternity. His ostracism by the various governors and some other colonial officials had nothing to do with any attempts at amelioration, but rather with his crude elimination of Scott from the office of assistant agent.

Walker blamed many of the economic and social ills affecting the department on the people's residence in the town. Town life was for him the root of all *winkel* evil. However, it allowed slaves to mix and form relationships more easily with free people of all colours. It also allowed greater opportunities of social mobility for themselves and their children. The distinctions between the different racial or ethnic groups became less sharp than on the plantations. Urban life in Berbice, as elsewhere in the Americas, weakened the social control of the masters over the slaves and offered slaves a measure of liberty which they could not enjoy on the plantations. Walker appeared unable to come to terms with this reality. He failed to realize that the basic problem was not the proximity of the village to town but the condition of slavery itself, which tended to have serious psychological effects on the enslaved, including low self-esteem and drunkenness. The attitudes and actions of the people were, in essence, cries for social justice which went unanswered on the plantation and in the village, and this forced them into resistance.

7

Oppression and Resistance, 1816–1825

Introduction

Caribbean slave society was oppressive and struggled with major problems of discipline. Slave masters often did not understand, or pretended not to understand, that no matter how light the physical bonds of slavery, the vast majority of enslaved persons wanted their freedom. The slaves therefore engaged in a wide range of resistant behaviours, including feigned sickness, go-slow, suicide, desertion and armed uprising. As Hilary Beckles has pointed out, "the perception of the need to resist . . . was uniform among all socially aware classes".¹ Some of the forms and patterns of resistance might also be viewed as mechanisms of survival, such as stealing, taking in work through the back door, engaging in forbidden rituals (which often acted as a vent for frustrated aggression) and desertion. What Beckles says about female resisters in Barbados is equally true of slaves everywhere in the Caribbean: "The assertion of their human needs above and beyond the interest of their owners was a central part of their search for self-definition and determination that constituted the basis of all their acts of resistance."² In this chapter we shall focus attention on the most significant acts of resistance by the *winkel* people, at the same time elaborating on those mechanisms of oppression mentioned in passing in the last three chapters.

It is quite common to find in any substantial group of people those who fail to comply with regulations, no matter how reasonable and necessary they are for the good of the community. Every society also has its "characters", humorous or serious, comic or tragic, and such persons were certainly present among the *winkel* people. There was Sim, the wife-beater; Hendrick II, the decrepit; Charles, the "deranged"; Betsy the "imbecile"; Thomas and Michael, the deserters; and so on.³ It is often difficult to determine whether the apparent idleness, laziness or other negative feature displayed by a slave was due to some inherent flaw in character or was simply a response to the drudgery and brutality of the slave system. But the actions and attitudes of the people had much to do with the lack of concern of the administrators for their welfare.

Walker veered very far from the system of rewards and punishments which he had advocated in 1818 in his *Letters on the West Indies*. In that work he had insisted that cruelty should be ruled out in matters of discipline: "As to cruelty, it is utterly excluded from all enlightened jurisprudence." He had also declared that Africans, no less than Europeans, were fully conscious of what constituted "just and reasonable sentence", and that "this fact is proverbial, even on every plantation". He had proposed that masters and managers should lend a patient ear to all of the slaves' complaints, and had enjoined white masters to accept that "the people in our hands are really persons of the same nature, passions, and feelings, in every respect as ourselves".⁴ These sentiments, if translated into practice, would have earned him a place among the most progressive slave owners and managers. However, his actual system of management (if it can be called a system) fell far short of these ideals. At the same time, he often played down the incidence of dissatisfaction and defiance within the department and gave the impression that all was well, until the lieutenant governor and the commissioners exposed him.

Rewards

Modern industrial practice places great emphasis on conferring recognition and rewards on deserving persons as a method of building individual and group morale, and increasing productivity. While not nearly to the same extent as today, a number of planters by the early nineteenth century had begun to recognize the importance of rewards, as part of the wider policy of amelioration. The commissioners for management had sought to make this a cardinal aspect of their administration, and punishment only a last resort.

While they had not achieved much success in this regard, it was still the policy that Walker was expected to follow. He himself had suggested that it was necessary to establish a "judicious system of *rewards*", since they were "a most powerful instrument of management".[5] Unfortunately, he paid very little attention to this matter and could hardly give a positive response when the commissioners of inquiry sought to find out his system of rewards.

All that he could answer on this score was that "a present of tobacco is given for good working, as this article, on the principle of economy is not made a regular allowance. Extra pieces of clothing of a better sort are sometimes given in the same manner, for comfort however, rather than finery, which I wish to discourage". He gave the women a "plain dress" as reward for "cleanliness, decent appearance and attendance on religious instruction".[6] He also claimed that he had recently (in 1825) instituted a system of offering a new house and a little furniture to newly married couples (that is, married according to the civil laws of the colony). But the only instances of such marriage had occurred three years before he instituted this system. He also alleged that he had offered to grant the young lady Juliana her freedom "by subscription" – by her purchasing it by degrees – if she should stay away from men and "listen only to offers of marriage", but that she did not comply.[7] In 1818 he had recommended that owners and managers should "promote virtuous connections by giving every young couple a present to set up house with".[8] But again there was a divorce between his principles and his practice.

By the 1820s it was quite common in all Caribbean jurisdictions to give monetary and other rewards and incentives to women to produce children and keep them alive for a certain period. The most liberal slave owners also exempted those with six or more living children from field work and only gave them light work.[9] The 1826 Berbice slave code required slave owners to give such rewards, with penal sanctions for breach of the law.[10] Even before the promulgation of the code mothers had begun to expect and sometimes demand such payment, although this should not be taken to mean that they were producing children for profit.[11]

Walker did give some monetary rewards to mothers within the department for new births, but the evidence concerning the consistency of this practice is ambiguous. The list of expenditures compiled by the commissioners mentions Susannah receiving f3 in 1815 for her child, possibly a reference to payment for a newborn baby. It also records two instances in 1816 of two mothers and their midwives being paid f18 (a total of f36), which if divided equally would amount to f6 to each of the parties.[12] How common such rewards were remains uncertain. The fact that Walker did not mention them in his testimony before the commissioners strongly suggests that they were given out in a very desultory fashion. This is corroborated by the rare mention of such rewards in the financial records and the absence of them from the day books, which record fairly regularly the birth of new infants. On the other hand, the testimony of Matilda (aged sixteen) before the commissioners implied that it was usual for Walker to give f6 in such circumstances. His selective approach to such rewards is indicated by two negative examples which have come to light. For some time he refused to give any money to Matilda, with whom he had developed strained relations, and eventually gave her only f1 seven months after the birth of her child. He also kept Christina I (aged forty-seven), the mother of six children, forcibly in his domestic employment, although he alleged that she was not required to work in order to earn her keep.[13]

Walker could give no cogent reason why he had never started a system of rewards among the men, declaring that they made enough money in their spare time to supply all their wants and this made it difficult to find any relatively inexpensive object which they would treasure as a reward.[14] Aside from his questionable ideas regarding the men's earning power, he seems to have been unaware that the social significance of a gift goes beyond its material value, or to have felt that the *winkel* people were not sufficiently refined to appreciate such significance. Nevertheless, it will be recalled that the department distributed red shirts periodically, which might have functioned as rewards. These half-hearted initiatives constituted the sum of Walker's "system" of rewards, a travesty of the policy outlined by the commissioners for management.

Disciplinary Policy

Walker's failure to develop a meaningful system of rewards meant that the administration would continue to enforce its policies with coercion. As already noted, he behaved no differently from other slave owners and managers in the colony; but this, in itself, is an indictment of his administration.

He was expected to conduct the management of the *winkel* people at the highest level, not the lowest common denominator. Walker – not unlike many slave managers – comes across as a cold, harsh spirit who sought to rule the people with an iron fist and whom the people resisted to the best of their ability. Terror was his favourite mode of punishment and main deterrent to acts of delinquency. From 1818 he signalled a clear preference for solitary confinement, one of the few matters on which he remained consistent over the years. His ideal in this respect was "a strong brick building", with thick walls to prevent communication among the inmates. This building should be "a place of dark confinement", comprising "dark cells". He spoke in apparent animation before the commissioners of inquiry of "the salutary influence of solitary and dark confinement above simple confinement in the stocks", as a means of creating fear in the hearts and minds of the people.[15]

Walker boasted of being the first person to introduce this form of punishment into the colony, in 1815, on one of the Crown estates. During his second period of administration he also introduced it among the *winkel* people, but temporarily abandoned it in 1824 when Lauw hung himself from the wooden rafters of his cell. He commenced the building of two new brick cells in March 1825, made urgent, in his view, by increasing idleness in the department since the commissioners' arrival. He anticipated that these new cells would to be "a powerful engine of punishment which would quicken the diligence & good conduct of the people in their work". He saw them as "an absolute necessity" for the women, whom he found difficult to control.[16]

While the commissioners for management had suggested that in extreme situations "confinement during the intervals of labour" might be used, they certainly did not envisage placing the people for lengthy periods in stocks or in the dark cells which the superintendent was about to erect. The cells bring to mind the dreaded French isolation cells of the *Réclusion* of Saint-Joseph, sister to Devil's island, just off the coast of the French Guiana mainland in the mid-1930s.[17] The dread with which slaves in Berbice viewed solitary confinement might be gleaned from the statement of the slave Woensdag of plantation Nieuw Stoop: "he is convinced that his master will flog him to death, or kill him by solitary confinement". Walker endorsed this view, declaring, "Many negroes would rather endure a flogging than such a confinement."[18]

While Walker resorted to solitary confinement in particular circumstances, he claimed that whipping was the chief mode of punishment used for the males, and stocks for the females. Confinement in stocks has received only passing notice in most works on the punishment of slaves, and writers seem generally to believe that this was a less inhumane form of punishment than whipping. However, long confinement in stocks could be as cruel, and sometimes more so, than whipping. Slaves confined in stocks for long periods usually suffered cramps and restrictions in the use of their limbs, and were sometimes permanently maimed, especially if the punishment was repeated over a period of months. Even confinement for a couple of weeks could have a damaging effect on the slave's health. August, for instance, of plantation Nieuw Stoop, testified that he begged his master to flog him instead of confining him in the stocks: "[he] knows that this confinement in the stocks is worse than any flogging, because, when locked up, they are not allowed to be unlocked to go to ease themselves, but [are] in such close confinement that they can scarcely walk when released".[19] Woensdag, referred to earlier, declared that after being confined in the stocks for a long time he was "severely attacked by the scurvy, and although he begged hard to be allowed to go and wash himself, was refused; he grew ill so that his master was afraid of losing him, and therefore released him . . . he was not allowed to go and ease himself, but lived in such a manner that it was impossible for any person to come near him".[20] The filth and stench in which management kept such slaves constituted an integral part of the degradation associated with the punishment.

There were several methods of confinement in stocks: one foot, both feet, all the limbs, head and limbs, in sitting, standing or lying positions, and (in particularly cruel cases) suspending the victims by the arms and legs (see chapter 1). Although the *winkel* documents do not indicate the precise methods that Walker employed or the impact of stocks on those being punished, it is difficult to believe that he showed greater humanity on this score than the average Berbice planter, especially in light of the cases of Cornelia III and Nancy, two of the persons whom he confined in stocks for extended periods (see below).

As regards whipping, Walker asserted that he disliked using it as a correctional tool, and that "if coercion and stripes had been my perpetual modes of management, I must have been the greatest flogger in Berbice". Dummett and McWatt, successive managers in the department, both concurred that Walker did not commonly resort to whipping, the latter criticizing his authority over the people as being "very deficient" and too restrained, thus leading to idleness and insubordination. McWatt, while much more approachable than Walker, believed in the salutary effects of the rod of correction,[21] the use of which became almost a reflex action in the hands of cruel drivers and masters. Walker alleged that the colonists knew of his own "notorious opposition to female flogging" and that there was only one instance of his having done so during his seven years as superintendent. However, elsewhere he confessed that once or twice he also gave females a few stripes over at least one garment on the shoulders, chiefly as a form of disgrace.[22] He himself might not have resorted to whipping on any appreciable scale, but some of his subordinates seem to have done so, although the perfunctory way in which the department kept the records makes it difficult to establish this point. The department failed to conform to the colonial law that a record of all punishments was to be made in the punishment book on the same day on which the event took place, including the alleged offence and the number of lashes.[23] The department entered details of punishment in the day books several days after the event, while it kept no record whatsoever of the most serious punishment of females by the superintendent.[24] The day books contain only two instances of the whipping of females, one apparently under Walker's authority and the other clearly on the orders of Dummett. Again, Walker violated his own precept that a record should be kept of "all crimes and punishments".[25]

The whipping of males extended, in the superintendent's own words, "according to the degree of the crime, from 6 lashes to the utmost amount of the law 39". Walker also alleged that he never permitted the manager to inflict the maximum number and that he could only recollect one occasion on which he ever inflicted that number. He estimated his average punishment as being ten to fifteen strokes.[26] The day books show that management administered thirty-nine lashes on at least two occasions (in 1821 and 1825).[27] They also record thirty-nine incidents of whipping of males, averaging just over sixteen lashes per person, slightly higher than the superintendent's upper limit of fifteen. This was not an excessive number of lashes by the standards of the time.

Fewer records exist of punishments on Berenstein, mainly comprising those complaints lodged before the commissioners of inquiry some years after the events, but we have already referred to the severity of the managers there and will deal with this matter more fully. Judicial punishments also need to be taken into account to get a true picture of the disciplinary record relating to the *winkel* people. In all, seventeen cases of judicial punishment appear in the day books, which fail to mention the celebrated case of the African ritualist Hans (see chapter 6). Of these cases, six entailed whipping alone; four, whipping and being placed in the chain gang; three, being placed in the chain gang alone; and four, being placed in the stocks.[28] The *winkel* people mentioned eighteen cases of arbitrary and unjust punishments (banishment, whipping, confinement and so on) to the commissioners of inquiry.[29]

A most disturbing feature of the whipping which took place in the *winkel* village is that it was commonly carried out at the hospital,[30] which was imprudent, since the sound of the lashes, the cries and the animated voices of the onlookers would have upset a number of the patients. Again, this injudicious way of dealing with discipline in the department proves that Walker was a less than sensitive and caring administrator. His hypocrisy is exposed by the fact that in 1818 he had criticized those who placed stocks in the hospital: "What alliance is there between sickness and crime? None but what a wise proprietor will rather destroy than promote."[31]

Capricious and Unjust Punishments

The *winkel* people felt that in a number of instances management had punished them capriciously and wrongfully. This, in itself, cannot indict the staff, since few persons consider their chastisement just in terms of either the alleged offence or the scale of the punishment. However, there were several instances in which the impartial observer would have been more persuaded by the viewpoint of the *winkel* people than the staff, as the examples below suggest. Matilda's punishment was one such instance. Between thirteen and sixteen years old at the time of the incident, she was one of the females who presented special management problems for the department. But the manner in which Mrs Stanley (to whom Walker had given permission to whip the girls in the workroom) attempted to discipline her for poor work caused her to retaliate in kind. In Stanley's words, "One day I slapped Matilda. . . ; she returned me slap for slap, and tried to turn up my clothes to lick me." Matilda's story, however, was quite different. According to her, the schoolmistress wanted her to kneel down and do a piece of work in the workroom but she was unable to do so because of a boil on her knee. As a result the schoolmistress beat her with a table foot and she returned the blow, for which action Walker punished her with a leather strap.[32]

Even at a young age Matilda was attempting to assert her rights as a human being. It should have been clear to the superintendent that Mrs Stanley had acted unwisely in slapping her, causing her to lose respect for the schoolmistress. Moreover, the superintendent should have realized that Mrs Stanley would encounter great difficulty in punishing the young ladies. She had once been a slave, which caused the people in the department to view her as being essentially no better than they, so that it was virtually impossible for her to become an authority figure in the department. She asserted that whenever she attempted to whip the young ladies they always resisted, telling her that they were as free as she.[33]

Matilda's case indicates one young girl's contempt for both the individual carrying out the punishment and the manner in which it was executed. But there were several other instances of capricious or unjust punishments. On one occasion Walker, suspecting that the people were harbouring two of their own who had absconded, retaliated by cutting off their supplies of salted fish until they should disclose the whereabouts of the fugitives. The records do not indicate how long this punishment lasted, but the two individuals were apprehended three weeks later on a private plantation. On another occasion he gave six individuals six lashes each for failing to turn up to witness one of their colleagues being whipped by the fiscal in the public marketplace for attacking the *winkel* manager.[34] This was the kind of tyranny to which the superintendent could descend in his exercise of power. These incidents suggest a certain measure of callousness or, at the very least, of naïveté in dealing with the disciplinary problems in the department.

Tyranny at Berenstein

One of the major points of conflict between the superintendent and the people was his assignment or banishment of them to Berenstein. He knew how profoundly they hated the place, and so he used it as a kind of penal plantation. The managers at Berenstein subjected the people to brutal punishments. As already noted, few records of actual punishments on Berenstein have survived, but this distant plantation gained notoriety for its severe managers, from whose presence the people sought to flee.

Finch, the first manager whom Walker appointed, proved completely unfit for the job. He did not exercise the care and control over the department which would have produced confidence in his administration. Susetta (alias Rosetta) complained to the fiscal in 1819 that Finch allowed the driver Zealand to mistreat the people, including herself. Zealand, she alleged, was always beating and cursing her, and had cut her once with a cutlass on her arm, where the mark was still visible. He had also hit her with a cutlass on her teeth. She further declared that Finch exercised little authority on the estate, leaving Zealand to do as he pleased. The last act of whipping, which occurred after those described above, caused her to desert the estate, remaining some days in the bush and eventually arriving at the hospital in town, where she miscarried. There was conflicting evidence on this matter. Dr Beresford, who examined Susetta very minutely a few days after the alleged miscarriage, found no evidence of such a circumstance and reported her fit for work. However, Elias, the "black doctor", testified that she had shown him a pot half-full of blood and water, "a thick substance". Mucalla and Mandarina likewise testified that they had seen the "substance", while the former added that Susetta's clothes had also had blood on them. Neither had seen the actual miscarriage and only Mucalla had been told about it.

Zealand claimed that Susetta had been disobedient and insolent to him and so he took "a thin piece of bush-rope, telling her not to be insolent, and licking her at the same time with this said instrument of correction on her mouth, stating, that as her mouth was so bad the same only deserved to be punished". Two witnesses testifying on behalf of Zealand supported his allegation that he had used a bush-rope (*carracarra*) to punish the slave woman, but both added the detail that the whipping drew blood from her mouth. Scott placed her in the stocks in town for about a week. On review of all the evidence, the fiscal simply reprimanded Susetta for her actions.[35] There can be little doubt that Susetta suffered a major trauma which drew blood, and she might well have miscarried. Beresford's failure to find evidence of such trauma cannot be taken as conclusive evidence that she was lying, for his and his brother's failure to find evidence of whipping was arguably a contributory cause of Cubinda's death (see below).

William Gattarel, the next manager (21 February to 5 April 1820), whom Walker recruited under the name William Richards and of whom he knew nothing at the time of recruitment, turned out to be a disreputable character. Later Walker alleged that Richards had lived as a planter in Demerara and Suriname for twenty-three years, and that he had recruited the man on a trial basis, because of the desperate need to place a white person on the estate or risk a fine for failing to conform to the colony's deficiency laws. He also asserted that the colonial authorities had permitted Richards to reside in the colony and that the individual had shown him character letters (from persons whom Walker did not know). The truth is that this man had been flogged twice under the gallows in Demerara and branded for robbery and piracy. He had subsequently migrated to Suriname before arriving in Berbice. Although Scott had notified Walker that he was harbouring a dangerous criminal, so deep was the hatred between the two men that the superintendent did not investigate the allegation. Shortly after, Cubinda, one of the people at Berenstein, died as a result of a whipping which he received on the orders of the manager. The story of this man's death offers a good example both of the cruelty of the manager and of the failure of Walker and other departmental personnel to take the people's complaints seriously, tending to view them instead as excuses for indolence.

Richards sent Cubinda, a boat builder, to town on the basis that he was unwell. According to Walker, he "had always been somewhat decrepit & weakly" and seemed "apparently rheumatic". However, Cubinda complained of pain in his right shoulder, extending down his ribs, and told the superintendent that his malady stemmed from a whipping with a stick by the manager, a complaint which neither the superintendent nor the two doctors who inspected him considered to be truthful. Cubinda suddenly took a turn for the worse and died within a few days; an autopsy revealed that he had suffered internal injuries consistent with a whipping. However, Richards was acquitted for lack of eyewitnesses. He later became the public hangman in Berbice.[36]

In the same month that he dismissed Gattarel, Walker recruited Deussen, whom he called an "extremely well recommended" and "industrious and intelligent" individual. However, with his appointment a new oppression replaced the old one. Deussen's relations with the people were, in the main, very poor, and under his administration production and social relations deteriorated more rapidly, forcing the superintendent to hire labour for six months. Among his negative attributes, Deussen was prone to flogging.

Paul II, a young man, testified that while at Berenstein the manager gave him thirty-nine lashes, which caused him to complain to Walker, but the latter sent him back to the manager, who gave him another twenty-five strokes. Deussen had given him between nine and ten lashes on other occasions.[37] Many others had similar tales to tell, including Primo III, Bernard, Lauw, Hercules, Ferdinand, Susannah II, Betsey I, and Leah I. Lauw, who could not tolerate the harsh discipline or understand why he had been posted to Berenstein in the first place (he was a cooper), deserted before the burgher officers had investigated his complaint. When apprehended and returned to Berenstein he was punished and, along with Primo II, Primo III, Susetta and Susannah, deserted again.[38]

There was also the case of Madelintje, a mulatto seamstress, just twenty-four years old at the time of her testimony before the commissioners. She had lived a chequered life and had been severely traumatized by her experiences. She first came to notice as a runaway at roughly the age of nineteen – an escapee from the stocks who was subsequently apprehended. In June 1821 she brought a complaint against Deussen, charging him with giving the people, including herself, heavy tasks to perform, and with hiring her out to Calmer to pick corn where she was kept past the expected time of her return, for which the manager had whipped her. She added an important detail concerning Deussen: "The manager is in the habit of taking the whip out of the driver's hand, and flogging us himself; his strokes are at random, and often very injurious, cutting away with the whip in all directions." Deussen refuted her testimony by declaring that he had put her to do light work and had assigned Helmaker, the best worker, to assist her. She had harvested less corn on Calmer's estate than a normal quota, he said, and she should have been back home earlier. He further alleged that he had never flogged her.[39] The records are silent on the fiscal's response to Madelintje's complaint but she was clearly dissatisfied with his judgment, for she was soon off again. Later she was picked up, or gave herself up, and was given a conditional pardon, subject to placing herself under the jurisdiction of Amelia, her mother. The latter, herself a *winkel* woman attached to

Government House as a laundress, had to hire her own daughter for an unspecified period at f33 per month.[40] Madelintje had further battles with the department, to which the schedules of testimony compiled by the commissioners make oblique reference. She alleged that she had once been hired out to a Mrs Drumgoole, who sent her for a month to plantation Prospect to huckster, but that after she had been there for three weeks the superintendent sent for her and placed her in the stocks for four weeks. Vital details are missing in her narrative, but we know that she was confined in the stocks. She clearly linked the beginning of her sorrows to some mishap or misunderstanding about her work.

The commissioners were convinced that in Madelintje's case distress had followed hard upon distress, and seemed inclined to be sympathetic towards her. This is what they had to say:

> From the girl's account it would appear that she has been for many years persecuted & punished by Mr. Walker. The instances she has mentioned are too numerous to be all inserted. The punishment consisted chiefly of frequent vexatious confinement in the stocks. She was frequently sent to the distant estate Berensteyn & once sent there chained or tied to the man Thomas. Was worked in the field (a thing unknown among women of her colour). The reason for this treatment appear[s] to have been with a view of compelling her to break the connexions she had formed with white men.[41]

The commissioners also noted her testimony that the superintendent once sent her in 1821 to be punished by the fiscal in the marketplace, but that this officer had considered the offence too slight to merit such punishment and had let her off on her begging forgiveness, a detail which they were able to verify through departmental records. Walker declared her to be unmanageable and insubordinate, and saw her complaint as a cheap cry for attention. However, Madelintje, distraught with her treatment and speaking with great bitterness, expressed a strong desire to be sold to anyone who would purchase her, since she did not want to remain any longer under Walker.[42] Madelintje's story was a sad and even tragic one, revealing damage done to body, soul and spirit. While unique in its details, it was not uncommon.

The superintendent was reluctant to part with Deussen because he believed that the people needed to be governed with a strong hand, he viewed their resistance as a test of will between himself and them, and he wanted to avoid the problem of finding a new manager. Eventually he had to dismiss Deussen, but only after his reign of terror had lasted for almost two years.[43] His replacement in the person of McConchie showed that, in Walker's case, thrice bitten was not enough, for this individual, exercising power without principle, took excessive liberties with the young women on the estate.

Julia, Betsey I and Mandarina testified that McConchie frequently coerced the young women to bathe in the creek with, or in the presence of, the young white boys from neighbouring plantations whom he allowed to visit Berenstein regularly.[44] He also beat one of the females severely for refusing to gratify his sexual lust. Julia, the daughter of Lauw and described as a "half cobb" and "nearly black", was about fifteen years old at the time and still classified in the records as a child when she rebuffed the manager's sexual overtures. The following day, a Sunday, which was a free day, she committed what would normally have been regarded as a minor offence by going to a neighbouring estate without a pass to obtain a "hoe stick", and this gave the manager an opportunity to vent his anger. He punished her transgression by having her whipped with a "supple jack" on her naked bottom "until her bowels were affected" and she could not get up. The most frightening aspect was the manner in which he punished her: by employing the "Spanish whip"[45] which Nepveu describes thus:

> the hands tied together, the knees drawn up between them, and a stick inserted through the opening between the knees and the hands and fixed firmly in the ground, around which they then lie like a hoop and are struck on the buttocks with a guava or tamarind rod; one side having been struck until the skin is completely broken they are turned over to have the other side similarly injured; some use hoopsticks for this, although this is an extremely dangerous practice, as it generally results in the slaves' death, even though the chastisement is less than with the abovementioned rods.[46]

Julia's mother, Flooda, reported the matter to Walker, who had Julia sent to town but sent her back to Berenstein within a few weeks without taking any further action. It was such abuses which helped to trigger recalcitrant behaviour by the people. The irony of the situation is that a few months earlier, Walker had spoken of his appointment of McConchie as though he had finally found the panacea for the ills affecting Berenstein: "I have placed a new manager on the plantation – the people are contented and healthy."[47]

The punishment of females for refusing sexual favours to the management was fairly common in Caribbean slave society. John Stedman cites the case of a young woman in Suriname whose manager gave her over two hundred lashes for rebuffing his advances. Wray also pointed out that several slaves in Berbice were coerced and sometimes whipped into conferring such favours on those with power over them.[48]

Walker claimed that he did not usually use Berenstein as a place of punishment but that "sometimes to detach a single young woman from her relations in town, and send her to that place 20 miles off, was used as a punishment". He also stated that "the punishment parties were sent singly and passes were refused". However, he contradicted himself by asserting that he "took much pains to explain to the people that Berenstein was no place of punishment".[49] Dummett confirmed that the superintendent banished several young women to the oblivion of the estate for "loose behaviour about town".[50] Walker's motives in doing so were defeated both by the women's stubborn resistance and by the lust of McConchie and his white friends, which often exposed the women to greater moral and physical harm.

Neither physical disability nor tender age offered any guarantee that an individual would be spared banishment to Berenstein. Hendrick II, "a decrepit Negro", was sent up in July 1824 for six months. Two more disturbing cases were those of Matilda and Maria III. In the case of the former, a child of thirteen or fourteen years old at the time, the superintendent explicitly stated that she was sent up because of an immoral situation ("a gross connection") in which she was involved. Maria III, only eleven years old, was probably also sent up for the same reason, although Walker later testified that she was a good girl and that he knew nothing bad about her.[51] Clearly, banishment was not the solution to this problem, but rather counselling and maternal care, which might have been given by the superintendent's wife, the schoolmistress or an elderly female inside or outside the department. Matilda's banishment, along with her confrontation with the schoolmistress (mentioned earlier) and other events, left an indelibly negative impression on her mind, causing her to tell the commissioners that she believed that the superintendent hated her.[52]

The General Problem of Desertion

Desertion, although occurring most commonly among those at Berenstein, was a problem which affected the department generally. It was the most frequently recorded expression of dissent. Few, if any, of the deserters attempted to strike a permanent blow for freedom, that is, to carve out a life of their own away from the department. One pattern of desertion, sometimes listed in the *winkel* day books as absence without permission, suggests that several of them did not really intend to abscond but simply to visit friends or relatives on other estates. Some of them were picked up and returned to the department, while others returned voluntarily. The day books record thirty incidents of desertion by males and five by females between 14 December 1820 and 15 September 1825,[53] but, given what we have said about record keeping in the department, this was probably not an accurate measure.

The fact that none of the *winkel* people became a long-term deserter[54] has multiple explanations. No African-born slaves had been introduced into the department since 1796, so that the vast majority of the young and robust, who would have been most likely to desert, would have been creoles. These had been socialized in the system of slavery and were therefore less likely than African-born slaves to desert. The deserters went in ones and twos, rather than in large groups, and this did not augur well for long-term survival in the Guyana jungles. But it is also possible that while the people found the *winkel* administration irksome and sometimes disgusting, they viewed the alternatives available to them as less viable. Whatever the reasons, desertion never posed a threat to the integrity of the department, seven persons being the largest number listed as deserters at any one time.[55] Indeed, desertion in Berbice was never as large-scale as in Demerara-Essequibo, where by the late eighteenth century it had become a chronic problem.[56]

So far we have discussed resistance in general terms, illustrating it by reference to a number of persons. However, some individuals stood out because of either their central role in resistance or the nature of their resistance, which served to throw into greater relief both the system of oppression and the people's reaction to it. Among these persons were Thomas and Michael, the two best-known deserters. Thomas, a creole blacksmith, was the brother-in-law of the "negro doctor" Lambert whose unhappy relations with management we shall discuss below. Thomas's life as a deserter began in

1819 at age twenty-five. He was dissatisfied with Scott's decision to hire him, along with others, on a long-term basis to Thomas Keen. Under the new administration that relocated the smithery some distance out of town, artisans possessed less opportunity than before for self-hire and so Thomas took matters into his own hands by absconding and shoeing horses for several persons surreptitiously. After about eight days he returned secretly to Keen's place, for some unknown reason, and was betrayed by two other slaves. Keen attempted to get him to return to the fold but he refused, threatening to drown himself in the river if anyone attempted to apprehend him. Pursued by Keen and some others, he actually made several attempts to make good his threat, staying under water for long periods, to Keen's utter dismay. However, Thomas had chosen a hard way to kill himself, if he really intended to do so. Exhaustion finally ended his brief dalliance with death. He was apprehended and taken to the fiscal, who sentenced him to a whipping at Keen's shop.[57]

In November 1820 Thomas received another whipping at the *winkel* hospital for an unspecified offence. The superintendent subsequently sent him to Berenstein where he came into conflict with Deussen and was placed in chains, from which he broke loose. Captured shortly after, he was bound once again and dispatched to Berenstein, but managed to break out of the chains *en route* and to abscond. When he was picked up a few weeks later on plantation De Kinderen and delivered to the public jail in town, the judicial authorities sentenced him to the chain gang for about three months. Upon his release, Walker dispatched him once again to Berenstein but he was not there long before he resumed his habit of desertion. Out on his own for several weeks, he decided to give himself up. The superintendent, in a decision which suggested conciliation but not wisdom, decided not to whip him on condition that he spend six months on Berenstein and pay an indemnity of f17:10 for thirty-five bunches of plantains for which he could give no account. Like other artisans, he hated going to the estate and apparently regarded this as punishment rather than forgiveness, as Walker had suggested, for he was off again within a short time. The record of his desertion closes with his recapture within a matter of weeks and his sentencing by the fiscal to fifty lashes and attachment to the colony's chain gang.[58]

Unfortunately, because of the poor way in which the records were kept, we know nothing for certain of how Thomas behaved after this series of incidents. However, it seems that he gradually came to lead a more sedentary life, and the superintendent allowed him to practise his trade once again after the abandonment of Berenstein in 1823 and the reopening of the smith's shop in 1824. Testifying before the commissioners, Thomas stated that at one time he had attended Wray's chapel, but no longer did so because he was too busy. He also declared that he was capable of making f3 per day by working at his trade on Sundays, and f1 in the two-hour lunch break (from 11 a.m. to 1 p.m.) during the week.[59] Walker testified that he was "a very clever smith and farrier, but not steady" and that he did a great deal of work for himself in his off time.[60] He was one of those individuals who saw slavery as a major hindrance to his personal development, and showed his resentment in no uncertain manner.

We have an equally brief but no less colourful picture of the boat builder Michael's life. He was the brother of Dominick (see chapter 4), and of Thomas Harvey who just one year later, at age fifteen, was to join the rank of deserters. The extant record of Michael's life as a deserter begins in July 1821 at age twenty-seven, the day book noting the superintendent's suspicion that the other members of the department had been providing asylum for him and Andries for the past month. These young men, like those mentioned earlier, were driven to desertion by the fiscal's failure to take their complaints against Deussen seriously. They had gone to him a little over a month earlier, complaining of heavy task work and unfair and cruel treatment. Michael was particularly peeved that he had "begged the manager for leave to go and see his mother, but could not gain permission" and that he, in common with the other people at Berenstein, was suffering from shortage of rations.[61] But the fiscal failed once again to respond to the people's concerns.

As a consequence, the young men chose to desert, moving from place to place until they were apprehended in August on plantation Prospect and delivered to the judicial authorities in town. The fiscal sentenced them to fifty-five lashes each at the public marketplace and to the chain gang for three months, but released them after a little over a month's confinement. The superintendent later dispatched them to Berenstein, from where Michael absconded in less than a week, but his freedom was once again abridged, this time within five days. On this occasion the fiscal gave the superintendent permission to work him in chains either on the estate or in town for three months. Gone again at a time not recorded, Michael was apprehended on plantation Smithson's Place, sent to town and given fifteen lashes in the department before being sent back to work.

Michael's career as a deserter was not yet over; six weeks later he deserted again, but this time for only three days before being hospitalized. About two weeks later he was in the public jail, awaiting trial as a deserter and subsequently receiving forty lashes on the fiscal's order. Released once again, he was picked up some months later (in December 1823) on plantation Vryheid, where he had beaten one of the slaves violently, for which he received twenty-four lashes.[62] Strangely, when questioned about him less than two years later, the superintendent responded that "he is generally well behaved". The day book listed him as a member of the Government House staff in January 1825, where he was fed and clothed, until being reassigned to the department when D'Urban, as acting lieutenant governor, cut down on his domestic staff. Management employed Michael, now back in the village, to dig the trench there. From later references to him it seems almost impossible to believe that this was the notorious deserter, but the records are unequivocal on this point.[63] He might well have come to an accommodation with Walker, after the abandonment of Berenstein, which turned his life around.

Suicidal Tendencies

The events of the mid-1820s, to which we shall now direct specific attention, constitute the high point of *winkel* resistance and of turbulence within the department. Documentation on these incidents is also richer than usual. These events, of course, built on those which preceded them and were punctuated by a series of petty acts of oppression, especially the superintendent's attempt in 1823 to abolish the extra day at Whitsuntide, traditionally allowed to the people (see below).

Walker alleged that increased agitation, indolence and insubordination occurred within the department in 1825, mainly due to news filtering through from England about amelioration and rumours that the commissioners had come to set the slaves free. Lieutenant Governor Beard, however, pointed out that the superintendent had given an entirely false impression to his superiors in London that all was quiet on the *winkel* front in

1824, when indeed there was "great insubordination", a fact well known in the colony. The disquiet and sometimes turbulence within the department in 1825 were clearly the residue of the events of 1823 and 1824, which might well have broken out into unprecedented violence had not the commissioners arrived in January 1825. Walker's main response to this turbulence was to build new engines of coercion, increase the incidence of solitary confinement and employ the whip more liberally. The commissioners noticed that the number of punishments had increased significantly since 28 March 1825.[64]

The three cases highlighted in this section were among the most disturbing incidents in the department's history. Sim threatened suicide, Lambert II attempted it, Lauw committed it – acts virtually unknown in the department before this time. The message was clear for those who had ears to hear, but the superintendent preferred to remain deaf. Bastide, among other writers, sees suicide as "an act of war", destroying self while also destroying the master's property.[65] It was often a sudden and spontaneous release of subterranean feelings of aggression, a view borne out in the threatened suicide of Sim and the attempted suicide of Lambert.

In April 1825 the manager accused Sim, a young man of age twenty-two, of leaving the field during working hours without permission and using "mutinous language" to him in the presence of the whole gang, daring the superintendent to punish him "wrongfully" and "threatening to destroy himself" if he were punished. The superintendent regarded Sim as being so suicidal that he took him to the public jail and had his hands tied before and after whipping him. The superintendent afterwards confined him in the stocks for some time. Sim finally submitted to the manager, who promoted him, and later on Sim apologized to that individual, in the commissioners' presence, for his behaviour.[66] While the evidence above seems to indicate that Sim's punishment was due entirely to his own indiscipline and insubordination, there were mitigating circumstances. He alleged that his supply of one and a half bunches of plantains, being too small for him, had run out and that he had gone to work without eating anything. At 2:30 p.m. he had left the field to get some "breakfast" from his mother and was away from his job for half an hour, for which management confined him and afterwards gave him thirty-five (the record says thirty-nine) lashes. This was why he felt that he was being punished wrongfully.[67] Walker attempted to rebut these allegations by stating that Sim complained of lack of food only after he had been disciplined, that he was known to dress in "a superior style", and that he was "one of the most plump stout young men to be seen in any land not only of slaves but of freemen – and always was so".[68] It is difficult to see the relationship between Sim's specific claim that hunger drove him to leave the field on a given day and the superintendent's comments about the way he looked or usually dressed.

But Sim's troubles with the department were not confined to this incident. On a former occasion, April 1821, he had received thirty-one lashes for disobedience, although the nature of the offence is unknown. Listed in 1819 as a domestic and in 1825 as a boat builder, for some unexplained reason he was sent to Berenstein as a field hand, and he was apparently working as such at the time that he ran afoul of the authorities in 1823. While there, manager McConchie gave him fifty lashes for objecting to having his sister Julia (dispatched to Berenstein as a punishment) go into the creek with some young white men. He must also have heard of, if not actually witnessed, the brutal whipping that his sister received on the orders of this same manager. He was one of six men who were whipped in 1824 for absenting themselves from the whipping of one of their colleagues. This was just five days after his father or stepfather Lauw had committed suicide, while the family was still grieving over this tragic loss.[69] Although he was the reputed husband of the *winkel* woman Lucia II, he did not have a house of his own but was forced to live with his mother, Flooda.[70]

Sim was not an exemplary character, for later on (after his imprisonment and punishment in 1825) he was known to ill-treat his reputed wife; he also cut up a piece of cloth belonging to Abraham II, another *winkel* person, for which he was put in the stocks for two days, until he repented and his wife intervened on his behalf. Conflicts with his wife might well have been the reason why they did not live together; Lucia was living in a recently rehabilitated house with her three children, the last of whom was his son.[71] In all, his was a far from happy life. Despite his character flaws, he was perhaps more sinned against than sinning. He had little reason to feel that justice could be expected from the administration, and this might well have explained his defiant reaction to the threat of punishment in 1825.

Given the observations above, it is easy to imagine the panic which must have hit the administration when Sim threatened to commit suicide less than a year after Lauw killed himself, especially as the men were from the same household. It explains why he was locked up and so heavily shackled before and after the punishment, and why efforts were finally made to effect reconciliation with him. His apology to the manager resulted from the direct efforts of that individual to conciliate him. He testified that when he was sick he received no comfort of any kind except a little soup for six days, but that it was "not fit for a dog to eat", so he threw it away. The manager, however, sent him good soup from his table, along with some rice and sugar. This gesture won his heart and changed his attitude to the manager, who went a step further and put him to deputize for Louis, the head boat builder, who was ill at the time.[72] Walker described Sim to the commissioners as "a saucy unmanageable Negro",[73] a characterization which does not accord with his elevation to the post of responsibility. His case shows how little acts of kindness and goodwill could go a long way towards reconciling seemingly inveterate foes. In this instance McWatt succeeded where Walker had failed.

Lambert II's case is more interesting, not only because of his attempt at self-destruction, but because of the antagonism which it bred between the superintendent and the members of this *winkel* man's family. A black man, thirty-one years old at the time of the incident, he is listed in the records as "doctor" and "principal hospital attendant". The commissioners regarded him as one of the most intelligent members of the department, with "apparently the best memory of any [*winkel* person] yet examined". Lieutenant Governor Beard's assessment was that he was "the most valuable and intelligent Negro of the gang".[74] His father, a free man, had taken pains to have him educated at a secular school in town, and he also went to Wray's school. Everything indicated that this was a literate individual, and even Walker had to admit that he was "a clever intelligent Negro", but quickly inserted the enigmatic remark that "his conduct is not answerable to his knowledge", and categorized his father as a "bad character".[75]

Lambert's troubles began in 1820 when he complained several times to the lieutenant governor that his house was so leaky and so bad that he could no longer live in it, as a result of which the lieutenant governor wrote to Walker about the matter. The superintendent, however, resented Lambert's actions and did little or nothing to repair the house, as attested by the fact that in 1825 Lambert was still complaining, this time to the commissioners, about his leaky house.[76] This was a grave discomfort and annoyance, but his

Oppression and Resistance, 1816–1825

life began to become really miserable in 1822 when, according to him, the superintendent gave him a "paper" to work outside the department. This offered him an opportunity to earn money for himself, which he did not have while working in the hospital. He claimed that after working for three days the superintendent placed him in the stocks for two days and then gave him thirty-nine lashes.

No direct confirmation of these allegations exists in the documents consulted, but a laconic entry in the day book of September 1821 (a year earlier than Lambert's recollection of the time of the incident) states that he received thirty-nine lashes for desertion for about ten days during that month. The day book does not mention him as being placed in the stocks, and so we may be looking at two separate incidents. It is, however, puzzling that the "negro doctor" should desert a profession which placed him at the pinnacle of the slave hierarchy. This was not a case of seeking out a spouse or another woman elsewhere, for the superintendent testified that Lambert was faithful to his wife Abinnaba, a *winkel* woman.[77] Lambert's real confrontation with the department came on 6 June 1824, during the Whitsuntide holidays, when he became intoxicated and was placed in the stocks. The records do not show that he threatened violence to anyone or was in any way insulting to the authorities, and it is therefore quite possible that he was making noise, not an unusual accompaniment to inebriation. The situation took a dramatic turn when he seized a bottle of "corrosive sublimate" and swallowed a portion. Timely medical assistance saved his life, but the department was never the same again.

The mood of the people became sour. In the superintendent's own words, "a considerable uproar arose among the Negroes", which he referred to elsewhere as a "riot" and which forced McWatt, the manager, to seek safety at the under-sheriff's house. There was clearly more to it than Walker cared to commit to writing, for the circumstances mentioned above would hardly have led to a riot had not the people thought that the administration was partly responsible for Lambert's attempted suicide. As noted above, McWatt believed in taking a hard line on the matter of discipline, and his attitude and actions might have incited the people. Walker himself, while testifying to the commissioners that he managed to bring the situation under control, nevertheless indicated that he had also found it prudent to seek the intervention of the fiscal in hopes that he would punish a couple of the ringleaders. The main targets were the victim's family, who had taken a strong stance against management's handling of their relative.

In the sequel, Abinnaba (Lambert's wife), Hendrick II (one of his brothers, lame from birth) and James II (his "kid brother", only fifteen years old) were arraigned before the Court of Criminal Justice for insubordination. The court acquitted Abinnaba, while it considered Hendrick to be too deformed to undergo punishment, although the superintendent later banished him to Berenstein for six months. (According to Walker, Hendrick was an assistant in the school and had engaged in "continued quarrels with the school-mistress". Dummett, however, could not remember any incident in which he had given cause to be punished, prior to his banishment.) The court sentenced James to thirty-nine lashes in the public marketplace and to work in chains for three months. Walker, in a tyrannical assertion of authority, insisted that the *winkel* people should be present to witness this flogging and, as noted above, he subsequently whipped six who absented themselves. It was while this trial was going on that Lauw committed suicide.[78]

During the period of unrest reports indicated that Lambert was "behaving in a very improper manner in the village, dancing before the manager's house", an act which was reflective of his defiant and perhaps neurotic state of mind. Walker had unwisely demoted him to the field gang before or after the incident, and that could only have given further umbrage to himself, his relatives and friends, for one of the worst insults to a nonpraedial slave in Caribbean society was to assign him to the praedial category. In the next few months Lambert was more in than out of hospital, only now as a patient – in hospital on 30 August 1824, out of hospital a month later, and back in hospital shortly after, where he remained up to 31 January 1825. When he testified before the commissioners in mid-1825 he was still not re-employed in the hospital but rather hired out to the Royal Engineers Department. Curiously, however, in June 1825 Walker awarded him a red shirt for some unspecified reason. Perhaps he was trying to effect reconciliation with Lambert, but up to May 1826 he had not been reinstated as hospital attendant.[79]

Lauw, forty-one years old at the time, succeeded where Lambert had failed, crossing the threshold of death in a state of depression and inebriation. But his apparently sudden rush to destruction was really the terminus of a series of unhappy events in his life. He was the eldest of Classina's four children, at least three of whom, including Lauw himself, ran afoul of the administration. The other two were Tannetje, who had several conflicts with the superintendent over her love relations, and Jacoba II, whom the superintendent whipped although she was seven months pregnant. He had also seen his daughter Julia banished to Berenstein, sexually harassed by the manager and brutally whipped by him subsequently.[80] His family's conflicts with the administration, and especially with Walker, went back to at least 1819, and threatened the destruction of this *winkel* family.

A cooper by trade, Lauw's troubles began either at Berenstein or shortly before he was dispatched there. He was among the nine persons mentioned above who complained in December 1820 about the heavy tasks Deussen usually assigned to them. Not getting any immediate redress from the superintendent, he absconded shortly after, but was apprehended about a month later, taken to jail and subsequently placed in the colony's chain gang. Released within about three weeks, he was sent back to Berenstein where he and his colleagues received a whipping (fifty lashes) on the orders of the fiscal for the alleged false complaint that they had made about the heavy workload. A short time later Lauw was on the run once again, but after a few months he decided to surrender to the authorities in town. An uneasy truce prevailed between him and the departmental administration until he ran off yet again, after stealing Braham's shirt and pawning his own. Caught soon after, he was dealt twenty-four lashes by the management and denied his allowance of salted fish for one month.

All these events happened between 28 December 1820 and 4 January 1823. Scarred in body and broken in spirit, he took to expressing his frustrated aggression through drinking; during one episode he allegedly began brandishing a cutlass, for which the driver in town placed him in solitary confinement. He finally snapped, taking his own life by hanging on 22 July 1824.[81] What is strange about this circumstance is that the driver, also a *winkel* person, should have been given or arrogated unto himself the authority to use solitary confinement as a mode of punishment. There is not the slightest indication in any of the documents that the driver exceeded his authority. From today's perspective the decision to commit suicide is always a tragic moral choice, but in slave society it was often seen as the ultimate escape from bondage and, according to African traditional religious philosophy, a transition to a higher life form.

The Case of Carolina II

The events described above manifest the many complex variables in the equation of power. They give the lie to Walker's assertion in April 1824 that the people were "for a considerable time not only orderly and well behaved, but contented, happy and attached to their service".[82] They also contradict his statement in August 1825 that the commissioners were digging up "old scenes of insubordination and punishment . . . which had been now for years lost in reform on the one side and forgiveness on the other", and that "after a considerable period of peace and good order, discord and dislike are introduced between the Negroes and myself".[83] While some of the incidents created only ripples, others created waves of greater magnitude. One such incident which occurred at Whitsuntide 1823, and which at the outset the superintendent hushed up, turned out to be his downfall, resulting in his dismissal two years later. This fact, along with the larger implications of the case, makes it necessary to discuss it in some detail.

The superintendent's desire to conform as closely as possible to plantocratic principles of administration comes out most clearly in his efforts to withdraw one of the major privileges which the Crown people had enjoyed for a long time and which continued to cause great uneasiness among the slave-holding fraternity. This was the granting of an extra day to them at Christmas, Easter and Whitsuntide. As noted in the previous chapter, this was not a legal holiday but one that was customarily given to the *winkel* people and many others in the country as a rest day. To Walker this day constituted simply "an extra day's idleness" and a period of "continued dissipation", although he was aware that the law forbade the people to fête on that day. He had tried in the past to abolish the extra day at Easter but the people had widely disobeyed his orders. He argued that there was no clear tradition regarding the extra days, which he alleged were of recent provenance, and that he could not ascertain "how far it was not always an innovation attempted by them, rather than an established practice".[84] This statement was disingenuous, for he must have known whether the practice existed during his first residence in the colony in 1815. Scott testified that the practice was time honoured, that it had developed into a kind of tradition in the department, and that it existed in a more desultory way on a number of estates, where the people often turned out to work later than usual and were given light tasks and sometimes the afternoon off. Management frequently turned a blind eye to those who did not report for work at all.[85]

As Walker himself testified, in an attempt to placate those persons who were against the granting of extra days he had sought the fiscal's assistance to stamp out the practice on the basis that it contravened the law governing holidays. However, that officer had responded that he had no authority to prevent masters or attorneys from giving their slaves extra days, provided they did not fête.[86] Walker therefore had no option if he wished to stop the practice but to do so himself. He attempted it in 1823, on a partial basis, by withdrawing the extra day at Whitsuntide, the least important of the holiday periods, and requiring the people to turn out for work. According to him, nearly all the people complied with his order, except about five males hired out to an estate and seven females – Tannetje, Jacoba II, Matilda, Fanny, Grietje, Adriana and Carolina II – employed in the workroom. The superintendent consented to have the men whipped by the estate personnel where they were hired out,[87] while he presided over the chastisement of the women. He assigned William Pitt, a nineteen-year-old member of his domestic staff, to perform the whipping with a leather strap doubled, and ordered him to strike the women hard. He insisted that the females lift up their outer clothing (but apparently not their petticoats or under dress) in order to receive the punishment. Among the women punished with twelve strokes was Jacoba II, a female seven months pregnant. Carolina II, a young lady fourteen years of age, refused to comply and Walker himself lifted up her dress and had the punishment administered.[88]

He made no record of this punishment in the day book, nor did he dispatch any correspondence to the Treasury on either the problem of the extra day or the punishment which took place. He mentioned to the commissioners the alleged insubordination, without going into specific details on the punishment. Later, however, Carolina testified before the commissioners that she had brought to the attention of the superintendent the fact that she was menstruating at the time of the punishment, that Walker had nevertheless lifted up all her clothes and had her whipped on her bare bottom, and that while the whipping was taking place blood was running down her legs.[89]

Imperial opinion strongly opposed the whipping of female slaves, resulting in the prohibition of this practice in the slave codes of St Lucia and

Trinidad. This was after the incident under discussion, but imperial sentiments on the subject were well known. Further, the commissioners viewed the whole circumstance of the females having their dresses lifted up, and Walker actually carrying out that act in the case of Carolina, as an event of a "low and disgusting . . . character", carried out in "revolting circumstances of indelicacy". They were particularly censorious of Jacoba's punishment, which was "if possible more objectionable decidedly dangerous and . . . even criminal".[90] They therefore decided to probe into the matter further, and the weight of the testimony proved to be clearly against the superintendent. All the females whipped, except Carolina, testified that only their outer clothing had been raised, although only some of them were certain that Carolina's underclothes had also been raised.[91] William Pitt, the young man who had carried out the whipping, initially confirmed Carolina's testimony. He declared that Walker lifted up Carolina's clothes himself, that she was whipped on her naked bottom and that Walker told him to "lay it on well". Later on, after speaking to Walker, he returned and sought to modify his statement. It was clear that the superintendent had sought to influence him, but he still maintained that Carolina was menstruating at the time, although he now asserted that the superintendent only lifted up her outer dress. He also contradicted himself in this second testimony, first by saying that he had spoken with Mrs Stanley after giving his original testimony and then denying that he had done so.[92]

Walker himself denied these accusations vigorously, alleging that he had taken pains to ensure that only the outer dress of the women was upraised, that he did not lift up Carolina's dress, and that no one had told him that she was menstruating. He claimed that he had "rather some indistinct recollection of something of the sort having been said in the case of Matilda". He also declared that he never saw Carolina's dress smeared with blood or any blood on the floor, although he did see her rubbing something with her foot after the punishment. He had distinctly ordered the whipping to be light (creating more fear than pain), through half a dozen or a dozen strokes – he could not remember exactly how many. He also alleged that he was not aware that Jacoba was pregnant at the time.[93]

In an undaunted and undignified way, Walker also sought to strip Carolina of whatever dignity she had, declaring her to be a loose young woman, of notoriously bad character and "almost incorrigibly bad habits", who went about the streets virtually naked, with nothing but a handkerchief wrapped around her. He further alleged that he had tried his best, but in vain, to reform her and that she was virtually a hopeless case from an educational and moral standpoint. He also engaged Mrs Stanley to have her say about Carolina that she was "a very bad girl", "a blackguard", as even her mother once confessed, and that she had finally been dismissed from the school. He presented several other written testimonies from his friends to his superiors at home, alleging that all that he had said about the young lady was correct. But the unkindest cut of all was Walker's comment about the allegation that her clothes were soiled at the time of the punishment, saying it suggested that "she might probably be of uncleanly habits".[94]

Walker failed to mention in his testimony that the handkerchief he had referred to was usually a substantial piece of cloth that the women commonly used as a head wrap. He had also conveniently forgotten his statement to the commissioners that the slaves in the colony generally went about almost naked (see chapter 5). In fact, it was not unusual for slaves in the various colonies to go about almost naked (and to be punished stark naked). Pinckard recorded that the washerwomen in Bridgetown wore nothing but a loincloth or petticoat, with their breasts exposed. John Waller, another observer, declared that "hundreds of naked negroes of both sexes" could be seen in Bridgetown, with the women wearing "only a short petticoat".[95] John Anderson, special magistrate of St Vincent, also wrote about the washerwomen presenting a "spectacle of African skins disincumbered [sic] of dress from the waist upwards, & their nether garments tucked to the knees".[96] So that in condemning Carolina (who was only fourteen years old at the time) for dressing in this way, Walker was condemning slave society as a whole.

In sullying Carolina's character and those of other witnesses Walker was appealing to white instincts about the inherent criminality of blacks, their lack of virtue and their gift for telling lies. Earl Bathurst, secretary of state for the colonies, became partially susceptible to his sophistry, advising the commissioners that "little dependence is to be placed on their veracity".[97] But the superintendent was unable to establish Carolina's alleged naughtiness; in fact, all the available evidence before the incident of 1823 places her in a very favourable light. Dummett, manager of the department from 1821 to 1824, declared that she had never been disciplined before, a view with which Walker was forced to concur,[98] while other evidence showed that management frequently employed her in the workroom and hired her out to individuals. For example, in July 1821 management hired her out (at age twelve) to Reverend Richard Austin, the Anglican minister, and in the next two years to one Mercy Harper and to Dr Joseph Jeffrey.[99] The obvious inference to be drawn from the fact that at least two of the three persons mentioned above were highly respected in the community was that the young lady carried herself with a certain measure of dignity and not with the complete lack of modesty later alleged. Walker must have felt quite comfortable at the time about hiring her out to these persons.

After the incident in 1823 Walker sent Carolina to Berenstein, but not for bad behaviour – like so many others, she had a white lover. Walker continued to hire her out and to employ her in other ways, for instance, as domestic to the department's bookkeeper in place of Susannah, who was hospitalized. She was actually on Walker's domestic staff as an apprenticed laundress at the time of the commissioners' investigations. But Walker attempted to extricate himself from this inconsistency by claiming that it was the last hope for her since she was unsuitable for the workroom, and that at the time of the punishment she had just returned from being hired out, where she had given much dissatisfaction.[100]

Walker's characterization of Carolina seems more like a caricature or a case of character assassination than an objective assessment. If she were as bad as he alleged, he would have taken measures long before 1823 to discipline her and dismiss her from his presence, as he had done with several others. He only released her from his domestic employ in July 1825, after the incident came to the attention of the commissioners. In September of the same year he gave her the extremely generous supply of ten yards of check[101] – his way of helping her to cover her nakedness, but also symbolically an attempt to cover his own error. Only crudity and insensibility could have caused him to direct a teenage lad to whip young ladies on their bottoms, naked or not. He provoked the young women into resistance in the first place by his abuse of authority in withdrawing the extra day, and followed this by an abuse of power in whipping them for not complying with his fiat. The fact is that he was caught in an undignified position and heaped indignities on a number of persons in order to extricate himself. Ultimately, it was his own hubris that occasioned his downfall.

After reviewing the evidence, the Lords Commissioners of the Treasury concluded that Walker was fully aware of the charge against him and that they had given him every opportunity to refute it, that "his own admissions established the charge in some of the most material features of it, and that he failed in his endeavours to repel the testimony of the witnesses in other material particulars". They therefore removed him from the superintendency "as wholly unfit under any circumstances to be any longer entrusted with such a charge". They also felt that he was unworthy to hold any public office, and therefore suspended him from the collectorship until he should have an opportunity to offer any further explanation or defence of his conduct. His dismissal and suspension from the two offices took effect on 5 December 1825.[102] Walker subsequently engaged his highly influential friends and acquaintances to send letters of character on his behalf and otherwise plead his cause. Among these were Reverend Dr Davidson of Edinburgh, a large landowner; Dr John Abercombie, a medical practitioner; George Ross, son of Admiral Sir John Lockart Ross and a judge of the Commissary Court of Scotland; Colonel Elliott Lockart, member of Parliament; and Lord Gillies, another high-court judge.[103] Faced with such an array of testimony, the Lords Commissioners eventually agreed to restore him to the collectorship, but refused to give him more than half-pay for his time of suspension from that office. He was reluctant to return to Berbice, and in the end (1827) he was given the collectorship of the Bahamas at a salary of £800 per annum.[104]

The case left a sour taste in everyone's mouth. Walker's attempts to cut down on the established holidays of the people represented an abuse of power and was recognized by them as such. It is interesting that it was the women who dared to defy him, underlining their role in slave resistance. They were engaging in a high level of struggle to maintain what had once been a privilege but had become a right by the time it was threatened. Their stand was eventually vindicated, even if not in the way that they had anticipated. When Kyte attempted at Easter 1826 to succeed where Walker had failed, the people defied him with all their might. Very few of them bothered to go to work at the ringing of the bell, although it was rung at the late hour of 11 a.m. When Kyte's actions came before the commissioners of inquiry, they wrote home requesting the imperial Treasury to establish suitable regulations to prevent anyone having control over the people making "a dangerous use of his authority".[105]

Conclusion

The impasse of 1823 contributed to the unrest in the department in 1824. We shall never know what might have come of the simmering discontent of these two years, because the commissioners' arrival caused a considerable reduction in resistant activities, despite Walker's allegations that they had stirred up new unrest among the people. The evidence concerning his equivocation and abuse of power is overwhelming in its detail. He was the source of endless vexations to the people, thus also enlarging the arena of conflict. The commissioners looked hard, but in vain, to find the method in his administrative madness. Historians often note the pressures on and sometimes the wreckage of the slave family by sale; this chapter shows how that family could be and was often severely tested, if not wrecked, by a number of other circumstances, including pressure to forgo certain relationships, brutal punishment, banishment, desertion and suicide.

Desertion – as part of the larger context of slave resistance – often emanated from a complexity of motives, including the desire for permanent or temporary freedom. The second motive was more characteristic of the *winkel* deserters, whose desertion was usually to escape the arm of the oppressor for a while, although they recognized that this might result in chastisement on their return. The limited objectives of this form of desertion were seen in the histories of some of them: roaming from estate to estate, being apprehended and sent to jail or returned to the department, falling sick and being sent to the "negro" hospital, running away again, and so on.

The dissonance and disharmony inherent in the slave system reached their high points in the defiance of the females over the withdrawal of the extra day at Whitsuntide, the suicide of Lauw and the attempted suicide of Lambert. Paulo Freire sees oppression, such as that inherent in the slave systems, as necrophilic, while Orlando Patterson views it as a form of "social death".[106] Frantz Fanon notes that one aspect of this kind of necrophilic behaviour is that the oppressed sometimes vent their anger on, and lash out at, each other. The *winkel* records offer glimpses of this kind of behaviour in the activities of Sim and Michael, who showed distinctly aggressive tendencies towards their oppressed brethren.[107] It was also there in the strong hand of the driver mercilessly whipping real and imagined transgressors.

The oppression within the department highlighted the function of slavery in degrading not only the slave but the master, not only the colonized but the colonizer.[108] Walker was an insecure individual who could not trust in his ability to influence the people by persuasion rather than coercion. He failed to understand the dynamics of human relationships and, like Bryan Edwards, felt that persuasion was lost on slaves and that coercion was a form of humanity and even charity towards them.[109] His wife was party to his mode of control and encouraged his insecurities and actions. Thus coercion became the kernel of his system of discipline, as it was in all New World slave societies. The practice of physical and psychological violence was rife, from the shortage of food, the scanty clothing, the unwelcome intrusion into the sexual lives of the females, to the banishment to Berenstein, the use of solitary confinement and so on.

8

The Road to Freedom, 1825–1831

> O, that I were free! . . . O, why was I born a man, of whom to make a brute! I am left in the hottest hell of unending slavery. O, God, save me! God deliver me! Let me be free![1]
>
> Frederick Douglass

To Free or Not to Free?

The main focus of the imperial government during the last few years of the *winkel* department's existence was what to do about it. In 1824 the commissioners of colonial audit saw only the bleakest future for it:

> We do not think that Mr. Walker's reports as to its present state and prospects, or the apparent demand for the work of the Winkels, warrant any expectation of pecuniary profit from it . . . we think there can be no doubt as to the expediency of discontinuing without delay, the Winkels as a public establishment altogether, and of disposing of the Negroes in such other manner as your Lordships shall deem fit.[2]

In the following year they referred to the department as "this more than useless concern" and once again advocated its demise: "We cannot conclude without strongly urging the necessity, as expressed in our former report, of altogether abolishing this ruinous and expensive establishment; so far from profit being derived from it, the loss upon it will annually increase."[3] They suggested that if the Lords Commissioners did not wish to sell the people they should consider transferring them to Trinidad, as part of the project mooted for the apprenticed Africans.⁴

However, some of those persons closer to the department were far more optimistic than the officials in the Department of Colonial Audit. In spite of his view that the people were lazy, McWatt believed that the establishment had the resources to be self-supporting.⁵ The commissioners of inquiry were even more certain that its potential could be translated into productivity under good management:

> That the Winkel Negroes are quite equal, not only to support themselves, but under a judicious system of management, are capable of being made a productive property, we entertain not the least doubt . . . but unless the most thorough and complete reform could be introduced, & effectually established in conducting the affairs of this Department, we cannot hold out much prospect of its being brought to that state, as a public establishment.⁶

The imperial government came increasingly to the conclusion that the *winkel* people's fate was inextricably linked with the wider problem of freedom for the rest of the slave population of the colonies. Foreign Secretary George Canning viewed the immediate or imminent emancipation of the slaves with trepidation, as he made clear in the following statement:

> In dealing with the negro, we must remember that we are dealing with a being possessing the form and strength of a man, but the intellect only of a child. To turn him loose in the manhood of his physical strength, in the maturity of his physical passions, but in the infancy of his uninstructed reason, would be to raise up a creature resembling the splendid fiction of a recent romance; the hero of which constructs a human form with all the corporeal capabilities of man, and with the thews and sinews of a giant, but being unable to impart to the work of his hands a perception of right and wrong, he finds too late that he has only created a more than mortal power of doing mischief, and recoils from the monster which he has made.⁷

In other words, Canning viewed the emancipation of the slaves at that point as analogous to the creation of Frankenstein's monster. Canning was the chief spokesman of the imperial government's position on the issue of emancipation, and while several persons in various government departments did not necessarily share his views, he was perhaps articulating the official government position.

At the same time, the imperial Treasury had mandated the commissioners of inquiry to investigate whether these slaves could manage on their own if liberated. The commissioners had come unequivocally to the view that, with few exceptions, all the effectives, both men and women, had the skills to provide for themselves and their children materially. However, they had expressed the reservation that since the people had acquired "idle habits", they were not ready for freedom but should be placed under a regime of industry which would in time allow them "to obtain the benefit of freedom by their own exertions". This was, in effect, a recommendation for a gradual approach to abolishing the department.[8] The imperial government was also concerned that the liberation of such a large body of slaves at once might create a political and social storm among the colonial whites in Berbice. In similar vein, Captain Gipps of the Royal Engineers Department, who was well acquainted with a number of the artisans, argued that "[t]o make them at once free, was to be objected to as dangerous".[9]

Financial and Administrative Reform

However, the government recognized the fact that the *winkel* department constituted a burden on the imperial Treasury, with little hope even in the long term that the situation would improve. True, the first few years after Walker's dismissal as superintendent were good ones for the department. Charles Kyte, the new acting part-time superintendent, was a much more experienced planter and attorney with wide political and social contacts in the colony. At various times he held such important offices as deputy vendue master (deputy auctioneer), president of the Board of Police (town council), treasurer of the town funds, acting comptroller of customs, member of the Court of Civil Justice, member of the Council of Government, and attorney for various planters, including Katz, the foremost planter. He was also the owner of a provision store.[10]

With such wide experience and contacts, Kyte was able to find employment for a much larger number of the effectives than formerly. However, the commissioners, while commending him for this achievement, were unhappy that it was won by methods which they considered to be against the best interests of the people, that is, by hiring them out as before as field hands, servants and drudges. They wanted to see Kyte develop a comprehensive programme of training the young men as artisans and re-establishing the shops that Scott had demolished. They mildly chastised him for withdrawing some artisan apprentices and hiring them out as regular domestics or field hands. Kyte, on the other hand, argued that sufficient work could not be found for the people as artisans, a view which the commissioners never accepted.

The two parties ran afoul of each other not only on this score but on a number of other issues: failure to repair the houses, disputes as to how much money should be spent on food and clothing, Kyte's complaint that the commissioners were taking up too much of his time and attention on trivia for the paltry sum of £300 per annum and would not allow him to get on with the administration of the department, and so on. In the end, Kyte resigned the office, effective 1 April 1826.[11] The commissioners eventually settled on Scott, the former assistant agent, as acting part-time superintendent, later to be confirmed in that office. During his tenure the department underwent extensive financial and administrative reforms to put it on a sounder footing and to prevent the recurrence of the major abuses which both the commissioners and the imperial officials agreed had crept into the operations. The superintendent's salary was reduced to £200 per annum, without any other perquisites of office, so that he now had to pay for all *winkel* labour which he utilized. The department's salary package was set at £450 per annum, with the exception of the medical practitioners. Like other senior colonial officials, the superintendent had to give financial security to help ensure probity in office – in his case amounting to £1,000 and two sureties of £500 each.

The new regulations also required the superintendent to turn over quarterly to the military chest in the colony all monies collected, with the exception of what he needed to meet routine expenses of the department. Further, he was forbidden to draw any drafts on the imperial Treasury without the express permission of that body. The Treasury, on the advice of the Department of Colonial Audit, also issued a comprehensive body of instructions on the keeping of the accounts, especially in relation to receipts of purchases, inventories of stores utilized and records of debtors to the department. They also appointed a new departmental staff (with the exception of the part-time medical practitioners), including a part-time debt collector. By 1829 the administration was functioning much more coherently and purposefully than formerly.[12]

The fortuitous circumstance of the ordnance department's building a new fort and a sawmill provided sufficient employment to keep the *winkel* department financially viable for a few years. On the recommendation of the commissioners, the ordnance department decided in 1826 to utilize the *winkel* people as much as possible in the erection of the new fort. Thus, for the next three years the department actually realized a surplus of income over expenditure, which amounted on 31 December 1828 to £1,019.[13] However, by 1829 dark clouds began to reappear on the financial horizon, with the realization that the building programme was nearing completion. By June 1830 the ordnance department was only employing a small number of artisans, and one year later the *winkel* department was in the red to the tune of £346. In 1832 the Treasury had to pay an overdraft of £1,267 owed to Katz for plantains over the past two years.[14] Serious financial problems faced the department once again.

Proposals for Financial Viability

Various local and overseas officials, both before and after 1826, offered suggestions on how to find a long-term solution to the financial dilemma, including hiring the *winkel* people out in batches to planters, leasing them to various persons who were interested in them, selling them, placing them on a new plantation or a woodcutting establishment, and setting them free. Selling them – a suggestion which, it may be recalled, the Department of Colonial Audit had put forward earlier, perhaps without any conviction – was out of the question, for the imperial government would not entertain the idea of making a financial gain from the sale of these people, not to mention the political repercussions of such an action. Nor was leasing them out any real solution, although between 1820 and 1826 William Armstrong, Charles Kyte, Wolfert Katz and William Campbell had made fresh offers to lease some or all of them. The position of the imperial government on leasing the people might be gleaned from Wilmot Horton's views on Kyte's proposal. He argued that while Kyte had focused attention on the health and comfort of the slaves, the objectives of the imperial government were far more "extensive, and the main hinge upon which [the] Government relies for extinguishing slavery in the spirit of the resolutions of the House of Commons is omitted". That hinge was moral and religious instruction, an issue which went far beyond monetary matters and the omission of which was "fatal to the reception of any proposals for the hire of the slaves".[15]

The Treasury received two other proposals on how to resolve the financial problems. The commissioners raised the issue of placing the *winkel* people on a fresh plantation, a proposal which they thought might be acceptable to the people, provided that the place was not too far from town and they understood that they would share directly in the proceeds of the enterprise. The plan involved allocating land to them as individuals or families and remunerating them according to the income gained from their crop yields. This was a kind of sharecropping arrangement, but one in which the only financial interest of the Crown would be to ensure that it was self-sufficient. The commissioners considered that a sugar estate was entirely out of the question, because of its symbolic association with all that was evil in slavery, but recommended that a good coffee and provision estate might prove workable, with artisan workshops located there.[16] Strangely, the commissioners themselves had little faith that it would work.[17] They probably put it forward as a suggestion made by Nicolay, a former member of the department. They were certainly correct in asserting that any plan which threatened to move the people from an urban to a rural settlement was likely to encounter grave difficulties. In any case, this proposal died a quick death, being overtaken in the correspondence and in imperial attention by a much more elaborate one put forward by Captain Gipps.

Gipps offered several reasons for putting forward his proposal. First, he considered it shameful to see the imperial government "not only still possessing slaves of its own, but actually jobbing them out". Second, by holding such property the government was "still a great encourager of slavery". Third, his close contact with the government slaves during his period as an officer in the ordnance department had convinced him that many of them fully deserved freedom. Fourth, the imperial government should be a pioneer, whenever possible, in putting into practice the ameliorative measures which it had recommended for the slave colonies. His proposal would give the government an opportunity to conduct an experiment to find out "whether a society of black people may not be formed in the West Indies, happy, and free". Fifth, it was necessary to introduce a transitional phase between slavery and full freedom, during which the people would develop into a wage-earning community and the government would be relieved of the financial burden of supporting them. Finally, this could be done with no threat of social unrest within the wider colonial slave society.[18]

Gipps suggested that the government should establish a settlement in the deep hinterland of the colony, at Barabakara, about six miles up the Wiruni River (not to be confused with the Wiruni Creek, as is sometimes the case), some fifty miles distant in a straight line from the coast, or about eighty-seven miles by the meandering course of the Berbice River. According to him, this site held a number of natural advantages in respect of fresh water, a healthy savannah environment, exceptionally good land for livestock and vegetables, and access to large timber supplies, which, however, he admitted might mean scouring the hinterland for miles to secure the best woods. Originally, he conceived the plan as simply a woodcutting establishment, but as his thoughts on it evolved he suggested that it should be one primarily for making boats, casks and vats, and that woodcutting should be only a secondary industry to which the people might resort in times of financial difficulty. They would keep the money that they had earned, paying a certain amount to maintain the administrative services of the settlement. The imperial government's obligation would be to finance the founding of the establishment and its maintenance for about the first two years. By that time it should become viable, paying all its costs, including those for a warden or ranger, a missionary-schoolteacher and a medical attendant, the last of these presumably on a visiting basis. Gipps estimated that the project would cost the imperial government a total of £4,000.[19]

The Treasury, after reviewing the plan carefully, decided to implement it, but only if Gipps would agree to become the first ranger. However, he had already left the colony, had recently married, and expressed no interest in returning to Berbice because of the adverse climate. In the end, therefore, the plan remained unrealized.[20] It is doubtful, in any case, that the plan would have met with any great measure of success, for a number of reasons. As already noted in respect of similar projects of resettlement, no significant number of *winkel* people were likely to favour leaving town, especially for resettlement so far upriver, although the government was prepared to offer them land on a freehold basis. The plan would also have meant certain financial ruin to a number of them, or at least, in the case of the men, redeployment of several of them as timber cutters. The only roles of the women would have been as cultivators of the provision fields, wives and mothers. But serious sexual and wider family problems were likely to arise, since the department had more men than women. To make matters worse, the plan proposed sought to bar other enslaved persons from approaching within the great distance of twenty straight miles (somewhat over thirty miles by the river's course) of the settlement, except accompanied by their masters or managers. This would have created a community completely isolated from the rest of the colony, apart from those times when its members went downriver for trade or other reasons.

The plan entailed subjecting the people to "strict vagrant law" both before and after they had achieved their freedom.[21] Whereas in town they had a certain degree of physical mobility, they would now be forbidden to leave the new settlement without permission, on pain of punishment. Likewise, those considered idle were to be coerced into working. The plan did not spell out the various punishments or other forms of coercion, except for the extreme one: banishment from the settlement and return to the *winkel* village. Obviously, Gipps had predicated this naïve plan on the assumption that the people would be anxious to go to the new settlement. Quite likely, those who disliked the place would deliberately have committed acts to provoke banishment back to town.

One of the main flaws of the plan was that it set no exact date for granting freedom to the people. They had to work out their salvation through their good behaviour and purchase of their freedom at two-thirds of their assessed value, over an estimated period of four to seven years, and longer for those not sufficiently thrifty or unable to find the necessary employment to do so. Since the women would have had no apparent means of income, it remains unclear how they would have achieved their freedom, especially if they were unmarried or unattached. The plan made provision for the purchase of family members, but this would have meant an exceedingly long time for a family of six. The fact is that while Gipps spoke about the proposed plan as one of free labour, it had many of the trappings of slavery. It was, at best, a transitional stage in which the people would be perceived as neither slaves nor free persons. He himself called it an "intermediate state between slavery and freedom".[22] Gipps's plan really did not offer anything attractive to entice the *winkel* people to consent to such a radical change in their way of life, and they might simply have ended up being gypped.

Resettlement schemes of bond or semifree persons were quite common in the history of European colonialism, but almost invariably they had to be introduced and maintained by naked force in the short term. The reservation schemes in the Americas and Africa speak eloquently to this point. In several instances they were brought to an end by widespread desertion or revolt by their inhabitants, as the Spanish experienced in Cuba and Vera Paz (Guatemala) in the sixteenth century. The early-nineteenth-century British experiment in Sierra Leone was also an example of misery which made life nasty, brutish and short there; and this was only slightly less true for the disbanded black soldiers resettled in Trinidad.[23] British efforts to get those apprenticed Africans who were first settled in various Caribbean territories to opt for resettlement in Sierra Leone or Trinidad came to nought, partly because of the people's reluctance to quit their places of residence.[24] History was likely to repeat itself in the case of the *winkel* people in Berbice.

Gipps's plan was not altogether unique, for several schemes of partial freedom had been mooted or were already in operation in different New World slave societies. The best known of these were the early Portuguese and Spanish practices of allowing people to purchase their freedom gradually through the system of *coartación*. After the Spanish American colonies won their freedom they generally instituted the system of granting theoretical freedom to newborn slave children, called *manumisos,* but forced these children into service to their mothers' owners until the age of eighteen to twenty-one years. Later on the British, Cubans and Brazilians instituted halffree institutions, called variously *apprenticeship, patronato* and *ingenuos,* to squeeze out the last vestiges of slave labour from their erstwhile human chattel.[25] Thus a state of "in-betweenity" pervaded the slave systems in their last years of existence, which frequently turned out to be a most unhappy state for those subjected to it. Even free(d) blacks and free coloureds were often in such a state, since the colonial regimes passed a battery of laws restricting their physical and other freedoms, and sometimes drawing little distinction between them and the slave community.[26]

The decision not to pursue Gipps's plan left the imperial government with few options. One of these was subsidizing the department indefinitely. Apart from day-to-day maintenance, the *winkel* houses had now become so dilapidated and the roofs so porous that almost all the structures needed to be demolished and new ones built. The imperial government, increasingly perceiving the *winkel* people simply as unprofitable servants, had now made up its mind about one thing: it was not going to spend good money on what it regarded as a bad cause. The Treasury declared that each of those not employed cost the government around £8 in annual maintenance.[27]

Preparing the *Winkel* People for Freedom

One option still remained open: immediate emancipation. Past and present *winkel* staff agreed that the *winkel* people were the most intelligent, and certainly the best-educated, slaves in the colony. Some believed that they were the most "civilised" ones in the entire Caribbean, while Scott opined that they had received "a greater degree of religious and moral instructions than perhaps any others of their unfortunate race in the world".[28] In such circumstances it appeared to make no sense to retain them in bondage any longer.

Already, in keeping with its policy of gradualism, and especially after the commissioners' report, the imperial government had begun to prepare the *winkel* people for emancipation through a new effort at industrial, social and moral reform. We have already discussed part of this new programme. Here it is important to mention the new policy established in the ordnance department, by which the artisans received payment for overtime work.[29] Although this was not a widespread practice, it was an important beginning that augured well for the future. The government also made provision for the people to place their money in a savings bank specially created within the colonial (Berbice) Treasury to receive funds from slaves. This was a consequence of the new slave code promulgated in 1826, which made provisions for such a bank. However, few slaves utilized this opportunity. Many of them continued to hoard what little savings they had accumulated, perhaps because they distrusted the government, which they often viewed as part of the system of oppression. Nevertheless, by 2 September 1830 several slaves, at least seven of whom belonged to the *winkel* department, had saved a total of f7,692. The *winkel* artisans Louis (f374) and Daniel (f518 and f797) made significant single-entry (that is, not accumulated) deposits, while Sophia (f1,320) and Harriet (f1,250), who belonged to other owners, made more impressive deposits (see Table 8.1, next page).[30]

Table 8.1 Deposits of Berbice Slaves in Savings Bank, 1 November 1826–16 March 1830 (guilders)

Slaves	Deposits
Zacharias	159:10
Daniel	1,699:0
William Henery	47:0
Maria	18:0
Louis	1,058:10
François	99:0
Jacob Benjamin	40:0
Sophia	1,465:0
Jacob Antony	63:0
Harriet	1,250:0
February	312:0
Elizabeth Anne	100:0
Total	6,311:0

Source: "Savings Bank", 16 March 1830, PRO, CO 111/110.

The main religious thrust of amelioration continued to lie with Reverend John Wray of the LMS, although he was no longer receiving a subvention from the department. The missionary's evangelical zeal drove his efforts to convert all and sundry to his faith, and he continued to view the *winkel* slaves as coming especially within his ambit. Also, by this time he had mellowed towards the prejudices of the plantocracy, who in turn became more conciliatory towards him. Some of them supported his work more liberally, so that the mission expanded considerably during this period. Specifically in relation to the *winkel* people, whose village was just five minutes' walk from the missionary chapel in town, attendance at worship grew considerably. The new spirit of revival also manifested itself in the prayer meetings which several of the people began to hold in their houses twice or thrice weekly, in the quiet observance of Christmas and Easter, and in more rigorous observance of Sunday as a day of rest.[31] In spite of this evidence that the *winkel* people had undergone significant acculturation, the imperial government was still disposed to proceed with extreme caution. Up to 1831 it refused to discuss in detail any plan for their general emancipation. Also, every proposal mooted by those who claimed that they had the people's interest at heart still suggested that the way forward should be marked by gradualism.

Scott put forward an elaborate plan whereby a small number of the most deserving males would be given a day's freedom (for example, free Mondays) every six months or every year, until through continued exemplary conduct they would be released fully from working for the department. According to this plan, their progress might be arrested at any point through misconduct, although they were not to have days already granted to them revoked. When they had been granted all seven days they were still to be regarded only as provisionally manumitted. They were to remain in the village and continue to contribute to its maintenance for a certain number of years, unless they could give an acceptable reason for wishing to reside outside of it. During this time their wives and children would also be manumitted over a number of years, the wives after three to five years, and one child yearly after that, provided the parent(s) continued to display good conduct. Where a provisionally manumitted male had even one child still enslaved, he was to pay one-sixth of his wages to ensure that child's education.

Scott argued that his plan was designed, among other things, to prevent the village from being divested suddenly of its most industrious and well-behaved persons and thus exposed to financial ruin and social depravity. These people would also be necessary to train new apprentices over a period of years. However, he did allow for some modification of his proposal, by which every year five or six of the most deserving people might be manumitted conditionally for three to five years, on the model of the apprenticed Africans, using coercion but not a return to slavery as an incentive to subsequent delinquents.[32] He envisaged a very gradual relief from the long night of slavery; indeed, so gradual that unless the imperial government were to accelerate it by significant modification the department was unlikely to disappear in the foreseeable future, especially since the main focus of the plan was on granting freedom to the males.

The imperial government considered this proposal while still working on Gipps's plan, and responded favourably to suggestions for the manumission of a few deserving slaves. So far the government had not developed any firm policy on the subject, but had simply allowed the department's personnel to do what they pleased. The department had manumitted no *winkel* persons officially between 1808 and 1820, although it had made a few attempts to do so – largely to sell *winkel* women (and their children) to their white lovers for manumission. However, neither the Council of Government nor the colonial courts recognized the superintendent's authority to alienate property without the express permission of the owners, a situation that the Treasury finally rectified. In all, the imperial government manumitted about forty-six persons before the abolition of the department.[33]

Apprenticed Africans and Government Slaves

Meanwhile, other events were taking place in the British Caribbean colonies which had a crucial bearing on the emancipation of the *winkel* people and the entire colonial slave population. As noted in chapter 4, in 1821 the government directed its attention to a number of Africans under Crown patronage in various forms of unfreedom. The most noteworthy of these were almost two thousand apprenticed Africans in its various Caribbean and other colonies, theoretically free, but in practice generally enjoying little or no freedom. After receiving the various reports of the commissioners sent out to investigate their condition and their capacity to live on their own, and reviewing the options available to them, the imperial officials decided in 1828 to set them free immediately and to give them lands within specially created villages. Their freedom was qualified, however, by the proviso that they might be transported to Trinidad should they become vagrants or a burden on the public within seven years, except for sickness or other unavoidable circumstances.[34]

The second main category of unfree persons under government control were the slaves purchased by the colonial governments, and others escheated to the Crown over the years, either as a result of their owners' dying intestate, forfeiture for acts of treason, or as prizes of war. The actual number of government slaves is difficult to ascertain because some colonial officials confused them in the returns with the apprenticed Africans. In 1803 there were two hundred government slaves in Essequibo who had belonged to the defunct estate Suyxbergen but had been left on their own for the past six years and were all but free. The lieutenant governor expressed the view that it would be too much trouble to restore them to slavery. At that period those in Demerara (Stabroek, the capital) numbered ninety-nine, in addition to one hundred Pioneers whom the colonial government had purchased to help defend the colony in place of regular troops. Contrary to the situation in Berbice, none of these enslaved persons was regarded as the private property of the Crown. The imperial government never paid any special attention to them, nor were they mentioned in the treaty of 1814 which restored the captured estates to the Dutch proprietors. They were reserved for colonial public works and private use by colonial officials. In the colonies as a whole the government slaves totalled at least 699 in 1823, apart from those in Berbice. The largest numbers were located in Grenada (292), Demerara-Essequibo (272) and Trinidad (103).

Apart from those on the two government estates in Grenada, the escheats numbered only about thirty-eight in 1823.[35] The escheats had experienced mixed fortunes up to that time. Colonial officials placed in charge of them disposed of them as they saw fit. For example, of the sixty-four escheats noted in the records of Trinidad between 1814 and 1823, fourteen were working with the colony's slave gang, three had died, seven had been manumitted and forty had been sold.[36] In Grenada three persons escheated to the Crown in 1812 were sold in 1822 on the orders of the governor, including a girl born to one of the escheats after the Crown had acquired them. The colonial government had given other escheats to relatives of the deceased owners periodically on application for them, but the government was unable to furnish specific details on the transactions. As late as August 1823 the Barbados government sold twenty-two escheats, while two were awaiting a similar fate. Eleven others were due to be sold, but the governor halted execution of the sale until he could determine how to respond to the request by the relatives of the deceased owner for them.[37]

James Stephen Jr, whose legal opinion the Colonial Office sought on the matter of the escheats, argued that the natural rights of the slaves to freedom should always be placed above the acquired rights of the relatives to property, particularly because there was no clear evidence that the deceased would have passed on such property to the survivors. Stephen went as far as to advise that all escheats should be liberated immediately, except for infants, young children, the aged and infirm, and those who were so depraved and ignorant that they were likely to be a charge on the public purse. The Colonial Office sent a few letters to the Treasury between 1819 and 1827 outlining their views on the subject, but the latter failed to respond to any of them.[38]

Meanwhile, the Treasury had granted to the surviving relatives of forfeited estates in Grenada half of the net profits of those properties, as a result of an application they had made to have the properties handed over to them in entirety. However, in 1828 that body became awakened from its slumber when both its attorney and the solicitor general advised that the entire properties should be passed on to the relatives of the deceased.[39] A long and interesting debate on this issue, only the main points of which can be dealt with here, engaged the attention of the Colonial Office and the Treasury.

The Treasury argued that the line of action suggested by its legal personnel conformed to long-established practice in Britain and the Caribbean where, except in rare instances, such property was returned to the relatives of the deceased upon application, and that to do otherwise would be to "inflict a great and undeserved hardship upon many persons having equitable claims to the property". The Treasury was prepared to grant the slaves their freedom only where such applications were not made.[40] By adopting this viewpoint the Treasury had placed property rights over natural rights, a stance which calls into question once again the seriousness with which that body viewed slave amelioration and abolition. Moreover, in this case the owners had forfeited the properties to the Crown by an act of attainder passed against them in 1795, for some act of treason or felony,[41] so that the Crown should have felt no obligation to restore them.

Strangely, the Colonial Office vacillated on the stand that it had adopted earlier on the question of the escheats. It now conceded that the Grenada escheats should not be set free, on the sole premise that it was impolitic, if not dangerous, to let loose such a large body of slaves on the local plantocracy in one fell swoop. At first it was only willing to grant the relatives the profits accruing from the plantations, which it felt government-appointed officials should continue to administer to ensure that the ameliorative measures of the imperial government remained in place. However, it later suggested that the relatives might be given a lease at a peppercorn rent, subject to periodic proofs of "good management". Oral and further written communication between the two branches of government settled that the lease should run for 999 years, subject to forfeiture at the absolute discretion of the Crown if at any time its officials felt that the relatives were not managing the estates in the best interests of the slaves.[42]

The larger issue of what to do with escheats generally remained unsettled. But by 1830 the Treasury had come around to the Colonial Office's earlier way of thinking, agreeing that the government should treat them exactly as it treated slaves forfeited for infringement of the slave trade abolition act of 1807, and grant them immediate freedom. The Colonial Office suggested that those in Tortola and the Bahamas might be granted Crown lands in the same areas where the apprenticed Africans were settled, those in Trinidad might join the disbanded black soldiers settled on similar lands in Trinidad, while those in Berbice and Demerara-Essequibo might join the settlement proposed for the *winkel* people in upper Berbice. The Colonial Office, therefore, sent a circular dispatch to the governors on 24 January 1831 ordering them to set free all escheated slaves immediately.[43]

The decision in respect of the escheats had much wider significance, also affecting the other groups of Crown slaves in the colonies. The imperial government recognized it as, in effect, a policy decision to liberate all of them. In 1831 Lord Goderich, the secretary of state for the colonies, made it clear to Governor D'Urban that the imperial government was in principle firmly committed to emancipation. He, like some other government officials, also began to refer to the slaves more often as "people", and once he even referred to them as a class of the King's "subjects".[44] Consequently, less than two months after the decision to liberate the escheats the government decided to emancipate the other Crown slaves, declaring that they constituted "a species of property which many considerations concur to recommend that the Crown should forthwith relinquish". By a circular dispatch of 12 March 1831, Lord Goderich instructed the governors to free all the Crown slaves within one month of receipt of the letter. He cited the success of the "experiment" of freeing the apprenticed Africans as one of the main reasons which led the government to this determination, declaring that their industry "affords a satisfactory assurance that the Negroes, now the property of the Crown, will, when manumitted, support themselves by their own exertions, in a manner equally innocuous".[45]

The Colonial Office sent the circular dispatch to D'Urban, who, it will be recalled, had been appointed on 4 March 1831 as governor of the united colony of British Guiana. In order to make it abundantly clear that the order applied also to the members of the *winkel* department, Goderich dispatched a follow-up letter to D'Urban on 14 March, directing him to set these people free and give them land grants. The *winkel* people should therefore have been set free by the middle of the year, but D'Urban's tardiness caused them to remain in bondage for another six months.[46] D'Urban, not keen on the emancipation of the Crown people, and still less on a general emancipation, used a wide range of arguments, hoping that the imperial government would revoke its decision to liberate the Crown slaves, or at least postpone it indefinitely. His main arguments had to do with the importance of the slaves to the public works department and high government officials; the slaves' dependence on the largesse of the Crown; their happiness with the state of comfort that they enjoyed; their inability to live on their own; the problems that they were likely to encounter through such precipitate manumission; and the dangers in freeing a fairly large group of people while retaining the mass of slaves in bondage. He put forward these arguments specifically in relation to the Crown slaves in Demerara, but they also applied to those in Berbice.[47]

Lord Goderich, however, dismissed all of these arguments as frivolous and once again ordered the governor to manumit the Crown slaves as soon as possible after receipt of his missive. His strong stance was based on the imperial government's decision, noted above, that the Crown had to divest itself of all its slaves at all costs. It was the first time that the government had taken a clear, ideological stand on this matter: the Crown could not be promoting amelioration and emancipation in the colonies for private slave owners while leaving "undone whatever is in the power of His Majesty's Government to render them effectual" by setting the example with its own slaves. More revolutionary was Goderich's view that slavery was incompatible with sovereignty, or at least British sovereignty. It was derogatory to the British monarch to stand as a proprietor of slaves in relation to any of his subjects, over whom he was expected to extend the same protection as to all other classes of "His people". The Roman emperors, Goderich opined, had also embraced this tenet.[48] Implicit in this position is the British doctrine of "trusteeship" which would surface frequently in the imperial government's dealings with colonized peoples in the Caribbean, Asia and Africa in the later nineteenth and the twentieth centuries.

Free at Last!

As a result of Goderich's further dispatch 298 *winkel* persons (160 males and 138 females) received certificates of freedom on 17 November 1831, although 29 males and 13 females remained in the dependent categories: aged, infirm or otherwise unable to take care of themselves. The imperial government decided to allow all who desired it to remain in the village, and to give land to those who wished to engage in agriculture. It also gave the manager's house to the LMS for a mission school.[49] Quite unexpectedly, from the viewpoint of the colonial officials, few if any of the people opted to receive land grants.[50] This was due primarily to two circumstances: the complete odium with which the colony's slaves, and especially the Crown people, regarded agricultural work, and the fact that most of them could engage in more profitable undertakings as artisans and so on. Scott stated that some of them refused to accept lands to cultivate because they could earn more money from raising livestock,[51] but it remains unclear why the government did not offer them lands expressly for that purpose.

Shortly after the *winkel* people had received their freedom Wray was rejoicing over the fact that now they were working for between f1:10 and f3 per day, in place of the scanty provisions offered to them as slaves. Contrary to those who had said that regular employment could not be found for them, Wray wrote that they had plenty of work, the men as artisans and the women as washers and seamstresses. Within a short period many of them had substantially rehabilitated their houses and were enjoying new comforts. As time went by, they began to scatter throughout the colony seeking new avenues of employment, some of the young adults migrating to Demerara. One of them even migrated to Barbados, where he was said to be working on the rehabilitation of the St Michael's Cathedral in 1833.[52]

An important footnote to these events is the reaction of the wider slave population to the liberation of the government slaves. In Demerara, where a large number of government slaves had been liberated[53] a little over a week before those in Berbice received a similar boon, the mood of the other slaves became very truculent. According to one colonist, some of them had conspired to set the town on fire two or three days after realizing that their owners were not going to free them at the same time as the government slaves. He also claimed that some slaves had carried out arson on several estates, and that the slaves throughout the entire colony were in a state of unrest because they felt that their masters were denying them the freedom which the king had decreed for them.[54] The governor's account of what took place was more vague and muted. He simply stated to his superiors in London that several of the slaves thought that the emancipation of their counterparts was the prelude to their own emancipation at Christmas. He therefore had to use his annual tour of inspection of the militia in various parts of the colony to explain to them that the imperial government had not decreed a general emancipation. This eventually quieted them and they were now "perfectly tranquil . . . contented and happy".[55] The governor had probably underplayed the extent of the agitation which prevailed in the colony for some weeks. It was not a happy determination for the enslaved people, for whom freedom would remain an elusive dream for the next few years.

Conclusion

The years following Walker's dismissal and the appointment of new personnel within the department saw slow and timid steps towards freedom. This was not surprising, given the fact that the imperial government continued to see the way forward as gradual amelioration and even more gradual emancipation. All the suggestions which emerged in the first few years after 1825 were for experiments at greater amelioration, with the vague hope of freedom for the most deserving persons. Imperial officials were still bogged down by the notion that freedom was not the natural condition of life but something to be earned by good conduct and commitment to industry – the kind of qualifications one makes for prisoners who are eligible for parole. But then, slavery *was* a form of imprisonment of the body and soul of the individual, a life sentence in the vast majority of instances, and manumission a sort of parole. There was really no "bend in the river", no change of course for the enslaved persons, until the very last years of slavery.

When circumstances finally drove the imperial government to set its slaves free, it pursued this objective in a rather *ad hoc* and piecemeal fashion over roughly a four-year span – first, the apprenticed Africans; then the escheated slaves; third, the Crown slaves in all the colonies except Mauritius; and finally those in Mauritius. It took the government another six years to abolish slavery entirely from its colonies – first the abolition of slavery as a legal institution and then the abolition of the apprenticeship system. In all, there were six phases of abolition in the decade 1828 to 1838.

Reflections

Charles Kyte observed in 1826 that the *winkel* establishment was "widely differing in it's [*sic*] formation and government from any other" in the colony.[1] This was true to the extent that it was by far the largest group of urban slaves in the colony and it belonged to the imperial government. It was subsidized by the imperial Treasury and was the focus of an experiment at amelioration over a fairly long period of time, some nineteen years, through special personnel appointed both in London and in the colonies to administer it. However, to the ordinary observer its unique features would have been less noticeable than its common ones. The daily lives of the Crown people basically replicated those of the vast majority of enslaved people in such important aspects as food, clothing, accommodation, access to medical care, reproductive health, punishment and leisure time. The slaves of the imperial government were not exempt from any of the slave laws governing the colony, the Crown having to pay the usual head taxes for them besides the various urban property taxes. For the most part, also, the administrators on the ground behaved like typical slave owners, and most of them either were slave owners themselves or had managed slaves at some point. They were clearly not imbued with any strong humanitarian sentiments and never administered the department with a view to emancipation. In all these respects the department bore a striking resemblance to the general pattern in the colony. When emancipation came in 1831 it was as the result of a sudden rush by the imperial government to get rid of its slaves generally, and especially the *winkel* department, which had become a serious burden, rather than proceeding from any reasoned policy and carefully crafted programme of emancipation.

The period when the properties were under the direct administration of the governors was marked by unprofessional and often sloppy management, and chequered with several instances of questionable financial practices and strong allegations of fraud. While the depreciation rate of the persons attached to the Crown properties was in keeping with that of the slave population in the colony as a whole, the wastage was still a matter of concern to the Treasury, especially since the population proved unable to reproduce itself by natural means. The Treasury perceived this as the ultimate indictment against the system of management. The question was whether the new management team, the (Berbice) Commission for Management, could do better.

The performance record of the commissioners was uneven, without any outstanding failures or successes. Looked at in absolute terms, it is reasonable to conclude that they failed to achieve their major objective – a decrease in the mortality rate of the persons under their charge – while many of their other initiatives barely got off the ground. They and their agents also had to deal with widespread hostility to their initiatives within the colony, not only from planters but also from some of the highest government officials. De la Court also turned out to be just the opposite of what the commissioners had anticipated. While not all the conflicts were of his own making, he never displayed the restraint and discretion which the commissioners had enjoined on him and which were necessary to the success of his mission. The task was never going to be easy, but he made it much more difficult than it might have been. If he did have any crusading zeal for the work, it became vitiated by the weight of antagonism against him and the mental corruption that often beset free persons living in slave societies. He also lost that singleness of vision which the commissioners required of him, becoming preoccupied with personal ventures and ingratiating himself into the ranks of the plantocracy, to the neglect of the proper management of the Crown properties.

At the end of the war the imperial government consciously aborted the main experiment at amelioration, much to the chagrin of the commissioners and the delight of the plantocracy, by returning the estates to the Berbice Association. This made nonsense of the experiment which had gone before, for, shortly after, all attempts at religious and other reforms ended and the association eventually sold the estates to a local planter who ran them as he did the rest of his property. The whole affair cast grave doubts on the depth of the imperial government's interest in the experiment in the first place. As regards the *winkel* department, the imperial government left it to drift along for several years after the return of the estates. This was the more surprising since Vansittart, a former member of the commission, was now chancellor of the exchequer and therefore in a strong position to guide Treasury (and, by implication, imperial) policy on the matter of amelioration within the department. But, arguably, the Treasury's concern about the *winkel* people was no greater than its concern about the escheated slaves.

As it turned out, the period between 1815 and 1826 was one of aimless drift in terms of amelioration, with the *winkel* people being treated in no way differently from other enslaved people. The fact that Walker had virtually no one to answer to for the day-to-day administration of the department, in the absence of the kind of overarching authority which the commission had exercised, allowed him great scope for abuse of authority and privilege. His main focus drifted from the amelioration of the people's condition to simply maintaining them on the minimum fare prescribed by law and custom, and sometimes he even breached the laws. It was only in the last five years or so before the department was abolished and the people emancipated that the imperial government made some effort, still on a rather *ad hoc* basis, to create limited opportunities for manumission, viewing emancipation as a distant objective. As noted already, when emancipation came it was sudden and largely unplanned, and was driven partly by the desire not to spend more money on an institution that had become economically unprofitable to the Crown. This factor and others dealt with in the study reinforce the view of Eric Williams that economic issues were central in the abolition of British slavery, as against the view of Seymour Drescher and others of his school that humanitarian issues were the most important.[2]

Another of the interesting features of our study is that, especially from the early 1820s, we have been able to follow fairly closely the day-to-day struggles of the *winkel* people to resist the forces of subjection and to lift themselves up by their own efforts. This was not through large-scale desertion or violent revolt, but through a host of acts of noncompliance, often viewed by management as insubordination for which the people were punished. These acts of noncompliance were embraced not only by adults but by children in their early teens. We can also follow the people through their agonies and feel their trauma through their testimony to the commissioners of inquiry, and the commissioners' own commentaries on what they observed and heard. The records therefore allow us to have an intimacy and immediacy with slave life in the department, and by extension the colony, which is rare in the history of slave societies in the Caribbean. In fact, at present it is impossible to make strong comparisons with any similar body of enslaved people in the region. The nearest comparisons are perhaps those of the Codrington and Newton slaves in Barbados, and of Worthy Park and Montpelier in Jamaica, but the studies by Bennett, Handler and Lange, Craton and Walvin, and Higman,[3] while giving considerable information on the material and social lives of the people, have little to say about their inner feelings and their aspirations for a better way of life. Slave testimonies in court cases involving rebellions, and complaints by slaves to the protectors appointed by the colonial governments in the French and Spanish Caribbean, and more selectively in the British Caribbean – in Trinidad, St Lucia, Demerara and Berbice – also give some indication of the inner feelings of the enslaved people, but in much more restricted circumstances than those of the *winkel* people with whom this study is concerned. Still, it may be argued persuasively that while the survival of this particular kind of record is unusual and perhaps unique, the experiences of the *winkel* people were certainly not unique, as this study has admitted, and therefore their views and aspirations reflected those of the wider community of slaves in the region.

The present study addresses the issue of ameliorating the conditions of slaves within the plantation and more particularly the urban context. Everywhere in the world that slave plantation regimes developed, enslaved persons suffered substantial loss of economic and social rights and in some instances were reduced almost completely to units of production. The phenomenon became more noticeable, for instance, in Dahomey in the later nineteenth century, during that country's transition from slave raiding and trading to palm-oil production and trade,[4] although it never reached the depths of human degradation associated with Caribbean plantation slavery. In other situations where persons were introduced in servile circumstances into new societies or households, their material and social conditions did not necessarily degenerate, and were sometimes even enhanced, where, for example, they became the wives, viziers or military personnel of wealthy persons.[5] But Caribbean slavery, even at its lightest, never ascended to such levels of material and social comfort. To the basic disabilities of natal alienation were added loss of civil rights, property rights and control over one's children.

There was also always the overarching disability of being of a darker hue than white – in short, racism. No matter how comparatively mild urban slavery might prove to be in a particular situation, all slaves suffered from an overt racist ideology and practice which had become endemic to Caribbean slave society by the eighteenth century. This fact, indeed, bound them to their free(d) black and coloured brethren, although these latter often attempted to distance themselves from persons held in slavery. The experience of the *winkel* people indicates quite clearly that no imperial or local official attempted to deal with this problem in a positive manner, not even missionary Wray, who pandered to the prejudices of the plantocracy by assigning the *winkel* people segregated seats in his chapel.[6] *Winkel* people found that it was true that the Ethiopian cannot change his skin or the leopard his spots.[7] The value of a black skin was of much economic worth but little social worth to the slave managers.

Caribbean slavery involved the exclusive right of individuals to own other individuals as property. That right remained unchallenged until the last years of the eighteenth century, and it was not until less than a decade before the demise of the slave system in the British Caribbean that the imperial government accepted the view that it was philosophically and ideologically incompatible with one's own humanity to hold individuals in such a condition. The discussions on the *winkel* people and the escheated slaves helped to draw them towards that conclusion. Still, the imperial government felt that the property rights of slave owners had to be recognized through the payment of compensation money consequent upon the abolition of slavery. The imperial government did not take into account the fundamental rights of the enslaved peoples to their freedom and the value of their labour. They took the position that the granting of freedom was sufficient payment for them, and left them to fend for themselves in the post-emancipation period. Of course, as already noted, in the specific case of the *winkel* people the imperial government undertook to support at a minimal level those incapable for providing for themselves who did not have relatives willing and able to do so. The government also offered them plots of land, provided they cultivated the same. However, no such facilities were made available to the other government slaves, indicating the imperial government's lack of concern with the ultimate welfare of these persons. The government therefore set the pattern in an important way for what was to follow in respect of the wider slave-owner interests in the colonies. The failure of the government to grant some form of compensation to the ex-slaves is the basis on which current demands for reparation to the descendants of these people are being made.

On the wider issue of freedom in slave societies, David Brion Davis has grappled with the problem of the slave holders in the American colonies actively pursuing their own freedom from imperial control while holding thousands of their fellow humans in bondage, for the most part without any compunction.[8] But most slave holders saw no contradiction in this situation, viewing slaves as lower life forms for whom freedom held little or no meaning. Many of them argued, and some of them felt, that slavery was the best milieu in which blacks could live, and that whites were in the best position to assist them to achieve what little human and social worth they were capable of achieving. Edward Long was sure that blacks were, in fact, a different species of humanity, if indeed they were human, in spite of the fact that their ability to reproduce with white partners proved that genetically they were human. He went as far as to assert that an ourang-outang would make a not unworthy husband for some of the Khoisan women of South Africa.[9] Others, not as extreme as Long, still believed that it would take a long while for Africans to reach the stage of "civilisation" where they could make positive use of their freedom.[10] A few persons, such as John Poyer, accepted the Aristotelian doctrine of natural slavery, applying it to Africans.[11]

The Berbice plantocracy embraced many of these sentiments and attitudes, and intensely resented the slightest metropolitan interference with their freedoms, including the freedom to order their society as they saw fit while denying the most elemental freedoms to their slaves. There, as elsewhere in the region, the basic division in the society was between free people and slave people. Slavery was the most significant social institution, defining almost all aspects of human relations in the slave colonies. As Patterson points out, "In a large-scale slave society, the slave relation, like a cancer in the blood, pervades all, degrades all, and magnifies in all the overwhelming goodness and desirability of freedom."[12] A Berbice slave named

Louisa expressed that sentiment about freedom in less elegant language, when asked whether she desired to be free: "[T]o be sure I do Massa, every body like free."[13]

Freedom, which is often taken as elemental today, a basic condition of human society and a precondition of social happiness, became in the slave societies almost an end in itself. But for many enslaved people the most important thing was simply to stay alive, especially given the exceptionally high mortality rate in slave plantation societies, where a newly imported slave lived on average for only a further seven to ten years.[14] This is one reason why Patterson referred to the institution as "a terrifying part of the human condition like warfare and piracy and plague and death".[15] That institution has left its mark on the psyche of many of the descendants of the slaves, one part of the multiple residues of slavery, as Vidiadhar Naipaul has noted so eloquently:

> So many things in these West Indian territories . . . speak of slavery. There is slavery in the vegetation. In the sugarcane brought by Columbus . . . In the breadfruit, cheap slave food . . . in the saltfish still beloved by the islanders. Slavery in the absence of family life, in the laughter in the cinema at films of German concentration camps, in the fondness of terms for racial abuse, in the physical brutality of strong to weak. . . .[16]

Notes

Preface

1. Walker to Harrison, 10 November 1821, Public Record Office (PRO), T1/3481: 287; Byng to Treasury, 4 August 1824, T1/3482/2: 14.

Introduction

1. Thomas Clarkson, *The History of the Rise, Progress and Accomplishment of the Abolition of the African Slave Trade by the British Parliament* (London: Longman, Hurst, Reese and Orme, 1808); James Stephen, *The Slavery of the British West India Colonies Delineated as It Exists Both in Law and Practice* (1824–1830; reprint, New York: Kraus, 1969).
2. Edward Long, *The History of Jamaica* (1774; reprint, London: Frank Cass, 1970); Bryan Edwards, *The History, Civil and Commercial, of the British Colonies in the West Indies*, 5th ed. (New York: AMS Press, 1966); James M'Queen, *The West India Colonies; The Calumnies and Misrepresentations Circulated against Them* (1825; reprint, New York: Negro Universities Press, 1969).
3. William L. Mathieson, *British Slavery and Its Abolition, 1823–1838* (London: Longman, Green and Co., 1926); Frank J. Klingberg, *The Anti-Slavery Movement in England: A Study in English Humanitarianism* (1926; reprint, Hamden, Conn.: Archon Books, 1968); Lowell Ragatz, *The Fall of the Planter Class in the British Caribbean, 1763–1833* (1928; reprint, New York: Octagon Books, 1963); Reginald Coupland, *The British Anti-Slavery Movement* (London: T. Butterworth, 1933); Eric Williams, *Capitalism and Slavery* (London: André Deutsch, 1944).
4. Adam Smith, *An Inquiry into the Nature and Causes of the Wealth of Nations* (1776; reprint, London: Murray, 1870).
5. For modern studies on the efficiency of slave labour see Stanley Engerman and Robert Fogel, *Time on the Cross: The Economics of American Negro Slavery* (Boston: Little, Brown, 1974); and David Brion Davis, *Slavery and Human Progress* (New York: Oxford University Press, 1984).
6. See, for instance, Seymour Drescher, *Econocide: British Slavery in the Era of Abolition* (Pittsburgh: University of Pittsburgh Press, 1977); Seymour Drescher, *Capitalism and Antislavery: British Mobilization in Comparative Perspective* (London: Macmillan, 1986); David Eltis, *Economic Growth and the Ending of the Transatlantic Slave Trade* (New York: Oxford University Press, 1987); Roger Anstey, *The Atlantic Slave Trade and British Abolition, 1760–1810* (London:

Macmillan, 1975); Walter Rodney, *How Europe Underdeveloped Africa* (London: Bogle L'Ouverture Publications, 1972); Selwyn Carrington, "The State of the Debate on the Role of Capitalism in the Ending of the Slave System", *Journal of Caribbean History* 22 (1988): 20–41; Barbara L. Solow, "Caribbean Slavery and British Growth: The Eric Williams Hypothesis", *Journal of Development Economics* 17, no. 1–2 (1985): 99–115; Stanley Engerman, "The Slave Trade and British Capital Formation in the Eighteenth Century: A Comment on the Williams Thesis", *Business History Review* 46 (1972): 430–43; Barbara L. Solow and Stanley Engerman, eds., *British Capitalism and Caribbean Slavery: The Legacy of Eric Williams* (New York: Cambridge University Press, 1987).

7. Barry Higman, *Slave Populations of the British Caribbean, 1807–1834* (Baltimore, Md.: Johns Hopkins University Press, 1984).

8. Kenneth Kiple, *The Caribbean Slave: A Biological History* (Cambridge: Cambridge University Press, 1984); Richard Sheridan, *Doctors and Slaves: A Medical and Demographic History of Slavery in the British West Indies, 1680–1834* (Cambridge: Cambridge University Press, 1985).

9. Barbara Bush, *Slave Women in Caribbean Society, 1650–1838* (Kingston, Jamaica: Heinemann, 1990).

10. Hilary McD. Beckles, *Natural Rebels: A Social History of Enslaved Black Women in Barbados* (London: Zed Books, 1989).

11. A few other important studies on gender in Caribbean slavery are Hilary McD. Beckles, "Historicizing Slavery in West Indian Feminism", *Feminist Review* 59 (1998): 34–56; Hilary McD. Beckles, "Sex and Gender in the Historiography of Caribbean Slavery", in *Engendering History: Caribbean Women in Historical Perspective*, ed. Verene Shepherd, Bridget Brereton and Barbara Bailey (Kingston, Jamaica: Ian Randle Publishers, 1995), 125–40; Bernard Moitt, "Women, Work and Resistance in the French Caribbean during Slavery, 1700–1848", in *Engendering History*, ed. Shepherd, Brereton and Bailey, 155–76; Marietta Morrissey, *Slave Women in the New World: Gender Stratification in the Caribbean* (Lawrence: University of Kansas Press, 1989); Barry Higman, "The Slave Family and Household in the British West Indies, 1800–1834", *Journal of Interdisciplinary History* 1, no. 2 (1975): 261–87.

12. Pedro Welch, "The Urban Context of the Slave Plantation System: Bridgetown, Barbados, 1680–1834" (PhD diss., University of the West Indies, 1994); Barry Higman, "Urban Slavery in the British Caribbean", in *Perspectives on Caribbean Regional Identity*, ed. Elizabeth Thomas-Hope (Liverpool: Centre for Latin American Studies, University of Liverpool, 1984), 39–56; Neville Hall, "Slavery in Three West Indian Towns: Christiansted, Frederiksted, and Charlotte Amalie", in *Trade, Government and Society in Caribbean History, 1700–1920*, ed. Barry Higman (Kingston, Jamaica: Heinemann, 1983), 21–38.

13. Robin Law, *The Oyo Empire, c.1600–c.1836: A West African Imperialism in the Era of the Atlantic Slave Trade* (Oxford: Clarendon Press, 1977), 67–70, 190.

14. For excellent discussions and bibliographies on this aspect of slavery see Orlando Patterson, *Slavery and Social Death: A Comparative Study* (Cambridge: Harvard University Press, 1982), 299–333; and Seymour

Drescher and Stanley Engerman, eds., *A Historical Guide to World Slavery* (Oxford: Oxford University Press, 1998), 27–50, 77–87, 189–92, 334–35. On *mamluk* rule see Ivan Hrbek, "Egypt, Nubia and the Eastern Deserts", in *The Cambridge History of Africa*, vol. 3, *From c.1050 to c.1600*, ed. Roland Oliver (Cambridge: Cambridge University Press, 1977), 39–69.
15. See, for instance, Treasury minutes, 1812–1817, PRO, T29/117–147.
16. See chapter 8 for a detailed discussion of the various categories of Crown slaves in the 1820s.
17. Henry Bolingbroke, *A Voyage to Demerary, Containing a Statistical Account of the Settlements There and Those of the Essequibo, the Berbice, and Other Contiguous Rivers of Guiana* (1808; reprint, Georgetown, Guyana: Daily Chronicle, 1947), 39.
18. The most detailed study on this subject is Roger N. Buckley, *Slaves in Red Coats: The British West India Regiments, 1795–1815* (New Haven, Conn.: Yale University Press, 1979).
19. Alvin O. Thompson, "African 'Recaptives' under Apprenticeship in the British West Indies, 1807–1828", *Immigrants and Minorities* 9, no. 2 (1990): 123–44.
20. James Rodway, *History of British Guiana from the Year 1688 to the Present Time*, vol. 3 (Georgetown, Guyana: J. Thomson, 1894), 269–70, 274–76; P.M. Netscher, "Laatste Levensjaren en Liquidatie der Societeit Van Berbice Als Particuliere Handelsvennootschap, 1815–1848", addendum to his *Geschiedenis Van De Kolonien Essequebo, Demerary en Berbice* (The Hague: Martinus Nijhoff, 1888).
21. Graham Cruickshank, "'King William's People': The Story of the Winkel Village, Berbice", *Timehri* 5 (1918): 104–19; Donald Wood, "Crown Slavery in Berbice" (seminar paper, Institute of Commonwealth Studies, University of London, 1984).
22. A.J. McR. Cameron, "Abolitionists Who Managed Slaves", *Stabroek News*, 19 August 1989; Cameron, "The Origins of the Winkle Village", *Stabroek News*, 26 August 1989.
23. Michael Craton, *Searching for the Invisible Man: Slaves and Plantation Life in Jamaica* (Cambridge: Harvard University Press, 1978).
24. Mary Prince, *The History of Mary Prince, a West Indian Slave, Related by Herself* (1831; reprint, Ann Arbor: University of Michigan Press, 1993).
25. Harriet Jacobs [Linda Brent, pseud.], *Incidents in the Life of a Slave Girl Written by Herself* (1861; reprint, Cambridge: Harvard University Press, 1987); William W. Brown, *Narrative of William W. Brown, a Fugitive Slave* (Boston: Anti-Slavery Office, 1847); Booker T. Washington, *Up from Slavery: An Autobiography* (1901; reprint, New York: Doubleday, 1963); Frederick Douglass, *My Bondage and My Freedom* (1855; reprint, New York: Dover, 1969); Douglass, *Narrative of the Life of Frederick Douglass* (1845; reprint, New York: Penguin Books, 1982). This last work was the most popular slave narrative of the American slavery period.

Chapter 1

1. Lloyd Best, "Outlines of a Model of Pure Plantation Economy", *Social and Economic Studies* 17, no. 3 (1968): 7–38; George Beckford, *Persistent Poverty: Underdevelopment in Plantation Economies of the Third World* (New York: Oxford University Press, 1972).
2. See, for instance, Gwendolyn Midlo Hall, *Social Control in Slave Plantation*

Societies: A Comparison of St. Domingue and Cuba (Baltimore, Md.: Johns Hopkins University Press, 1971), 81–112; and Elsa Goveia, *The West Indian Slave Laws of the Eighteenth Century* (Bridgetown, Barbados: Caribbean Universities Press, 1970).
3. See the following texts, from which much of the data that follow are derived: Barry Higman, *Slave Populations of the British Caribbean, 1807–1834* (Baltimore, Md.: Johns Hopkins University Press, 1984); Pedro Welch, "The Urban Context of the Slave Plantation System: Bridgetown, Barbados, 1680–1834" (PhD diss., University of the West Indies, 1994); Edward Brathwaite, *The Development of Creole Society in Jamaica, 1770–1820* (Oxford: Oxford University Press, 1971); Elsa Goveia, *Slave Society in the British Leeward Islands at the End of the Eighteenth Century* (1965; reprint, Westport, Conn.: Greenwood Press, 1980); Karl Watson, *The Civilized Island Barbados* (Bridgetown, Barbados: Caribbean Graphics, 1979); Colin Clarke, *Kingston, Jamaica: Urban Development and Social Change, 1692–1962* (Berkeley: University of California Press, 1975); Neville Hall, "Slaves and the Law in the Towns of St Croix, 1802–1807", *Slavery and Abolition* 8 (1987): 147–65; Neville Hall, "Slavery in Three West Indian Towns: Christiansted, Fredericksted, and Charlotte Amalie", in *Trade, Government and Society in Caribbean History, 1700–1920*, ed. Barry Higman (Kingston, Jamaica: Heinemann, 1983), 21–38.
4. The Dutch ceded the colony in 1814 to the British, who amalgamated it to its sister colony Demerara-Essequibo in 1831 to form British Guiana. The Colonial Office sent the letter of amalgamation to Lieutenant Governor Sir Benjamin D'Urban on 4 March 1831 and he published it on 21 July 1831. See A.R.F. Webber, *Centenary History and Handbook of British Guiana* (Georgetown, Guyana: Argosy Co., 1931), 158.
5. Henry Dalton, *The History of British Guiana, Comprising a General Description of the Colony*, vol. 1 (London: Longman, 1855), 6–14.
6. Richard Schomburgk, *Travels in British Guiana, 1840–1844*, vol. 1, trans. and ed. W.E. Roth (Georgetown, Guyana: Daily Chronicle, 1922), 55.
7. Van Batenburg to Portland, 30 November 1799, PRO, CO 111/73.
8. Ibid.; Beard to Murray, 22 February 1830, CO 111/109, enc.
9. Van Batenburg to Hobart, 26 January 1804 and July 1804, CO 111/74; Van Batenburg to Castlereagh, 10 October 1805, CO 111/75; Woodley to Castlereagh, 14 June 1809, CO 111/77; Managers of Wolfert Katz's estates to Beard, 14 February 1826, CO 111/103.
10. Van Batenburg to Portland, 30 November 1799, CO 111/73; Beard to Murray, 22 February 1830, CO 111/109, enc.
11. Walker to Harrison, 24 July 1823 and 30 December 1823, PRO, T1/3481: 197, 386; Walker to Harrison, 2 April 1825, T1/3482/2: 38–39; "Report of the Commission of Inquiry", November 1826, T1/3483/1: 199; Memorial of Walker to Bathurst, 3 March 1827, T1/3484: 133–36.
12. George Pinckard, *Notes on the West Indies . . . and . . . the Coast of Guiana*, vol. 2 (London: Longman, Hurst, Rees and Orme, 1806), 308.
13. James Williams, *Dutch Plantations on the Banks of the Berbice and Canje Rivers in the Country Known since 1831 as the Colony of British Guiana, and the Village Evolved from the Plantation* (Georgetown, Guyana: Daily Chronicle, 1940), passim.

14. See Alvin O. Thompson, "The Guyana-Suriname Boundary Dispute: An Historical Appraisal, c.1683–1816", *Boletín de Estudios Latinoamericanos y del Caribe* 39 (1985): 63–84.
15. See Alvin O. Thompson, *Colonialism and Underdevelopment in Guiana, 1580–1803* (Bridgetown, Barbados: Carib Research and Publications, 1987), 62–68.
16. Ibid., 82–83.
17. Van Batenburg to Portland, 30 November 1799, CO 111/73.
18. *Berbice Gazette*, 8 April 1815.
19. Berbice Court of Policy to Bathurst, 28 May 1816, CO 111/85; "Extract from minutes of the Council of Government of Berbice", 8 January 1818, CO 111/88, and enc.; Scott to Macaulay, 29 December 1818, T1/3484: 1013–28.
20. James Rodway, *History of British Guiana from the Year 1688 to the Present Time*, vol. 2 (Georgetown, Guyana: J. Thomson, 1893), 265–66.
21. "Slave Population of Berbice in 1822", 23 December 1823, CO 111/97.
22. *Berbice Gazette*, 30 September 1815.
23. Higman, *Slave Populations*, 310. He did not give figures for 1831 to 1834, probably because the colony lost its specific identity in 1831 through amalgamation with Demerara-Essequibo.
24. Higman, *Slave Populations*, 309–10; Beard to Murray, 22 February 1830, CO 111/109, enc.
25. A. Thornborrow, "Berbice, 7 October 1811", CO 111/78; J. Lyons Nixon, "White and Free Coloured population . . . for 1822", 13 January 1824, CO 111/97; "Population of Berbice on 15 September 1829", 16 January 1830, CO 111/109.
26. Beard to Horton, 13 January 1824, CO 111/97.
27. Compiled from Stanley Engerman and Barry Higman, "The Demographic Structure of the Caribbean Slave Societies in the Eighteenth and Nineteenth Centuries", in *General History of the Caribbean*, vol. 3, *The Slave Societies of the Caribbean*, ed. Franklin Knight (London: UNESCO Publishing/Macmillan Education, 1997), 50–52.
28. We cannot account for the size of the population decrease in 1817, except by suggesting that the figures were inaccurate, taken as they were before the first official census in 1819, which gives a significantly higher figure. Higman's data contain discrepancies concerning the figures for selected years (see, for instance, *Slave Populations*, 415, 435, 468).
29. Court of Policy and Criminal Justice of Berbice (CPCJB), Sessional Papers, 1 October 1810, Guyana National Archives (GNA).
30. Welch, "Urban Context", 327.
31. "Return of the population of Berbice on 15 September 1829", 16 January 1830, CO 111/109.
32. CPCJB, Sessional Papers, 8 January 1812, CO 114/2.
33. "Complaints of slaves to the protector of slaves", 1 July–1 September 1827, in Bird to Beard, 1 September 1827, CO 111/104.
34. For slaves', and occasionally masters', complaints to the fiscal or protector see House of Commons, "Copies of the Record of the Proceedings of the Fiscals of Demerara and Berbice, in their Capacity of Guardians and Protectors of the Slaves . . . from the 1st January 1814", *PP*, 1825, XXV (476); and "Copies of the Record of the Proceedings of the Fiscals of Demerara and Berbice, in their Capacity of Guardians and Protectors of the Slaves . . . from the 1st January 1814 . . . In Continuation of the Papers Presented 23 June 1825; No. 476", *PP*, 1826, XXVI (401).

35. Beard to Power, 27 January 1829, CO 111/107; Beard to Murray, 18 March 1829, CO 111/107. There are two letters from Beard to Murray on this subject bearing the same date.
36. *PP,* 1826, XXVI (401): 8.
37. Bennett to Bentinck, 19 May 1817, CO 111/88 and enc.; Wray to Hankey, 19 August 1818, London Missionary Society manuscripts (LMS), Box 1A; House of Commons, "Further Papers Relating to the Treatment of Slaves in the Colonies", *PP,* 1818, XVII (433): 228–41.
38. *PP,* 1825, XXV (476): 25–27; *PP,* 1826, XXVI (401): 15–16.
39. *PP,* 1818, XVII (433): 243–49; Wray to Hankey, 19 August 1818, LMS, Box 1A.
40. *PP,* 1818, XVII (433): 249.
41. Gipps to Twiss, 17 February 1830, CO 111/112.
42. *PP,* 1826, XXVI (401): 12.
43. Ibid., 13.
44. *PP,* 1825, XXV (476): 63, 66.
45. *PP,* 1826, XXVI (401): 17.
46. *PP,* 1825, XXV (476): 47.
47. He was the chief judicial officer and forerunner of the attorney general. However, for a long time the governor sat as president of the Court of Criminal Justice.
48. House of Commons, "Copy of the Report of the Commissioners Appointed for the Management of the Crown Estates in the Colony of Berbice, to the Lords Commissioners of His Majesty's Treasury", *PP,* 1816, VIII (528): 36; *Berbice Gazette,* 14 November 1818; Berbice slave registry, 1819, T1/438; Wray to Hankey, 6 February 1822, LMS, Box 1A; Rodway, *History of British Guiana,* vol. 3, 273; Pinckard, *Notes on the West Indies,* vol. 2, 352–53. In 1831 a total of sixteen government officers owned slaves, the largest slave owner being the fiscal, who was joint owner of plantation Woodley Park with eighty-seven slaves. See "Govt. slaves in Berbice and Govt. officers owning slaves", 18 April 1831, in Beard to Goderich, 21 April 1831, CO 111/114.
49. *PP,* 1826, XXVI (401): 4.
50. House of Commons, "An Account of the Final Disposal of the Slaves Escheated to the Crown in the Colonies of the West Indies, since 1st January 1821, and whose Cases have been referred to the Decision of His Majesty's Government", *PP,* 1830–31, XVI (121): 9–15.
51. J.R. Ward, *British West Indian Slavery, 1750–1834: The Process of Amelioration* (Oxford: Clarendon Press, 1988), 198.
52. Ibid., 1–7, 190–232, 261–79.
53. White and McLean to Beard, 30 October 1826, CO 111/102.
54. Beard to Horton, 1 October 1826, CO 111/102.
55. "Regulations for the treatment of servants and slaves" (translated by British Imperial Government), 1 October 1784, CO 111/44; Berbice Legislature, "Proclamations", in appendix to minutes of the Council of Government of Berbice, 1817–18, GNA; "Report of the Commission of Inquiry", T1/3483/1: 99–100.
56. Conversion rates for the Dutch guilder (f) ranged from about f12 to £1 around 1803, to f14:5 to £1 around 1831. We have often rounded off the monies cited in this study to whole guilders or pounds as the case may be.
57. Berbice Legislature, "Proclamations", in appendix to minutes of the Council of Government of Berbice, 1817–18, GNA.
58. James Walker, *Letters on the West Indies* (London: Camberwell Press, 1818), 73, 74, 77.
59. Pinckard, *Notes on the West Indies,* vol. 2, 201. The Berbice protector of slaves also employed the cart whip sometimes

(Stephen to Twiss, 6 November 1828, CO 111/106).
60. Schwiers to White, May 1818, CO 111/88.
61. Walker, *Letters*, 70.
62. Thomas Rain, *The Life and Labours of John Wray, Pioneer Missionary in British Guiana, Compiled from His Own Mss. and Diaries* (London: John Snow and Co., 1892), 256.
63. Beard to Murray, 2 January 1829, CO 111/107; "Regulations for the treadmill", 29 July 1828, CO 111/107. For a short statement on the use of the treadmill in the British colonies in general see Higman, *Slave Populations*, 243–44.
64. Blue Book, Berbice, 1828, CO 116/176; Higman, *Slave Populations*, 201; William L. Burn, *Emancipation and Apprenticeship in the British West Indies* (London: Jonathan Cape, 1937), 282–84.
65. Blue Book, Berbice, 1828, CO 116/176; Beard to Murray, 2 January 1829, CO 111/107; "Regulations for the treadmill", 29 July 1828, CO 111/107; "Monthly returns of slaves worked on the treadmill", August–December 1828 and January–October 1829, in Beard to Murray, 2 January 1829 and 5 November 1829, CO 111/107.
66. Cited in Rain, *John Wray*, 301.
67. Bryan Edwards, *The History, Civil and Commercial, of the British Colonies in the West Indies*, 5th ed., vol. 2 (New York: AMS Press, 1966), 13; italics in original.
68. Stephen to Twiss, 6 November 1828, CO 111/106.
69. Ibid.
70. CPCJB, Sessional Papers, 8 August 1808, GNA; "Return of slaves taken up and sold in execution of debt . . .", 1 January 1821–10 August 1825, d. 15 December 1825, CO 111/101.

71. "Manumissions", 4 April 1808–4 October 1820, CO 111/94; "Manumissions", 1 January 1825–15 November 1830, in Beard to Murray, 18 November 1830, CO 111/110.
72. Bird to Beard, 1 September 1827, CO 111/104.
73. See Alvin O. Thompson, "'Happy – Happy Slaves!': Slavery as a Superior State to Freedom", *Journal of Caribbean History* 29, no. 2 (1995): 93–119.
74. "Complaints of slaves", 2 November 1826–2 January 1827, in Power to Beard, 21 January 1827, CO 111/104.
75. Beard to Goderich, 21 July 1827, CO 111/104.
76. "Complaints of slaves", 2 November 1826–2 January 1827, in Power to Beard, 21 January 1827, CO 111/104.
77. Bird to Beard, 1 September 1827, CO 111/104.
78. Stephen to Horton, 9 July 1827, CO 111/105; Beard to Murray, 22 September 1828, 18 March 1829 and 15 May 1830, CO 111/106, 107 and 109.
79. "Extract from the register of the minutes of the Court of Policy and Criminal Justice . . .", 1 August 1812, CO 111/79.
80. Paul Beatty, *A History of the Lutheran Church in Guyana* (Georgetown, Guyana: Daily Chronicle, 1970), 24; Wray to Burder, 25 October 1817, LMS, Box 1A; Wray to Hankey, 30 October 1824 and 24 February 1831, LMS, Box 1B; Austin to Beard, 30 April 1821, CO 111/93; Wray to Beard, 28 December 1823, CO 111/97; Blue Book, Berbice, 1829, CO 116/177. Beatty gives the date for the coming of a new pastor to the Lutheran church as around 1818, but other evidence shows that there was a pastor in 1816.
81. Cited in Rain, *John Wray*, 278, 294. See also Wray to Hankey, 26 March and 21 September 1830, LMS, Box 2.

82. CPCJB, Sessional Papers, 11 April 1808, GNA.
83. Beatty, *Lutheran Church*, 27.
84. Vos to Power, November 1826, CO 111/104. See also Power to Beard, 16 April 1827, CO 111/104. Wray claimed that up to the time of his death Vos had left the slaves on his church's plantation in total neglect. However, in 1832 he declared that the Lutherans were teaching their slaves to read and write: "What a change!!!" (Wray to Hankey, 26 March 1830 and 8 March 1832, LMS, Box 2).
85. Rain, *John Wray,* 284–310; Wray to Hankey, 11 July 1832, LMS, Box 2.
86. Extract from *Berbice Royal Gazette,* 30 January 1827, CO 111/104; Beard to Murray, 8 July 1829, CO 111/107; Blue Books, Berbice, 1829 and 1831, CO 116/177 and 178.
87. The former site, often referred to as Old Dageraad, was located some forty-five miles up the left bank of the Berbice River. Government of Guyana, *Gazetteer of Guyana* (Georgetown, 1974), 107.
88. Thompson, *Colonialism,* 80; Rain, *John Wray,* 87, 102; Guyana, *Gazetteer of Guyana,* 52, 103, 123; Williams, *Dutch Plantations,* 101–2, 153–54, 172–73.
89. Van Batenburg to Nicholson, 18 July 1804, CO 111/75.
90. "Lyste van der edelen societyts steenbakkery in Rio Berbice . . .", 1 January–31 December 1791, CO 116/127, folio (f.) 133; "Jaarlykse lyste van der edele societyts steenbakkerye . . .", 1 January–31 December 1792, CO 116/127, f. 105; "Lyste der afgeleveerde stenen in't jaar 1792 . . . aan de colonie . . .", CO 116/127, f. 406; "Lyste van het extra werk der edelen societyts steenbakkerye slaaven gedaan in 't jaar 1792", CO 116/127, ff. 407–8; "Veranderinge der steenbakkerys slaaven, in 't jaar 1792", d. 31 December 1792, CO 116/127, f. 408; "Jaarlykse lyste van der edelen societyts steenbakkerye . . .", 1 January–31 December 1793, CO 116/127, f. 404; "Lyste van der edelen societyts steenbakkery in Rio de Berbice van de veranderinge der slaaven . . . en waar dezelve geemployeert in 1793", d. 31 December 1793, CO 116/127, ff. 399–402.
91. Ibid.
92. "Report of the Commission of Inquiry", T1/3483/1: 49–50.
93. *PP,* 1816, VIII (528): 3–4.
94. Montgomerie to Castlereagh, 1 July 1807, CO 111/76; Woodley to Castlereagh, 17 July 1809, CO 111/77.

Chapter 2

1. See Colonist [sic], *Kort Historisch Verhaal Van den Eersten Aanleg, Lotgevallen en Voortgang der Particuliere Colonie Berbice* (Amsterdam: Sepp Jansz., 1807), 296–97.
2. Convention of 12 August 1815, Article 11, in Bathurst to Bentinck, 19 February 1816, PRO, CO 111/85.
3. Hobart to Van Batenburg, 31 March 1804, CO 112/8.
4. "Inventories of estates", October 1803, in Moncrieff to Hobart, 6 January 1804, CO 111/73; "Inventory of sundry articles belonging to the Winkel Department delivered over to A.A. de la Court . . .", 19 November 1812, in Murray to Bathurst, 20 January 1813, CO 111/80. See also chapter 5 on the *winkel* village in the mid-1820s.
5. "Inventories of estates", October 1803, in Moncrieff to Hobart, 6 January 1804, CO 111/73.
6. Nicholson to Grinfield, 17 November 1803, CO 111/73.
7. Van Batenburg to Camden, 15 November 1804, CO 111/74.
8. Ibid.

9. Ibid.; Van Batenburg to Secretary of State, February 1805, CO 111/75; Lohman to Van Batenburg, c. July 1804, CO 111/75.
10. See Karl Watson, *The Civilized Island Barbados* (Bridgetown, Barbados: Caribbean Graphics, 1979).
11. A.R.F. Webber, *Centenary History and Handbook of British Guiana* (Georgetown, Guyana: Argosy Co., 1931), 127, 141; Henry Dalton, *The History of British Guiana, Comprising a General Description of the Colony*, vol. 1 (London: Longman, 1855), 280–81.
12. "Report of the Commission of Inquiry", PRO, T1/3483/1: 233.
13. "Inventory of books and papers belonging to the Winkel Department delivered over to A.A. de la Court . . .", 12 November 1812, in Murray to Bathurst, 20 January 1813, CO 111/80.
14. Nicholson to Van Batenburg, 12 July 1804, CO 111/75.
15. Van Batenburg to Camden, 15 November 1804, CO 111/75; Woodley to Liverpool, 3 January 1810, CO 111/78.
16. "List of buildings, crafts, materials and slaves of the shopkeepers department", 7 October 1803, CO 111/73, enc. no. 5 of Moncrieff to Hobart, 6 January 1804; "Inventory of the Negroes and other slaves belonging to the Winkel Department", in Murray to Peel, 7 August 1812, CO 111/79.
17. CPCJB, Sessional Papers, 11 January 1811, CO 114/1.
18. CPCJB, Sessional Papers, 1 August 1812 and 26 July 1813, CO 114/1.
19. "Account of the revenue and expenditure of the Colony of Berbice, 1811–1814", c.1815, CO 111/83.
20. "Inventory of the Negroes and other slaves belonging to the Winkel Department", in Murray to Peel, 7 August 1812, CO 111/79.
21. "Inventory of books and papers belonging to the Winkel Department . . .", 12 November 1812, in Murray to Bathurst, 20 January 1813, CO 111/80.
22. "The Colonial Treasury of the settlement of Berbice's account current", in Van Batenburg to Secretary of State, 16 October 1802, CO 111/73.
23. Gordon to Bathurst, 27 February 1813, CO 111/80; House of Commons, "Papers Relating to the Crown Estates in the Colony of Berbice", *PP*, 1816, VIII (509): 30. The original document contains a couple of errors, the major one being a calculation error, with a difference of f300 in the total underpayments. The document published in *PP*, 1816, VIII (509): 30 incorrectly cites the figures as pounds sterling instead of guilders, thus considerably inflating them.
24. Liverpool to Gordon, 19 November 1811, CO 112/8.
25. Ibid.
26. Ibid. In 1811 the Court of Policy acknowledged that if the imperial government were to liquidate the *winkel* department it would result in the loss of "a considerable part" of the lieutenant governor's income (CPCJB, Sessional Papers, 11 January 1811, CO 114/1).
27. "Report of the Commission of Inquiry", T1/3483/1: 230.
28. Ibid.
29. Ibid., 50–51. See the introduction and chapter 4 for a description of the establishment of this commission.
30. "Lyste van het extra werk der edelen societyts steenbakkerye slaaven gedaan in 't jaar 1792", CO 111/127, ff. 407–8; CPCJB, Sessional Papers, 8 August 1808, GNA; Woodley to Castlereagh, 19 July 1809, CO 111/77; "Inventory of the Negroes", in Murray to Peel, 7 August 1812, CO 111/79; CPCJB, Sessional Papers, 1

August 1812, CO 114/2. The value of *winkel* labour is based on an estimate of 280 working days, deductions being made for one and a half days' free time per week and a few holidays. In the last days of the association's administration of the department the hire of a *winkel* male was usually f1 (1s. 8d) per day and of a female f0:75 (1s. 3d). In 1808 a year's hire of a prime male was f300 (£25); the figure for a female was probably f225 (£18:15).
31. CPCJB, Sessional Papers, 18 January 1811, 4, 5 and 14 February 1811, 1 and 9 April 1811, CO 114/1.
32. CPCJB, Sessional Papers, 14 February 1811, 1 April 1811, 1 February 1813, CO 114/1-2.
33. CPCJB, Sessional Papers, 7 July 1807, CO 114/1.
34. "Report of Court of Policy", 25 November 1808, in Montgomerie to Jenkinson, 20 March 1810, CO 111/78.
35. "Account of produce made and delivered from the colony estates at Berbice ... September 1804 to December 1808 inclusive", in Woodley to Castlereagh, 19 July 1809, CO 111/77.
36. Dalrymple to Liverpool, 13 December 1810, CO 111/78.
37. Gordon to Goulburn, 12 November 1812, CO 111/79.
38. "Account of produce made and delivered from the colony estates at Berbice, with the general expences of management ... from September 1804 to December 1808, inclusive", in Woodley to Castlereagh, 19 July 1809, CO 111/77; "Inventory of books and papers belonging to the Crown estates delivered over to A.A. de la Court ...", 9 November 1812, in Murray to Bathurst, 20 January 1813, CO 111/80; Gordon to Goulburn, 12 November 1812, CO 111/79.
39. Dalrymple to Liverpool, 4 May 1810, CO 111/78.
40. Gordon to Liverpool, 2 May 1811, CO 111/78.
41. Nicholson to Grinfield, 17 November 1803, CO 111/73; Staple to Harrison, 28 February 1809, CO 111/77; Woodley to Castlereagh, 19 July 1809, CO 111/77; Staple to Liverpool, 6 November 1809, CO 111/77; Montgomerie to Jenkinson, 20 March 1810, CO 111/78.
42. Montgomerie to Jenkinson, 20 March 1810, CO 111/78; Gordon to Liverpool, 16 December 1810, CO 111/78.
43. Montgomerie to Jenkinson, 20 March 1810, CO 111/78.
44. Deposition of Unger, 3 April 1806, CO 111/76; Colonist, *Kort Historisch*, 296–309. The British government also paid 5 per cent commissions to the administrators of its estates in Suriname and Grenada (see Sampson Sharp and Batard to Henry Fagel and Granville Penn, 23 May 1814, T75/17, and several similar letters in this set of documents; also Shipley to Bathurst, 10 May 1815, CO 101/55).
45. Gordon to Liverpool, 2–3 May 1811, CO 111/76.
46. Gordon to Harrison, 3 May 1811, CO 111/78. The appraisal of the estates was as follows: Sandvoort – f534,980; St Jan – f213,015; Dankbaarheid – f393,110; and Dageraad – f297,020, together amounting to f1,438,125 (£110,625) (ibid.).
47. Gordon to Goulburn, 12 November 1812, CO 111/79; CPCJB, Sessional Papers, 7 January 1812, CO 114/2.
48. Montgomerie to Jenkinson, 20 March 1810, CO 111/78; Gordon to Liverpool, 2 May 1811, CO 111/78.
49. Van Batenburg to Hobart, 26 January and July 1804, CO 111/74; Van Batenburg to Camden, 15 November 1804, CO 111/74; Van Batenburg to

Castlereagh, 10 October 1805, CO 111/75.
50. Woodley to Castlereagh, 6 and 14 June 1809, CO 111/77.
51. Gordon to Liverpool, 16 December 1810, CO 111/78.
52. Gordon to Goulburn, 12 November 1812, CO 111/79.
53. CPCJB, Sessional Papers, 22 February 1813, CO 114/2.
54. Staple to Harrison, 28 February 1809, CO 111/77; Staple to Liverpool, 6 November 1809, CO 111/77; Treasury minutes, 8 and 25 May 1810, T29/105; Court of Policy to Bentinck, 28 October 1815, CO 111/83; James Williams, *Dutch Plantations on the Banks of the Berbice and Canje Rivers in the Country Known since 1831 as the Colony of British Guiana, and the Village Evolved from the Plantation* (Georgetown, Guyana: Daily Chronicle, 1940), 172.
55. Cited in Castlereagh to Woodley, 30 March 1809, CO 112/8.
56. Woodley to Castlereagh, 19 July 1809, CO 111/77; Treasury minutes, 28 August 1810, T29/107; Dalrymple to Liverpool, 4 May 1810, CO 111/78; Wharton to Bunbury, 3 September 1810, CO 111/78. We have noted earlier that an accounting error led to an overestimate of the profits from the estates between 1804 and 1808.
57. Treasury minutes, 25 May 1810, T29/105.
58. Treasury minutes, 15 June 1810, T29/106; Treasury minutes, 26 March 1811, T29/110.
59. House of Commons, "Copy of the Report of the Commissioners Appointed for the Management of the Crown Estates in the Colony of Berbice, to the Lords Commissioners of His Majesty's Treasury", *PP,* 1816, VIII (528): 1.
60. Ibid., 2–3.
61. Treasury minutes, 26 March 1811, T29/110.
62. Gordon to Liverpool, 4 October 1811, CO 111/78. Gordon also claimed that the government had manumitted a few persons but did not specify the number (ibid.).
63. Barry Higman, *Slave Populations of the British Caribbean, 1807–1834* (Baltimore, Md.: Johns Hopkins University Press, 1984), 414–18.
64. *PP,* 1816, VIII (528): 3.
65. Treasury minutes, 26 March 1811, T29/110. See also Wharton to Peel, 23 July 1811, CO 111/78; Colonist, *The Edinburgh Review and the West Indies, with Observations on the Pamphlets of Stephen, Macaulay, etc.* (Glasgow: John Smith and Son, 1816), 296; Joseph Marryat, *More Thoughts Occasioned by Two Publications* (London: J.M. Richardson and J. Ridgway, 1816), 10.
66. *PP,* 1816, VIII (528): 3, 13.
67. *Dictionary of National Biography,* compact ed., s.v. "Wilberforce, William"; Reginald Coupland, *Wilberforce: A Narrative* (Oxford: Clarendon Press, 1923); Robin Furneaux, *William Wilberforce* (London: Hamish Hamilton, 1974); John Pollock, *Wilberforce* (London: Constable and Co., 1977).
68. *Dictionary of National Biography,* compact ed., s.v. "Stephen, James". See James Stephen, *Reasons for Establishing a Registry of Slaves in the British Colonies: Being a Report of a Committee of the African Institution* (London: African Institution, 1815); and Stephen, *Slavery of the British West India Colonies Delineated as It Exists Both in Law and Practice* (1824–1830; reprint, New York: Kraus, 1969).
69. *Dictionary of National Biography,* compact ed., s.v. "Macaulay, Zachary". See also George Trevelyan, *The Life and Letters of Lord Macaulay* (London: Longman Green, 1878).

70. Karen Racine, "Brittania's Bold Brother: British Cultural Influence in Haiti during the Reign of Henry Christophe (1811–1820)", *Journal of Caribbean History* 33, no. 1–2 (1999): 125–45.
71. J. Harry Bennett, Jr, *Bondsmen and Bishops: Slavery and Apprenticeship on the Codrington Plantations of Barbados, 1710–1838* (Berkeley: University of California Press, 1958).
72. William Dickson, *Mitigation of Slavery* (1814; reprint, Westport, Conn.: Negro Universities Press, 1970).
73. Joshua Steele, *Letters on Slavery* (1789), in Dickson, *Mitigation of Slavery*, 9–14, 115–25, and passim; also introduction by Dickson, xviii–xxiv; Thomas Clarkson, *Thoughts on the Necessity of Improving the Condition of the Slaves in the British Colonies* (London, 1823), 31–44; John Newman, "The Enigma of Joshua Steele", *Journal of the Barbados Museum and Historical Society* 19, no. 1 (1951): 6–20; Lowell Ragatz, *The Fall of the Planter Class in the British Caribbean, 1763–1833* (1928; reprint, New York: Octagon Books, 1963), 70–71. There is some difference among writers as to the date of Steele's death.
74. *PP*, 1816, VIII (528): 5. See also House of Commons, "Copies of Commissions of the Lords of the Treasury, Appointing Commissioners for the Management of the Crown's Estates in Berbice and on the Continent of South America; dated 23 April 1811 and 22 July 1811", *PP*, 1812, X (355): 357–59.

Chapter 3

1. Treasury minutes, 26 March 1811, PRO, T29/110; House of Commons, "Copy of the Report of the Commissioners Appointed for the Management of the Crown Estates in the Colony of Berbice, to the Lords Commissioners of His Majesty's Treasury", *PP*, 1816, VIII (528): 3–5; *Parliamentary Debates*, 1st ser., vol. 34, sec. 1269 (26 June 1816).
2. *PP*, 1816, VIII (528): 3–8.
3. Treasury minutes, 26 March 1811, T29/110; *PP*, 1816, VIII (528): 4. See the introduction for the location of these other estates. Apart from Berbice, those in Suriname came under the commissioners' jurisdiction, but only from 1813 until the end of the war, so that the commissioners did not have time to accomplish anything substantial.
4. *PP*, 1816, VIII (528): 7–9.
5. Ibid., 33.
6. For a detailed study of the Sierra Leone experiment see Christopher Fyfe, *A History of Sierra Leone* (London: Oxford University Press, 1962). See also Johnson Asiegbu, *Slavery and the Politics of Liberation, 1787–1861: A Study of Liberated African Emigration and British Anti-Slavery Policy* (London: Longman, 1969).
7. *PP*, 1816, VIII (528): 9.
8. Ibid.
9. House of Commons, "Papers Relating to the Crown Estates in the Colony of Berbice", *PP*, 1816, VIII (509): 28; Joseph Marryat, *An Examination of the Report of the Berbice Commissioners* (London: Hughes and Baynes, 1817), 16.
10. Gordon to Liverpool, 4 October 1811, PRO, CO 111/78; *PP*, 1816, VIII (509): 21–22.
11. *PP*, 1816, VIII (528): 11.
12. *PP*, 1816, VIII (509): 14.
13. Ibid., 29, 30; Gordon to Bathurst, 27 February 1813, CO 111/79.
14. Gordon to Bathurst, 27 February 1813, CO 111/79; *PP*, 1816, VIII (509): 29.

15. *PP,* 1816, VIII (528): 35–36.
16. Colonist, *The Edinburgh Review and the West Indies, with Observations on the Pamphlets of Stephen, Macaulay, etc.* (Glasgow: John Smith and Son, 1816), 295–96.
17. Joseph Marryat, *More Thoughts Occasioned by Two Publications* (London: J.M. Richardson and J. Ridgway, 1816), 14–15; Marryat, *An Examination,* 20–21.
18. James Stephen, *The Speech of James Stephen, Esq. at the Annual Meeting of the African Institution* (London: J. Butterworth and Son, and J. Hatchard, 1817), 32–33.
19. Ibid., 39; *Parliamentary Debates,* 1st ser., vol. 34, sec. 1268 (26 June 1816).
20. Macaulay to Bathurst, 2 April 1813, CO 111/80.
21. Thomas Rain, *The Life and Labours of John Wray, Pioneer Missionary in British Guiana, Compiled from His Own Mss. and Diaries* (London: John Snow and Co., 1892), 120–21.
22. *PP,* 1816, VIII (509): 26–39.
23. Ibid., 35, 40; *PP,* 1816, VIII (528): 21.
24. *PP,* 1816, VIII (509): 14.
25. Ibid., 51.
26. Ibid., 45, 49–50.
27. Ibid., 38.
28. Ibid., 39.
29. De la Court, "Administration account respecting the Crown estates in Berbice", January 1812–February 1815, T89/1.
30. "Copy of the *Berbice* Commissioners Instructions to their Agent", 27 August 1811, in *PP,* 1816, VIII (509): 7–16.
31. Ibid., 7–8.
32. Ibid., 10.
33. Ibid.
34. Ibid., 10, 15.
35. Ibid., 11–12; Bryan Edwards, *The History, Civil and Commercial, of the British Colonies in the West Indies,* 5th ed., vol. 2 (New York: AMS Press, 1966), 41.
36. *PP,* 1816, VIII (509): 11, 32; *PP,* 1816, VIII (528): 30, 31; Barry Higman, *Slave Populations of the British Caribbean, 1807–1834* (Baltimore, Md.: Johns Hopkins University Press, 1984), 164, 179–80, 188, 200; William A. Green, *British Slave Emancipation: The Sugar Colonies and the Great Experiment, 1830–1865* (New York: Oxford University Press, 1976), 135, 194, 197 n.21; Hugh Tinker, *A New System of Slavery: The Export of Indian Labour Overseas, 1838–1920* (London: Oxford University Press, 1974), 182–83.
37. *PP,* 1816, VIII (509): 11.
38. Ibid., 10–11.
39. Ibid., 12
40. Ibid.; *PP,* 1816, VIII (528): 31.
41. "Inventories of the estates, October 1803", in Moncrieff to Hobart, 6 January 1804, CO 111/73.
42. *PP,* 1816, VIII (509): 13.
43. Alvin O. Thompson, *Colonialism and Underdevelopment in Guiana, 1580–1803* (Bridgetown, Barbados: Carib Research and Publications, 1987), 112–13; CPCJB, Sessional Papers, 1 October 1810, CO 114/1.
44. *PP,* 1816, VIII (509): 11, 16; *PP,* 1816, VIII (528): 9–12, 31–32; Rain, *John Wray,* 138; *Berbice Gazette,* 23 April 1814, 9 July 1814, 3 and 31 December 1814; Wray to Burder, 29 October 1813 and Wray to Langton, 30 October 1813, LMS, Box 1A.
45. Rain, *John Wray,* 137; *PP,* 1816, VIII (528): 12; Walker to Macaulay, 28 December 1815, CO 111/83. For Walker's early views concerning amelioration see James Walker, *Letters on the West Indies* (London: Camberwell Press, 1818). We will discuss his second period of administration in chapters 4 to 7.
46. Rain, *John Wray,* 137.

47. Stephen, *Speech,* 38–41; Walker, *Letters,* 258, 259; Macaulay to Harrison, 21 May 1816, CO 111/87.
48. *PP,* 1816, VIII (509): 9.
49. Marryat, *An Examination,* 12–13; *PP,* 1816, VIII (509): 19–20. See chapter 5 for a more detailed discussion of food.
50. Wray to Directors of LMS, 4 October 1813, LMS, Box 1A; Rain, *John Wray,* 131.
51. CPCJB, Sessional Papers, 8 March 1814, CO 114/2.
52. Walker, *Letters,* 256.
53. Wray to Directors of LMS, 23 February 1814, LMS, Box 1A; Rain, *John Wray,* 130, 131, 135–37; *PP,* 1816, VIII (528): 12.
54. Rain, *John Wray,* 131; *PP,* 1816, VIII (528): 12.
55. "Inventory of Sandvoort", 18–20 February 1815, T1/3482/2: 94–95. Scott, Walker, De la Court and White signed this document.
56. Rain, *John Wray,* 136–37; *Berbice Gazette,* 23 April 1814, 2 July 1814.
57. *PP,* 1816, VIII (528): 12. The Berbice law, published in 1806, required each estate providing plantains as the staple food to cultivate two full-grown bunches per slave, except for nursing children. In order to meet this stipulation the estate was to grow seventy-five healthy trees per slave on the coast and sixty on the rivers (where better yields were normal; see CPCJB, Sessional Papers, 11 February 1806, GNA).
58. *PP,* 1816, VIII (528): 13, 24.
59. Ibid., 24.
60. Ibid., 19–20, 22, 24; Walker, *Letters,* 257. See also *Berbice Gazette,* 1 April 1815.
61. *PP,* 1816, VIII (509): 19–20; *PP,* 1816, VIII (528): 14.
62. Higman, *Slave Populations,* 223.
63. Bird to Beard, September 1830, CO 111/110, and enc.; "Report of the Commission of Inquiry", T1/3483/1: 204–5; see also House of Commons, "Papers Presented to Parliament by His Majesty's Command, in Explanation of the Measures Adopted by His Majesty's Government, for Giving Effect to the Act for the Abolition of Slavery Throughout the British Colonies. Part II", *PP,* 1835, L (278–1): 44–45.
64. J. Harry Bennett, Jr, *Bondsmen and Bishops: Slavery and Apprenticeship on the Codrington Plantations of Barbados, 1710–1838* (Berkeley: University of California Press, 1958), 36–37; A.C. Carmichael, *Domestic Manners and Social Conditions of the White, Coloured and Negro Populations of the West Indies,* vol. 1 (London: Whittaker, 1833), 142–43. For comparative figures for clothing distributed by planters in different colonies see Higman, *Slave Populations,* 233–35.
65. *PP,* 1816, VIII (509): 20; *PP,* 1816, VIII (528): 40.
66. *PP,* 1816, VIII (509): 20; Rain, *John Wray,* 131–32; Walker, *Letters,* 258.
67. *PP,* 1816, VIII (528): 38, 40.
68. Wray to Burder, 11 January 1816, LMS, Box 1A. See chapter 5 for quantities of clothing distributed to the *winkel* people in the mid-1820s.
69. *PP,* 1816, VIII (509): 15; Marryat, *An Examination,* 10.
70. Walker, *Letters,* 254–55; *PP,* 1816, VIII (528): 13.
71. "Inventory of Sandvoort", 18–20 February 1815, T1/3482/2: 98–99; *PP,* 1816, VIII (528): 13; Wray to Burder, 11 January 1816, LMS, Box 1A; Rain, *John Wray,* 124.
72. *PP,* 1816, VIII (509): 19; "Inventory of Sandvoort", 18–20 February 1815, T1/3482/2: 97; Walker, *Letters,* 256.
73. *PP,* 1816, VIII (528): 10, 31, 32; *PP,* 1816, VIII (509): 11.
74. *PP,* 1816, VIII (528): 19, 32; Wray to Tracy, 21 June 1814, LMS, Box 1A.
75. Wray to Langton, 4 July 1815, LMS, Box 1A. Sunday work had been pro-

hibited in the colony, except for emergencies, since at least 1810 (see the government proclamation of 14 November 1810, renewed on 4 October 1814 and published in the *Berbice Gazette* on 15 October 1814).
76. *Dictionary of National Biography*, compact ed., s.v. "Macaulay, Zachary".
77. Wray to Directors, 23 February 1814, LMS, Box 1A; Wray to Tracy, 21 June 1814, LMS, Box 1A; *PP,* 1816, VIII (528): 30.
78. *PP,* 1816, VIII (528): 32; Rain, *John Wray,* 109, 110, 111, 135.
79. Wray to Burder, 6 August 1815, LMS, Box 1A; Rain, *John Wray,* 140–41.
80. *PP,* 1816, VIII (528): 16; *PP,* 1816, VIII (509): 17.
81. *PP,* 1816, VIII (528): 16–17.
82. Ibid., 17; Walker, *Letters,* 255–56; *PP,* 1816, VIII (509): 51–54.
83. *PP,* 1816, VIII (509): 19–20.
84. *PP,* 1816, VIII (528): 20, 22; Wray to Burder, 11 January 1816, LMS, Box 1A; Rain, *John Wray,* 116, 138–39; Walker, *Letters,* 56.
85. *PP,* 1816, VIII (528): 18. See also Marryat, *An Examination,* 26–28.
86. Gordon to Liverpool, 4 October 1811, CO 111/78; Treasury minutes, 26 March 1811, T29/110; *PP,* 1816, VIII (528): 18. See also Walker, *Letters,* 254.
87. *PP,* 1816, VIII (528): 18, 24; Walker, *Letters,* 254. See also *PP,* 1816, VIII (509): 17.
88. *PP,* 1816, VIII (528): 36. The figures exclude those *winkel* persons under the control of the military and civil establishments. Figures are unavailable for children on the estates around this time.
89. Walker, *Letters,* 253.
90. Macaulay to De la Court, 21 April 1813, in *PP,* 1816, VIII (528): 32.
91. Rain, *John Wray,* 146.
92. *PP,* 1816, VIII (528): 11, 31; Wray to Beard, 18 June 1821, LMS, Box 1A; Rain, *John Wray,* 32, 84–85, 101.
93. Cited in Wray to Directors, 4 October 1813, LMS, Box 1A. Note also Walker's statement about Wray: "I can bear witness, that he conforms to the directions, which, in fulfilment of my own instructions from the Commissioners, I have uniformly given him, to inculcate upon the Slaves all submission to their masters, implicit obedience and orderly conduct" (Walker to Macaulay, 3 January 1816, in *PP,* 1816, VIII [528]: 42).
94. Wray to Directors, 18 May 1813, LMS, Box 1A.
95. Rain, *John Wray,* 96–97, 124–25, 131; Wray to Burder, 29 October 1813, LMS, Box 1A.
96. Wray to Directors, 18 May 1813, LMS, Box 1A; Rain, *John Wray,* 119, 127, 134, 148.
97. Wray to Directors, 18 May 1813 and 4 August 1813, LMS, Box 1A.
98. Rain, *John Wray,* 88; Wray to Directors, 4 August 1813, LMS, Box 1A. It is said that Murray threatened to expel John Smith if he ever found him teaching enslaved persons how to read (Rain, *John Wray,* 107).
99. Rain, *John Wray,* 54, 56, 60, 62, 64, 70, 124, 147. Rain states that Bentinck searched the private property of missionary Davies of Demerara for potentially subversive literature (ibid., 65–66).
100. Mary Turner, *Slaves and Missionaries: The Disintegration of Jamaican Slave Society, 1787–1834* (Urbana: University of Illinois Press, 1982), 86, 89.
101. Wray to Directors, 18 May 1813 and 29 October 1813, LMS, Box 1A.
102. Wray to Burder, 2 January 1814, and Wray to Langton, 4 July 1815, LMS, Box 1A; Rain, *John Wray,* 109–10, 131, 135, 140.

Notes to pages 95–102

103. *PP,* 1816, VIII (528): 33; Rain, *John Wray,* 130, 135.
104. Rain, *John Wray,* 89–90.
105. Ibid., 130, 135; Wray to Burder, 2 January 1814, LMS, Box 1A. The details of the sermon have not come to light.
106. Rain, *John Wray,* 103, 108; Wray to Directors, 4 August 1813 and 4 October 1813, LMS, Box 1A. See also Wray to Directors, 2 August 1814, LMS, Box 1A.
107. Wray to Directors, 23 February 1814, LMS, Box 1A; Wray to Tracy, 21 June 1814, LMS, Box 1A; Rain, *John Wray,* 131.
108. Wray to Directors, 2 August 1814, LMS, Box 1A; Rain, *John Wray,* 120–21, 130; *Berbice Gazette,* 26 March 1814, 9 April 1814 and 16 July 1814.
109. Wray to Langton, 4 July 1815, LMS, Box 1A; Wray to Burder, 11 January 1816 and 25 October 1817, LMS, Box 1A; *PP,* 1816, VIII (528): 23; Rain, *John Wray,* 116–17, 133, 140, 144–46; Walker, *Letters,* 257.
110. *PP,* 1816, VIII (509): 13–14.
111. *PP,* 1816, VIII (528): 3, 5, 8, 10, 14; Walker, *Letters,* 260.
112. *PP,* 1816, VIII (528): 14–15.
113. Ibid., 15–16; *PP,* 1816, VIII (509): 20. The auditors in the imperial Treasury found the commissioners' financial statement to be accurate, with satisfactory vouchers (Treasury minutes, 18 July 1817, T29/151).
114. Walker, *Letters,* 255, 259–60.
115. The commissioners gave somewhat different population and production figures for the Crown estates, but we have used the official returns as published in the *Berbice Gazette.* The population figures given by the former are Sandvoort – 235, Dageraad – 157, and Dankbaarheid – 351 (*PP,* 1816, VIII [509]: 17). The discrepancies seem to relate to absolute population figures recorded in the commissioners' statement, as against those given in the government gazette for taxation purposes that exempted infants and treated other children less than ten years old as half an adult (see, for instance, *Berbice Gazette,* 1 October 1814).
116. *PP,* 1816, VIII (509): 7.
117. *PP,* 1816, VIII (528): 36. No record is available of the actual number of sick and superannuated persons at the time that the commission took control of the department.
118. Ibid., 37–40.
119. "Account of the revenue and expenditure of the Colony of Berbice, 1811–1814", CO 111/83; Bentinck to Bathurst, 26 June 1816, CO 111/84.
120. *Parliamentary Debates,* 1st ser., vol. 34, sec. 1267–69 (26 June 1816). See above for Marryat's publications on the subject.
121. CPCJB, Sessional Papers, 8 March 1814, CO 114/2.
122. Convention of 12 August 1815, Article 11, in Bathurst to Bentinck, 19 February 1816, CO 111/85. The imperial government had decided in the previous year to return the estates to the association (Treasury minutes, 19 April 1814, T29/128).
123. *PP,* 1816, VIII (528): 20–24; extract of a letter from Macaulay to Walker, 14 September 1815, CO 111/84; extracts of letters from Macaulay to Scott, 11 January 1816 and 9 May 1816, CO 111/84; petition of Swaving and Staal to Governor of Berbice, c.4 July 1816, CO 111/84; Bentinck to Bathurst, 12 August 1816, CO 111/84; Directors of Berbice Society to Baron Fagel, July 1816 and 27 December 1816, Fagel Family Papers, Algemeen Rijksarchief; P.M. Netscher, *Geschiedenis Van De Kolonien Essequebo, Demerary en Berbice* (The Hage: Martinus Nijhoff, 1888), addendum, 5–7.

124. *Berbice Gazette*, 12 December 1818; Netscher, *Geschiedenis*, addendum, 6–7. The transaction was, however, not legally completed until 1821.
125. Gordon to Harrison, 3 May 1811, CO 111/78; Gordon to Liverpool, 4 October 1811, CO 111/78; Netscher, *Geschiedenis*, addendum, 7.

Chapter 4

1. See chapter 1. For a general discussion of the urban context of slavery in the Caribbean, see Barry Higman, *Slave Populations of the British Caribbean, 1807–1834* (Baltimore, Md.: Johns Hopkins University Press, 1984), 92–99, 257–59, 396. For a specialized study on Barbados, see Pedro Welch, "The Urban Context of the Slave Plantation System: Bridgetown, Barbados, 1680–1834" (PhD diss., University of the West Indies, 1994).
2. Council of Government of Berbice, Sessional Papers, 3 November 1818, 28 November 1818 and 8 January 1819, GNA.
3. Burdett to Kyte, 28 March 1826, PRO, T1/3482/1: 330; "Report of the Commission of Inquiry", T1/3483/1: appendix comprising sketch of town and *winkel* village.
4. Henry Dalton, *The History of British Guiana, comprising a General Description of the Colony*, vol. 2 (London: Longman, 1855), 36.
5. George Pinckard, *Notes on the West Indies . . . and . . . the Coast of Guiana*, vol. 2 (London: Longman, Hurst, Rees and Orme, 1806), 316–17; Henry Bolingbroke, *A Voyage to Demerary, Containing a Statistical Account of the Settlements There and Those of the Essequibo, the Berbice, and Other Contiguous Rivers of Guiana* (1808; reprint, Georgetown, Guyana: Daily Chronicle, 1947), 111–12.
6. James Rodway, *History of British Guiana from the Year 1688 to the Present Time*, vol. 2 (Georgetown, Guyana: J. Thomson, 1893), 90; Van Batenburg to Portland, 15 November 1804, PRO, CO 111/74.
7. Pinckard, *Notes*, vol. 2, 338.
8. Van Batenburg to Camden, 15 November 1804, CO 111/74; Woodley to Major General Dalrymple, 28 April 1809, CO 111/78.
9. Woodley to Liverpool, 3 January 1810, CO 111/78.
10. House of Commons, "Papers Relating to the Crown Estates in the Colony of Berbice", *PP*, 1816, VIII (509): 52.
11. Thomas Rain, *The Life and Labours of John Wray, Pioneer Missionary in British Guiana, Compiled from His Own Mss. and Diaries* (London: John Snow and Co., 1892), 101.
12. Dalton, *History*, vol. 2, 36.
13. M. Shahabuddeen, *The Legal System of Guyana* (Georgetown: Guyana Printers, 1973), 472.
14. Reynolds to Walker, 9 October 1823, and Walker to Reynolds, 22 November 1823, T1/3483/1: 148, 149.
15. "Capitation tax", 1812–1822, CO 111/94; Blue Book, 31 December 1824, CO 116/173; "Report of the Commission of Inquiry", T1/3483/1: 57.
16. Beard to Horton, 13 January 1824, CO 111/97.
17. Higman, *Slave Populations*, 94.
18. Ibid., 93–94, 226.
19. Bentinck to Bathurst, 22 February 1814 and 29 April 1814, CO 111/81; *Berbice Gazette*, 16 July 1814; Council of Government of Berbice, Sessional Papers, 21 and 22 August 1823, GNA.
20. Walker to Macaulay, 28 December 1815, CO 111/83; Scott to Arbuthnot, 25 October 1819, T1/3481: 350; Walker to Bentinck, 8 November 1819, T1/3481: 440;

Walker to Reynolds, 2 July 1823, T1/3482/3: 4.
21. Wray to Goulburn (?), 26 November 1817, CO 111/90.
22. Treasury minutes, 8 December 1818, T29/168.
23. Walker to Lushington, 1 June 1820, T1/3481: 108.
24. Walker to Lushington, 13 May 1820, T1/3481: 615; Walker to Harrison, 20 August 1820, T1/3481: 502. Protested bills attracted interest of 25 per cent if settled out of court and 50 per cent if settled in court (Kyte to Barron, 21 November 1825, T1/3482/1: 42–43).
25. "Report of the Commission of Inquiry", T1/3483/1: 12–13. The official statistics in 1825 included three deserters.
26. Ibid., 12.
27. Ibid., 162, 206, 246–47.
28. Ibid., 93–94; "*Winkel* employment on 3 January 1822", CO 318/90: 248. The figure given excludes thirty-eight persons who were at Government House and Fort St Andrew at the time.
29. "Report of the Commission of Inquiry", T1/3483/1: 207.
30. These figures appear to include all employable persons not hired out (that is, sick, in jail, deserters and so on), with the exception of the (three or four) apprentices.
31. "Report of the Commission of Inquiry", T1/3843/1: 230.
32. Ibid., 32.
33. "Sworn testimony of G.W. Rolfe", 27 February 1826, CO 318/85.
34. Ibid.
35. Walker to Harrison, 19 June 1821 and 20 April 1824, T1/3481: 488, 827–28; "Report of the Commission of Inquiry", T1/3483/1: 58.
36. "Commissioners of Inquiry's summary of receipts and expenditures", CO 318/91: 315–16. There is a discrepancy between the amount listed here for receipts and that in Table 4.3, perhaps because the commissioners of inquiry omitted from the document that constitutes the table small incomes derived in 1819 from the sale of livestock, plantains and other small items during Scott's administration.
37. *PP,* 1816, VIII (509): 14.
38. "Report of the Commission of Inquiry", T1/3483/1: 33, 38–39.
39. Byng and Harrison to Treasury, 12 August 1825, T1/3482/3: 74.
40. "Report of the Commission of Inquiry", T1/3483/1: 231. Several years earlier, in 1817, one individual wishing to hire six slaves was willing to pay f350 per annum for each, indicating that even at that time labour prices were high (*Berbice Gazette,* 23 August 1817).
41. "Return of Negroes", 20 January 1825, T1/3483/1: 76.
42. Walker to Katz, 8 July 1825, T1/3482/2: 126; Campbell to Kyte, 9 January 1826, T1/3482/1: 88–89. Campbell's alternative proposal would have meant that, in effect, he was only offering f200 (£14:5:9) per annum for the hire of the women. He declared that he was not really interested in hiring them since "they will only be a source of annoyance on the property, not having been accustomed to field labour" (ibid., 93–94).
43. "Report of the Commission of Inquiry", T1/3483/1: 207–8, 234.
44. Ibid., 58–59.
45. Walter Rodney, *A History of the Guyanese Working People, 1881–1905* (Baltimore, Md.: Johns Hopkins University Press, 1981), 32.
46. "Report of the Commission of Inquiry", T1/3483/1: 207, 233–34; Walker to Harrison, 31 December 1823, T1/3481: 198; Kyte to Burdett and Kinchela, 10 March 1826, T1/3482/1: 294–95.
47. The source records the earnings of the artisans as composite figures from 1822, as shown in the table, making it

impossible to calculate the total earnings of individual artisan groups for the entire period. We have omitted the earnings from the sale of small quantities of plantains and coffee in 1819 (f270) and 1820 (f2,651:10), and from "stock and produce" in 1821 (f1,308) and 1822 (f2,020:18), because the commissioners omitted them from the heads mentioned above ("Winkel accounts", 28 February 1815–31 December 1824, CO 318/91: 305–8).
48. "Report of the Commission of Inquiry", T1/3483/1: 24, 152.
49. "Schedules", CO 318/91: 179.
50. "Report of the Commission of Inquiry", T1/3483/1: 215.
51. For modern studies on the efficiency of slave labour see Stanley Engerman and Robert Fogel, *Time on the Cross: The Economics of American Negro Slavery* (Boston: Little, Brown, 1974); David Brion Davis, *Slavery and Human Progress* (New York: Oxford University Press, 1984).
52. "Report of the Commission of Inquiry", T1/3483/1: 150, 152, 163, 186, 207, 231.
53. Ibid., 152, 166, 170.
54. Ibid., 43–44, 58.
55. Ibid., 105.
56. Ibid., 49, 121.
57. Ibid., 46, 119, 155.
58. Ibid., 272–73; Walker to Lushington, 6 December 1819, T1/3481: 373; Walker to Harrison, 10 November 1821, T1/3481: 285–86.
59. *Berbice Gazette*, 14 July 1818; Day Book 6, 31 January 1824, CO 318/90: 498; "Report of the Commission of Inquiry", T1/3483/1: 272–73.
60. Walker to Harrison, 31 October 1823, T1/3481: 745; "Report of the Commission of Inquiry", T1/3483/1: 14, 32, 118.
61. Walker to Arbuthnot, 25 March 1822, T1/3481: 247; "Report of the Commission of Inquiry", T1/3483/1: 91; Commissioners of Inquiry to Horton, 30 November 1826, T1/3483/2: 168–69.
62. "Report of the Commission of Inquiry", T1/3483/1: 46.
63. Commissioners' minutes, 7 March 1826, T1/3482/1: 170–71.
64. "Report of the Commission of Inquiry", T1/3483/1: 49–50.
65. *Berbice Gazette*, 17 December 1817.
66. Walker to Barron, 11 July 1825, T1/3482/2: 127; Walker to Harrison, 16 July 1825, T1/3482/2: 123–24. In 1817 and 1818 the military department had put out tenders for the supply of artisans (carpenters, coopers, masons and so on) and ordinary field hands, instead of giving the *winkel* department first option to supply these persons (*Berbice Gazette*, 3 December 1817 and 20 October 1818).
67. "Report of the Commission of Inquiry", T1/3483/1: 73–83, 118.
68. Ibid., 17; Walker to Arbuthnot, 25 March 1822, T1/3481: 247; Walker to Harrison, 25 March 1822, T1/3481: 198; Walker to Harrison, 21 October 1823, T1/3481: 279; Walker to Harrison, 31 December 1823, T1/3481: 744.
69. "Schedules", CO 318/91: 171.
70. See Higman, *Slave Populations*, 179–80.
71. James Walker, *Letters on the West Indies* (London: Camberwell Press, 1818), 66–67.
72. "Report of the Commission of Inquiry", T1/3483/1: 162, 248; Beard to Bathurst, 16 January 1824, CO 111/97; Memo. of Katz's Managers, 14 February 1826, CO 111/103.
73. "Report of the Commission of Inquiry", T1/3483/1: 99, 162, 168, 248; Day Book 1, 28 December 1820, 19 March 1821 and 29 March 1821, CO 318/90: 178, 182, 183.
74. "Schedules", CO 318/91: 186; "Report of the Commission of Inquiry",

T1/3483/1: 141. The day books (CO 318/90) contain several instances of self-hire, but these are invariably short term. On 20 January 1825 only one person, Frederick III, was on self-hire ("Return of Negroes", in "Report of the Commission of Inquiry", T1/3483/1: 76).
75. "Report of the Commission of Inquiry", T1/3483/1: 15; Byng to Treasury, 4 August 1824, T1/3482/2: 12–13. The commissioners did not give separate annual figures of expenditure for 1818–23.
76. White estimated the average maintenance at f90 and Nicolay at f100, while Walker estimated it at f120 to f125 for adults and half that for children ("Report of the Commission of Inquiry", T1/3483/1: 98–99, 230, 247).
77. "Report of the Commission of Inquiry", T1/3483/1: 15.
78. Ibid., 15, 231; "Winkel accounts", 28 February 1815–31 December 1824, CO 318/91: 301–14; Byng to Treasury, 4 August 1824, T1/3482/2: 12–13.
79. Higman, *Slave Populations*, 244–47; Howard Johnson, "A Slow and Extended Abolition: The Case of the Bahamas, 1800–1838", in *From Chattel Slaves to Wage Slaves: The Dynamics of Wage Bargaining in the Americas*, ed. Mary Turner (London: James Currey, 1995), 172; Roger Bastide, *The African Religions of Brazil: Towards a Sociology of the Interpenetration of Civilizations*, trans. Helen Sebba (Baltimore, Md.: Johns Hopkins University Press, 1978), 51–52.
80. "Report of the Commission of Inquiry", T1/3483/1: 161; "Schedules", CO 318/91: 181.
81. Day Books 4 and 6, 31 December 1823 and 31 March 1824, CO 318/90: 487, 511; "Schedules", CO 318/91: 176; "Report of the Commission of Inquiry", T1/3483/1: 105. In 1827 he finally received his freedom, on application to the Treasury (Treasury minutes, 23 January 1827, T29/265; Beard to Horton, 29 January 1827, CO 111/104).
82. Cited in John W. Blassingame, *The Slave Community: Plantation Life in the Antebellum South*, rev. and enl. ed. (New York: Oxford University Press, 1979), 193.
83. "Schedules", CO 318/91: 176; "Report of the Commission of Inquiry", T1/3483/1: 105.
84. "Schedules", CO 318/91: 176; Day Books, CO 318/90: passim.
85. Day Books, CO 318/90: passim.
86. "Schedules", CO 318/91: 176; Rain, *John Wray,* 270.
87. Day Book 1, CO 318/90: 195, 202–3, 213, 217.
88. "Schedules", CO 318/91: 168, 174–76.
89. Ibid., 200; Day Book 2, 24 June 1822 and 1 July 1822, CO 318/90: 316, 319; "Report of the Commission of Inquiry", T1/3483/1: 64, 226.
90. Beard stated that he left the assignment of tasks to his housekeeper and that since stock for domestic use was usually obtained by barter, "he should not be able to supply his household by other means" than such activity ("Report of the Commission of Inquiry", T1/3483/1: 45, 74).
91. Ibid., 64; Burdett and Kinchela to Scott, 28 June 1826, T1/3482/1: 436; Wray to Burder, 26 March 1821, LMS, Box 1A.
92. "Schedules", CO 318/91: 195, 207, 209, 210.
93. Johnson, "A Slow and Extended Abolition", 174–75; Higman, *Slave Populations,* 246.
94. Johnson, "A Slow and Extended Abolition", 176.
95. Higman, *Slave Populations,* 244. For further discussion on self-hire see

Woodville K. Marshall, ed., *The Colthurst Journal: Journal of a Special Magistrate in the Islands of Barbados and St. Vincent, July 1835–September 1838* (Millwood, N.Y.: KTO Press, 1977), 211; Howard Johnson, *The Bahamas from Slavery to Servitude* (Gainesville: University of Florida Press, 1996), 33–46.
96. Higman, *Slave Populations*, 245, 246.
97. Higman, *Slave Populations*, 244–45.
98. Walker to Lushington, 31 January 1820, T1/3481: 148–49; Wray to Walker, 3 October 1820, T1/3481: 176; Walker to Harrison, 10 November 1821, T1/3481: 287–88; Walker to Arbuthnot, 10 January 1822, T1/3481: 265; "Report of the Commission of Inquiry", T1/3483/1: 114, 157, 224.
99. Burdett and Kinchela to Horton, 12 October 1825, T1/3483/2: 126; Abstract of the accounts of Walker, T1/3483/2: 78; "Report of the Commission of Inquiry", T1/3483/1: 15, 32.
100. Walker, "Winkel Work Room", 1821–24, T1/3482/2: 40–41; Burdett and Kinchela to Horton, 12 October 1825, T1/3482/3: 126; "Report of the Commission of Inquiry", T1/3483/1: 32, 157, 224; Appendix Z to final report of Commissioners, 15 November 1826, CO 318/91: 258.
101. "Report of the Commission of Inquiry", T1/3483/1: 157; Day Books 1 and 2, CO 318/90: 195, 252, 293, 316, 319.
102. "Report of the Commission of Inquiry", T1/3483/1, 203, 206, 239, 241.
103. Walker to Harrison, 20 January 1823, CO 111/96; Walker to Harrison, 24 March 1826, T1/3482/2: 189.
104. "Mr Gannon's Report on the Conditions of Apprenticed Africans", *PP,* 1826–27, XXII (355): 35.
105. Wray to Vansittart, 1 May 1822, T1/3481: 321.
106. Walker to Katz, 29 June 1823, in Walker to Harrison, 31 July 1823, T1/3481: 379. Katz allowed his slaves one working day every four weeks to themselves (Memo. of Katz's Managers, 14 February 1826, CO 111/103).
107. "Report of the Commission of Inquiry", T1/3483/1: 104.
108. "Observations", in Walker to Harrison, 24 March 1826, T1/3482/2: 189; "Report of the Commission of Inquiry", T1/3482/1: 113, 224.
109. "Schedules", CO 318/91: 166, 211, 217, 219.
110. "Report of the Commission of Inquiry", T1/3483/1: 20, 35.
111. Scott to Bentinck, 19 November 1819, T1/3481: 870–71; "Report of the Commission of Inquiry", T1/3483/1: 36–38, 116. In October 1824 he rented separate accommodation for the *winkel* and customs offices but it is unclear whether he paid additional rental fees ("Report of the Commission of Inquiry", T1/3483/1: 116).
112. "Report of the Commission of Inquiry", T1/3483/1: 37–38, 89, 111–19, 153, 157; "Mrs Stanley's evidence", 3 April 1826, T1/3482/1: 248–49.
113. "Report of the Commission of Inquiry", T1/3483/1: 151, 152, 165.
114. Ibid., 224–26; "Schedules", CO 318/91: 200.
115. "Report of the Commission of Inquiry", T1/3483/1: 35–36, 38, 161.
116. Ibid., 38.
117. Ibid., 117.
118. Ibid., 47.
119. Ibid., 150, 152, 166; Albert Memmi, *The Coloniser and the Colonised,* trans. Howard Greenfield (New York: Orion Press, 1965), xviii.

Chapter 5

1. Orlando Patterson, *Freedom*, vol. 1, *Freedom in the Making of Western Culture* (New York: Basic Books, 1991), 311.
2. "Report of the Commission of Inquiry", PRO, T1/3483/1: appendix comprising sketch of town and *winkel* village. There was some debate as to whether the village should properly be classified as being a part of the town, since it paid town taxes (Kyte to Barron, 23 February 1826, T1/3482/1: 199; Burdett and Kinchela to Kyte, 1 March 1826, T1/3482/1: 204).
3. Walker to Barron, 2 April 1825, T1/3482/2: 58.
4. Walker to Harrison, 25 May 1821 and 10 November 1821, T1/3481: 286, 484; Day Book 1, 10 August 1821, PRO, CO 318/90: 202.
5. Day Book 1, 10 August 1821, CO 318/90: 202; "Report of the Commission of Inquiry", T1/3483/1: 148, 207.
6. "Report of the Commission of Inquiry", T1/3483/1: 16.
7. Reynolds to Walker, 9 October 1823, and Walker to Reynolds, 22 November 1823, T1/3483/1: 148, 149.
8. House of Commons, "Papers Relating to the Crown Estates in the Colony of Berbice", *PP,* 1816, VIII (509): 44–46, 52.
9. Kyte to Barron, 23 February 1826, T1/3482/1: 199; "Report of the Commission of Inquiry", T1/3483/1: 17, 91, 151 and appendix showing ground plan of village. The site of the original workshops is unknown but they seem to have been located in the town proper. In 1819 Scott agreed to remove the smitheries to "a place less inconvenient for the inhabitants of the new Town to be selected by His Excellency" (Council of Government of Berbice, Sessional Papers, 28 November 1818 and 9 January 1819, GNA).
10. *PP,* 1816, VIII (509): 44–46, 52.
11. *"Winkel* expenditure", 1815–25, CO 318/91: 368; Burdett to Kyte, 28 March 1826, T1/3482/1: 333–34.
12. Council of Government of Berbice, Sessional Papers, 28 November 1818 and 9 January 1819, GNA; Kyte to Barron, 23 February 1826, T1/3482/1: 199; "Extract from the examination of Mr. Andrew McWatt", 23 February 1826, T1/3482/1: 207–8.
13. Council of Government of Berbice, Sessional Papers, 28 November 1818, GNA.
14. "Report of the Commission of Inquiry", T1/3483/1: 98.
15. Walker to Harrison, 10 November 1821, T1/3481: 286.
16. The manicole palm: "a clumped palm of four to sixteen slender, spineless stems that can exceed 50 ft in height, each with a crown of dense arching fronds; the stems and hard, reddish bark are used in building huts" (Richard Allsopp, ed., *Dictionary of Caribbean English Usage* [Oxford: Oxford University Press, 1996], 369).
17. "Report of the Commission of Inquiry", T1/3483/1: 322.
18. Ibid., 23–24, 273–74.
19. "Schedules", CO 318/91: 236; Kinchela to Kyte, 27 March 1826, T1/3482/1: 352–53; "Examination", 25 March 1826, in Burdett to Kyte, 28 March 1826, T1/3482/1: 340–47.
20. Walker to Harrison, 2 April 1825, T1/3482/2: 38; "Report of the Commission of Inquiry", T1/3483/1: 24, 98, 151, 301.
21. Burdett to Kyte, 28 March 1826, T1/3482/1: 334; Kinchela to Kyte, 28 March 1821, T1/3482/1: 353; "Report of the Commission of Inquiry", T1/3483/1: 319.
22. "Schedules", CO 318/91: 235–36.

23. Kyte to Barron, 21 March 1826, T1/3482/1: 328.
24. Burdett to Kyte, 28 March 1826, T1/3482/1: 334–35.
25. Aimé Césaire, *Discourse on Colonialism*, trans. Joan Pinkham (New York: Monthly Review Press, 1972), 20.
26. "Examination", in Burdett to Kyte, 28 March 1826, T1/3482/1: 344.
27. "Schedules", CO 318/91: 175–77, 184, 192.
28. "Report of the Commission of Inquiry", T1/3483/1: 322.
29. "Materials purchased by the Department", 1815–24, CO 318/91: 263.
30. Barry Higman, *Montpelier, Jamaica: A Plantation Community in Slavery and Freedom, 1739–1912* (Kingston, Jamaica: University of the West Indies Press, 1998), 148–56; Kyte to Barron, 21 March 1826, T1/3482/1: 328; "Report of the Commission of Inquiry", T1/3483/1: 322; "Return of the number of houses", 20 January 1825, T1/3483/1: 893–95.
31. "Schedules", CO 318/91: 181.
32. Ibid., 236; Walker to Barron, 2 April 1825, T1/3482/2: 59.
33. Burdett to Kyte, 28 March 1826, T1/3482/1: 334; Kinchela to Kyte, 27 March 1826, T1/3482/1: 353.
34. George Pinckard, *Notes on the West Indies . . . and . . . the Coast of Guiana*, vol. 2 (London: Longman, Hurst, Rees and Orme, 1806), 204–5, 208.
35. [Bernard Senior], *Jamaica, as It Was, as it Is, and as It May Be* (1835; reprint, New York: Negro Universities Press, 1969), 45.
36. "Report of the Commission of Inquiry", T1/3483: 96.
37. Walker to Ross and Downer, 11 December 1823, T1/3481: 193–94; "Report of the Commission of Inquiry", T1/3483/1: 60.
38. Scott to Macaulay, 29 May 1818 and 29 December 1818, T1/3484: 1009–10, 1028.
39. Scott to Bentinck, 19 November 1819, T1/3481: 873–74; "Abstract of an Account . . . for Receipts and Payments of Mr William Scott", 1 January 1818–30 September 1820, T1/3482/3: 79.
40. "Report of the Commission of Inquiry", T1/3483/1: 60; Walker to Harrison, 23 August 1823 and 15 November 1823, T1/3481: 657, 757; Walker to Ross and Downer, 11 December 1823, T1/3481: 193–94.
41. Walker to Lushington, 13 May 1820, T1/3481: 615–16; Scott to Bentinck, 19 November 1819, T1/3481: 873–74.
42. *"Winkel* expenditure", 1815–25, CO 318/91: 293–384.
43. Walker to Lushington, 24 May 1820, T1/3481: 622–24; Scott to Walker, 11 March 1820, T1/3481: 627.
44. House of Commons, "Copies of the Record of the Proceedings of the Fiscals of Demerara and Berbice, in their Capacity of Guardians and Protectors of the Slaves . . . from the 1st January 1814", *PP*, 1825, XXV (476): 24, 36–43.
45. Walker to Harrison, 29 December 1823, T1/3481: 196; Byng to Treasury, 4 August 1824, T1/3482/2: 13.
46. Day Books 6, 7 and 8, CO 318/90: 533, 586, 596; "Report of the Commission of Inquiry", T1/3483/1: 16–17, 151, 162–63.
47. Walker to Harrison, 23 August 1823, T1/3481: 658–59; Walker to Harrison, 27 April 1824, T1/3482/2: 6.
48. Bennett to Burdett and Kinchela, 31 January 1826, T1/3482/1: 107–8; Bird to Beard, September 1830, CO 111/110; "Report of the Commission of Inquiry", T1/3483/1: 163.

49. House of Commons, "Papers Presented to Parliament by His Majesty's Command, in Explanation of the Measures Adopted by His Majesty's Government, for Giving Effect to the Act for the Abolition of Slavery Throughout the British Colonies. Part II", *PP,* 1835, L (278-1): 144-45.
50. Managers of Katz's estates to Beard, 14 February 1826, CO 111/103; Barry Higman, *Slave Populations of the British Caribbean, 1807-1834* (Baltimore, Md.: Johns Hopkins University Press, 1984), 209.
51. "Disbursements in the Dept., 1815-24", CO 318/91: 260-61.
52. "Schedules", CO 318/91, 240-42; "Observations", 13 March 1826, in Walker to Harrison, 24 March 1826, T1/3482/2: 190; "Report of the Commission of Inquiry", T1/3483/1: 96-97, 303-4. See also "Report of the Commission of Inquiry", T1/3483/1: 20. Scott refuted Walker's suggestion that it had always been the practice to give the people the quantities of plantains specified above, declaring that he used to give all adults two bunches ("Report of the Commission of Inquiry", T1/3483/1: 21).
53. "Report of the Commission of Inquiry", T1/3483/1: 96-97.
54. Wray to Burder, 21 March 1821, LMS, Box 1A.
55. "Report of the Commission of Inquiry", T1/3483/1: 97. The law specified seven to nine pounds of rice.
56. Ibid., 154; McWatt to Kyte, 16 December 1825, in Kyte to Barron, 17 December 1825, T1/3482/1: 70-71.
57. Ibid.
58. "Schedules", CO 318/91: 240.
59. "Report of the Commission of Inquiry", T1/3483/1: 155, 163, 237; Day Book 4 and 7, 31 March 1823 and 25 December 1824, CO 318/90: 402, 583.
60. *PP,* 1835, L (278-1): 144-45.
61. Wray to Tracy, 21 June 1814, LMS, Box 1A.
62. For the importance of slaves' provision grounds see Roderick A. McDonald, *The Economy and Material Culture of Slaves: Goods and Chattels on the Sugar Plantations of Jamaica and Louisiana* (Baton Rouge: Louisiana State University Press, 1993); Howard Johnson, *The Bahamas in Slavery and Freedom* (Kingston, Jamaica: Ian Randle Publishers, 1991); Hilary McD. Beckles, "An Economic Life of Their Own: Slaves as Commodity Producers and Distributors in Barbados", *Slavery and Abolition* 12, no. 1 (1991): 31-48; Woodville K. Marshall, "Provision Ground and Plantation Labour in Four Windward Islands: Competition for Resources during Slavery", *Slavery and Abolition* 12, no. 1 (1991): 48-67; Sidney W. Mintz and Douglas Hall, *The Origins of the Jamaican Internal Marketing System,* Yale University Publications in Anthropology, no. 57 (New Haven, Conn.: Yale University Press, 1960); Mary Turner, ed., *From Chattel Slaves to Wage Slaves: The Dynamics of Wage Bargaining in the Americas* (London: James Currey, 1995).
63. Wray to Burder, 26 March 1821, LMS, Box 1A.
64. "Report of the Commission of Inquiry", T1/3483/1: 20.
65. "Schedules", CO 318/91: 195.
66. Higman, *Montpelier,* 245; see also 230.
67. Steeve O. Buckridge, "The 'Colour and Fabric' of Jamaican Slave Women's Dress", *Journal of Caribbean History* 33, no. 1-2 (1999): 84-124. For a detailed discussion of the African aesthetics in dress see John Thornton, *Africa and the Africans in the Making of the Atlantic World, 1400-1680* (Cambridge: Cambridge University Press, 1992), 221-34.

68. Kyte to Barron, 20 December 1825, T1/3482/1: 76.
69. Pinckard, *Notes,* vol. 2, 208–9.
70. Walker to Kyte, 16 December 1825, T1/3482/1: 69; "Report of the Commission of Inquiry", T1/3483/1: 263, 305.
71. "Report of the Commission of Inquiry", T1/3483/1: 99.
72. Ibid., 97–98, 156, 238.
73. Ibid., 225–26, 238. According to Kyte, the annual distribution of clothing in the colony was as follows: men (including boys fourteen to fifteen years old) – one inferior hat, one jacket, two laps and one blanket (the last of these every three years); headmen – one superior hat, one jacket, one pair trousers, one check shirt, two laps and one blanket every three years; younger boys – one check shirt, one lap and one hat; women – one woollen wrapper, one osnaburg or check petticoat, one handkerchief, one hat and one blanket every three years; domestics and drivers' wives received in addition a piece of calico; female children – petticoats of check, osnaburg or salempore; infirm persons received the same as effectives. "Humane" masters gave extra clothing as rewards to industrious persons and those who kept their children well (ibid., 204–5).
74. Ibid., 98.
75. Walker to Kyte, 16 December 1825, T1/3482/1: 68–69.
76. "Winkel Negro Ledger", CO 318/90: 4, 5, 85.
77. "Report of the Commission of Inquiry", T1/3483/1: 262–64.
78. Ibid., 226, 262–63, 305, 308–9.
79. Ibid., 22.
80. Ibid., 255–56, 262–63.
81. Ibid., 18, 21–23.
82. Ibid., 227.
83. Walker to Harrison, 27 August 1823, T1/3481: 662–63.
84. "Report of the Commission of Inquiry", T1/3482/1: 295, 304; "Schedules", CO 318/91: 188. The commissioners noted that, in fact, February seemed to have received his last set of clothing at Christmas 1824 ("Report of the Commission of Inquiry", 304).
85. Barron to Kyte, 21 December 1825, T1/3482/1: 82–83.
86. Alvin O. Thompson, *Colonialism and Underdevelopment in Guiana, 1580–1803* (Bridgetown, Barbados: Carib Research and Publications, 1987), 126. See also Thomas St Clair, *A Soldier's Sojourn in British Guiana, 1806–1808* (Georgetown, Guyana: Daily Chronicle, 1947), 244–48; Henry Bolingbroke, *A Voyage to Demerary, Containing a Statistical Account of the Settlements There and Those of the Essequibo, the Berbice, and Other Contiguous Rivers of Guiana* (1808; reprint, Georgetown, Guyana: Daily Chronicle, 1947), 39.
87. Walker to Kyte, 16 December 1825, T1/3482/1: 68–69; Kyte to Barron, 17 December 1825, T1/3482/1: 66–67.
88. Check, salempore and osnaburg are the ones most commonly mentioned in the documents, while jaconet, derries, union stripe, dimity, linsey woolsey and linen platilla are each mentioned only once ("Disbursements in the Dept.", 1815–24, CO 318/91: 255–60). The following is the usage of some of these cloths: check – for men's shirts, women's frocks and so on; osnaburg – for petticoats and trousers of the field people; blue salempore – for petticoats and men's laps; bengal – for use by smiths, cooks and so on; gingham and calico – for better quality dresses; sheeting – for better quality petticoats, trousers and jackets; cotton and white salempore – most commonly used for hospital bandages and so on; canvas – for aprons (ibid., 258; "Report of the Commission of Inquiry", T1/3483/1:

220, 224). We have no information on the uses of the other cloths.
89. "Report of the Commission of Inquiry", T1/3483/1: 102.
90. "Disbursements in the Department", 1815–24, CO 318/91: 255–57; "Report of the Commission of Inquiry", T1/3483/1: 157, 224, 238, 266. North American masters sometimes distributed shoes to their slaves in winter (Ulrich Phillips, "Southern Negro Slavery: A Benign View", in *American Negro Slavery: A Modern Reader*, ed. Allen Weinstein and Frank Otto Gatell [New York: Oxford University Press, 1968], 37).
91. Day Books 8 and 9, CO 318/90: 659, 684, 688, 713; "Disbursements in the Dept.", 1815–24, CO 318/91: 256–58; "Report of the Commission of Inquiry", T1/3483/1: 301.
92. CPCJB, Sessional Papers, 14 May 1814, CO 114/2; J. Harry Bennett, Jr, *Bondsmen and Bishops: Slavery and Apprenticeship on the Codrington Plantations of Barbados, 1710–1838* (Berkeley: University of California Press, 1958), 35–36; Eugene Genovese, *Roll, Jordan, Roll: The World the Slaves Made*, First Vintage Books (1972; reprint, New York: Random House, 1976), 555.
93. "Disbursements in the Dept.", 1815–24, CO 318/91: 260–61, 288; Memo. of Katz's Managers to Beard, 14 February 1826, CO 111/103.
94. "Schedules", CO 318/91: 168, 196, 198, 207, 228–33; "Observations", in Walker to Harrison, 24 March 1826, T1/3482/2: 190–91.
95. Walker to Burder, 16 June 1823, LMS, Box 1B.

Chapter 6

1. Barry Higman, *Montpelier, Jamaica: A Plantation Community in Slavery and Freedom, 1739–1912* (Kingston, Jamaica: University of the West Indies Press, 1998); Jerome Handler and Frederick W. Lange, *Plantation Slavery in Barbados: An Archaeological and Historical Investigation* (Cambridge: Harvard University Press, 1978).
2. Walker to Harrison, 31 July 1823, PRO, T1/3481: 376; Walker to Harrison, 21 September 1824, T1/3482/2: 35.
3. James Walker, *Letters on the West Indies* (London: Camberwell Press, 1818), 40–53; italics in original.
4. Ibid., 52–54.
5. Ibid., 62–63.
6. Walker to Vansittart, 10 January 1822, T1/3481: 258–59; Walker to Katz, 29 June 1823, in Walker to Harrison, 31 July 1823, T1/3481: 378.
7. Walker to Harrison, 27 December 1823, T1/3482/3: 15, 20. Sections of this document are separated from each other in the archives and given pagination that is not sequential.
8. Macaulay to Scott, in Scott to Arbuthnot, 25 October 1819, T1/3481: 354–56.
9. Walker to Burdett and Kinchela, 19 March 1825, T1/3482/2: 49; "Report of the Commission of Inquiry", T1/3483/1: 102–3, 107.
10. "Report of the Commission of Inquiry", T1/3483/1: 12–13, 93–94; "Crown", in Scott to D'Urban, 17 November 1831, PRO, CO 111/117; House of Commons, "Copy of the Report of the Commissioners Appointed for the Management of the Crown Estates in the Colony of Berbice, to the Lords Commissioners of His Majesty's Treasury", *PP*, 1816, VIII (528): 36; House of Commons, "Accounts of the Total Number of Captured Negroes who were Liberated in each of the Different Colonies; and of the Number of Crown Slaves who

have been Liberated in each of the Colonies", *PP*, 1833, XXVI (542): 18.
11. A few of these figures exclude or include single individuals who were not actually in the department at the time that the censuses were taken (who, for example, had deserted, were in jail for life, or had been given to individuals for manumission).
12. Alvin O. Thompson, *Colonialism and Underdevelopment in Guiana, 1580–1803* (Bridgetown, Barbados: Carib Research and Publications, 1987), 65.
13. "Return", 27 February 1819, T71/438: 723–32; *Berbice Gazette*, 12 April 1820. The figures for 1820 include 727 persons whom the document designates as "foreigners". We have excluded from our calculation the 113 runaways listed in the population for 1820.
14. "Report of the Commission of Inquiry", T1/3483/1, 185.
15. "Register of slaves in Berbice", 1819–31, as follows: 27 February 1819, T71/438: 723–32; 27 February 1822, T71/440: 751–54; 26 February 1825, T71/442: 59–64; 16 January 1828, T71/443: 605–8; 25 January 1831, T71/444: 105–10; see also "Normal list of Winkel people maintained by the Crown", 22 August 1832, CO 111/122.
16. "Register of slaves in Berbice", 1819, T71/438: 723–32; "Report of the Commission of Inquiry", T1/3483/1: 24.
17. "Register of slaves in Berbice", 1819, T71/438: 723–32.
18. Ibid.
19. Walker to Harrison, 24 July 1823 and 30 December 1823, T1/3481: 197, 386; "Report of the Commission of Inquiry", T1/3483/1: 199; Walker's memorial, 3 March 1827, T1/3484: 133–36.
20. "Report of the Commission of Inquiry", T1/3483/1: 93–94.
21. Barry Higman, *Slave Populations of the British Caribbean, 1807–1834* (Baltimore, Md.: Johns Hopkins University Press, 1984), 260–302; Richard Sheridan, *Doctors and Slaves: A Medical and Demographic History of Slavery in the British West Indies, 1680–1834* (Cambridge: Cambridge University Press, 1985), 16–41, 115–20; House of Commons, West India Royal Commission, *Report 1938–1939* (London: Her Majesty's Stationery Office, 1945), 141–42.
22. "Observations", in Walker to Harrison, 24 March 1826, T1/3482/2: 189; "Report of the Commission of Inquiry", T1/3483/1: 119, 160; Day Books, CO 318/90: passim.
23. *"Winkel* expenditures", 1817–1820, T1/3481: 985–89; Juan Francisco Manzano, *Poems by a Slave in the Island of Cuba Recently Liberated,* cited in Philip Foner, *A History of Cuba and Its Relations with the United States,* vol. 1 (New York: International Publishers, 1963), 195.
24. "Report of the Commission of Inquiry", T1/3483/1: 98, 185–200; *"Winkel* expenditure", 1815–25, CO 318/91: 275.
25. Day Book 6, CO 318/90: 530–31; "Schedules", CO 318/91: 188, 240; Beard to Horton, 24 September 1825, T1/3482/2: 149.
26. House of Commons, "Extract From the Proceedings on the Trial of a Slave, in Berbice, for the Crime of Obeah, and Murder", *PP,* 1823, XVIII (348): 1–45.
27. "Schedules", CO 318/91; "Report of the Commission of Inquiry", T1/3483/1: 19.
28. "Schedules", CO 318/91: 182, 183, 202, 205–6, 208.
29. "Report of the Commission of Inquiry", T1/3483/1: 199–200.
30. Ibid., 237–38, 242.
31. Ibid., 158–59, 175.

32. "Schedules", CO 318/91: 234, 237, 238.
33. Ibid., 237; "Report of the Commission of Inquiry", T1/3483/1: 301.
34. "Schedules", CO 318/91: 238.
35. Ibid., 242.
36. Ibid., 241.
37. Ibid., 193, 194.
38. "Report of the Commission of Inquiry", T1/3481/1: 19. They stated that forty-one persons had complained to them about inadequate food (ibid.).
39. House of Commons, "Papers Relating to the Crown Estates in the Colony of Berbice", *PP,* 1816, VIII (509): 26.
40. "Schedules", CO 318/91: 206, 208; Day Book 2, 11 February 1822, CO 318/90: 276.
41. "Schedules", CO 318/91: 206, 207, 208; Day Book 1, 28 December 1820, 29 March 1821 and 14 December 1821, 3 January 1822, CO 318/90: 178, 183, 239.
42. Three houses were unoccupied for reasons not recorded. Perhaps they were too dilapidated, or being used as nurseries or administrative buildings ("Return of the number of houses", 20 January 1825, T1/3483/1: 893–95).
43. Wray to Burder, 11 January 1816 and 25 October 1817, LMS, Box 1A.
44. Schwiers to White (Government Secretary), May 1818, CO 111/88.
45. "Return of the number of houses", 20 January 1825, T1/3483/1: 893–95; "Return of the Men and Women", 20 January 1825, T1/3483/1: 889–92. The children of the husbands by a former relationship can be found in "Schedules", CO 318/91.
46. For more detailed studies on this topic see Barbara Bush, *Slave Women in Caribbean Society, 1650–1838* (Kingston, Jamaica: Heinemann, 1990), 84–93; Higman, *Slave Populations,* 164–73; Barry Higman, "The Slave Family and Household in the British West Indies, 1800–1834", *Journal of Interdisciplinary History* 1, no. 2 (1975): 261–87; Michael Craton, "Changing Patterns of Slave Families in the British West Indies", in *Caribbean Slave Society and Economy: A Student Reader,* ed. Hilary McD. Beckles and Verene Shepherd (Kingston, Jamaica: Ian Randle Publishers, 1991), 228–49; Herbert Gutman, *The Black Family in Slavery and Freedom,* First Vintage Books (New York: Random House, 1977), 3–44.
47. "Report of the Commission of Inquiry", T1/3483/1: 161; "Schedules", CO 318/91: 181.
48. "Slaves belonging to the Crown in 1819", T1/3481: 1017; "Schedules", CO 318/91: 196–99.
49. "Schedules", CO 318/91.
50. Ibid., 196; "Return of the number of Houses", 20 January 1825, T1/3483/1: 893–95; "Return of the Unmarried Women", 20 January 1825, T1/3483/1: 891.
51. Burdett to Kyte, 28 March 1826, T1/3482/1: 337.
52. "Schedules", CO 318/91.
53. "Report of the Commission of Inquiry", T1/3483/1: 105.
54. Wray to Langton, 4 July 1815, LMS, Box 1A; see also Thomas Rain, *The Life and Labours of John Wray, Pioneer Missionary in British Guiana, Compiled from His Own Mss. and Diaries* (London: John Snow and Co., 1892), 145–46; Walker to Burder, 16 June 1823, LMS, Box 1B.
55. Wray to Burder, 26 March 1821, LMS, Box 1A.
56. "Report of the Commission of Inquiry", T1/3483/1: 110, 111; Walker to Burder, June 1823 LMS, Box 1B.
57. "Return of slaves", 2 August 1819, T71/438: 723–32; Day Books, 31 October 1823, 31 December 1823,

12 January 1824 and 20 July 1824, CO 318/90.
58. "Schedules", CO 318/91: 196, 198, 207, 228–33.
59. "Report of the Commission of Inquiry", T1/3483/1: 107.
60. Day Books, CO 318/90: 195, 202, 222, 327, 540; "Schedules", CO 318/91: 206, 207, 214, 217; "Examination of Tannetje", 28 July 1825, T1/3483/2: 566, 568.
61. Roger Bastide, *The African Religions of Brazil: Towards a Sociology of the Interpenetration of Civilizations*, trans. Helen Sebba (Baltimore, Md.: Johns Hopkins University Press, 1978), 54.
62. John G. Stedman, *Narrative of Five Years' Expedition against the Revolted Negroes of Surinam in Guiana on the Wild Coast of South America from the Years 1772 to 1777* (1796; reprint, Amherst: University of Massachusetts Press, 1972), 18–19.
63. Douglas Hall, *In Miserable Slavery: Thomas Thistlewood in Jamaica, 1750–1786* (London: Macmillan, 1989), 60–62, 67, 215.
64. Stedman, *Narrative*, 18–19. According to a young Dutchman writing about Berbice around 1735, the white females whom he found there were "ugly as sin. Girls of fourteen years old are like thirty, thin, yellow, and without teeth, so that there will be no fight for them, and I cross myself three times at the sight of them" (G.T. Galbano-Elephantius, ed., *A Voyage to the New Colony of Berbice in 1735* [Georgetown, Guyana: Daily Chronicle, 1877], 9).
65. "Schedules", CO 318/91: 207, 210.
66. "Report of the Commission of Inquiry", T1/3483/1: 57.
67. "Schedules", CO 318/91. All three of the men listed specifically as having coloured partners were artisans (ibid., 170, 183, 190).

68. Government Proclamation, published 21 November 1817, T1/3482/1: 401–2.
69. Burdett and Kinchela to Horton, 22 April 1826 and enc. d. 31 March 1826, T1/3482/1: 362–64, 380–85; Barron to Kyte, 29 March 1826, T1/3482/1: 364–65; Joshua Steele, *Letters on Slavery* (1789), in William Dickson, *Mitigation of Slavery* (1814; reprint, Westport, Conn.: Negro Universities Press, 1970), 149.
70. George Pinckard, *Notes on the West Indies . . . and . . . the Coast of Guiana*, vol. 2 (London: Longman, Hurst, Rees and Orme, 1806), 208–9.
71. Pinckard, *Notes*, vol. 2, 352–53; Richard Schomburgk, *Travels in British Guiana, 1840–1844*, vol. 1 (1847; reprint, trans. and ed. W.E. Roth, Georgetown, Guyana: Daily Chronicle, 1922), 47–48.
72. Wray to Hankey, 22 April 1826, LMS, Box 1B; Wray to Hankey, 11 January 1827, LMS, Box 2; see also "Report of the Commission of Inquiry", T1/3483/1: 150.
73. Pinckard, *Notes*, vol. 2, 352–53; CPCJB, Sessional Papers, 5 January 1807, CO 114/1; Wray to Langton, 25 May 1820, LMS, Box 1A.
74. Pinckard, *Notes*, vol. 2, 352–53; Schomburgk, *Travels*, vol. 1, 47–48; Wray to Langton, 25 May 1820, LMS, Box 1A.
75. Day Book, 6 September 1824, CO 318/90: 553; Wray to Hankey, 11 January 1827, LMS, Box 2.
76. Wray to Langton, 4 July 1825, LMS, Box 1A.
77. Day Books, 6 September 1824 and 9 May 1825, CO 318/90: 553, 646; "Walker's notes", enc. in Customs to Treasury, 27 April 1826, T1/3482/3: 224; "Report of the Commission of Inquiry", T1/3483/1: 100, 117.
78. Government Proclamation of 8 March 1814, cited in Wray to Burder, 20 February 1826, LMS, Box 1B. See

Thompson, *Colonialism,* 131–35 for a fuller discussion of this matter in the context of Guyana.
79. Wray to Tracy, 30 October 1813, LMS, Box 1A.
80. Wray to Burder, 20 February 1826, LMS, Box 1B; "Report of the Commission of Inquiry", T1/3483/1: 161.
81. House of Commons, "Copy of any Reports Which may have been Received from the Protectors of Slaves in the Colonies Demerara, Berbice, Trinidad, St. Lucia, the Cape of Good Hope and Mauritius. Part II", *PP,* 1831, XV (262): 48–49.
82. "Register of slaves in Berbice", 1819, T71/438: 726; "Copy of Proclamation", 7 August 1819, in Walker to Lushington, 6 December 1819, T1/3481: 367.
83. House of Commons, "Copies of the Record of the Proceedings of the Fiscals of Demerara and Berbice, in their Capacity of Guardians and Protectors of the Slaves . . . from the 1st January 1814", *PP,* 1825, XXV (476): 28.
84. Ibid., 29.
85. Ibid., 30.
86. Ibid., 28–30.
87. "Copy of Proclamation", 7 August 1819, in Walker to Lushington, 6 December 1819, T1/3481: 367–69; Wray to Wilberforce, 29 October 1819, LMS, Box 1A.
88. *PP,* 1816, VIII (509): 32–33.
89. Scott to Walker, 24 April 1818, T1/3481: 704; Macaulay to Walker, 9 January 1819, T1/3481: 705.
90. Wray to Vansittart, 1 May 1822, T1/3481: 320.
91. Ibid., 320–22.
92. Wray to Beard, 18 June 1821, LMS, Box 1A; Burder to Walker, 1 December 1819, T1/3481: 707.
93. Wray to Walker, 4 October 1820, T1/3481: 171–72; Wray to Vansittart, 1 May 1822, T1/3481: 320–22.
94. Walker to Harrison, 17 July 1823, T1/3481: 385; Walker to Harrison, 16 June 1823, T1/3482/3: 11.
95. "Schedules", CO 318/91: 180.
96. Wray to Directors, 16 October 1823 and 10 May 1824, LMS, Box 1B; copy of letter from Wray to Directors, 27 August 1823, CO 111/96.
97. Wray to Directors, 16 October 1823, LMS, Box 1B.
98. "Report of the Commission of Inquiry", T1/3483/1: 110–11; *PP,* 1816, VIII (509): 29.
99. "Duties of slaves", in Wray to Hankey, 27 January 1823, LMS, Box 1B; Wray to Directors, 10 May 1824, LMS, Box 1B.
100. Orlando Patterson, *Freedom,* vol. 1, *Freedom in the Making of Western Culture* (New York: Basic Books, 1991), 294.
101. Gal. 3:13; Gal. 5:1; Eph. 6:5.
102. Michael A. Gomez, *Changing Our Country Marks: The Transformation of African Identities in the Colonial and Ante-Bellum South* (Chapel Hill: University of North Carolina Press, 1998), 1–3, 257.
103. Exod. 2–14; "Schedules", CO 318/91: 220. Slaves used Christianity as a catalyst in some revolts, such as those led by Quamina in Demerara in 1823 and Sam Sharpe in Jamaica in 1831–32 (see Mary Turner, *Slaves and Missionaries: The Disintegration of Jamaican Slave Society, 1787–1834* [Urbana: University of Illinois Press, 1982], 94, 149–78; Michael Craton, *Testing the Chains: Resistance to Slavery in the British West Indies* [Ithaca, N.Y.: Cornell University Press, 1982], 241–321).
104. Wray to Vansittart, 1 May 1822, T1/3481: 322; "Subscribers", in Wray to Hankey, 18 January 1823, LMS, Box 1B.
105. Wray to Raynor, 27 August 1823, LMS, Box 1B; Wray to Hankey, 4 September 1823, LMS, Box 1B; Wray

to Directors, 18 November 1823, LMS, Box 1B.
106. "Schedules", CO 318/91.
107. "Extracts from extraordinary meetings of Council of Govt.", 1–2 February 1822, CO 111/94; Beard to Bathurst, 6 February 1822, CO 111/94; Beard to Bathurst, 16 January 1824, CO 111/97.
108. "Slaves attending school", 31 October 1823, T1/3481: 202.
109. Wray to Hankey, 18 June 1825 and 20 July 1825, LMS, Box 1B.
110. "Slaves attending school", 31 October 1823, T1/3481: 200–2.
111. "Report of the Commission of Inquiry", T1/3483/1: 37–38.
112. Ibid., 112.
113. Ibid., 225; "Slaves attending school", 31 October 1823, T1/3481: 200–2.
114. Day Book 1, 18 July 1821, CO 318/90: 195; "Children attending *winkel* school", March 1825, T1/3482/2: 53.
115. George Trevelyan, *English Social History: A Survey of Six Centuries from Chaucer to Victoria* (1944; illus. ed., London: Longman, 1978), 425, 478–80. See also M. Dorothy George, *London Life in the Eighteenth Century* (1925; reprint, Harmondsworth, Engl.: Penguin, 1965), 183–95, 250–56.
116. "Report of the Commission of Inquiry", T1/3483/1: 123, 224; "Schedules", CO 318/91: 220.
117. "Schedules", CO 318/91: 179, 182, 186.
118. "Report of the Commission of Inquiry", T1/3483/1: 54–55.
119. "Schedules", CO 318/91: 222, 224, 232. For other cases of private instruction see ibid., 191, 228.
120. Ibid., 191–231, passim.
121. Walker to Barron, 27 March 1825, T1/3482/2: 52; Wray to Hankey, 23 October 1821, LMS, Box 1A; Wray to Hankey, 28 September 1824 and 6 February 1826, LMS, Box 1B.
122. "Report of the Commission of Inquiry", T1/3483/1: 53, 55, 143; Byng to Treasury, 4 August 1824, T1/3482/2: 14.
123. "Schedules", CO 318/91.

Chapter 7

1. Hilary McD. Beckles, *Natural Rebels: A Social History of Enslaved Black Women in Barbados* (London: Zed Books, 1989), 152.
2. Ibid., 166. See pp. 153–74 of this study for his discussion on female resistance in Barbados.
3. Day Books, PRO, CO 318/90: 181–86, 202–3, 211, 340, 711.
4. James Walker, *Letters on the West Indies* (London: Camberwell Press, 1818), 72–79.
5. Ibid., 77.
6. "Report of the Commission of Inquiry", PRO, T1/3483/1: 102, 141.
7. Ibid., 105–7, 141; Walker to Beard, 30 March 1822, T1/3481: 102; Power to Beard, 21 January 1827, CO 111/104.
8. Walker, *Letters*, 92.
9. William A. Green, *British Slave Emancipation: The Sugar Colonies and the Great Experiment, 1830–1865* (New York: Oxford University Press, 1976), 132.
10. "Slave Code of 1826", sec. 21, CO 111/102.
11. "Schedules", CO 318/91: 199, 211.
12. "*Winkel* expenditure", 1815–25, CO 318/91: 270, 368.
13. "Schedules", CO 318/91: 199, 211.
14. "Report of the Commission of Inquiry", T1/3483/1: 141.
15. Ibid., 100, 113; Walker, *Letters*, 74.
16. "Report of the Commission of Inquiry", T1/3483/1: 100, 113; Walker to Bathurst, 25 February 1826, T1/3482/2: 238–39.
17. House of Commons, "Papers Relating to the Crown Estates in the Colony of Berbice", *PP,* 1816, VIII (509): 28; Henri Charrière, *Papillon,* trans. June P. Wilson and Walter B. Michaels

(New York: Pocket Books, 1971), 227–30. See also Blair Niles, *Condemned to Devil's Island: The Biography of an Unknown Convict* (London: Jonathan Cape, 1928).
18. House of Commons, "Copies of the Record of the Proceedings of the Fiscals of Demerara and Berbice, in their Capacity of Guardians and Protectors of the Slaves . . . from the 1st January 1814", *PP,* 1825, XXV (476): 47; Walker, *Letters,* 74.
19. *PP,* 1825, XXV (476): 46.
20. Ibid., 46–47.
21. Walker to Harrison, 24 March 1826, T1/3482/2: 185; "Examination of Dummett", 1 September 1825, T1/3482/2: 206; "Report of the Commission of Inquiry", T1/3483/1: 113, 141, 166.
22. "Report of the Commission of Inquiry", T1/3483/1: 99–100; "Statement concerning Walker's dismissal", 30 June 1826, T1/3483/2: 681.
23. Berbice Legislature, "Proclamations", in appendix to minutes of the Council of Government of Berbice, 1817–18, GNA.
24. See the case of Carolina II later in this chapter.
25. Walker, *Letters,* 73.
26. "Report of the Commission of Inquiry", T1/3483/1: 99–100.
27. Day Books 1 and 8, 21 September 1821 and 26 April 1825, CO 318/90: 213, 643.
28. Ibid., 181, 183, 186, 203, 217, 270, 345, 539–40. Eight of the cases had to do with desertion and nine with insubordination in the department.
29. "Schedules", CO 318/91.
30. See Day Books 1–2, CO 318/90: 177, 183, 270, 322, 333 and passim.
31. Walker, *Letters,* 75.
32. "Schedules", CO 318/91: 211.

33. "Evidence of Mrs. Stanley", in Walker to Customs, 22 March 1826, T1/3482/2: 229.
34. Day Book 7, 27 July 1824, CO 318/90: 540.
35. *PP,* 1825, XXV (476): 24–25.
36. "Extracts from *The Guiana Chronicle and Demerara Gazette*", 9 and 23 January 1824, in Walker to Harrison, 21 February 1824, T1/3481: 210, 214; Walker to Lushington, 10 and 24 May 1820, T1/3481: 524–27, 622–24; Scott to Walker, 11 March 1820, T1/3841: 627; "Copy of Walker's letter to editor of *The John Bull* ", 27 December 1823, T1/3482/3: 15; "Report of the Commission of Inquiry", T1/3483/1: 269–71.
37. "Report of the Commission of Inquiry", T1/3483/1: 295–97.
38. Day Books 1–2, CO 318/90: 180, 199, 203, 221, 248, 272.
39. *PP,* 1825, XXV (476): 43–44.
40. Day Book 1, 14 December 1820, 2 and 22 August 1821, CO 318/90: 177, 199, 203; "Schedules", CO 318/91: 195.
41. "Schedules", CO 318/91: 210.
42. Ibid.
43. Walker to Harrison, 10 November 1821, T1/3481: 284; "Report of the Commission of Inquiry", T1/3483/1: 238–39, 297; Wray to Burder, 26 March 1821, LMS, Box 1A.
44. "Schedules", CO 318/91: 205.
45. Ibid., 204–5. This term is not used in the document, but the manner of punishment leads to this conclusion.
46. R.A.J. Van Lier, *Frontier Society* (The Hague: Martinus Nijhoff, 1971), 916.
47. Walker to Harrison, 25 March 1822, T1/3481: 279.
48. John G. Stedman, *Narrative of Five Years' Expedition against the Revolted Negroes of Surinam in Guiana on the Wild Coast of South America from the Years 1772 to 1777* (1796; reprint, Amherst: University of Massachusetts

Press, 1972), 177–78; Thomas Rain, *The Life and Labours of John Wray, Pioneer Missionary in British Guiana, Compiled from His Own Mss. and Diaries* (London: John Snow and Co., 1892), 133. See also Van Lier, *Frontier Society*, 64.
49. "Report of the Commission of Inquiry", T1/3483/1: 114.
50. Ibid., 114, 239, 241.
51. Walker, "Remarks on the evidence", 25 February 1826, T1/3482/2: 222. Both of them suffered banishment to Berenstein during the period of management of the immoral McConchie ("Schedules", CO 318/91: 209, 211; "Return of slaves", 31 October 1823, T1/3481: 202).
52. "Schedules", CO 318/91: 211.
53. Day Books 1–9, 14 December 1820–15 September 1825, CO 318/90: 177–714.
54. The day book referred to Lauw, who absconded from 16 July to 20 October 1821, as a long-time deserter (Day Book 1, CO 318/90: 199, 220).
55. Day Book 1, 2 August 1821, CO 318/90: 199.
56. Alvin O. Thompson, *Some Problems of Slave Desertion in Guyana, 1750–1814*, Occasional Paper, no. 4 (Cave Hill, Barbados: Institute of Social and Economic Research, University of the West Indies, 1976).
57. *PP*, 1825, XXV (476): 25.
58. CO 318/90, Day Books 1 and 2, 28 November 1820–23 January 1822: passim; *PP*, 1825, XXV (476): 36, 40.
59. "Schedules", CO 318/91: 186.
60. Ibid., 172, 186.
61. *PP*, 1825, XXV (476): 43–44.
62. Day Books 1–4, 18 July 1821–30 December 1823, CO 318/90: passim.
63. A search of several departmental records revealed only one person named Michael, the son of Maria (see "Schedules", CO 318/91: 172; "Register of slaves in Berbice", 1817, T71/437: 428; "Register of slaves in Berbice", 1819, T71/438: 727; "Report of the Commission of Inquiry", T1/3483/1: 74).
64. Walker to Burdett and Kinchela, 19 March 1825, T1/3482/2: 49; Beard to Horton, 24 September 1825, T1/3482/2: 149; "Report of the Commission of Inquiry", T1/3483/1: 100, 105, 141–42, 167–68.
65. Roger Bastide, *The African Religions of Brazil: Towards a Sociology of the Interpenetration of Civilizations*, trans. Helen Sebba (Baltimore, Md.: Johns Hopkins University Press, 1978), 81.
66. "Case of Sim", in Walker to Harrison, 24 March 1826, T1/3482/2: 190–92.
67. "Schedules", CO 318/90: 193.
68. Ibid.; "Case of Sim", in Walker to Harrison, 24 March 1826, T1/3482/2: 190–91.
69. Lauw was the reputed husband of Flooda, Sim's mother, but the sources do not identify him as Sim's father ("Schedules", CO 318/91, 193).
70. Ibid.; Day Books 1, 7 and 9, 3 April 1821, 22 and 27 July 1824 and 7 September 1825, CO 318/90: 183, 539, 540, 711; "Register of slaves in Berbice", 1819, T71/438: 727–28.
71. Day Book 9, 7 September 1825, CO 318/90: 711; "Schedules", CO 318/91: 202.
72. "Schedules", CO 318/90: 193.
73. Ibid.
74. Ibid., 188; Beard to Horton, 24 September 1825, T1/3482/2: 149.
75. "Schedules", CO 318/91: 188; "Remarks by Walker", T1/3484: 340–41.
76. Bentinck to Walker, 2 May 1820, in "Report of the Commission of Inquiry", T1/3483/1: 251; "Schedules", CO 318/91: 188.
77. Ibid.; Day Book 1, 21 September 1821, CO 318/90: 213.
78. "Report of the Commission of Inquiry", T1/3483/1: 114, 117; Day

Book 7, 30 July 1824, CO 318/90: 539–41; Beard to Horton, 24 September 1825, T1/3482/2: 149–50; Burdett and Kinchela to Horton, 8 March 1826, T1/3482/3: 240–41; Walker to Barron, 22 February 1826, T1/3482/3: 232; Walker to Burdett and Kinchela, 9 March 1826, T1/3482/3: 233; "Remarks by Walker", 25 February 1826, T1/3484: 340–41.
79. Walker to Beard, 23 June 1824, in Beard to Horton, 24 September 1825, T1/3482/2: 151; "Report of the Commission of Inquiry", T1/3483/1: 273; Day Books 7–8, CO 318/90: 541, 549, 558, 576, 596, 659.
80. "Register of slaves in Berbice", 1819, T71/438: 729–30. The cases of Tannetje and Julia have already been discussed above, while that of Jacoba II will be discussed later in this chapter.
81. Day Books, CO 318/90: passim; Walker to Beard, 23 June 1824, in Beard to Horton, 24 September 1825, T1/3482/2: 150; "Report of the Commission of Inquiry", T1/3483/1: 100.
82. Walker to Harrison, 20 April 1824, T1/3481: 829.
83. Walker to Harrison, 13 August 1825, T1/3482/3: 86.
84. "Examination of Walker", in Burdett and Kinchela to Horton, 22 April 1826, T1/3482/1: 380–84; "Special case", in Burdett and Kinchela to Bathurst, 13 August 1825, T1/3483/2: 553.
85. "Examination of Scott", in Kinchela to Horton, 22 April 1826, T1/3482/1: 376–79, 379; "Special case", in Burdett and Kinchela to Bathurst, 13 August 1825, T1/3483/1: 553.
86. "Examination of Walker", in Burdett and Kinchela to Horton, 22 April 1826, T1/3482/1: 382–83; "Special case", in Burdett and Kinchela to Bathurst, 13 August 1825, T1/3483/2: 554.
87. "Examination of Walker", in Burdett and Kinchela to Horton, 22 April 1826, T1/3482/1: 385.
88. "Special case", in Burdett and Kinchela to Bathurst, 13 August 1825, T1/3483/2: 544–73.
89. Ibid., 544–45, 559.
90. Ibid., 536–37.
91. Ibid., 536–41, 562–68. Carolina herself testified incorrectly that all the women were whipped on their naked bottoms (ibid., 548–50, 560–62, 570).
92. Ibid., 546–52.
93. "Examination of Walker", in Burdett and Kinchela to Bathurst, 13 August 1825, T1/3483/2: 553–58; "Reply of Walker", 13 August 1825, reproduced 25 February 1826, T1/3483/2: 242.
94. Memorial of Walker to Treasury, 31 July 1826, T1/3482/2: 250; "Evidence of Mrs. Stanley", in Walker to Commissioners of Customs, 22 March 1826, T1/3482/2: 228. See also 230–33 of this document for other testimonies along the same lines.
95. George Pinckard, *Notes on the West Indies . . . and . . . the Coast of Guiana*, vol. 3 (London: Longman, Hurst, Rees and Orme, 1806), 258; John A. Waller, *A Voyage to the West Indies* (London: Sir Richard Phillips, 1820), 3, 4.
96. Roderick A. McDonald, ed., *Between Slavery and Freedom: Special Magistrate John Anderson's Journal of St Vincent during the Apprenticeship* (Kingston, Jamaica: University of the West Indies Press, 2001), 66.
97. Bathurst to Commissioners, 25 August 1825, CO 319/28.
98. Burdett and Kinchela to Horton, 8 March 1826, T1/3482/3: 240–41; Memorial of Walker to Treasury, 31 July 1826, T1/3482/2: 250.
99. Day Books 1–3, 18 July 1821, 29 March 1822, 20 June 1822 and 1

March 1823, CO 318/90: 195, 293, 316, 393.
100. "Special case", in Burdett and Kinchela to Bathurst, 13 August 1825, T1/3483/2: 556; Day Books 4, 6, 7 and 8, 31 October 1823, 31 December 1823, 12 January 1824, 20 July 1824 and 31 January 1825, CO 318/90: 468, 490, 493, 538, 600; "Schedules", CO 318/91: 201. While she was at Berenstein McConchie had her whipped naked by the driver ("Schedules", CO 318/91: 201).
101. Day Book 9, 30 July 1825 and 10 September 1825, CO 318/90: 690, 712.
102. Treasury minutes, 5 December 1825, T29/252; Memorial of Walker to Treasury, 31 July 1826, T1/3482/2: 249.
103. Letters enc. in Walker to Bathurst, 3 March 1827, T1/3484: 346–59.
104. Treasury minute, 7 April 1826, 28 August 1827 and 21 September 1827, T29/256, 272 and 273 respectively; Memorial of Walker to Huskisson, 23 May 1828, T1/3484: 22.
105. Barron to Kyte, 29 March 1826, T1/3482/1: 364–65; Kyte to Barron, 29 March 1826, T1/3482/1: 366–67; Burdett and Kinchela to Horton, 22 April 1826, T1/3482/1: 362–63; "Examination of McWatt", in Burdett and Kinchela to Horton, 22 April 1826, T1/3482/1: 372–76.
106. Paulo Freire, *Pedagogy of the Oppressed*, trans. Myra Bergman Ramos (Harmondsworth, Engl.: Penguin, 1972), 36; Orlando Patterson, *Slavery and Social Death: A Comparative Study* (Cambridge, Mass.: Harvard University Press, 1982).
107. Frantz Fanon, *The Wretched of the Earth*, trans. C. Farrington (Harmondsworth, Engl.: Penguin Books, 1967), 42; Day Books 4, 8 and 9, 30 December 1823, 9 May 1825 and 7 September 1825, CO 318/90: 487, 646, 711. See also Eugene Genovese, *Roll, Jordan, Roll: The World the Slaves Made*, First Vintage Books (1972; reprint, New York: Random House, 1976), 625–37.
108. Albert Memmi, *The Coloniser and the Colonised*, trans. Howard Greenfield (New York: Orion Press, 1965), xviii.
109. Bryan Edwards, *The History, Civil and Commercial, of the British Colonies in the West Indies*, 5th ed., vol. 2 (New York: AMS Press, 1966), 41.

Chapter 8

1. Cited in John W. Blassingame, *The Slave Community: Plantation Life in the Antebellum South*, rev. and enl. ed. (New York: Oxford University Press, 1979), 192.
2. Byng to Treasury, 4 August 1824, PRO, T1/3482/2: 14.
3. Byng and Harrison to Treasury, 12 August 1825, T1/3482/3: 74.
4. Ibid.; Alvin O. Thompson, "African 'Recaptives' under Apprenticeship in the British West Indies, 1807–1828", *Immigrants and Minorities* 9, no. 2 (1990): 137–39.
5. McWatt to D'Urban, 6 May 1826, T1/3482/3: 270.
6. "Report of the Commission of Inquiry", T1/3483/1: 61–62.
7. Cited in Frank J. Klingberg, *The Anti-Slavery Movement in England: A Study in English Humanitarianism* (1926; reprint, Hamden, Conn.: Archon Books, 1968), 227–28.
8. "Report of the Commission of Inquiry", T1/3483/1: 61–62, 65; "Schedules", PRO, CO 318/91; Burdett and Kinchela to Treasury, 30 June 1825, T1/3484: 546–48.
9. "Appendix to a proposal for a settlement of free blacks", in Gipps to Beard, 31 March 1829, T1/3484: 411.

Notes to pages 244–250

10. *Berbice Gazette*, 13 August 1817; Kyte to Barron, 7 and 23 March 1826, T1/3482/1: 206, 288–89; Burdett and Kinchela to Horton, 22 April 1826, T1/3482/1: 7; Kyte to D'Urban, 28 March 1826, T1/3482/3: 176; "Extract from register of Court of Civil Justice", 22 November 1822, T1/3483/2: 407; Walker to Daly, 23 February 1822, T1/3483/2: 474; "Extract from minutes of Council of Government of Berbice", 20 December 1826, CO 111/102.
11. Kyte to Burdett and Kinchela, 10 March 1826: 294–95; Kyte to Barron, 23 January 1826, T1/3482/1: 98–99; Barron to Kyte, 23 January 1826, T1/3482/1: 100–1; Burdett and Kinchela to Horton, 22 April 1826, T1/3482/1: 5–8; Barron to Kyte, 18 March 1826, T1/3482/3: 197–98; Kyte to D'Urban, 27 and 28 March 1826, T1/3482/3: 171–72, 175–78.
12. Treasury minutes, 30 October 1827 and 22 August 1828, T29/274 and 284; Byng and Kingston to Treasury, 6 August 1827: 211–13; Byng and Kingston to Treasury, "Draft memorial of additional instructions . . .", 6 August 1827: 288–91; Huskisson to Beard, 21 November 1827, CO 112/9.
13. *Berbice Gazette*, 7 January 1826; Treasury minutes, 5 February 1830, T29/302; "Memo. of the Report of the Commissioners", 4 December 1826, T1/3482/2: 349; "Report of the Commission of Inquiry", T1/3483/1: 62–64; "Berbice – Winkel Department", c.1830, T1/3484: 455.
14. Scott to Twiss, 8 June 1830, T1/3484: 1229; Scott to Stewart, 6 January 1832, T1/3484: 1128–29; Treasury minutes, 13 December 1831, T29/324.
15. Memo. of Horton, c.6 September 1825, in Horton to Harrison, 17 October 1825, T1/3484: 534–44.
16. "Report of the Commission of Inquiry", T1/3483/1: 64–66; Burdett and Kinchela to Treasury, 30 June 1825, T1/3484: 553–54.
17. "Report of the Commission of Inquiry", T1/3483/1: 65–66.
18. "Proposal for the settlement of free blacks in the upper part of the River Berbice", 5 May 1828, T1/3484: 592–649; "Appendix, to a proposal for a settlement of free blacks", 31 March 1829, T1/3484: 384–441.
19. "Proposal for the settlement of free blacks in the upper part of the River Berbice", 5 May 1828, T1/3484: 592–649; "Appendix, to a proposal for a settlement of free blacks", 31 March 1829, T1/3484: 384–441.
20. Howick to Stewart, 24 March 1831, T1/3484: 1140; Treasury minutes, 9 December 1828, 5 February 1830 and 26 October 1830, T29/288, 302 and 310 respectively; Gipps to Howick, 3 January 1831, CO 111/119.
21. "Proposal for the settlement of free blacks in the upper part of the River Berbice", 5 May 1828, T1/3484: 621.
22. Ibid., 622.
23. For some examples of these settlements see Alvin O. Thompson, *Colonialism and Underdevelopment in Guiana, 1580–1803* (Bridgetown, Barbados: Carib Research and Publications, 1987), 216–17; Lewis Hanke, *The Spanish Struggle for Justice in the Conquest of America* (1949; reprint, Boston: Little, Brown and Co., 1965), 42–82; Christopher Fyfe, *A History of Sierra Leone* (London: Oxford University Press, 1962), 38–126; K.O. Laurence, "The Settlement of Free Negroes in Trinidad before Emancipation", *Caribbean Quarterly* 9, no. 1–2 (1963): 26–52.
24. Thompson, "Recaptives", 137–38.
25. Michael Craton, "Reshuffling the Pack: The Transition from Slavery to Other Forms of Labour in the British

Caribbean, c.1790–1890", *Nieuwe Westindische Gids* 68 (1995): 23–75; William A. Green, "Apprenticeship", in *A Historical Guide to World Slavery*, ed. Seymour Drescher and Stanley Engerman (Oxford: Oxford University Press, 1998), 63–65; Michael Twaddle, ed., *The Wages of Slavery: From Chattel Slavery to Wage Labour in Africa, the Caribbean and England* (London: Frank Cass, 1993); Howard Johnson, "A Slow and Extended Abolition: The Case of the Bahamas, 1800–1838", in *From Chattel Slaves to Wage Slaves: The Dynamics of Wage Bargaining in the Americas*, ed. Mary Turner (London: James Currey, 1995), 165–81.

26. See Jerome Handler, *The Unappropriated People: Freedmen in the Slave Society of Barbados* (Baltimore, Md.: Johns Hopkins University Press, 1974); David Cohen and Jack Greene, eds, *Neither Slave nor Free: The Freedmen of African Descent in the Slave Societies of the New World* (Baltimore, Md.: Johns Hopkins University Press, 1972).

27. William Scott, "Report", 18 May 1829, T1/3484: 496–97; Howick to Stewart, 24 March 1831, T1/3484: 1141–42; Treasury minutes, 5 February 1830, T29/302.

28. Scott, "Report", 18 May 1829, T1/3484: 488.

29. Wray to Hankey, 29 June 1827, LMS, Box 2.

30. "Deposits in the Savings Bank", 1 April–30 June 1826, 1 November–31 December 1826, and 10 May 1827–16 March 1830, CO 111/104 and 110; William Bine, "Statement of monies deposited in the Savings Bank", 16 March 1830, CO 111/110; "Account of the Savings Bank", 12 March–2 September 1830, CO 111/110. For the existence of similar banks in Demerara and Trinidad see James Rodway, *The Story of Georgetown* (1920; reprint, Georgetown: Guyana Heritage Society, 1997), 201; Henry Coleridge, *Six Months in the West Indies in 1825* (1825; reprint, New York: Negro Universities Press, 1970), 98–102.

31. Burdett and Kinchela to Bathurst, 22 April 1826, T1/3482/1: 418–21; "Examination of certain Winkel Negroes", in Burdett to Kyte, 28 March 1826, T1/3482/1: 344; Wray to Power, 9 November 1826, CO 111/104; Wray to Hankey, 20 July 1825, 22 April 1826 and 25 October 1826, LMS, Box 1B; Wray to Hankey, 11 January 1827 and 14 April 1828, LMS, Box 2; Thomas Rain, *The Life and Labours of John Wray, Pioneer Missionary in British Guiana, Compiled from His Own Mss. and Diaries* (London: John Snow and Co., 1892), 254–55, 267, 274–83.

32. Scott to Beard, 12 January 1829, T1/3484: 755–64.

33. House of Commons, "Copy of the Report of the Commissioners Appointed for the Management of the Crown Estates in the Colony of Berbice, to the Lords Commissioners of His Majesty's Treasury", *PP*, 1816, VIII (528): 36; House of Commons, "Accounts of the Total Number of Captured Negroes who were Liberated in each of the Different Colonies; and of the Number of Crown Slaves who have been Liberated in each of the Colonies", *PP*, 1833, XXVI (542): 18; Walker to Treasury, 31 October 1820, T1/3481: 514–16; Walker to Harrison, 22 April 1822 and 15 August 1822, T1/3481: 311–12, 333, 345; "Declaration and demand made in the Court of Civil Justice", 12 April 1822, T1/3481: 314; "Report of the Commission of Inquiry", T1/3483/1: 12–14, 40–43, 93–94, 110–11; "Return of manumissions", 4 April 1808–4 October 1820, CO 111/94.

34. For further details on these Africans see Thompson, "Recaptives".
35. House of Commons, "Account of all Slaves now in Possession of His Majesty's Government, in any of the Colonies", *PP,* 1824, XXIV (423); "Inventory", 26 September 1803, in Moncrieff to Hobart, 6 January 1804, CO 111/73; D'Urban to Goderich, 21 May 1831, CO 111/72; Thompson, *Colonialism,* 61–62. Wherever possible, we have omitted the apprenticed Africans from the number of government slaves given in this study.
36. *PP,* 1824, XXIV (423): 33.
37. Ibid., 10, 27.
38. House of Commons, "An Account of the Final Disposal of the Slaves Escheated to the Crown in the Colonies of the West Indies, since 1st January 1821, and whose Cases have been referred to the Decision of His Majesty's Government", *PP,* 1830–31, XVI (121): 3–7.
39. Ibid., 7.
40. Ibid., 7–8.
41. Ibid., 7. "Attainder" is defined as "the legal consequences of judgement of death or outlawry, in respect of treason or felony, viz. forfeiture of estate real and personal, corruption of blood, so that the condemned could neither inherit nor transmit by descent, and generally, extinction of all civil rights and capacities" (*The Shorter Oxford English Dictionary,* 3rd ed., s.v. "attainder"). The circumstance in question was perhaps a consequence of the rebellion of Julian Fédon, the free-coloured small planter in 1795 (see Michael Craton, *Testing the Chains: Resistance to Slavery in the British West Indies* [Ithaca, N.Y.: Cornell University Press, 1982], 207–10).
42. *PP,* 1830–31, XVI (121): 8–10.
43. Ibid., 9–15.
44. Goderich to D'Urban, 2 September 1831, CO 112/15.
45. House of Commons, "Copies of the Several Orders sent to the Colonies for Emancipating the Slaves Belonging to the Crown", *PP,* 1831, XIX (305): 3. See also *PP,* 1833, XXVI (542).
46. Goderich to D'Urban, 14 March 1831, CO 112/7. See also *PP,* 1831, XIX (305): 4–6; Howick to Stewart, 24 March 1831, T1/3484: 1138–42.
47. D'Urban to Goderich, 21 May 1831, CO 111/72.
48. Goderich to D'Urban, 2 September 1831, CO 112/15.
49. Howick to Stewart, 24 March 1831, T1/3484: 1141–42; D'Urban to Goderich, 7 November 1831, CO 111/117; Scott to D'Urban, 17 November 1831, CO 111/117; "Manumitted Crown Slaves", in Scott to D'Urban, 17 November 1831, CO 111/117; Treasury minutes, 22 April 1831 and 13 March 1832, T29/316 and 327 respectively; Wray to Clayton, 9 August 1832, LMS, Box 2.
50. Scott to D'Urban, 30 November 1831, CO 111/122; D'Urban to Goderich, 10 October 1832, CO 111/122; Howick to Stewart, 24 March 1831, T1/3484: 1141–42; Blue Books, 1832 and 1833, CO 116/179 and 180 respectively. See also Rain, *John Wray,* 296.
51. Scott to D'Urban, 30 November 1831, CO 111/122.
52. Wray to Ellis, 1831, LMS, Box 2; Wray to Hankey, 8 March 1832, LMS, Box 2; Wray to Clayton, 9 August 1832, LMS, Box 2; Wray to Arundel, 19 December 1832, LMS, Box 2; Rain, *John Wray,* 296.
53. A total of 316 (comprising 149 males and 167 females) were manumitted in Demerara and Essequibo ("Abstract", 7 November 1831, CO 111/117).
54. John McClean to John Gladstone, 14 November 1831, CO 111/119.
55. D'Urban to Goderich, 31 December 1831, CO 111/117; see also Wray to Hankey, 8 March 1832, LMS, Box 2.

Reflections

1. Kyte to Barron, 20 December 1825, PRO, T1/3482/1: 79.
2. See Eric Williams, *Capitalism and Slavery* (London: André Deutsch, 1944); and Seymour Drescher, *Econocide: British Slavery in the Era of Abolition* (Pittsburgh, Penn.: University of Pittsburgh Press, 1977).
3. J. Harry Bennett, Jr, *Bondsmen and Bishops: Slavery and Apprenticeship on the Codrington Plantations of Barbados, 1710–1838* (Berkeley: University of California Press, 1958); Jerome Handler and Frederick W. Lange, *Plantation Slavery in Barbados: An Archaeological and Historical Investigation* (Cambridge: Harvard University Press, 1978); Michael Craton and James Walvin, *A Jamaican Plantation: The History of Worthy Park, 1670–1970* (London: W.H. Allen, 1970); Barry Higman, *Montpelier, Jamaica: A Plantation Community in Slavery and Freedom, 1739–1912* (Kingston, Jamaica: University of the West Indies Press, 1998). See also Michael Craton, *Searching for the Invisible Man: Slaves and Plantation Life in Jamaica* (Cambridge: Harvard University Press, 1978).
4. Patrick Manning, *Slavery, Colonialism and Economic Growth in Dahomey, 1640–1960* (Cambridge: Cambridge University Press, 1982), 13, 54.
5. Seymour Drescher and Stanley Engerman, eds, *A Historical Guide to World Slavery* (Oxford: Oxford University Press, 1998), 189–92.
6. Wray to Burder, 13 December 1816, LMS, Box 1A; Wray to Hankey, 18 June 1825, LMS, Box 1B.
7. Jer. 13:23.
8. David Brion Davis, *The Problem of Slavery in Western Culture* (Ithaca, N.Y.: Cornell University Press, 1966).
9. Edward Long, *The History of Jamaica*, vol. 2 (1774; reprint, London: Frank Cass, 1970), 364–65.
10. See Alvin O. Thompson, "'Happy – Happy Slaves!': Slavery as a Superior State to Freedom", *Journal of Caribbean History* 29, no. 2 (1995): 93–119.
11. John Poyer, *The History of Barbados, from the First Discovery of the Island, in the Year 1605, till the Accession of Lord Seaforth, 1801* (London: J. Mawman, 1808), 42; Henry Dalton, *The History of British Guiana, comprising a General Description of the Colony*, vol. 1 (London: Longman, 1855), 153.
12. Orlando Patterson, *Freedom*, vol. 1, *Freedom in the Making of Western Culture* (New York: Basic Books, 1991), 294.
13. Gipps to Twiss, 17 February 1830, PRO, CO 111/112.
14. Alvin O. Thompson, *Colonialism and Underdevelopment in Guiana, 1580–1803* (Bridgetown, Barbados: Carib Research and Publications, 1987), 129. See also Barry Higman, *Slave Populations of the British Caribbean, 1807–1834* (Baltimore: Md.: Johns Hopkins University Press, 1984), 303–77.
15. Patterson, *Freedom*, 321.
16. V.S. Naipaul, *The Middle Passage: Impressions of Five Societies – British, French and Dutch – in the West Indies and South America* (London: André Deutsch, 1974), 182–83.

Bibliography

A. Manuscript Sources

Guyana National Archives, Georgetown
Sessional Papers. Berbice, 1807–1831 (incomplete).

The Hague, Netherlands
Algemeen Rijksarchief. Fagel Family Papers.

Public Record Office, London

CO 101/55–56. Governor's Dispatches, Enclosures and Other Papers, Grenada, 1815–1816.
CO 111/72, Governor's Dispatches, Enclosures and Other Papers, Demerara-Essequibo, 1831.
CO 111/73–114. Governor's Dispatches, Enclosures and Other Papers, Berbice, 1799–1831.
CO 111/115–127. Governor's Dispatches, Enclosures and Other Papers, Essequibo, Demerara and Berbice, 1828–1833.
CO 112/1. Précis of Secretary of State's Correspondence, Berbice, 1801–1807.
CO 112/7. Secretary of State's Dispatches, Demerara-Essequibo, 1831.
CO 112/8–9. Secretary of State's Dispatches, Berbice, 1801–1831.
CO 112/11, 12, 14. Secretary of State's Miscellaneous Correspondence, Offices and Individuals, Demerara-Essequibo and Berbice, 1815–1831.
CO 112/15. Secretary of State's Dispatches, British Guiana, 1831.
CO 114/1–5. Sessional Papers, Court of Policy and Criminal Justice (called Council of Government from 1817) of Berbice, 1806–1830.
CO 114/12. Sessional Papers, British Guiana, 1831–1832.
CO 116/127. Statistics, etc., Berbice, 1791–1795.
CO 116/143–153. Reports of Protectors of Slaves, Berbice, 1826–1834.
CO 116/170–181. Blue Books, Berbice, 1821–1834.

CO 318/85, 87–89. Correspondence, Berbice Commission of Inquiry, 1824–1826.
CO 318/90–92. Day Books, Schedules of Examination, etc. of the *Winkel* Department, Berbice, 1820–1826.
CO 318/93, 95, 98. Correspondence, Commission of Inquiry, Berbice, 1827–1830.
CO 319/27. Commission of Legal Inquiry, 1826.
CO 319/28. Secretary of State's Dispatches and Colonial Office–Treasury Correspondence *re* Commissioners of Apprenticed Africans and Berbice Commissioners of Inquiry, 1822–1835.
CO 714/71–73. Index to Governors' Dispatches, Berbice, 1815–1833 (included as part of British Guiana from 1831).
T1/3481–3484. Correspondence, Crown Slaves in Berbice, 1815–1832.
T6/1–8. Letters from Treasury to Colonial Audit, 1810–1832.
T29/80–348. Treasury Minutes, 1803–1833.
T71/438, 440, 442–444. Registers of Slaves in Berbice, 1819–1831.
T75/17. Sequestered Estates, Suriname, 1814.
T89/1. Berbice Commission for Management of Crown Slaves, 1811–1818.

SCHOOL OF ORIENTAL AND AFRICAN STUDIES, UNIVERSITY OF LONDON

London Missionary Society, Boxes 1A, 1B and 2. Berbice, 1813–1834.

B. GOVERNMENT DOCUMENTS

Government of Guyana. *Gazetteer of Guyana*. Georgetown, 1974.
House of Commons. *Commons Journals*, LXXI, 1 February 1816–2 January 1817.
———. West India Royal Commission. *Report 1938–1939*. London: Her Majesty's Stationery Office, 1945.
Parliamentary Debates, 1st ser., vol. 34 (1816).
Parliamentary Papers. House of Commons (Accounts and Papers):
1806, XII (84). "Copy of an Order of His Majesty in Council, dated 15th of August 1805; made for Prohibiting the Importation of Slaves into any of the Settlements, Islands, Colonies, or Plantations, on the Continent of America, or in the West Indies, Which have been Surrendered to His Majesty During the Present War".
1812, X (355). "Copies of Commissions of the Lords of the Treasury, Appointing Commissioners for the Management of the Crown's Estates in Berbice and on the Continent of South America; dated 23 April 1811, and 22 July 1811".
1816, VIII (509). "Papers Relating to the Crown Estates in the Colony of Berbice".
1816, VIII (528). "Copy of the Report of the Commissioners Appointed for the Management of the Crown Estates in the Colony of Berbice, to the Lords Commissioners of His Majesty's Treasury".
1818, XVII (433). "Further Papers Relating to the Treatment of Slaves in the Colonies".

1823, XVIII (348). "Extract From the Proceedings on the Trial of a Slave, in Berbice, for the Crime of Obeah, and Murder".
1824, XXIV (423). "Account of all Slaves now in Possession of His Majesty's Government, in any of the Colonies".
1825, XXV (476). "Copies of the Record of the Proceedings of the Fiscals of Demerara and Berbice, in their Capacity of Guardians and Protectors of the Slaves . . . from the 1st January 1814".
1826, XXVI (401). "Copies of the Record of the Proceedings of the Fiscals of Demerara and Berbice, in their Capacity of Guardians and Protectors of the Slaves . . . from the 1st January 1814 . . . In Continuation of the Papers Presented 23 June 1825; No. 476".
1826–27, XXII (128). "Slaves Manumitted in Each Colony for the Last Five Years".
1826–27, XXII (355). "Mr Gannon's Report on the Conditions of Apprenticed Africans".
1828, XXV (204). "Further Returns from the Slave Colonies . . . Antigua, Mauritius, Montserrat, St. Lucia".
1828, XXV (261). "Minutes of Evidence Taken Before His Majesty's Privy Council, in the Matter of the Berbice and Demerara Manumission Order in Council".
1829, XXV (301). "Copy or Copies of any Order or Orders in Council Respecting the Manumission of Slaves in Demerara or Berbice, Which Have Been Issued Since the Examination of Evidence Upon the Subject Before the Privy Council".
1829, XXV (333). "Measures Adopted by His Majesty's Government, for the Melioration of the Condition of the Slave Population in His Majesty's Possessions in the West Indies, on the Continent of South America and at Mauritius".
1829, XXV (335). "Copy of any Reports Which May Have Been Received From the Protectors of Slaves in the Colonies of Demerara, Berbice, Trinidad, St. Lucia, and the Cape of Good Hope".
1830–31, XVI (121). "An Account of the Final Disposal of the Slaves Escheated to the Crown in the Colonies of the West Indies, since 1st January 1821, and whose Cases have been referred to the Decision of His Majesty's Government".
1831, XV (262). "Copy of any Reports Which may have been Received from the Protectors of Slaves in the Colonies Demerara, Berbice, Trinidad, St. Lucia, the Cape of Good Hope and Mauritius. Part II".
1831, XIX (305). "Copies of the Several Orders sent to the Colonies for Emancipating the Slaves Belonging to the Crown".
1831–32, XLVII (660). "Return from all the Slave Colonies Belonging to the British Crown, Including the Cape of Good Hope and the Mauritius, of the Following Particulars, Commencing on the 1st January 1825, and Continued to the Latest Period . . . List of all Slaves Escheated to the Crown".

1833, XXVI (542). "Accounts of the Total Number of Captured Negroes who were Liberated in each of the Different Colonies; and of the Number of Crown Slaves who have been Liberated in each of the Colonies".

1835, L (278–1). "Papers Presented to Parliament by His Majesty's Command, in Explanation of the Measures Adopted by His Majesty's Government, for Giving Effect to the Act for the Abolition of Slavery Throughout the British Colonies. Part II".

C. Books

Allsopp, Richard, ed. *Dictionary of Caribbean English Usage.* Oxford: Oxford University Press, 1996.

Anstey, Roger. *The Atlantic Slave Trade and British Abolition, 1760–1810.* London: Macmillan, 1975.

Asiegbu, Johnson. *Slavery and the Politics of Liberation, 1787–1861: A Study of Liberated African Emigration and British Anti-Slavery Policy.* London: Longman, 1969.

Bastide, Roger. *The African Religions of Brazil: Towards a Sociology of the Interpenetration of Civilizations.* Translated by Helen Sebba. Baltimore, Md.: Johns Hopkins University Press, 1978.

Beatty, Paul. *A History of the Lutheran Church in Guyana.* Georgetown, Guyana: Daily Chronicle, 1970.

Beckford, George. *Persistent Poverty: Underdevelopment in Plantation Economies of the Third World.* New York: Oxford University Press, 1972.

Beckles, Hilary McD. *Black Rebellion in Barbados: The Struggle against Slavery, 1627–1838.* Bridgetown, Barbados: Antilles Publications, 1984.

———. *Natural Rebels: A Social History of Enslaved Black Women in Barbados.* London: Zed Books, 1989.

Beckles, Hilary McD., and Verene Shepherd, eds. *Caribbean Slave Society and Economy: A Student Reader.* Kingston, Jamaica: Ian Randle Publishers, 1991.

———. *Caribbean Slavery in the Atlantic World: A Student Reader.* Kingston, Jamaica: Ian Randle Publishers, 2000.

Bennett, J. Harry, Jr. *Bondsmen and Bishops: Slavery and Apprenticeship on the Codrington Plantations of Barbados, 1710–1838.* Berkeley: University of California Press, 1958.

Bergad, Laird. *Cuban Rural Society in the Nineteenth Century: The Social and Economic History of Monoculture in Matanzas.* Princeton, N.Y.: Princeton University Press, 1990.

Blackburn, Robin. *The Overthrow of Colonial Slavery, 1776–1848.* London: Verso, 1988.

Blassingame, John W. *The Slave Community: Plantation Life in the Antebellum South.* Rev. and enl. ed. New York: Oxford University Press, 1979.

Bolingbroke, Henry. *A Voyage to Demerary, Containing a Statistical Account of the Settlements There and Those of the Essequibo, the Berbice, and Other Contiguous Rivers of Guiana.* 1808. Reprint, Georgetown, Guyana: Daily Chronicle, 1947.

Brathwaite, Edward. *The Development of Creole Society in Jamaica, 1770–1820.* Oxford: Oxford University Press, 1971.

Brereton, Bridget. *Law, Justice and Empire: The Colonial Career of John Gorrie, 1829–1892.* Kingston, Jamaica: The Press, University of the West Indies, 1997.

Brown, William W. *Narrative of William W. Brown, a Fugitive Slave.* Boston: Anti-Slavery Office, 1847.

Buckley, Roger N. *Slaves in Red Coats: The British West India Regiments, 1795–1815.* New Haven, Conn.: Yale University Press, 1979.

Burn, William L. *Emancipation and Apprenticeship in the British West Indies.* London: Jonathan Cape, 1937.

Bush, Barbara. *Slave Women in Caribbean Society, 1650–1838.* Kingston, Jamaica: Heinemann, 1990.

Campbell, Mavis. *The Maroons of Jamaica, 1655–1796: A History of Resistance, Collaboration and Betrayal.* Trenton, N.J.: Africa World Press, 1990.

Carey, Bev. *The Maroon Story: The Authentic and Original History of the Maroons in the History of Jamaica, 1490–1880.* Gordon Town, Jamaica: Agouti, 1997.

Carmichael, A.C. *Domestic Manners and Social Conditions of the White, Coloured and Negro Populations of the West Indies.* 2 vols. London: Whittaker, 1833.

Carrión, Arturo M., ed. *Puerto Rico: A Political and Cultural History.* New York: Norton and Co., 1983.

Césaire, Aimé. *Discourse on Colonialism.* Translated by Joan Pinkham. New York: Monthly Review Press, 1972.

Charrière, Henri. *Papillon.* Translated by June P. Wilson and Walter B. Michaels. New York: Pocket Books, 1971.

Clarke, Colin. *Kingston, Jamaica: Urban Development and Social Change, 1692–1962.* Berkeley: University of California Press, 1975.

Clarkson, Thomas. *The History of the Rise, Progress and Accomplishment of the Abolition of the African Slave Trade by the British Parliament.* 2 vols. London: Longman, Hurst, Reese and Orme, 1808.

———. *Thoughts on the Necessity of Improving the Condition of the Slaves in the British Colonies.* London, 1823.

Cohen, David, and Jack Greene, eds. *Neither Slave nor Free: The Freedmen of African Descent in the Slave Societies of the New World.* Baltimore, Md.: Johns Hopkins University Press, 1972.

Coleridge, Henry. *Six Months in the West Indies in 1825*. 1825. Reprint, New York: Negro Universities Press, 1970.
Colonist. *The Edinburgh Review and the West Indies, with Observations on the Pamphlets of Stephen, Macaulay, etc.* Glasgow: John Smith and Son, 1816.
Colonist. *Kort Historisch Verhaal Van den Eersten Aanleg, Lotgevallen en Voortgang der Particuliere Colonie Berbice*. Amsterdam: Sepp Jansz., 1807.
Coupland, Reginald. *Wilberforce: A Narrative*. Oxford: Clarendon Press, 1923.
———. *The British Anti-Slavery Movement*. London: T. Butterworth, 1933.
Craton, Michael. *Searching for the Invisible Man: Slaves and Plantation Life in Jamaica*. Cambridge: Harvard University Press, 1978.
———. *Testing the Chains: Resistance to Slavery in the British West Indies*. Ithaca, N.Y.: Cornell University Press, 1982.
Craton, Michael, and James Walvin. *A Jamaican Plantation: The History of Worthy Park, 1670–1970*. London: W.H. Allen, 1970.
Da Costa, Emília Viotti. *Crowns of Glory, Tears of Blood: The Demerara Slave Rebellion of 1823*. New York: Oxford University Press, 1994.
Dalton, Henry. *The History of British Guiana, Comprising a General Description of the Colony.* 2 vols. London: Longman, 1855.
Davis, David Brion. *The Problem of Slavery in Western Culture*. Ithaca, N.Y.: Cornell University Press, 1966.
———. *The Problem of Slavery in the Age of Revolution, 1770–1823*. Ithaca, N.Y.: Cornell University Press, 1975.
———. *Slavery and Human Progress*. New York: Oxford University Press, 1984.
De la Beche, H.T. *Notes on the Present Condition of the Negroes in Jamaica*. London: Cadell, 1825.
Dickson, William. *Mitigation of Slavery.* 1814. Reprint, Westport, Conn.: Negro Universities Press, 1970.
Dirks, Robert. *The Black Saturnalia: Conflict and Its Ritual Expression on British West Indian Plantations*. Gainesville: University of Florida Press, 1987.
Dookhan, Isaac. *A History of the British Virgin Islands, 1672–1970*. Epping, Engl.: Caribbean Universities Press, 1975.
Douglass, Frederick. *Narrative of the Life of Frederick Douglass*. 1845. Reprint, New York: Penguin Books, 1982.
———. *My Bondage and My Freedom*. 1855. Reprint, New York: Dover Publications, 1969.
Drescher, Seymour. *Econocide: British Slavery in the Era of Abolition*. Pittsburgh, Penn.: University of Pittsburgh Press, 1977.
———. *Capitalism and Antislavery: British Mobilization in Comparative Perspective*. London: Macmillan, 1986.

Drescher, Seymour, and Stanley Engerman, eds. *A Historical Guide to World Slavery.* Oxford: Oxford University Press, 1998.
Edwards, Bryan. *The History, Civil and Commercial, of the British Colonies in the West Indies.* 5th ed. New York: AMS Press, 1966.
Eltis, David. *Economic Growth and the Ending of the Transatlantic Slave Trade.* New York: Oxford University Press, 1987.
Engerman, Stanley, and Robert Fogel. *Time on the Cross: The Economics of American Negro Slavery.* 2 vols. Boston: Little, Brown, 1974.
Engerman, Stanley, and E.D. Genovese, eds. *Race and Slavery in the Western Hemisphere: Quantitative Studies.* Princeton, N.J.: Princeton University Press, 1975.
Fanon, Frantz. *Black Skins White Masks.* Translated by Charles Lain Markmann. New York: Grove Press, 1967.
———. *The Wretched of the Earth.* Translated by C. Farrington. Harmondsworth, Engl.: Penguin Books, 1967.
Foner, Philip. *A History of Cuba and Its Relations with the United States.* Vol. 1. New York: International Publishers, 1963.
Fouchard, Jean. *The Haitian Maroons: Liberty or Death.* New York: Edward W. Blyden Press, 1981.
Fox-Genovese, Elizabeth. *Within the Plantation Household: Black and White Women of the Old South.* Chapel Hill: University of North Carolina Press, 1988.
Frazier, Franklin. *The Negro Family in the United States.* 1939. Reprint, Chicago: University of Chicago Press, 1966.
Freire, Paulo. *Pedagogy of the Oppressed.* Translated by Myra Bergman Ramos. Harmondsworth, Engl.: Penguin Books, 1972.
Furneaux, Robin. *William Wilberforce.* London: Hamish Hamilton, 1974.
Fyfe, Christopher. *A History of Sierra Leone.* London: Oxford University Press, 1962.
Galbano-Elephantius, G.T., ed. *A Voyage to the New Colony of Berbice in 1735.* Georgetown, Guyana: Daily Chronicle, 1877.
Genovese, Eugene. *Roll, Jordan, Roll: The World the Slaves Made.* First Vintage Books. 1972. Reprint, New York: Random House, 1976.
George, M. Dorothy. *London Life in the Eighteenth Century.* 1925. Reprint, Harmondsworth, Engl.: Penguin Books, 1965.
Giuseppi, M.S., ed. *Guide to the Contents of the Public Record Office.* Vol. 2. London: Her Majesty's Stationery Office, 1963.
Gomez, Michael A. *Changing Our Country Marks: The Transformation of African Identities in the Colonial and Ante-Bellum South.* Chapel Hill: University of North Carolina Press, 1998.
Goodrich, Derek H. *History of All Saints Parish New Amsterdam, 1811–1979.* New Amsterdam, Guyana, c.1979.

Gordon, Shirley C. *God Almighty Make Me Free: Christianity in Preemancipation Jamaica.* Bloomington: Indiana University Press, 1996.
Goveia, Elsa. *The West Indian Slave Laws of the Eighteenth Century.* Bridgetown, Barbados: Caribbean Universities Press, 1970.
———. *Slave Society in the British Leeward Islands at the End of the Eighteenth Century.* 1965. Reprint, Westport, Conn.: Greenwood Press, 1980.
Green, William A. *British Slave Emancipation: The Sugar Colonies and the Great Experiment, 1830–1865.* New York: Oxford University Press, 1976.
Gutman, Herbert. *The Black Family in Slavery and Freedom.* First Vintage Books. New York: Random House, 1977.
Hall, Douglas. *In Miserable Slavery: Thomas Thistlewood in Jamaica, 1750–1786.* London: Macmillan, 1989.
Hall, Gwendolyn Midlo. *Social Control in Slave Plantation Societies: A Comparison of St. Domingue and Cuba.* Baltimore, Md.: Johns Hopkins University Press, 1971.
Handler, Jerome. *The Unappropriated People: Freedmen in the Slave Society of Barbados.* Baltimore, Md.: Johns Hopkins University Press, 1974.
Handler, Jerome, and Frederick W. Lange. *Plantation Slavery in Barbados: An Archaeological and Historical Investigation.* Cambridge: Harvard University Press, 1978.
Hanke, Lewis. *The Spanish Struggle for Justice in the Conquest of America.* 1949. Reprint, Boston: Little, Brown and Co., 1965.
Hart, Richard. *Slaves Who Abolished Slavery.* Vol. 1, *Blacks in Bondage.* Kingston, Jamaica: Institute of Social and Economic Research, 1980.
Hartsinck, Jan J. *Beschrijving van Guiana of de Wildekust in Zuid-America.* Amsterdam: G. Tielenburg, 1770.
Higman, Barry. *Slave Population and Economy in Jamaica, 1807–1834.* Cambridge: Cambridge University Press, 1976.
———. *Slave Populations of the British Caribbean, 1807–1834.* Baltimore, Md.: Johns Hopkins University Press, 1984.
———. *Montpelier, Jamaica: A Plantation Community in Slavery and Freedom, 1739–1912.* Kingston, Jamaica: University of the West Indies Press, 1998.
———, ed. *Trade, Government and Society in Caribbean History, 1700–1920.* Kingston, Jamaica: Heinemann, 1983.
Hoetink, Harry. *Slavery and Race Relations in the Americas: Comparative Notes on Their Nature and Nexus.* New York: Harper and Row, 1973.
Jacobs, Harriet [Linda Brent, pseud.]. *Incidents in the Life of a Slave Girl Written by Herself.* 1861. Reprint, Cambridge: Harvard University Press, 1987.
Jakobssen, Stiv. *Am I Not a Man and a Brother? British Missions and the Abolition of the Slave Trade and Slavery in West Africa and the West Indies, 1786–1838.* Uppsala, Sweden: Wicksells Boktryckeri, 1972.

Johnson, Howard. *The Bahamas in Slavery and Freedom.* Kingston, Jamaica: Ian Randle Publishers, 1991.

———. *The Bahamas from Slavery to Servitude, 1787–1933.* Gainesville: University of Florida Press, 1996.

Kiple, Kenneth. *The Caribbean Slave: A Biological History.* Cambridge: Cambridge University Press, 1984.

Klingberg, Frank J. *The Anti-Slavery Movement in England: A Study in English Humanitarianism.* 1926. Reprint, Hamden, Conn.: Archon Books, 1968.

Knight, Franklin, ed. *General History of the Caribbean.* Vol. 3, *The Slave Societies of the Caribbean.* London: UNESCO Publishing/Macmillan Education, 1997.

Knutsford, Margaret-Jean Holland, Viscountess. *Life and Letters of Zachary Macaulay.* London: Edward Arnold, 1900.

Law, Robin. *The Oyo Empire, c.1600–c.1836: A West African Imperialism in the Era of the Atlantic Slave Trade.* Oxford: Clarendon Press, 1977.

List of Colonial Office Records. New York: Kraus, 1963.

List of the Records of the Treasury, the Paymaster General's Office, the Exchequer and Audit Department and the Board of Trade to 1837. New York: Kraus, 1963.

Long, Edward. *The History of Jamaica.* 2 vols. 1774. Reprint, London: Frank Cass, 1970.

Lovett, Richard. *The History of the London Missionary Society.* 2 vols. London: Henry Frowde, 1899.

Lowenthal, David. *West Indian Societies.* London: Oxford University Press, 1972.

Manning, Patrick. *Slavery, Colonialism and Economic Growth in Dahomey, 1640–1960.* Cambridge: Cambridge University Press, 1982.

Marryat, Joseph. *More Thoughts Occasioned by Two Publications.* London: J.M. Richardson and J. Ridgway, 1816.

———. *An Examination of the Report of the Berbice Commissioners.* London: Hughes and Baynes, 1817.

———. *More Thoughts Still on the State of the West India Colonies.* London: Hughes and Baynes, 1818.

Marshall, Woodville K. *The Colthurst Journal: Journal of a Special Magistrate in the Islands of Barbados and St. Vincent, July 1835–September 1838.* Millwood, N.Y.: KTO Press, 1977.

Mathieson, William L. *British Slavery and Its Abolition, 1823–1838.* London: Longman, Green and Co., 1926.

McDonald, Roderick A. *The Economy and Material Culture of Slaves: Goods and Chattels on the Sugar Plantations of Jamaica and Louisiana.* Baton Rouge: Louisiana State University Press, 1993.

———, ed. *Between Slavery and Freedom: Special Magistrate John Anderson's Journal of St Vincent during the Apprenticeship.* Kingston, Jamaica: University of the West Indies Press, 2001.

McGowan, Winston, James Rose and David Granger, eds. *Themes in African-Guyanese History.* Georgetown, Guyana: Free Press, 1998.
Memmi, Albert. *The Coloniser and the Colonised.* Translated by Howard Greenfield. New York: Orion Press, 1965.
Mintz, Sidney W., and Douglas Hall. *The Origins of the Jamaican Internal Marketing System.* Yale University Publications in Anthropology, no. 57. New Haven, Conn.: Yale University Press, 1960.
Mintz, Sidney W., and Richard Price. *An Anthropological Approach to the Afro-American Past: A Caribbean Perspective.* Philadelphia: Institute for the Study of Human Issues, 1976.
Morrissey, Marietta. *Slave Women in the New World: Gender Stratification in the Caribbean.* Lawrence: University of Kansas Press, 1989.
M'Queen, James. *The West India Colonies; The Calumnies and Misrepresentations Circulated against Them.* 1825. Reprint, New York: Negro Universities Press, 1969.
Naipaul, V.S. *The Middle Passage: Impressions of Five Societies – British, French and Dutch – in the West Indies and South America.* London: André Deutsch, 1974.
Netscher, P.M. *Geschiedenis Van De Kolonien Essequebo, Demerary en Berbice.* The Hague: Martinus Nijhoff, 1888.
Nieboer, H.J. *Slavery as an Industrial System: Ethnological Researches.* 1900. Reprint, New York: B. Franklin, 1971.
Niles, Blair. *Condemned to Devil's Island: The Biography of an Unknown Convict.* London: Jonathan Cape, 1928.
Oliver, Roland, ed. *The Cambridge History of Africa.* Vol. 3, *From c.1050 to c.1600.* Cambridge: Cambridge University Press, 1977.
Patterson, Orlando. *The Sociology of Slavery: An Analysis of the Origins, Development, and Structure of Negro Slave Society in Jamaica.* London: MacGibbon and Kee, 1967.
———. *Slavery and Social Death: A Comparative Study.* Cambridge: Harvard University Press, 1982.
———. *Freedom.* Vol. 1, *Freedom in the Making of Western Culture.* New York: Basic Books, 1991.
Pinckard, George. *Notes on the West Indies . . . and . . . the Coast of Guiana.* 3 vols. London: Longman, Hurst, Rees and Orme, 1806.
Pollock, John. *Wilberforce.* London: Constable and Co., 1977.
Poyer, John. *The History of Barbados, from the First Discovery of the Island, in the Year 1605, till the Accession of Lord Seaforth, 1801.* London: J. Mawman, 1808.
Prince, Mary. *The History of Mary Prince, a West Indian Slave, Related by Herself.* 1831. Reprint, Ann Arbor: University of Michigan Press, 1993.
Pugh, R.B. *The Records of the Colonial and Dominions Offices.* London: Her Majesty's Stationery Office, 1964.

Ragatz, Lowell. *The Fall of the Planter Class in the British Caribbean, 1763–1833.* 1928. Reprint, New York: Octagon Books, 1963.

Rain, Thomas. *The Life and Labours of John Wray, Pioneer Missionary in British Guiana, Compiled from His Own Mss. and Diaries.* London: John Snow and Co., 1892.

Ramsay, James. *An Essay on the Treatment and Conversion of African Slaves in the British Sugar Colonies.* London: James Phillips, 1784.

Richardson, David, ed. *Abolition and Its Aftermath: The Historical Context, 1790–1916.* London: Frank Cass, 1985.

Rodney, Walter. *How Europe Underdeveloped Africa.* London: Bogle L'Ouverture Publications, 1972.

———. *A History of the Guyanese Working People, 1881–1905.* Baltimore, Md.: Johns Hopkins University Press, 1981.

Rodway, James. *History of British Guiana from the Year 1688 to the Present Time.* 3 vols. Georgetown, Guyana: J. Thomson, 1891–94.

———. *The Story of Georgetown.* 1920. Reprint, Georgetown: Guyana Heritage Society, 1997.

Roth, Walter E. *An Introductory Study of the Arts, Crafts, and Customs of the Guiana Indians.* 1924. Reprint, New York: Johnson Reprint Corporation, 1970.

Rousseau, Jean Jacques. *The Social Contract.* Translated by Maurice Cranston. Harmondsworth, Engl.: Penguin Books, 1968.

Schomburgk, Richard. *Travels in British Guiana, 1840–1844.* 2 vols. 1847. Reprints, translated and edited by W.E. Roth. Georgetown, Guyana: Daily Chronicle, 1922–23.

[Senior, Bernard]. *Jamaica, as It Was, as It Is, and as It May Be.* 1835. Reprint, New York: Negro Universities Press, 1969.

Shahabuddeen, M. *The Legal System of Guyana.* Georgetown: Guyana Printers, 1973.

Shepherd, Verene, Bridget Brereton and Barbara Bailey, eds. *Engendering History: Caribbean Women in Historical Perspective.* Kingston, Jamaica: Ian Randle Publishers, 1995.

Sheridan, Richard. *Doctors and Slaves: A Medical and Demographic History of Slavery in the British West Indies, 1680–1834.* Cambridge: Cambridge University Press, 1985.

Smith, Adam. *An Inquiry into the Nature and Causes of the Wealth of Nations.* 1776. Reprint, London: Murray, 1870.

Smith, M.G. *Culture, Race and Class in the Commonwealth Caribbean.* Kingston, Jamaica: Department of Extra Mural Studies, University of the West Indies, 1984.

Solow, Barbara L., and Stanley Engerman, eds. *British Capitalism and Caribbean Slavery: The Legacy of Eric Williams.* New York: Cambridge University Press, 1987.

St Clair, Thomas. *A Soldier's Sojourn in British Guiana, 1806–1808.* Georgetown, Guyana: Daily Chronicle, 1947.

Stedman, John G. *Narrative of Five Years' Expedition against the Revolted Negroes of Surinam in Guiana on the Wild Coast of South America from the Years 1772 to 1777.* 1796. Reprint, Amherst: University of Massachusetts Press, 1972.

Stephen, James. *Reasons for Establishing a Registry of Slaves in the British Colonies: Being a Report of a Committee of the African Institution.* London: African Institution, 1815.

———. *The Speech of James Stephen, Esq. at the Annual Meeting of the African Institution.* London: J. Butterworth and Son, and J. Hatchard, 1817.

———. *The Slavery of the British West India Colonies Delineated as It Exists Both in Law and Practice.* 2 vols. 1824–1830. Reprint, New York: Kraus, 1969.

Substance of the Debate in the House of Commons on the 15th May, 1823, on a Motion for the Mitigation and Gradual Abolition of Slavery Throughout the British Dominions. 1823. Reprint, New York: Negro Universities Press, 1969.

Thomas-Hope, Elizabeth, ed. *Perspectives on Caribbean Regional Identity.* Liverpool: Centre for Latin American Studies, University of Liverpool, 1984.

Thompson, Alvin O. *Some Problems of Slave Desertion in Guyana, 1750–1814.* Occasional Paper, no. 4. Cave Hill, Barbados: Institute of Social and Economic Research, 1976.

———. *Colonialism and Underdevelopment in Guiana, 1580–1803.* Bridgetown, Barbados: Carib Research and Publications, University of the West Indies, 1987.

Thornton, John. *Africa and the Africans in the Making of the Atlantic World, 1400–1680.* Cambridge: Cambridge University Press, 1992.

Tinker, Hugh. *A New System of Slavery: The Export of Indian Labour Overseas, 1838–1920.* London: Oxford University Press, 1974.

Titus, Noel. *The Development of Methodism in Barbados, 1823–1883.* Berne: Peter Lang, 1994.

Trevelyan, George Macaulay *English Social History: A Survey of Six Centuries from Chaucer to Victoria.* Illus. ed. 1942. Reprint, London: Longman, 1978.

Trevelyan, George Otto. *The Life and Letters of Lord Macaulay.* London: Longman Green, 1878.

Turner, Mary. *Slaves and Missionaries: The Disintegration of Jamaican Slave Society, 1787–1834.* Urbana: University of Illinois Press, 1982.

———, ed. *From Chattel Slaves to Wage Slaves: The Dynamics of Wage Bargaining in the Americas.* London: James Currey, 1995.

Twaddle, Michael, ed. *The Wages of Slavery: From Chattel Slavery to Wage Labour in Africa, the Caribbean and England.* London: Frank Cass, 1993.

Van Lier, R.A.J. *Frontier Society.* The Hague: Martinus Nijhoff, 1971.

Walker, James. *Letters on the West Indies.* London: Camberwell Press, 1818.

Waller, John A. *A Voyage to the West Indies.* London: Sir Richard Phillips, 1820.

Walne, P., ed. *A Guide to Manuscript Sources for the History of Latin America and the Caribbean in the British Isles.* London: Oxford University Press, 1973.
Ward, J.R. *British West Indian Slavery, 1750–1834: The Process of Amelioration.* Oxford: Clarendon Press, 1988.
Washington, Booker T. *Up from Slavery: An Autobiography.* 1901. Reprint, New York: Doubleday, 1963.
Watson, Karl. *The Civilized Island Barbados.* Bridgetown, Barbados: Caribbean Graphics, 1979.
Webber, A.R.F. *Centenary History and Handbook of British Guiana.* Georgetown, Guyana: Argosy Co., 1931.
Weiner, Marli F. *Mistresses and Slaves: Plantation Women in South Carolina, 1830–1880.* Urbana: University of Illinois Press, 1997.
Weinstein, Allen, and Frank Otto Gatell, eds. *American Negro Slavery: A Modern Reader.* New York: Oxford University Press, 1968.
Wesley, John. *Thoughts on Slavery.* London: John Cruickshank, 1774.
West India Royal Commission. *Report 1938–1939.* London: Her Majesty's Stationery Office, 1945.
White, Deborah. *Ar'n't I a Woman? Female Slaves in the Plantation South.* New York: W.W. Norton, 1985.
Williams, Eric. *Capitalism and Slavery.* London: André Deutsch, 1944.
Williams, James. *Dutch Plantations on the Banks of the Berbice and Canje Rivers in the Country Known since 1831 as the Colony of British Guiana, and the Village Evolved from the Plantation.* Georgetown, Guyana: Daily Chronicle, 1940.

D. Articles, Papers and Dissertations

Anstey, Roger. "The Volume and Profitability of the British Slave Trade, 1761–1807". In *Race and Slavery in the Western Hemisphere: Quantitative Studies,* edited by Stanley Engerman and E.D. Genovese, 3–31. Princeton, N.J.: Princeton University Press, 1975.
Beckles, Hilary McD. "Rebels without Heroes: Slave Politics in Seventeenth-Century Barbados". *Journal of Caribbean History* 18, no. 2 (1984): 1–21.
———. "Caribbean Anti-Slavery: The Self-Liberation Ethos of Enslaved Blacks". *Journal of Caribbean History* 22, no. 1–2 (1988): 1–19.
———. "An Economic Life of Their Own: Slaves as Commodity Producers and Distributors in Barbados". *Slavery and Abolition* 12, no. 1 (1991): 31–48.
———. "Sex and Gender in the Historiography of Caribbean Slavery". In *Engendering History: Caribbean Women in Historical Perspective,* edited by Verene Shepherd, Bridget Brereton and Barbara Bailey, 125–40. Kingston, Jamaica: Ian Randle Publishers, 1995.

———. "Historicizing Slavery in West Indian Feminism". *Feminist Review* 59 (1998): 34–56.
Best, Lloyd. "Outlines of a Model of Pure Plantation Economy". *Social and Economic Studies* 17, no. 3 (1968): 7–38.
Bolland, Nigel. "Systems of Domination after Slavery: The Control of Land and Labor in the British West Indies after 1838". *Comparative Studies in Society and History* 23, no. 4 (1981): 591–619.
Buckridge, Steeve O. "The 'Colour and Fabric' of Jamaican Slave Women's Dress". *Journal of Caribbean History* 33, no. 1–2 (1999): 84–124.
Cameron, A.J.McR. "Abolitionists Who Managed Slaves". *Stabroek News,* 19 August 1989.
———. "The Origins of the Winkle Village". *Stabroek News,* 26 August 1989.
Carrington, Selwyn. "The State of the Debate on the Role of Capitalism in the Ending of the Slave System". *Journal of Caribbean History* 22 (1988): 20–41.
Costas, Aida R.C. "The Organization of an Institutional and Social Life". In *Puerto Rico: A Political and Cultural History,* edited by Arturo M. Carrión, 25–40. New York: Norton and Co., 1983.
Craton, Michael. "The Passion to Exist: Slave Rebellions in the British West Indies, 1650–1832". *Journal of Caribbean History* 13 (1980): 1–20.
———. "Changing Patterns of Slave Families in the British West Indies". In *Caribbean Slave Society and Economy: A Student Reader,* edited by Hilary McD. Beckles and Verene Shepherd, 228–49. Kingston, Jamaica: Ian Randle Publishers, 1991.
———. "Reshuffling the Pack: The Transition from Slavery to Other Forms of Labour in the British Caribbean, *c.*1790–1890". *Nieuwe Westindische Gids* 68 (1995): 23–75.
Cruickshank, Graham. "'King William's People.' The Story of the Winkel Village, Berbice". *Timehri* 5 (1918): 104–19.
De Groot, Silvia. "The Maroons of Surinam: Agents of Their Own Emancipation". In *Abolition and Its Aftermath: The Historical Context, 1790–1916,* edited by David Richardson, 55–79. London: Frank Cass, 1985
De Groot, Silvia, Catherine Christen and Franklin Knight, "Maroon Communities in the Circum-Caribbean". In *General History of the Caribbean.* Vol. 3, *The Slave Societies of the Caribbean,* edited by Franklin Knight, 169–93. London: UNESCO Publishing/Macmillan Education, 1997.
Engerman, Stanley. "The Slave Trade and British Capital Formation in the Eighteenth Century: A Comment on the Williams Thesis". *Business History Review* 46 (1972): 430–43.
Engerman, Stanley, and Barry Higman. "The Demographic Structure of the Caribbean Slave Societies in the Eighteenth and Nineteenth Centuries". In *General History of*

the Caribbean. Vol. 3, *The Slave Societies of the Caribbean,* edited by Franklin Knight, 45–104. London: UNESCO Publishing/Macmillan Education, 1997.
Furley, O.W. "Moravian Missionaries and Slaves in the West Indies". *Caribbean Studies* 5, no. 2 (1965): 3–16.
Green, William A. "Apprenticeship". In *A Historical Guide to World Slavery,* edited by Seymour Drescher and Stanley Engerman, 63–65. Oxford: Oxford University Press, 1998.
Hall, Neville. "Slavery in Three West Indian Towns: Christiansted, Fredericksted, and Charlotte Amalie". In *Trade, Government and Society in Caribbean History, 1700–1920,* edited by Barry Higman, 21–38. Kingston, Jamaica: Heinemann, 1983.
———. "Slaves and the Law in the Towns of St Croix, 1802–1807". *Slavery and Abolition* 8 (1987): 147–65.
Higman, Barry. "The Slave Family and Household in the British West Indies, 1800–1834". *Journal of Interdisciplinary History* 1, no. 2 (1975): 261–87.
———. "Urban Slavery in the British Caribbean". In *Perspectives on Caribbean Regional Identity,* edited by Elizabeth Thomas-Hope, 39–56. Liverpool: Centre for Latin American Studies, University of Liverpool, 1984.
Hrbek, Ivan. "Egypt, Nubia and the Eastern Deserts". In *The Cambridge History of Africa.* Vol. 3, *From c.1050 to c.1600,* edited by Roland Oliver, 10–97. Cambridge: Cambridge University Press, 1977.
Johnson, Howard. "The Liberated Africans in the Bahamas, 1811–1860". *Immigrants and Minorities* 7, no. 1 (1988): 16–40.
———. "A Slow and Extended Abolition: The Case of the Bahamas, 1800–1838". In *From Chattel Slaves to Wage Slaves: The Dynamics of Wage Bargaining in the Americas,* edited by Mary Turner, 165–81. London: James Currey, 1995.
Knight, Franklin. "Pluralism, Creolization and Culture". In *General History of the Caribbean.* Vol. 3, *The Slave Societies of the Caribbean,* edited by Franklin Knight, 271–86. London: UNESCO Publishing/Macmillan Education, 1997.
Laurence, K.O. "The Settlement of Free Negroes in Trinidad before Emancipation". *Caribbean Quarterly* 9, no. 1–2 (1963): 26–52.
Manigat, Leslie F. "The Relationship between Marronage and Slave Revolts and Revolution in St Domingue-Haiti". In *Comparative Perspectives on Slavery in New World Plantation Societies,* edited by Vera Rubin and Arthur Tuden, 420–58. New York: Annals of the New York Academy of Sciences, 1977.
Marshall, Woodville K. "Provision Ground and Plantation Labour in Four Windward Islands: Competition for Resources during Slavery". *Slavery and Abolition* 12, no. 1 (1991): 48–67.
Martínez-Fernandez, Luis. "The Havana Anglo-Spanish Mixed Commission for the Suppression of the Slave Trade and Cuba's *Emancipados*". *Slavery and Abolition* 16, no. 2 (1995): 205–25.

Moitt, Bernard. "Women, Work and Resistance in the French Caribbean during Slavery, 1700–1848". In *Engendering History: Caribbean Women in Historical Perspective*, edited by Verene Shepherd, Bridget Brereton and Barbara Bailey, 155–76. Kingston, Jamaica: Ian Randle Publishers, 1995.

Newman, John. "The Enigma of Joshua Steele". *Journal of the Barbados Museum and Historical Society* 19, no. 1 (1951): 6–20.

Phillips, Ulrich. "Southern Negro Slavery: A Benign View". In *American Negro Slavery: A Modern Reader*, edited by Allen Weinstein and Frank Otto Gatell, 37–50. New York: Oxford University Press, 1968.

Racine, Karen. "Brittania's Bold Brother: British Cultural Influence in Haiti during the Reign of Henry Christophe (1811–1820)". *Journal of Caribbean History* 33, no. 1–2 (1999): 125–45.

Sheridan, Richard. "The Wealth of Jamaica in the Eighteenth Century". *Economic History Review*, 2d ser., 18, no. 2 (1965): 292–311.

Solow, Barbara L. "Caribbean Slavery and British Growth: The Eric Williams Hypothesis". *Journal of Development Economics* 17, no. 1–2 (1985): 99–115.

Thompson, Alvin O. "Race and Colour Prejudices and the Origin of the Trans-Atlantic Slave Trade". *Caribbean Studies* 16, no. 3–4 (1976–77): 251–73.

———. "The Guyana-Suriname Boundary Dispute: An Historical Appraisal, c.1683–1816". *Boletín de Estudios Latinoamericanos y del Caribe* 39 (1985): 63–84.

———. "African 'Recaptives' under Apprenticeship in the British West Indies, 1807–1828". *Immigrants and Minorities* 9, no. 2 (1990): 123–44.

———. " 'Happy – Happy Slaves!': Slavery as a Superior State to Freedom". *Journal of Caribbean History* 29, no. 2 (1995): 93–119.

Vergne, Teresita Martínez. "The Allocation of Liberated African Labour through the Casa de Beneficiencia: San Juan, Puerto Rico, 1859–1864". *Slavery and Abolition* 12, no. 1 (1991): 200–16.

Welch, Pedro. "The Urban Context of the Slave Plantation System: Bridgetown, Barbados, 1680–1834". PhD diss., University of the West Indies, Cave Hill, 1994.

Wood, Donald. "Crown Slavery in Berbice". Seminar paper, Institute of Commonwealth Studies, University of London, 1984.

Woodman, Harold D. "The Profitability of Slavery: A Historical Perennial". *Journal of Southern History* 29 (1963): 303–25.

E. Newspapers

Berbice Gazette, 1803–1826 (incomplete).
Courier (London), July 1816.
Stabroek News, August 1989.

Index

Aaron, 177
Abercrombie, John, 239
Abinnaba, 231–32
abolition
   advocates of, 64–66
   and economics, 2–3
   effects in Berbice, 25, 42, 53
   phases of, 260–61
Abraham, 178
Abraham II, 229
Abrammaker, 166, 184
abuse. *See also* punishment
   of children, 34
   sexual, 34, 222–23, 229
   spousal, 229
accommodations for slaves, 66–67
   in Barbados, 66–67
   Commission for Management on, 77
   complaints about, 146–47, 184, 230–31
   on estates, 50–51, 60–61, 86
   maintenance of, 77, 86, 106, 144–49, 259
Adam I, 166
Adolphe, 146, 184
Adolphe II, 184
Adonis, 136
Adrian, 146–47
Adriana, 235
Africa, 4–5. *See also* apprenticed Africans
African culture, 141–42, 181–82, 195, 197–98
African Institution, 65
age. *See also* elderly people
   of *winkel* people, 176–77
agriculture. *See also* Crown estates; provision grounds
   in Berbice, 21, 24–25, 27, 61
   tools of, 86

alcohol. *See* drinking
Alexander, 170
Amelia, 146–47, 220–21
amelioration, 36–44, 173–75, 263–66
   and Crown estates, 52–53
   as experiment, 46–48, 65–70
   and government slaves, 64, 108
   humanitarians and, 52, 100–101
   obstacles to, 35, 43
   planters' response to, 38, 42–43, 74
   and productivity, 35–36, 52, 97, 120
   rewards as part of, 210–11
America (slave woman), 29–30
Andries, 226
Anglican Church, 44–45, 67, 201–2, 204
Anna I, 130, 162–63
Anna II, 136
Antigua, 26
Anti-Slavery Monthly Reporter, 65
Anti-Slavery Society, 65
Antoinette, 129
apprenticed Africans, 134, 250, 253–58, 260
apprenticeship system, 250
   and emancipation, 253, 260–61
   slaves in, 7
Aqueshaba, 34
Armstrong, William, 246–51
Arsenia, 190
artisans. *See also winkel* department; *winkel* people
   demand for, 116–18
   morale of, 122, 155
   overtime pay for, 251
   as plantation workers, 135, 154–55
   training of, 54–55, 121, 123–25
Asia, 4–5
August (slave man), 214

Index

Austin, Richard, 204, 238
Auxiliary Bible Society, 94

Baatje, 178
Bahamas, 126, 131, 132, 257
Balter, 129–30
banking, 251–52
baptisms, 96–97
Barabakara, 248
Barbados, 12, 26–28. *See also* Codrington estates
   amelioration in, 66–68
   escheated slaves in, 6, 255
   mortality in, 25, 52–53, 175
   self-hire in, 132
   slavery in, 14, 52–53, 65, 66–68, 172, 265
   winkel migration to, 259
   women slaves in, 4, 209
Bastiaan, 178, 186
Bastide, Roger, 192, 228
Batavian Republic, 22, 49, 102
Bathurst, Earl of, 237
Beard, Henry, 35, 130, 203
   on government slaves, 43, 124, 227–28, 230
   views of, 20, 38, 107
Beatty, John, 45
Beckles, Hilary, 4, 209
Benfield, Paul, 47
Benin. *See* Dahomey
Bennett, J. Harry, Jr., 265
Bennett, M.S., 35, 85, 157
Bentinck, Henry, 35, 75, 94, 100
   concern about hospital, 144, 145
Berbice, 16–22, 46. *See also* British Guiana; Council of Policy; New Amsterdam; treasury
   administration of, 53
   agriculture in, 21, 24–25, 27, 61
   amelioration in, 37–44, 46–48
   British occupation of, 24, 49, 52, 69–70
   climate of, 20, 61, 89
   coloured people in, 26, 28, 107–8
   currency of, 61–62
   difficulties of colonizing, 46, 61–62
   disease in, 20–21, 69, 88–89, 179
   Dutch occupation of, 18, 21–22, 49, 92
   education in, 44–46, 230
   history of, 22–25
   hospitals in, 75, 89, 144, 145
   labour costs in, 116
   military establishments in, 106–7, 108
   miscegenation in, 192
   mortality in, 25, 46, 69, 89, 179
   population of, 25–27, 28, 107–8, 257
   punishment laws in, 38–40
   religion in, 44–46, 95–96
   slavery in, 25–27, 107–8, 267
Berbice Agricultural Society, 25
Berbice Association, 22
   as owner of estates, 46–48, 102, 263–64
   return of estates to, 81, 102, 109, 153, 181, 263
   and *winkel* department, 47, 175
Berbice Commission for Management. *See* Commission for Management
Berbice (slave), 177
Berenstein estate, 153–56
   desertions from, 218, 220, 224, 225, 233
   disciplinary problems on, 120, 156
   food shortage at, 226
   managers of, 155, 201, 218–23
   as punishment, 128, 133–34, 156, 175, 187, 191, 217–23, 225, 229, 232, 238
   punishments at, 216, 218–27
Beresford, James, 118, 119, 181
Beresford, John, 177, 179, 181, 218–19
Bernard, 184, 220
Betje, 202
Betsey, 156, 178, 182–83, 210, 220, 222
Betsey II, 191–92
Bird, Charles, 44, 85, 157
birth rates, 79, 90, 176
Black Rangers, 6–7
blacks. *See* free blacks
Blassingame, John, 127
Board of Police, 142–44
boat builders, 115, 121–23, 126–27, 145
Bolingbroke, Henry, 6
Bone, James, 121
Boyer, Jean-Pierre, 66

Braham, 233
Brandes, Charles, 146
Brathwaite, John, 66
Brazil, 250
bricklayers, 128–29
Britain. *See* imperial government
British
   and Crown estates, 102
   Dutch attitude to, 92
   and education, 44
   occupation of Berbice by, 24, 49, 52, 69–70
   and *winkel* department, 53–54
British and Foreign Bible Society, 66
British and Foreign School Society, 66
British Guiana, 11, 16n4, 26n23, 257
British Honduras, 132
British West India Regiment, 6–7
Brutus, 34
Buckridge, Steeve, 163
buildings. *See* accommodations for slaves; government buildings
Burdett, Commissioner, 105, 147, 148
Burn, William, 40
Bush, Barbara, 3–4
Buxton, Thomas Fowell, 65

Cadet, 177
Calmer (planter), 220
Cameron, A.J. McR., 8
Cameron, Donald Charles, 102
Campbell, William, 115–16, 246
Canning, George, 243–44
Capitalism and Slavery (Williams), 2
Caribbean
   education in, 66–68
   government slaves in, 6–7, 126, 255
   health care in, 179–80
   religion in, 66, 68
   self-hire in, 126, 131, 132
   slave laws in, 235–36
   slavery in, 1–4, 12–16, 101, 108, 265–67
   whites in, 27–28, 108
Carmichael, Mrs, 85
Carolina II, 135, 191, 235–38
carpenters, 115, 117, 118, 121, 129
carracarra, 39

Catherina, 191
Catherine, 187
Césaire, Aimé, 148
chain gangs, 6, 216, 225, 226
chains, 39, 221, 225
Chanton, 130
Charles, 210
Charles II (slave man), 191
Chester's estate, 67
child abuse. *See* abuse
child labour, 67, 87, 205
children. *See also* infant mortality; schools
   care of, 90, 165
   family life of, 188–89
   health of, 177–78, 179
Christianity. *See also specific religious institutions*
   civilizing influence of, 79
   conversion to, 91–97
   and unrest, 203n103
Christian Observer, 65
Christina I, 212
Christina II, 206
Christmas, 193–95
   clothing distribution at, 163–64, 166
Christophe, Henri, 65–66
churches. *See also individual churches*
   buildings for, 106, 203–4
   slaves owned by, 7, 45
Church Missionary Society, 201–2
Clapham Sect, 64–65. *See also* humanitarians
Clarissa, 189, 191
Clarkson, Thomas, 2, 52, 65–66
Classina, 232–33
clothing for slaves, 77, 163–71. *See also* red shirts; *winkel* workroom
   for children, 165
   Christmas distribution of, 163–64, 166
   inadequacy of, 29, 166–68
   provision of, 60, 84–85, 164–70
coartación, 250
cobbs. *See* coloured people
Codrington estates, 66–67, 85, 170, 265
coffee production, 21–22, 24, 31–32, 48, 61
Colonial Office, 50, 255–57. *See also* Department of Colonial Audit

Index

coloured people, 15, 16, 134, 266
　in Berbice, 26, 28, 107–8
　as competition for *winkel* people, 116, 118–19
　in *winkel* population, 190
Commission for Management, 10, 64, 68–70, 72, 263. *See also* humanitarians
　achievements of, 100–101, 263
　agents chosen by, 70–76, 101
　Alexander De la Court and, 81, 263
　expenses of, 97
　hostility towards, 71–74, 91
　instructions of, 71, 76–82, 86–87, 97, 114, 174, 186, 200
　Charles Kyte and, 244–45
　and slave unrest, 240
　James Walker and, 174, 239
　and *winkel* department, 74–76, 109, 186
Commission of Inquiry (1824), 10, 111, 113–14, 243
coopers, 117, 129–30
copyholds, 67
Cornelia, 191
Cornelia II, 188–89
Cornelia III, 191–92, 214
corruption, 57, 60, 97
cotton production, 24, 61
Council for American Plantations, 49
Council of Elders, 67, 68
Coupland, Reginald, 2
Court of Policy, 50, 55, 60, 82
Craton, Michael, 8–9, 265
creolization, 36, 141, 176, 182, 224
Crown estates, 60, 74–76. *See also specific estates;* Berbice Association; managers
　administration of, 58–62, 97–100
　and amelioration, 52–53
　finances of, 58–59, 62–63, 69, 98–99
　maintenance of, 58–59, 63, 86
　mismanagement of, 59, 82–83
　ownership of, 69–70, 101–2
　performance of, 58, 60–63, 98–99
　rental proposals for, 62–68
"Crown Slavery in Berbice" (Wood), 7–8
Crown slaves. *See* government slaves
Cruickshank, Graham, 7–8
Cuba, 12, 26, 126, 250

Cubinda, 219
currency, 29n56, 61–62

Dageraad estate, 47, 48, 60n46, 86, 98
Dahomey, 5, 265
Dalrymple, Lieutenant Governor, 58, 63
Dalton, Henry, 105, 106
dancing, 194–95
Daniel, 251–52
Dankbaarheid estate, 47, 48, 60n46, 61
　accommodations at, 50–51, 86
　hospital at, 89
David, 29
Davidson, Dr, 239
Davis, David Brion, 267
deficiency laws, 80
De la Court, Alexander, 58, 71, 72, 95
　and accommodations, 86, 106
　and Commission for Management, 81, 263
　conflicts of, 74–76, 81
　and food production, 82–83, 84
　and health care, 89–90
　and payments to slaves, 85–87
　and John Wray, 74, 83, 94–95
Demerara-Essequibo, 22, 24–25, 26n23. *See also* British Guiana
　banks in, 251n30
　desertions in, 224
　freed slaves in, 257, 259
　plantations in, 12, 27
　punishment laws in, 38–39
　religious instruction in, 91–92
　revolts in, 45, 91–92, 108, 168, 203, 228
　shipping in, 20, 24
　slavery in, 6, 26, 108, 132, 254–55
　transfers of slaves to, 25, 98
demography. *See also* Higman, Barry
　of Berbice, 25–27, 28, 257
　of government slaves, 63–64, 90, 175–77
　of slavery, 3, 26–27, 52–53, 63–64, 90, 175
Department of Colonial Audit, 113–15, 242–43, 245
Derrick, 207
desertions, 176n13, 224–27, 240

instances of, 111n25, 125, 128–29, 187, 218, 220, 233
Deussen, J., 155–56, 219–22
   complaints about, 187, 201, 226, 233
   mistreatment by, 192, 220, 225
Deutichem estate, 198
Dickson, William, 67
Diena II, 182
disabilities, 177–79
discipline. *See also* punishment
   Commission for Management on, 77–78, 87
   James Walker's approach to, 39–40, 210–16, 223, 228, 232
disease, 20–21, 69, 88–89, 179
domestics, 117, 130, 135
   assignment of, 56–57, 130
   clothing of, 164
   and prostitution, 190–91
Dominick, 126, 128–29, 146, 226
Drescher, Seymour, 2–3, 264
drinking, 195–97, 231, 233
Drumgoole, Mrs, 221
drumming, 195
Dummett, Francis, 161, 183
   on Carolina II, 237
   and provision of clothing, 164, 165
   on James Walker, 161, 214–15, 223, 232
D'Urban, Benjamin, 161, 227, 257–58
Dutch
   in Berbice, 18, 21–24, 49, 92
   and education, 44
   and slave clothing, 168–69
   and *winkel* department, 53–54
Dutch Reformed church, 44–45, 106
Dyos, Pryce, 129

Econocide (Drescher), 2–3
education
   in Berbice, 44–46, 206, 230, 259
   in Caribbean, 66–68
   slaves and, 46, 91–97, 191, 201, 202, 205–7
Edwards, Bryan, 2, 41, 241
Edwards, Mr, 130
Eenhuys, J.H., 181
Egypt, 5

elderly people, 67, 88–89, 177–78, 184–86
Elias, 218
Eliza, 191
Elizabeth, 187, 191–92
Elizabeth Anne, 252
emancipation, 173, 174, 242–44, 257–60, 264
   imperial government and, 251, 257, 260–61, 266
   lack of support after, 266–67
   and punishment, 36–37
   reactions to, 259–60
Emmanuel, 169
escheated slaves, 6, 254–57, 260
Esdaile (slave child), 191
estates. *See also specific estates;* Crown estates; plantations
   abandonment of, 21, 24–25, 46, 98, 102, 156
   accommodations at, 50–51, 60–61, 86
   owned by Berbice Association, 46–48, 102, 263–64
   provision grounds on, 83–84, 158

families, 43, 188–89, 231–33
Fanny, 235
Fanon, Frantz, 240
Farley, Thomas, 155
fathers, 188–89
February (slave man), 168, 177, 252
Fédon, Julian, 256n41
Ferdinand, 220
Ferrell, Thomas, 207
fêting, 193–95
Finch (Fink), John, 155, 218
Flooda, 222, 229
Flora, 177
food for slaves, 14, 60, 77, 82–84, 153–63. *See also* provision grounds
   in Barbados, 66–67
   complaints about, 29, 153, 156, 182–85, 228–29
   for invalids, 89, 182–83, 185–86
   for urban slaves, 14, 158–60
footwear, 169–70
Fort St Andrew (Andries), 108
François, 252

Index

François II, 186
Frantze, 202
Frederica, 207
Frederick, 43, 198–99
Frederick II, 129, 131
Frederick III, 125n74, 126, 127–28
Frederick IV, 182
free blacks, 13, 15, 107, 266
  as *winkel* competition, 118–19
free coloured. *See* coloured people
freedom, 243, 249. *See also* emancipation;
  gradualism; manumission
  attempts to purchase, 126–27
  desire for, 209, 240, 268
  partial, 250, 251, 254
  preparations for, 251–54
Freire, Paulo, 240
French revolutionary wars, 12
Friday (slave man), 43
Fruitje, 177
funerals, 197

Galley (Gallez), L.F., 34, 202
Gattarel, William, 155, 219
gender issues, 3–4, 79
George, 118
Georgetown. *See* Demerara-Essequibo
Geschiedenis (Netscher), 7
Gillies, Lord, 239
Gipps, George, 162–63, 244
  proposal for *winkel* department, 247–51
Goderich, Lord, 257–58
Gordon, James, 64
Gordon, Mary, 207
Gordon, William, 55, 74, 93, 160
  on Commission for Management, 71–73
  and conflict of interest, 35, 73
  and Crown estates, 58–61, 64, 82
Gorée, 130, 149
government. *See specific departments;* Court
  of Policy; imperial government; lieutenant governors
government buildings, 105–7, 246
Government House, 99, 105
government slaves, 4–7, 15, 35, 108,
  254–58, 262. *See also* emancipation

acquisition of, 6–7, 254–57
in Caribbean, 6–7, 126, 255
health of, 88–90, 177–87
neglect of, 60–61
population of, 63–64, 90, 175–77
studies of, 7–8
Grade, C.J., 30
gradualism, 250, 251, 253, 254, 260
graft. *See* corruption
Graham (*winkel* bookkeeper), 129
Great Britain. *See* imperial government
Grenada, 6, 60n44, 255–56
Grieta, 195
Grietje, 191, 235
grooms, 124
Guadeloupe, 12
Guatemala, 250
Guianas, 11. *See also* British Guiana
  difficulty of civilizing, 22
  disease in, 20–21, 179
  shipping in, 18–20

Haiti, 12, 65–68
Hall, Neville, 4
Hallett's estate, 67
Handler, Jerome, 172, 265
Hannah, 138
Hans, 182, 197–200
Harper, Mercy, 238
Harriet, 138, 206, 251–52
hats, 85
head tax, 25–26, 107
health care, 88–90, 179–87. *See also*
  hospitals; invalids
Hector, 136
Helmaker, 220
Hendrick I, 129, 170
Hendrick II, 178, 205, 210, 223, 232
Henson, Josiah, 127
Hercules (slave man), 220
Highbury estate. *See* Dankbaarheid estate
Higman, Barry, 3, 4, 265
  on clothing, 163
  on house designs, 149
  on punishments, 40
  on self-hire, 131–32
  on slave populations, 26, 64, 108
  on social culture, 172

Index

History of British Guiana (Rodway), 7
Hobson, Webbe, 57
holidays, 30–33, 34, 193–95, 234–35
Horton, Wilmot, 246
hospitals
   in Barbados, 67
   in Berbice, 75, 89, 144, 145
   Commission for Management on, 78, 79
   as place of punishment, 216
hucksters, 130
humanitarians, 2–3, 52, 94, 174, 205
   in Commission for Management, 64–66, 70, 71, 76–82
   in Haiti, 65–66

Iantje, 149
imperial government
   and amelioration, 53, 263–64
   and colonized peoples, 258
   and emancipation, 251, 257, 260–61, 266
   and *winkel* department, 109, 246–47, 264
infant mortality, 79, 90, 205
ingenuos, 250
insubordination, 120, 232, 234, 235
intermarriage, 190–93
invalids, 89, 165, 182–86
inventories, 50–51, 86

Jack, 115
Jacoba II, 233, 235–36
Jacob Antony, 252
Jacob Benjamin, 252
Jacobus, 178
Jacobus II, 130, 146–47
Jamaica
   effects of amelioration in, 36–37
   plantation culture in, 12, 37
   revolts in, 203n103
   slavery in, 8–9, 14, 26, 132, 153, 163, 172, 265
James II (slave man), 232
Janetje, 191
janissaries, 5
January (slave), 200
Jeffrey, Joseph, 181, 238

Jemima, 207
Johanna, 177
Johnson, Howard, 131
Johnstone, A., 181
Jonetta, 185
judicial system, 35. *See also* laws
   punishment under, 40–41, 88, 107, 216
Julia, 191, 222, 229, 233
Juliana, 130–31, 138, 187, 191, 211

Katz, Wolfert, 47, 72, 203, 244
   Crown estate lease proposal of, 62–63
   treatment of slaves by, 135, 138
   and *winkel* department, 115, 123, 124, 157, 246
Keen, Thomas, 121, 225
Kendal's estate, 67–68
Kinchela, John, 10, 147. *See also* Commission of Inquiry (1824)
"King William's People" (Cruickshank), 7–8
kinship, 141. *See also* families
Kiple, Kenneth, 3
Klingberg, Frank, 2
Kyte, Charles, 244–45
   on free blacks and coloureds, 118
   and slave resistance, 239
   on slaves, 85, 148, 152, 163, 169
   and *winkel* department, 111, 116–19, 246–47, 262

labourers, 117
labour force
   creolization of, 36
   slaves in, 118–19
   transfer from estates, 25, 82, 86, 98
   in *winkel* department, 56–57, 111–13, 131
   women in, 79, 115, 130–31, 134–35, 162–63, 249
labour market, 115–20
Lambert, 93, 195, 224, 240
Lambert, James, 47
Lambert II, 181, 230–32
land grants, 257–58, 259
Lange, Frederick, 172, 265
language, 204

laundresses, 130
Lauw, 220, 222, 224n54
    suicide of, 195–97, 213, 229, 232–33, 240
Lavinia, 207
laws, 28, 30–33, 53. *See also* judicial system; slave laws
    on amelioration, 38–39
    on clothing provision, 85, 164
    deficiency, 80
    on food provision, 157–62
    on manumission, 42
    planters' flouting of, 28, 30–33
    and punishment, 35–42, 88, 107, 216
    against self-hire, 132
Leah I, 156, 220
Lena, 185
Le Resouvenir estate, 91–92
Letters on the West Indies (Walker), 173–74, 210
lieutenant governors, 35, 50, 169–70. *See also specific governors*
    as administrators, 53, 55–56, 263
    commissions paid to, 56, 58, 97
    Alexander De la Court's conflicts with, 74–76
    and *winkel* department, 56, 122
literacy, 93–94, 202, 203n103, 206
livestock, 155–56, 162
Lizetta, 147
LMS. *See* London Missionary Society
Lockart, Elliott, 239
Lohman, B., 51
London Missionary Society (LMS), 44–46. *See also* Wray, John
    missionary work by, 45, 92–93, 252
    monetary support from, 201
    schools run by, 206, 259
Long, Charles, 64
Long, Edward, 2, 267
Louis, 122, 123, 152, 230
    marriage of, 188–89
    savings of, 251–52
    self-hire by, 126–27
Louisa, 34, 178, 267–68
Louisa II, 206
Lucia, 177
Lucia II, 191, 229

Lucretia II, 207
Lutheran Church, 44–46
Lysje I, 177, 185

Macalister, Duncan, 71, 74, 76–77, 84
Macaulay, Zachary, 10, 52, 73, 87
    on Commission for Management, 65–66, 70
    and James Walker, 174
Madelintje, 131, 191, 220–21
mamluks, 5
managers, 87–88, 94–95. *See also specific managers and estates*
    whipping by, 87–88, 218–20, 222–23, 225, 229
Mandarina, 218, 222
manicole palm, 146, 150–51
manumission, 64n62, 253–54, 257
    for mothers, 79
    obstacles to, 42–43
    in *winkel* department, 175
Manzano, Juan Francisco, 180
Maria I, 189, 227n63, 252
Maria III, 223
Marietje, 146–47
marriages, 97, 188–89, 211
    between races, 190–93
    reputed, 189–91, 229
Marryat, Joseph, 73, 86, 100
Martinique, 12, 26
masons, 117, 128–29
Mathieson, William L., 2
Matilda, 135, 212, 216–17, 223, 235
Mauritius, 259
McConchie, William, 155, 222–23, 229
McIntosh, Mrs, 206
McRae (Mac Rae), John, 155
McWatt, Andrew, 197, 231
    kindnesses of, 182, 230
    on Louis, 126–27, 189
    on medical care, 183–84
    on provisions to slaves, 157, 161, 169–70
    on James Walker, 161, 214–15
    and *winkel* department, 111, 118–20, 124, 139, 145, 147, 243
Meadowcroft (John Wray's assistant), 93, 97

Memmi, Albert, 139
men. *See* slave men
Mentor, 184
Michael, 129, 156, 210, 221, 225–27, 240
midwives, 181, 212
military departments, 106–7, 108
    winkel work for, 122–23
    women working for, 162–63
miscegenation, 192. *See also* intermarriage
missionaries, 92, 96. *See also specific missionary societies;* Christianity
Mitigation of Slavery (Dickson), 67
Moanda, 147, 152
Montgomerie, Lieutenant Governor, 58–59
Moravian Missionary Society, 201–2
morbidity, 88–89, 177, 179. *See also* disease
mortality
    among infants, 79, 90, 205
    among slaves, 53, 64, 176, 268
    in Barbados, 25, 52–53, 175
    in Berbice, 25, 46, 69, 89, 179
Moses I, 115, 148–49
Moses II, 124
Moses III, 206–7
mothers, 79
    and childcare, 34–35
    rewards for, 211–12
Moyne Commission Report (1939), 179–80
M'Queen, James, 2
Mucalla, 218
mulattoes. *See* coloured people
murder, 28
Murray, John, 35, 74–75, 93–94
music, 195
mustees. *See* coloured people

Naipaul, V.S., 268
Nancy, 136, 138, 191–92, 214
Napoleonic Wars, 6, 7
Nassau (Berbice), 21
Nassau (slave man), 184
Nathaniel, 207
Natural Rebels (Beckles), 4
Netherlands, 101–2. *See also* Dutch
Netscher, P.M., 7

New Amsterdam, 21, 103–8
    administration of, 107, 122
    prostitution in, 190
    punishments in, 40–41
    religious life of, 95–97
Nicholson, Lieutenant Governor, 59–60
Nicolay, Frederick
    on *winkel* department, 54, 111, 247
    on *winkel* profitability, 56–57, 115–18, 126
Nieuw Stoop estate, 35, 213–14
Nigeria, 5
nudity, 168–69, 237

Obermuller, Johan Frederic, 74
obeah, 197–200
Ottoman empire, 5
Overeem, Jacobus, 29–33
Oyo empire, 5

Pamba, 115
Parliament, 2, 100–101. *See also* imperial government
patronato, 250
Patterson, Orlando, 141, 240, 267–68
Paul II, 115, 168, 220
Perceval, Spencer, 63, 70
Peter, 182
Phibbah, 192
Pinckard, George
    on Berbice, 21, 105
    on Christmas, 194
    on slaves, 153, 163–64, 195, 237
    on whipping, 39
pipes (tobacco), 85
Pitt, William, 235–36
plantains, 154, 155–56
    distribution of, 83n57, 158–60
plantations, 12–13, 27. *See also* estates
    coffee, 21–22, 24, 31, 48
    productivity of, 36–37
    slavery on, 3, 13–14, 27–28
    sugar, 24, 48, 61
    in Suriname, 27, 60n44, 70n3
planters, 47, 202–3
    flouting of laws by, 28, 30–33
    opposition to amelioration by, 38, 80–81

and religious instruction, 92–93, 202
and John Wray, 96, 202–3, 252, 266
Pontje, 178
Port of Spain. *See* Trinidad
Poyer, John, 267
pregnancy, 79, 89–90
   punishment during, 29–30, 191–92, 218, 235
Primo, 115, 178
Primo II, 146, 220
Primo III, 146, 168, 220
Prince, Mary, 9
Profit estate, 153
property
   owned by slaves, 34, 43–44
   slaves as, 4–7, 6, 15, 45, 47, 255–56, 265–66
Prospect estate, 221
prostitution, 14, 130, 190–91
protector of slaves, 29, 39n59, 44, 265
Proteus, Beilby, 67
provision grounds
   in Barbados, 66–68
   on estates, 83–84, 158
   time allowed to cultivate, 77, 79–80, 82–83, 135
   of *winkel* department, 156–57, 162
public works, 54, 122
   slaves used for, 6, 15, 99
Puerto Rico, 26
punishment, 28–38, 178. *See also specific types of punishment;* Berenstein; managers
   Commission for Management on, 77–78
   complaints about, 216–17, 228–29, 231
   and emancipation, 36–37
   of families, 231–33
   as instrument of repression, 41–42, 187
   judicial, 40–41, 88, 107, 216
   laws about, 35–36, 38–42
   for obiah practice, 199–200
   official response to, 30–33, 35–36
   for outside relationships, 191–93
   during pregnancy, 29–30, 191–92, 218, 235
   of women, 191–93, 214, 218–20, 222–23, 235–36

Quamina, 203n103
Quassie, 33

racism, 134, 180, 236–37, 265
Ragatz, Lowell, 2
Ramsay, James, 52
Reasons for Establishing a Registry of Slaves in the British Colonies (Stephen), 65
rebellions. *See* revolts
red shirts, 170, 212, 232
reform, 71, 76–82, 101
   in Haiti, 66–68
   of *winkel* department, 244–46, 251
religion, 197–204. *See also* religious instruction
   African, 197–98
   in Berbice, 44–46, 95–97
religious instruction, 44–46, 91–97, 174, 247, 252. *See also specific religious institutions;* religion
   in Caribbean, 66, 68
   Commission for Management on, 79–80, 200
   planters' views of, 92–93, 202
resettlement schemes, 250, 257
resistance. *See* unrest
rest periods, 29, 79–80, 148. *See also* holidays; provision grounds
revolts, 5, 231
   in Berbice, 24, 74, 96, 108
   in Demerara-Essequibo, 45, 91–92, 108, 168, 203, 228
   fear of, 74, 108, 131–32, 168, 173, 228
   and literacy, 93–94, 203n103
   in St Domingue, 9, 12, 24, 94
Rodway, James, 7
Rolfe, G.W., 113
Roosje (Rosa), 30
Rosalia, 130, 136
Rose, Tom, 189
Ross, George, 239
Roxanna, 181
rum, 72

St Domingue, 12, 164
   slave revolts in, 9, 12, 24, 94
St Eustatius, 14

Index

St Jan estate, 47, 48, 102, 153
   accommodations at, 51
   removal of slaves from, 82, 86
St Kitts, 12
St Lucia, 235–36
St Thomas, 14
St Vincent, 85, 237
Sandvoort estate, 47, 48, 60n46
   accommodations at, 50–51, 86
   church attendance at, 96
   free time at, 82–83
   maintenance of, 59, 86
   managers at, 94–95, 98, 202
   provision for slaves at, 83, 85, 89, 90
   revenues of, 48, 58
Sanetje, 191
Sarah, 146
Schomburgk, Richard, 195
schools, 46, 87, 95, 205–7
   mission-run, 206, 259
   for *winkel* people, 201, 205–6
Schwiers, Conrad, 39, 188
Scott, John, 146
Scott, John (slave child), 207
Scott, Nancy, 43
Scott, William, 82, 95, 202, 203, 234–35
   emancipation plan of, 253
   and provision for slaves, 84, 86, 90, 145, 147, 153–54
   and James Walker, 109–13, 120, 154–55, 208, 219
   and *winkel* department, 109, 113, 121, 139, 245–46, 251
seamstresses, 85, 130–33. See also *winkel* workroom
Searching for the Invisible Man (Craton), 8–9
self-hire, 14–15, 125–32
   in Caribbean, 126, 131, 132
Senior, Bernard, 153
sexual abuse. *See* abuse
sexual relations
   between non-whites and whites, 28, 190–93
   between slaves and owners, 34
   between *winkel* women and free men, 189–90
Sheridan, Richard, 3

shipping, 18–20, 24
shoes, 169–70
Sierra Leone, 73, 250
Sierra Leone Company, 65
Sim, 170, 210, 228–30, 240
Simon, 178, 185
slave laws, 38–41. *See also* amelioration
   in Caribbean, 235–36
   slave code (1826), 38, 42, 43, 251
   slave registry bill (1817), 25
slave men
   clothing provided for, 165, 170, 212, 232
   oppression of, 35, 214–15
   rates of hire for, 115
   rewards for, 212
Slave Populations of the British Caribbean 1807–1834 (Higman), 3
slavery, 258. *See also* abolition; slaves
   in Caribbean, 1–4, 12–16, 101, 108, 265–67
   debate about, 2, 52
   in Demerara-Essequibo, 6, 26, 108, 132, 254–55
   inhumanity of, 101, 127
   in Jamaica, 8–9, 14, 26, 132, 153, 163, 172, 265
   on plantations, 3, 13–14, 27–28
   religious groups and, 7, 45
   studies of, 2, 265
The Slavery of the British West India Colonies Delineated (Stephen), 65
slaves, 9–10, 13–14, 25–26, 43, 267. *See also specific locations and types of slaves*; revolts; slave men; slavery; slave women
   appraisal of, 42–43
   aspirations of, 207–8, 265
   in Berbice, 25–27, 107–8, 267
   control of, 131–32
   and education, 46, 91–97, 191, 201, 202, 205–7
   elderly, 67, 88–89, 177–78, 184–86
   mortality among, 53, 64, 176, 268
   ownership of, 4–7, 6, 15, 45, 47, 255–56, 265–66
   payments to, 67, 85–87
   population of, 26–27, 52–53, 63–64, 90, 175

property rights of, 34, 43–44
protectors of, 29, 39n59, 44, 265
resistance by, 209, 224, 228
as soldiers, 6–7
slave unrest
  Commission for Management and, 240
slave women, 3–4, 34–35, 188. *See also* domestics; gender issues; pregnancy; *winkel* workroom
  clothing provided for, 165
  Commission for Management on, 79
  outside relationships of, 189–90, 191
  punishment of, 191–93, 214, 218, 220, 222–23, 235–36
  resistance by, 135–36, 191, 209, 221–22, 238, 239, 240
  rewards for, 211–12
  sexual abuse of, 34, 222–23, 229
  as workers, 79, 115, 130–31, 134–35, 162–63, 249
Slave Women in Caribbean Society, 1650–1838 (Bush), 3–4
Smith, John, 94n98, 203
Smith, William, 64, 73, 100
smiths, 117, 121, 127, 225, 226
Smyth, Sir James Carmichael, 41
Society for Effecting the Abolition of the Slave Trade, 64
Society for the Amelioration and Gradual Abolition of Slavery Throughout the British Dominions, 65
Society for the Propagation of the Gospel, 66–67
Society of Berbice. *See* Berbice Association
solitary confinement, 213, 233
Sophia I, 130, 187, 191, 251–52
Sophia II, 131, 178
South Africa, 92
Stanley, Elizabeth, 165, 237
  and punishments, 216–17, 236
  as schoolmistress, 137, 205–6
  and *winkel* workroom, 130, 132–33, 137–38, 167
Staple, Colonel, 59, 62–64
Stedman, John, 192, 223
Steele, Joshua, 67–68
Stephen, James, 2, 41–42, 63, 94, 255

on Commission for Management, 64–65, 73
stocks, 28, 30, 191–92
  laws about, 39
  as punishment for women, 214, 218, 220
sugar production, 24, 48, 61
suicide, 195–97, 213, 225, 227–33, 240
Suriname, 22, 192, 223
  estates in, 27, 60n44, 70n3
Susannah, 189, 191, 211–12, 238
Susannah II, 187, 220
Susetta (Rosetta), 156, 218–19, 220
Suxybergen, 254
Suzette, 191

tailors, 116
Tannetje, 130, 138, 191, 233, 235
task work, 15, 78, 86–87, 124–25
taxes. *See* head tax
Taylor (slave man), 178
technology, 78, 86–87
Tellaway (slave man), 147
theft, 34
Theurer, L., 181, 183
Thistlewood, Thomas, 192
Thomas, 125, 210, 224–26
Thomas Eden & Co., 50
Thomas Harvey, 129, 226
tobacco, 24, 85
Tom, 206
Tortola, 14, 257
trade, 61, 72–73, 98, 164
training, 54–55, 85
treadmill, 40–41, 107
treasury
  of Berbice, 61, 68
  imperial, 255–57
Treaty of Amiens (1802), 49
Trinidad, 12, 250, 251n30
  freed slaves in, 257
  slave code in, 235–36
  slaves in, 6, 26, 108, 255

Unger, Godlieb (George) Willem, 60
United States, 61, 126, 170n90, 267
unrest, 224, 228. *See also* revolts

among slave women, 135–36, 191, 209, 221–22, 238–40
among *winkel* people, 120, 168, 207–8, 222, 240, 264–65
Christianity and, 203n103
in *winkel* workroom, 135, 167, 235
urban slaves, 4, 13–16, 107–8, 141, 265–66. *See also* self-hire; *winkel* people
mobility of, 14–15
provision of food for, 14, 158–60

Van Batenburg, A.J. Imbyze, 20, 50, 61, 105
and Crown estates, 53, 59–60
financial irregularities of, 57, 60
and *winkel* department, 54
Vander Brock, Johannes, 30–33
Van Hattem (bookkeeper), 60
Van Pere family, 22
Vansittart, Nicholas, 64, 264
Venus (slave woman), 199, 200
Vesey, Denmark, 203
Vos, Johannes, 45–46
Vryberg estate, 128
Vryheid estate, 115–16

Walker, James, 88, 123–24, 173–75. *See also* Berenstein; Commission of Inquiry; Department of Colonial Audit
and accommodations for slaves, 86, 145–47, 149
and clothing for slaves, 85, 164–70
as collector of customs, 134–37, 239
disciplinary approach of, 39–40, 210–16, 223, 228, 232
and education, 205–6
and food for slaves, 83–84, 153, 156–63
and health care, 89–90, 180
and holidays, 234–35
improprieties of, 137–39, 167, 239, 240, 264
on insubordination, 120, 235
management practices of, 98, 234–35
mismanagement by, 113–15, 120, 131, 134–36, 139, 157, 187, 201, 208
and prostitution, 190–91
racism of, 134, 236–37
and religious instruction, 174, 200
and William Scott, 109–13, 120, 154–55, 208, 219
and slavery, 173–74, 205–6
as superintendent of *winkel* department, 81–82, 95, 109–10, 114–15, 138–39, 239
and task work, 124–25
on *winkel* department, 75, 85, 100, 116, 208, 227–28
and *winkel* men, 127–29
and *winkel* women, 133–34, 170–71, 175, 187, 190–93, 213, 221–23, 236–38
and *winkel* workers, 121, 125, 130, 132–33, 137–38
and John Wray, 96, 132, 193, 200–202, 204
Walker, Mrs James, 192, 241
Waller, John, 237
Warburton, William, 67
Ward, John R., 36–37
Waring, G., 181
wars, 6, 7, 12, 61
Welch, Pedro, 4, 28
Welcome (slave man), 178
whipping, 29–30, 39, 214–15
elimination of, 67, 78, 87
laws about, 38–40
by managers, 87–88, 218–20, 222–23, 225, 229
during pregnancy, 218, 235
of women, 235–36
White, Henry, 82–83, 111
whites, 13, 15, 148
in Berbice, 25, 26, 107–8
in Caribbean, 27–28, 108
sexual relationships with non-whites, 28, 190–93
Whitfield, Reverend, 204
Wilberforce, William, 10, 52, 94
on Commission for Management, 64–66, 100
Willem, 181–82
William, 123, 130, 195
William Henery, 252
Williams, Eric, 2, 264

Index

winkel department, 53–57, 109–13, 262–63. *See also* Walker, James; *winkel* workroom
  administration of, 55–57, 97–100, 125, 262
  Berbice Association and, 47, 175
  Commission for Management and, 74–76, 109, 186
  competition of, 116, 118–19, 121–23
  costs of, 125–26, 159, 167, 180
  effectives in, 111–13, 131
  financial problems of, 55–57, 157, 246
  hiring out from, 57n30, 111–13, 115–16, 121–22, 133, 237–38, 244–45
  imperial government and, 109, 246–47, 264
  Charles Kyte and, 111, 116–19, 246–47, 262
  and labour market, 115–20
  Andrew McWatt and, 111, 118–20, 124, 139, 145, 147, 243
  mismanagement of, 109, 113–15, 121–24, 139
  population of, 55, 64, 90, 98–100, 173–77
  proposals for, 246–51
  provision grounds of, 156–57, 162
  record-keeping in, 55–56, 113–15, 120–21, 124, 166, 215, 245
  reforms in, 244–46, 251
  William Scott and, 109, 113, 121, 139, 245–46, 251
  social policy of, 173–75
  as source of revenue, 47–48, 54–57, 100, 111–13, 125–26
  workforce of, 56–57, 99, 110–13, 135–36
winkel people, 140–42, 187–97. *See also* artisans; *winkel* village
  African culture among, 141–42, 181–82, 195, 197–98
  church attendance by, 96, 204
  clothing of, 85, 168–71
  discontent among, 120, 168, 207–8, 222, 240
  emancipation of, 243–44, 251–54, 259–60, 262–63

  food of, 157–62
  furnishings of, 152–53
  health of, 177–87
  oppression of, 240–41
  outside relationships of, 189–90, 191
  as public slaves, 1, 6, 15, 99, 102, 111–13
  resistance by, 135–36, 191, 209, 221–22, 238–40, 264–65
  rewards offered to, 210–12
  savings bank for, 251–52
  self-hire by, 14–15, 125–32
  social life of, 193–97
  unemployment among, 115–18, 259
  urban preference of, 247, 248
  as workers, 118, 119–20
winkel store, 137
winkel village, 51, 107, 142–53, 250–51
  construction of, 149–52
  drainage problems of, 142–44
  during holidays, 194–95
  households in, 188–89
  maintenance of, 142–44
winkel workroom, 132–33, 137, 201
  clothing produced by, 58, 133, 164–65, 167
  earnings of, 117, 133–34
  unrest in, 135, 167, 235
Woensdag (slave man), 213–14
Wood, Donald, 7–8
woodcutting, 123–24
Woodley, William, 56, 61, 105
  and Crown estates, 58–59, 62–63
work, 86–87. *See also* child labour; labour force; task work
  by animals and machines, 78, 86–87
  extra, 86–87, 124–25
  on Sundays, 87, 93, 96, 201, 202
  by *winkel* people, 118, 119–20
  by women, 79, 115, 130–31, 134–35, 162–63, 249
Wray, John, 91–96, 200–202. *See also* Meadowcroft
  and Alexander De la Court, 74, 83, 94–95
  and humanitarians, 94
  on LMS work, 46
  payments to, 97, 200–201

and planters, 96, 202–3, 252, 266
on provisions for slaves, 83–86, 161–62
on religious instruction, 95–96
religious instruction by, 91–94, 96, 202, 252
supporters of, 203–4, 252
views of, 41, 88, 90, 118, 190, 194–95, 197
and James Walker, 96, 132, 193, 200–202, 204

Wray, Mrs John, 85, 88, 132, 187
Wyndham, Sir Charles, 10. *See also* Commission of Inquiry (1824)

Yorubaland, 5
Young, Ben, 190

Zacharias, 146–47, 252
Zamore, 147, 152
Zanj slaves, 5
Zealand (slave man), 218

www.ingramcontent.com/pod-product-compliance
Lightning Source LLC
Chambersburg PA
CBHW021817300426
44114CB00009BA/212